Implementing Oracle Integration Cloud Service

Understand everything you need to know about Oracle's Integration Cloud Service and how to utilize it optimally for your business

Robert van Mölken
Phil Wilkins

BIRMINGHAM - MUMBAI

Implementing Oracle Integration Cloud Service

First published: January 2017

Production reference: 1130117

Published by Packt Publishing Ltd.
Livery Place
35 Livery Street
Birmingham
B3 2PB, UK.
ISBN 978-1-78646-072-1

www.packtpub.com

Credits

Authors

Robert van Mölken

Phil Wilkins

Reviewer

Rolando Carrasco

Commissioning Editor

David Barnes

Acquisition Editor

Nitin Dasan

Content Development Editor

Mayur Pawanikar

Technical Editor

Prasad Ramesh

Copy Editor

Safis Editing

Project Coordinator

Nidhi Joshi

Proofreader

Safis Editing

Indexer

Aishwarya Gangawane

Graphics

Disha Haria

Production Coordinator

Nilesh Mohite

Foreword

As the digital age embraces each of us, our businesses and the world around us, the importance of Software as a Service (SaaS), Cloud Integration, and API Management and is higher than ever before. Today, every business is not only expected to lead but also be able to pivot and flex to ride over disruptions or even disrupt age old industries themselves--be it banking, public sector, hospitality, music or any other, even the 300 year old taxi industry. Today businesses expect their IT to be agile and rapid enough to enable them to compete and lead in an environment where the next technology-led disruption is always just around the corner.

Enterprises, large, and small, are seeing rapid uptake of best of breed SaaS applications, often led not by the CIO or IT, but by the Line of Business (LOB) such as the HR manager, the sales VP or the marketing officer. SaaS bring unprecedented advantages of the cloud with rapid deployments, ease of use and huge savings in time and money. While SaaS undoubtedly brings these benefits, it doesn't take long for the LOB to realize the importance of their SaaS applications integrating with each other, with existing on-premises applications and with business processes across the enterprise – without this SaaS is nothing but silos as a service. This is where the rapid development and elevated user experience of the leading Integration Platform as a Service (iPaaS)--Oracle Integration Cloud Service (ICS) comes in.

In this book, *Phil Wilkins* and *Robert van Mölken*, take us through an exciting and insightful journey of how Oracle ICS solves exactly this crucial and urgent need that businesses face today – an iPaaS solution that complements your SaaS and on-premises application landscape allowing SaaS business users to rapidly build cloud and hybrid integrations, while allowing IT to have visibility of these integrations at design time and runtime, across the enterprise.

Phil and *Robert*, bring years of rich experience solving integration problems for market leading businesses across the globe. Through this book, they not only share their expertise of Oracle ICS through in-depth information on leveraging the service but also take us through an exciting journey weaving through various aspects of rapidly building cloud and on-premises integrations--simple as well as complex, multi-step orchestrations – leveraging tens of out of the box connectivity adapters and monitoring capabilities that Oracle ICS brings, for the SaaS user as well as IT. *Phil* and *Robert*, have not only shared when and how to use Oracle ICS for your business but have also articulated how to effectively solve modern business integration problems.

Your drive and expertise will always have the biggest impact on your IT and business, but I hope the knowledge you gain from this book of Oracle ICS enables you further to build the technical, architectural, and integration capabilities your business critically needs today, whether in the cloud, on-premises or both, to innovate and to future proof your business and IT.

Vikas Anand

Vice President, Product Management, Oracle Integration Platform Oracle Corporation

About the Authors

Robert van Mölken lives in Utrecht, the Netherlands, and is a Fusion Middleware specialist. He has over 9 years of experience in IT. Robert studied computer science at the University of Applied Sciences in Utrecht and received his BCS in 2007. Before his graduation, he started as a graphic designer and web developer, but soon shifted his focus to Fusion Middleware. His career started just before the release of Oracle SOA Suite 10gR3 and progressed heavily from there. Currently, Robert is one of the expertise leads on integration and cloud at AMIS. Before he started working at AMIS, he already had 4 years of experience in SOA Suite 10g and 11g. AMIS is specialized in most of the facets of the Oracle Red Stack and is an initiator of the Red Expert Alliance, a group of well-known Oracle partners. His main emphasis is on building service-oriented business processes using SOA Suite 12c, but lately his focus has shifted towards cloud and on-premise integrations, using Oracle's offerings and custom JEE solutions. Robert is a speaker at international conferences and is frequently on the AMIS Technology blog, the Oracle Technology Network, and OTN ArchBeat Podcasts. He is one of the two SOA/BPM SIG leads for the Dutch Oracle User Group (OGh) and organizes these meetups. He also works closely with the SOA Oracle Product Management team by participating in the Beta programs. In 2016, Robert was named Oracle ACE, promoted from ACE Associate, for SOA and middleware, because of these contributions. He served as a technical reviewer for the book *Applied SOA Patterns on the Oracle Platform*. It was published in 2014.

I would like to thank the people who have helped me over the years to shape my professional career. I'm most thankful of the people at AMIS who gave me the chances to excel in my career. Without them, I wouldn't have come this far. My utmost gratitude goes to my friends and family for their loving support in writing this book. And finally, a special thanks goes out to my coauthor, Phil Wilkins, for his efforts and hard work in making this title a reality.

Phil Wilkins has spent over 25 years in the software industry with a breadth of experience in different businesses and environments, from multinationals to software start-ups and customer organizations, including a global optical and auditory healthcare provider. He started out as a developer on real-time, mission-critical solutions and has worked his way up through technical and development leadership roles, primarily in Java-based environments. Phil now works for Capgemini, specializing in cloud integration and API technologies and more generally with Oracle technologies. Outside of his work commitments, he has contributed his technical capabilities to support others in a wide range of activities, from the development of local community websites to providing input and support to the development of technical books (particularly with Packt) and software ideas and businesses. He has also had a number of articles published in technical journals in his own right and is an active blogger. The journal contributions have been part of a wider commitment to the UK Oracle User Group (UKOUG), where Phil is also a member of the Middleware Special Interest Group Committee. He has been recognized as an Oracle ACE Associate. When not immersed in work and technology, he spends his time pursuing his passion for music and with his wife and two sons.

> *I would like to thank those who, over the years, have offered me opportunities, encouraged me, and supported me to reached the point where this book has become a reality. I would also like to thank my coauthor, Robert van Mölken, not only for his hard work but for also his passion and commitment that has taken an idea to a conclusion. Lastly, but most importantly to me, I would like to take this opportunity to thank my wife, Catherine, and our two sons, Christopher and Aaron, for their tolerance of the many hours I spent in front of a computer, not only on this project but also many that have preceded and those that will surely follow.*

Acknowledgement from both the authors

We would like to thank the Oracle middleware team, particularly Ramkumar Menon, Yogesh Sontakke, and Jürgen Kress, who have been very supportive and engaging; they shared with us the details of the ICS Roadmap, providing access and an early glance of the product and answering the questions we posed.

We would also like to thank the Packt team, particularly David Barnes, who took the time to help us get this project up and running.

About the Reviewer

With a passion for system and application integration, **Rolando Carrasco** has spent most of his professional career working with customers to solve a common long-time problem: application integration. He started working with Hewlett Packard (Mexico) back in 2001, when he was in college. Even though his tenure with HP was short, as he realized very early that his professional career should be focused on Applications Integration. He started to implement integration solutions with JAVA, XML, Web Services, and EAI. He graduated with honors and was the best student of his batch (1997-2001). He studied in Mexico at Universidad Iberoamericana. The HP and Compaq fusion initiated a lot of changes in HP, so Rolando moved to Oracle, and that changed his professional career. At Oracle, he was always focused on the integration technology that Oracle had at that time; it was not as many products as today, but it was something to start with.

Then the Collaxa acquisition by Oracle happened, and that was the first step in this journey that turned Rolando into one of the most respected professionals in the Oracle SOA space for the Latin-American market. Rolando started to work with Oracle BPEL PM and had the opportunity to join the Oracle Product Management Team. He was the first PM for LAD in those days, covering Mexico to Brazil.

From 2005 to 2010, he was a Principal Product Manager for the Latin-American region and was the in charge the whole Fusion Middleware stack. Oracle acquired most of the components that are the foundation of the current Middleware offering: BEA, Thor, SUN, Oblix, Tangosol, and so on, at that time. Rolando had to be proficient in the whole stack, which was great challenge because of the extension of every product. All this kept Rolando very busy in the whole region and gave him the opportunity to work with the most important customers of the region. From Mexico to Argentina, Rolando collaborated with the different Oracle subsidiaries to promote the usage of Fusion Middleware.

Then in 2010 he joined S&P Solutions as an associate. S&P Solutions is one of the most important Oracle partners in the Latin-American region. In S&P, Rolando has had the opportunity to implement most of the Oracle Fusion Middleware stack, with the top companies in Mexico (telcos, financial institutions, retailers, manufacturing, and construction). Rolando is an Oracle ACE and is also one of the leaders of the ORAMEX Oracle Users Group in Mexico. He has a lot of articles and posts published on his blog, (`http://oracleradio.blogspot.com/`) as well as in the Oracle Technology Network for the Spanish speaking community.

Rolando wrote, back in 2015, the Oracle API Management 12c implementation book together with some other friends and colleagues, and this has been one of the greatest achievements in his career.

I would like to thank, first and foremost, my savior and lord Jesus Christ. Everything I do is to thank him and for him. I also thank my wife, Cristina, and my daughter, Constanza, as well as my parents, Rolando and Mercedes, and my brother, Manuel, for being my support. I would also like to thank my company, S&P Solutions, and my friends, in particular Paola, Erick, Ricardo, and Leonardo. I would also like to thank Robert van Mölken and Phil Wilkins, who are the authors of this book. I want to thank them for allowing me to be the technical reviewer. It was a very interesting and fun time to be reviewing all the chapters and sharing my thoughts with such a great Oracle professionals.

www.PacktPub.com

For support files and downloads related to your book, please visit www.PacktPub.com.

Did you know that Packt offers eBook versions of every book published, with PDF and ePub files available? You can upgrade to the eBook version at www.PacktPub.com and as a print book customer, you are entitled to a discount on the eBook copy. Get in touch with us at service@packtpub.com for more details.

At www.PacktPub.com, you can also read a collection of free technical articles, sign up for a range of free newsletters and receive exclusive discounts and offers on Packt books and eBooks.

https://www.packtpub.com/mapt

Get the most in-demand software skills with Mapt. Mapt gives you full access to all Packt books and video courses, as well as industry-leading tools to help you plan your personal development and advance your career.

Why subscribe?

- Fully searchable across every book published by Packt
- Copy and paste, print, and bookmark content
- On demand and accessible via a web browser

Customer Feedback

Thank you for purchasing this Packt book. We take our commitment to improving our content and products to meet your needs seriously--that's why your feedback is so valuable. Whatever your feelings about your purchase, please consider leaving a review on this book's Amazon page. Not only will this help us, more importantly it will also help others in the community to make an informed decision about the resources that they invest in to learn. You can also review for us on a regular basis by joining our reviewers club. **If you're interested in joining, or would like to learn more about the benefits we offer, please contact us**: customerreviews@packtpub.com.

Table of Contents

Preface

As you are reading this, we can assume you will have some sense of what Oracle Integration Cloud Service (ICS) is; if you don't, then do not worry, as this book will guide you through the product and the underlying concepts. We start by putting ICS into context in terms of the rapidly growing cloud marketplace, and given that we are writing for the benefit of a broad audience, let's try to get a common understanding. As you probably know, enterprise cloud solutions can be roughly split into three layers: Software as a Service (SaaS), Platform as a Service (PaaS), and Infrastructure as a Service (IaaS). ICS fits into the broad band of PaaS, which itself is divided into many forms, but we will come back to that in a moment. IaaS services such as Amazon Web Services, Microsoft Azure, and Oracle IaaS are well understood–effectively, the provision of virtualized hardware and the idea is not that new. We just have cool new names and have developed the concept. If you were involved with websites 10 years ago, you would have talked about hosting using a third-party server on which you would have installed a chosen website tool or written something from scratch. The difference between then and now is primarily the hyperscales, the speed of provisioning, and the ability to provision as many servers as you need. SaaS, at the end of the scale, is essentially a full-blooded application that users may be able to configure to meet their specific needs, but fundamentally, there is no major development involved. Illustrations include commodity blogging solutions such as WordPress and enterprise-class capabilities such as Salesforce and Office 365.

PaaS differentiates itself from the top and the bottom tiers by the fact that the platform will give you a foundation far greater than just the operating system and network, but not a complete solution that is ready to configure and use. PaaS represents the cloud-based provision of the resources you would need to build a contemporary enterprise solution such as an empty database and an application container. To return to our IaaS analogy, if in setting up a hosted website you were given all the software preinstalled to then build the website (for example, a MySQL database and perhaps a CMS solution such as Drupal) and your provider took care of the patching and so on, of the software (that is, deployment of the latest software versions with new features, bug fixes, and security fixes for the O/S, MySQL, and Drupal), then you were buying into the idea of PaaS. The challenge in understanding is the vast breadth of functionality here – from almost SaaS-like offerings such as WordPress (which can be used to build whole websites) to cloud-hosted databases, which are only a bit more than IaaS. As a result of all the flavors of PaaS we talk about, the different areas of PaaS have developed their own terms to make them distinct from other PaaS offerings; for example, integration platforms have adopted the term of iPaaS (integration Platform as a Service), and cloud databases are referred to as DBaaS, and so on.

This fragmentation, as well as the desire for a similar acronym for all layers, has spawned the adoption of the expression XaaS—anything (or X) as a Service.

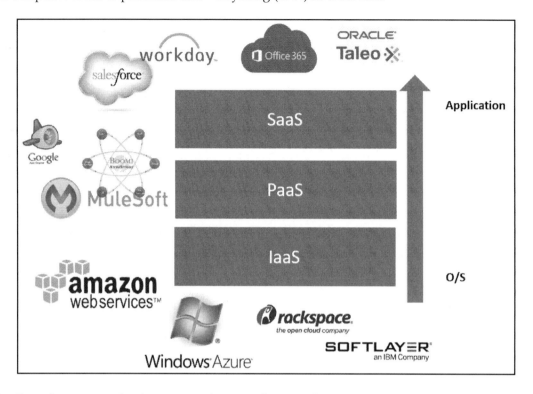

iPaaS can be commonly characterized in two flavors of products—the heavily technical solutions such as Oracle SOA Suite (known as SOA CS) and IBM's WebSphere Application Server on Cloud, along with the second type with graphical user interface-driven solutions in which ICS competes, which includes products such as MuleSoft, Dell Boomi, and SnapLogic. These more visual and often less technical tools can often draw on more consumer-like experiences, and you can trace the origins of this group of iPaaS solutions to consumer predecessors such as products in the form of solutions such as IFTTT (If This Then That – `https://ifttt.com/`) and Zapier (`https://zapier.com`), where you could set up in a fairly visual manner integrations like, when a favorite RSS feed posts something, you can get it to be tweeted by on your Twitter account by exploiting the APIs provided.

The difference between solutions such as IFTTT and iPaaS at the enterprise end of the spectrum is sophistication, capability, security, and reliability; that is, you expect enterprise solutions to be 24/7 resilient and very robust, not to mention, having a focus on connecting enterprise solutions such as Salesforce, Workday, Oracle Taleo, Office 365, and SuccessFactors. That said, as more social and collaborative platforms influence more and more of the workplace, we will see this line blur.

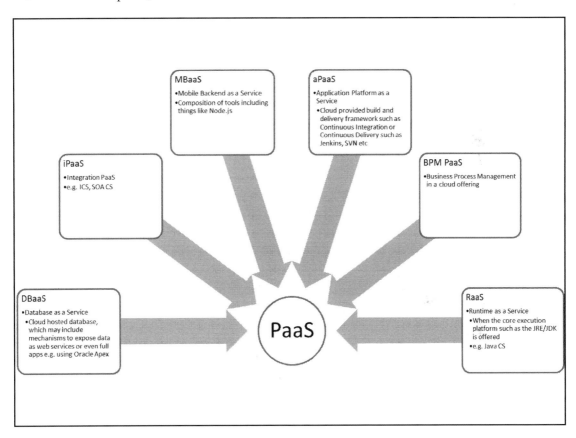

The last thing to keep in mind with our first iPaaS group is that these more technical products are typically cloud-enabled versions of their mature on-premises solutions. As mentioned previously, SOA CS is Oracle SOA Suite when deployed on-premises (with a few additional tools added to address the need to hide the platform considerations of the deploying SOA). The newer generation products, such as ICS, Boomi, and MuleSoft, are largely focused on a cloud delivery approach and cannot be deployed as on-premises solutions in the traditional manner (such as SOA Suite), although vendors such as Oracle are leading innovative thinking in this space.

Before we look at why ICS is a significant product in the iPaaS space, it is important to remember that you do not need to have acquired any other products from Oracle to use it. In simple terms, ICS can be used to integrate with any application/service if it complies with one of a number of supported standards or has an adaptor. The ability to offer adapters that simplify integration is going to be an area of growth and market differentiation.

Oracle has several distinct advantages in the marketplace that makes ICS a very significant player. Setting aside the arguments of Oracle's deep pockets, the factors you might consider are as follows:

- Mature leading integration solutions that can be exploited to create a new feature rich tool. Even while Oracle had focused on on-premises solutions, they have had to build connectors to major cloud solutions such as Salesforce and Workday, and these are being ported to the cloud.
- Oracle has a very large partner base and has created an ecosystem for partners, customers, and the wider community to build, sell, or donate their adaptors to work with ICS (and potentially for SOA CS and other parts of their PaaS offering).
- ICS can be easily adopted by both its middleware (SOA Suite and so on) and customer base, as well as its applications customers (E-Business Suite, Seibel, Fusion applications, and so on).

- Hyper-convergence means that Oracle owns solutions from microchips and other hardware all the way to SaaS, which in turn creates economies and optimizations as the hardware is tailored to provide optimal performance for the different product elements. It also allows Oracle to make market propositions the competition cannot, for example, protecting cloud services against attacks that exploit very low-level vulnerabilities because there is logic in the microprocessors to detect it.
- You can buy full Oracle cloud stack and run on-premises and even have a financial model based upon cloud concepts such as compute utilization (not hardware and license cost) and some other major vendors as recognizing this idea as well.
- If you are an Oracle customer, then your existing products will have the benefit of connectors that have been developed for Oracle's own products, making integration easier and simpler (something we will explore further in this book).
- Oracle's portfolio has been broadened and is now exploiting open source initiatives far more quickly within the PaaS space with the arrival of Application Container Cloud Service (based on Docker), Kafka service, and `Node.js`. In many respects, this approach appears a lot like that of Red Hat in so far as they take versions of open source offerings and then make them sufficiently robust enough that they can offer a service with them. This is something that can be done in a cost-effective manner, as Oracle can drive the continued updates and patching rather than needing to offer long-term support agreements for on-premises solutions.

The last point here is worth exploring a little further. Oracle's application portfolio has grown through build as well as acquisition. This has meant Oracle has needed to have a story for making these products working together easily. This approach has changed over the years, starting when Oracle effectively owned multiple discrete products and having overtime brought the best of the different products together to form what is now known as Fusion applications. The Fusion applications are also the core of many of Oracle's SaaS solutions (and the foundation of Fusion applications is Fusion Middleware and is the basis of nearly all Oracle products today).

The following diagram illustrates how Oracle has evolved and enabled integration between the different portfolio offerings over the last decade to arrive at where they are today:

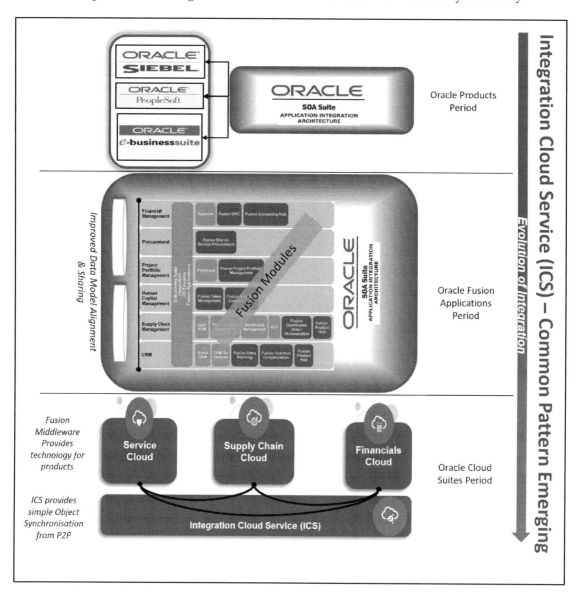

We can characterize the different periods and their approaches to integration along the following lines:

- Oracle Products Period:
  - Completely discrete solutions with integration offered by middleware and licensed PIPs
  - Applications built on own technologies
  - Applications that effectively share nothing out-of-the-box
- Oracle Fusion Applications Period:
  - Rebuilt applications using Fusion technology stack
  - Here, product features overlapped the best ideas, which were carried forward to the Fusion generation
  - Integration needs that were sought to be reduced by making data models more common and exploit Fusion integration mechanisms internally
- Oracle Cloud Suites Period:
  - Grouping of related Fusion applications/components
  - Each cloud offering is now decoupled from other clouds—so, ICS is invoked by cloud solution event framework
  - The customer configures ICS to respond to Create, Read, Update, Delete (CRUD)-based services – interface data model mapping is kept easy through a recommendation engine populated with standard Oracle provided mappings

What this book covers

The book's goal is to illustrate the capabilities of ICS and how they can be applied. The book will introduce some concepts and technologies that will allow you to develop integrations not only quickly but in a way that means they are maintainable and extensible. The book will also help guide the reader as to where more information can be found, as a single volume can't cover every aspect of integration.

Chapter 1, *Introducing the Concepts and Terminology*, is an overview of the ideas and terms that anyone working with ICS and integration generally needs to have a basic handle on, and it also introduces common characteristics of integration with ICS.

Chapter 2, *Integrating Our First Two Applications*, is the first practical use of ICS, which will illustrate integrating two systems together.

Chapter 3, *Distribute Messages Using the Pub-Sub Model*, reworks the integration demonstrated in the previous chapter to use the pub-sub model to help demonstrate the differences and benefits of the different approaches.

Chapter 4, *Integrations between SaaS Applications*, builds upon the ideas presented so far, explores how to integrate SaaS solutions, and shows how you can test your integration without affecting a live system.

Chapter 5, *Going Social with Twitter and Google*, looks at how connecting social applications differ. As social capabilities become ever more important, how do you connect and authenticate against such services?

Chapter 6, *Creating Complex Transformations*, explains that simply connecting systems together and performing data mappings is only the beginning of integration. Often, integration will need to enrich the data from simple things like transforming different representations and beyond.

Chapter 7, *Routing and Filtering*, demonstrates how things can be done when you need rules to determine who will receive data.

Chapter 8, *Publish and Subscribe with External Applications*, takes the concept of subscribing to events a step further using other Oracle middleware capabilities.

Chapter 9, *Managed File Transfer with Scheduling*, looks at how some processes follow the older file-based integrations with ICS and the use of file transfer, because not all integrations are event-driven.

Chapter 10, *Advanced Orchestration with Branching and Asynchronous Flows*, demonstrates the latest capabilities of ICS that include the ability to make parts of the integration asynchronous, so the process is not limited by the slowest part of an integration.

Chapter 11, *Calling an On-Premises API*, look at how ICS enables a cloud integration platform to work systems in different clouds or on-premises easily with forecasts for enterprises needing to run hybrid environments (that is, any combination of public, private, and normal on-premises solutions).

Chapter 12, *Are My Integrations Running Fine, and What If They Are Not?*, examines how to determine if things are running well or not, and when they are not, how to diagnose problems because, in the ideal world, nothing ever fails, but the world is not perfect.

Chapter 13, *Where Can I Go from Here?*, presents the other resources that are available to you to further exploit ICS because, with everything presented so far, we have not distinguished between a live environment and a development environment.

How we have approached this book

The approach we have adopted with this book is worth explaining. If you read the section on the target audience you'll note that we're not aiming only at the developer community but at a wider potential user audience of ICS. To help us do this, we have set ourselves some parameters that will help you understand why things have been done a particular way:

1. Using tools that the entire target audience can use and understand; so, nice integrated developer tools are not used for most of the book – there are a couple of areas where they are relevant, though.

2. Not forcing the reader to buy lots of extra products to allow the majority of the examples to be exercised – this does mean that rather than real end systems, we use tools to allow us to pretend they exist. If you are a developer seeing this, you will recognize this as simply implementing the idea of mocking. We have used apiary and `Mockable.io` for this in the book. We will also make use of several different but well-known tools to demonstrate triggering of web services such as SoapUI, cURL, and Postman to help give a sense of the different choices, although we make strong use of SoapUI as it is a leading tool.

3. Not getting caught up in any unnecessary complexities that can arise to ensure data can flow from A to B. All the examples should work from your home or work computer without needing to talk with your Internet provider or network manager about IP addresses.

4. Trying to build the examples around a plausible idea that anyone could relate to. To achieve this, we have drawn on the idea of services that can be connected to the FlightAware API, which provides the ability to get events and query information relating to flights, airports, and air travel generally at one end and other systems at the other, for example, Salesforce or a Flight Progress notification. The example will only be a vehicle to help illustrate the product's utilization, though:
   - The FlightAware API can be found at `https://uk.flightaware.com/commercial/flightxml/`
   - The services we have used are not fully aligned with the FlightAware

API to simplify the amount of effort in the reader implementing the examples

- The simplification also enables us to focus on the parts that are central to explaining ICS and the ideas behind it (so not all elements are used in the example)

5. Rather than explaining every step in each example, we have reduced the amount of explanation provided as certain activities need to be repeated, such as setting up connections.

6. Conveying the ideas and concepts will always take priority of being puritan with best practices.

7. ICS is a growing and maturing product—everything in this book will hold largely true for a few years—even if the occasional screen label changes or stylesheets get updated, the reader should understand what they are being shown as well as how.

What you need for this book

Beyond the use of ICS, we have taken the approach of utilizing additional services and tools that are free wherever possible. We will explain in more detail the different tools and services, but let's start by just introducing what is needed:

- An Oracle Cloud account. A trial ICS account will be sufficient for most things (as long as you have tried everything in the book within the trial period obviously).

- Free accounts with apiary (https://apiary.io/) and Mockable (https://www.mockable.io/). We will introduce these in more detail shortly.

- A free edition of SoapUI (https://www.soapui.org/), as we will be using this to initiate many of our use cases. We also make use of Postman (https://www.getpostman.com/) as an alternate option, which can be retrieved freely.

- To follow the book, it will be necessary to look at and make minor changes to the XML Schemas. The changes needed are simple enough that they can be done with a simple text editor, you would rather use your preferred development tool, such as JDeveloper. If you want to use JDeveloper, we would recommend adopting a 12.x version, which can be obtained from http://www.oracle.com/technetwork/developer-tools/jdev/overview/index.html. There is, of course, the middle ground with tools such as Xsemmel (https://xsemmel.codeplex.com/) as an open source option, or the market-leading XMLSpy (http://www.altova.com/).

- A copy of the schemas and related resources that go with this book. These can be found via the Packt website or via the author's own site at `https://oracle-integration.cloud`.
- The CURL command-line tool to allow us to make simple calls to the ICS API (`https://curl.haxx.se/`).
- VirtualBox is a freely available desktop style virtualization tool and is used to help quickly create an environment in which we can run the Oracle agent technology (`https://www.virtualbox.org/`).

Several of the chapters also make use of additional external services to demonstrate some of the features such as file-level integration and social web services. To demonstrate such capabilities, we have created accounts with the following services. To follow these chapters, you may wish to do them. The services are as follows:

- Google (`https://console.developers.google.com/`)
- Salesforce (`https://developer.salesforce.com/`)
- TimeDB (`https://timezonedb.com`)
- Twitter (`https://dev.twitter.com/overview/api`)
- Trello (`https://trello.com/`)
- Oracle Messaging Cloud Service (`https://cloud.oracle.com/messaging`)

This book is intended for web developers with no knowledge of WebStorm yet, but who are experienced in JavaScript, `Node.js`, HTML, and CSS, and reasonably familiar with frameworks such as AngularJS and Meteor.

Introduction to apiary

To be able to describe, work with, and simulate (mock) web services that use the REST paradigm (explained in Chapter 1, *Introducing the Concepts and Terminology*) easily and in a way that reflects the sort of integrations you are likely to build with ICS, we have chosen to use `Apiary.io` (although there are other services on the Internet that offer similar capabilities). We chose `Apiary.io` as Oracle are developing a closer relationship with apiary with other products, so it may be possible that Oracle will develop its ecosystem for ICS to further incorporate apiary in the future. Apiary also offers a pricing model that allows you to get started without any additional expenditure.

Introducing Mockable

Cloud services that offer support for SOAP mocking are limited, in part as REST is overtaking SOAP as a more popular way to provide web services and define them using definition syntaxes such as Blueprint and Swagger. We have adopted `Mockable.io` for this book – driven by its ease of use and simplicity and again free startup model.

Creating an instance of Integration Cloud Service

When you first start using ICS, you will use Oracle's cloud managed website, which will allow to select the service(s) that you want and configure users. In this book, we have deliberately chosen not to write about this process so that we can concentrate on the application of ICS, which generally will be of greater value to you, we believe. The process of managing users is relatively simple. In addition to this, both Oracle and their partners will surely assist any customers in managing environment setup as it is in their interests to see customers using their services successfully.

Who this book is for

This book seeks to support a broad range of readers ranging from Citizen Integrators to software architects and developers. This brings in the question – what is a Citizen Integrator? The term Citizen Integrator can be traced back to at least 2009 with Gartner (`htt p://www.gartner.com/newsroom/id/1212813`) as a variation on the idea of Citizen Developer. Gartner proposes and we are now seeing the idea that you no longer need to be a technologist to be able to integrate solutions. A Citizen Integrator can be characterized as anyone who can as easily be part of an organizations, business community as much as the IT part of a business. These individuals will have a level of technical appreciation, and will certainly understand the semantics of the data being exposed. For example, a business analyst is as likely to use ICS to build integrations as an IT specialist.

Conventions

In this book, you will find a number of text styles that distinguish between different kinds of information. Here are some examples of these styles and an explanation of their meaning.

Code words in text, database table names, folder names, filenames, file extensions, pathnames, dummy URLs, user input, and Twitter handles are shown as follows: "An XSLT style sheet is an XML document containing the root node `<xsl:stylesheet>`, which is declared by the `xsl` prefix and is mandatory."

A block of code is set as follows:

```
<html>
  <body>
    LET $book := doc("bookstore.xml")/book
    FOR $ch in $book/chapter
    WHERE $book/chapter/num < 10
    ORDER BY $ch/pagecount DESC
    RETURN <h2>{ $ch/title }</h2>
  </body>
</html>
```

Any command-line input or output is written as follows:

```
curl -u username:password -H "HTTP header attribute settings inquotes" -X
HTTP operation e.g. GET target URL
```

New terms and **important words** are shown in bold. Words that you see on the screen, for example, in menus or dialog boxes, appear in the text like this: "Besides the home page, all the functions are part of the **Designer Portal**."

Warnings or important notes appear in a box like this.

Tips and tricks appear like this.

Reader feedback

Feedback from our readers is always welcome. Let us know what you think about this book – what you liked or disliked. Reader feedback is important for us as it helps us develop titles that you will really get the most out of. To send us general feedback, simply e-mail feedback@packtpub.com, and mention the book's title in the subject of your message. If there is a topic that you have expertise in and you are interested in either writing or contributing to a book, see our author guide at www.packtpub.com/authors.

Customer support

Now that you are the proud owner of a Packt book, we have a number of things to help you to get the most from your purchase.

Downloading the example code

To complete the integrations, it will be necessary to download the schemas and WSDLs from the Packt site or the author's site at `https://www.oracle-integration.cloud`. You may also want to download the exported implementations from the different chapters which will also be available that these sites.

The XSDs, WSDLs, and related artifacts have not been written to reflect best practice (such as separating the WSDL and XSD content) but to provide the material in a form that keeps the content simple and easy to follow as our goal in the book is about mastering ICS, rather than best practices for web standards.

You can download the example code files for this book from your account at `http://www.packtpub.com`. If you purchased this book elsewhere, you can visit `http://www.packtpub.com/support` and register to have the files e-mailed directly to you.

You can download the code files by following these steps:

1. Log in or register to our website using your e-mail address and password.
2. Hover the mouse pointer on the **SUPPORT** tab at the top.
3. Click on **Code Downloads & Errata**.
4. Enter the name of the book in the **Search** box.
5. Select the book for which you're looking to download the code files.
6. Choose from the drop-down menu where you purchased this book from.
7. Click on **Code Download**.

Once the file is downloaded, please make sure that you unzip or extract the folder using the latest version of:

- WinRAR / 7-Zip for Windows
- Zipeg / iZip / UnRarX for Mac
- 7-Zip / PeaZip for Linux

The code bundle for the book is also hosted on GitHub at `https://github.com/PacktPublishing/Implementing-Oracle-Integration-Cloud-Service`. We also have other code bundles from our rich catalog of books and videos available at `https://github.com/Packt`

`Publishing/`. Check them out!

Downloading the color images of this book

We also provide you with a PDF file that has color images of the screenshots/diagrams used in this book. The color images will help you better understand the changes in the output. You can download this file from `https://www.packtpub.com/sites/default/files/down` `loads/ImplementingOracleIntegrationCloudService_ColorImages.pdf`.

Errata

Although we have taken every care to ensure the accuracy of our content, mistakes do happen. If you find a mistake in one of our books—maybe a mistake in the text or the code—we would be grateful if you could report this to us. By doing so, you can save other readers from frustration and help us improve subsequent versions of this book. If you find any errata, please report them by visiting `http://www.packtpub.com/submit-errata`, selecting your book, clicking on the **Errata Submission Form** link, and entering the details of your errata. Once your errata are verified, your submission will be accepted and the errata will be uploaded to our website or added to any list of existing errata under the Errata section of that title.

To view the previously submitted errata, go to `https://www.packtpub.com/books/conten` `t/support` and enter the name of the book in the search field. The required information will appear under the **Errata** section.

Piracy

Piracy of copyrighted material on the Internet is an ongoing problem across all media. At Packt, we take the protection of our copyright and licenses very seriously. If you come across any illegal copies of our works in any form on the Internet, please provide us with the location address or website name immediately so that we can pursue a remedy.

Please contact us at `copyright@packtpub.com` with a link to the suspected pirated material.

We appreciate your help in protecting our authors and our ability to bring you valuable content.

Questions

If you have a problem with any aspect of this book, you can contact us at `questions@packtpub.com`, and we will do our best to address the problem.

1
Introducing the Concepts and Terminology

This chapter gives us an overview of the concepts and terminology that apply when implementing integrations with **Oracle Integration Cloud Service**. It explains the components a general integration consists of, with a step-by-step approach.

When we talk about integration, we mean the act of bringing components together into one single system. In the context of IT, we refer to a process that stitches together different subsystems, so that the data contained in each system becomes part of a larger single system that can share data more quickly and easily.

Oracle Integration Cloud Service is a solution that enables you to simplify integrations between cloud applications, and between cloud and on-premises applications. It helps you create connections to well-known and less-known SaaS and PaaS applications, using the available cloud adapters, publish or subscribe to the Messaging Cloud Service, or use industry standards such as **SOAP, REST, FTP, File,** and **JMS.** Most of these technologies will be explained in more detail later. **Integration Cloud Service (ICS)** provides enterprise-grade connectivity regardless of the application you are connecting to or where they are hosted.

The concepts and terminology can be categorized into three major areas:

- Connections describe the inbound and outbound applications that we are integrating with
- Integrations describe how information is shared between applications
- Transformations and lookups describe how to interact with the data

We can engage with Oracle Cloud Services and especially with ICS by going to `http://cloud.oracle.com/integration`. Here we can try the service for free, which we can use when going through this book.

Typical workflow and steps to execute

Before we dive deep into the major three areas, let's first take a look at the typical workflow when creating integrations with Oracle Integration Cloud Service. Since ICS is a cloud service, you only need to open a browser and enter the URL of your Cloud instance, for example: `https://instancex-domainy.integration.us2.oraclecloud.com/ics`.

We can sign into Oracle Integration Cloud Service by entering our credentials. Just like any Oracle Cloud Service users can be provisioned after subscribing to a service. After logging in we are welcomed by the home page:

The home page gives an overview of all major functionalities that ICS has to offer. On this page we can easily navigate to each of these functions or to the help pages to learn the details. Besides the home page, all the functions are part of the **Designer Portal**. We use the **Designer Portal** to create the five pillars of ICS: **Integrations**, **Connections**, **Lookups**, **Packages**, **Agents** and **Adapters**. We will discuss the pillars in the chapters to come, but we specifically address the agents in Chapter 11, *Calling an On-Premises API* and adapters in Chapter 13, *Where Can I Go From Here?*:

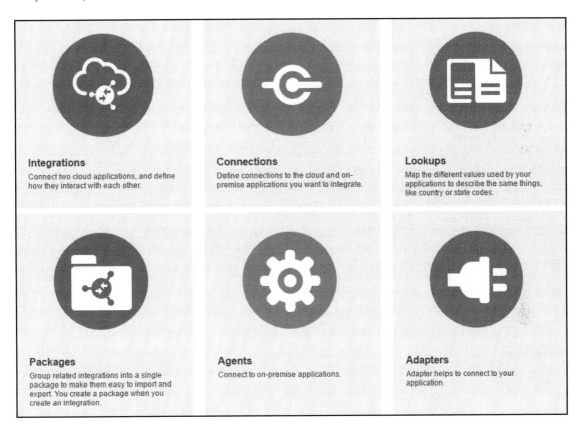

Integrations

Connect two cloud applications, and define how they interact with each other.

Connections

Define connections to the cloud and on-premise applications you want to integrate.

Lookups

Map the different values used by your applications to describe the same things, like country or state codes.

Packages

Group related integrations into a single package to make them easy to import and export. You create a package when you create an integration.

Agents

Connect to on-premise applications.

Adapters

Adapter helps to connect to your application.

Let's investigate the most important pillars. Each integration starts with a blank canvas:

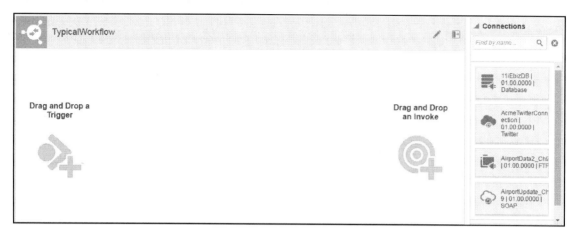

An integration always consists of a **Trigger** (source) and an **Invoke** (target). A **Trigger** means the connection where the integration receives the message from. An **Invoke** means the connection where the integration sends the message to. These two connections are the first two objectives before creating an integration.

In the following figure, both **Trigger** and **Invoke** connections use a SOAP connector. Just simply drag and drop the connection to use from the **Connections** panel onto the drop zone:

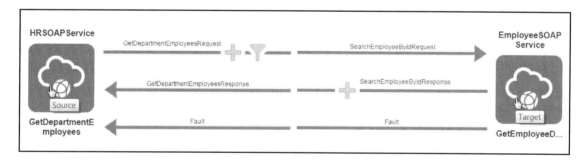

When integrating two applications with each other, it is likely that the data structure which the **Trigger** and **Invoke** applications understand is different. The next objective is to map the data between the two applications:

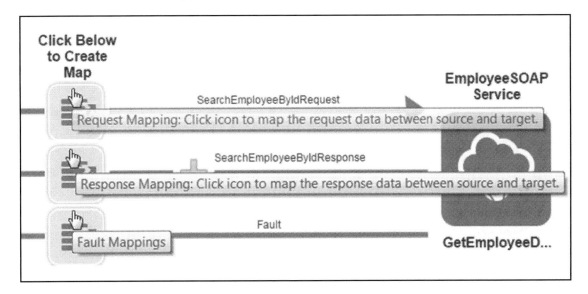

It depends on the type of connection pattern which mappings you can create. For example, when dealing with an asynchronous/one-way operation you only have a request mapping. When dealing with a synchronous operation you have both request and response mappings. The only time you can create a fault mapping is when both trigger and invoke connections define faults. For instance, in the preceding case where both WSDLs define a business fault in their specification.

For point-to-point integrations these are the objectives to reach. But if you are dealing with more complex integrations a typical workflow can consist of a few more objectives.

For instance, if the data received from the **Trigger** needs to be enriched (that is, locating and adding additional data based on data included in the message) before it can be sent to the **Invoke**. The next objective would be to add a call to an enrichment service. This enrichment service can be a different connector from your trigger or invoke:

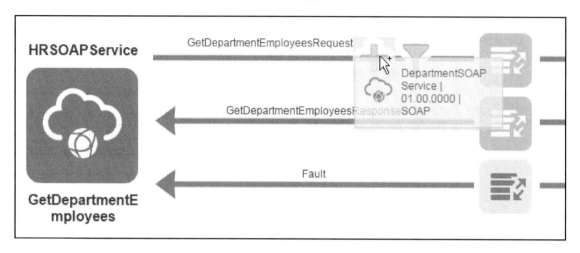

An enrichment service can easily be added with a simple drag and drop of the connection. Another objective can be to route to a different target based on the source data:

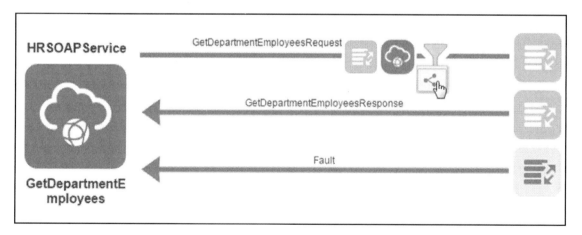

All of these objectives are going to be discussed in detail, but first let's explore the concepts and terminology behind them.

Connections define our integration points

It all starts with creating connections. A connection defines the application you want to integrate with. If an application has a public API then ICS can integrate with it. For example, a well-known or lesser-known SaaS application, a public SOAP or REST API for weather or flight information, a custom application using the Messaging Service, or an on-premises **Enterprise Resource Planning (ERP)** application.

Oracle Integration Cloud Service comes with a large set of out-of-the-box Cloud adapters, to provide easy access to these applications. The amount of available adapters is constantly growing. Most of these adapters are built by Oracle, but through the marketplace it is also possible for customers and partners to build their own adapters.

Each connection can be used for inbound and outbound communication. The majority of available adapters support both ways. A connection commonly describes the type of application, the location of the API definition or endpoint, and the credentials needed to connect securely with the application.

Connections can be divided into four categories: SaaS adapters, Technology adapters, Social adapters, and on-premises adapters:

SaaS adapters

Oracle Integration Cloud Service offers a large collection of adapters to connect to SaaS applications natively. **Software as a Service (SaaS)**, also called on-demand software, is software that is offered as a hosted service. SaaS applications are typically accessed by users using a browser, but most offer API's to access and modify the data or to send events to the SaaS application to perform a task. For the most popular SaaS vendors, Oracle supplies Cloud adapters that can be used by Integration Cloud Service. New adapters are released on monthly cycles. The SaaS adapters can also be developed by customers, partners, and even you.

Most SaaS applications that Oracle offers as the vendor have their own adapter in Integration Cloud Service, such as the ERP, HCM, and the Sales Cloud:

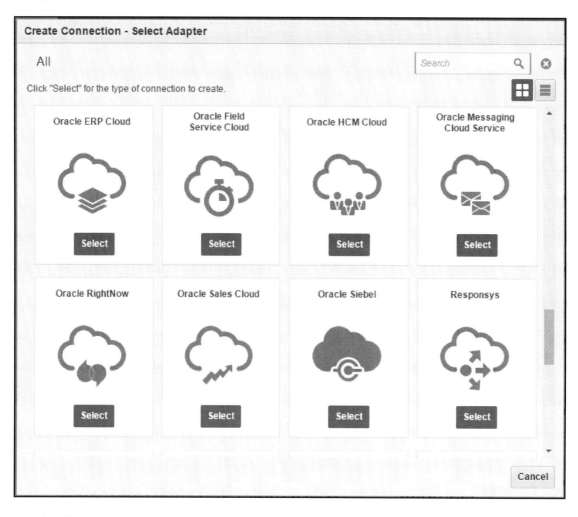

Besides that, ICS supports solutions such as Salesforce, Eloqua, and NetSuite out-of-the-box.

What's the difference with native APIs?

Because the SaaS application offers their API, you might wonder why a special adapter is necessary. The adapters offer a much more simplified experience through a powerful wizard. For example, the Oracle RightNow and Salesforce adapters support the automatic provisioning of Business Objects in the wizard. These adapters also handle security and provide standard error handling capabilities.

In Chapter 4, *Integrations between SaaS Applications*, we will integrate applications with some of these SaaS applications.

Technology adapters

Not all applications we see on a daily basis are SaaS applications with prebuilt adapters. Industry standards such as SOAP and REST are used by the majority of APIs. SOAP is mostly used for system-to-system integrations, whereas the lightweight REST protocol is used to provide access to mobile applications. For both protocols Oracle Integration Cloud Service provides an adapter.

SOAP adapter

Originally an acronym for **Simple Object Access Protocol**, SOAP is an industry standard protocol originated around 2000. This specification is used in the implementation of web services and describes exchanging structured information. The SOAP protocol uses XML as the markup language for its message format. SOAP itself is not a transport protocol, but relies on application layer protocols, such as HTTP and JMS.

Web services that are built to communicate using the SOAP protocol use the **Web Service Description Language** (**WSDL**). This is an XML-based interface and describes the functionality a web service offers. The acronym WSDL also describes the physical definition file. There are two versions of the WSDL, 1.1 and 2.0, but version 1.1 is still the most commonly used.

The WSDL structure consists of five building blocks; **types**, **messages**, **porttypes**, **bindings**, and **services**:

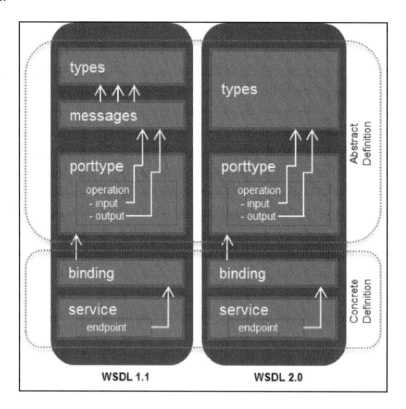

The first three describe the abstract definition and are separated from the latter two that describe the concrete use, allowing the reuse in multiple transports. Where concrete means that a specific instance of a service is referenced (meaning that you have a URI).

Types are nothing more than placeholders that describe the data. An embedded or external referenced XML Schema definition is used to describe the message structure.

Messages are an abstraction of the request and/or response messages used by an operation. The information needed to perform the operation is described by the message. It typically refers to an element in the embedded or referenced XML Schema definition.

PortTypes or Interfaces define a web service, with a set of operations it can perform and direct which messages are used to perform the operation. An operation can only have a request message (one-way), a response message (call-back), or both request and response message (synchronous).

Bindings describe the first part of a concrete WSDL. It specifies the interface with its operations and binds a porttype to a specific protocol (typically SOAP over HTTP).

Services expose a set of bindings to the web-based protocols. The port or endpoint typically represent where consumers can reach the web service:

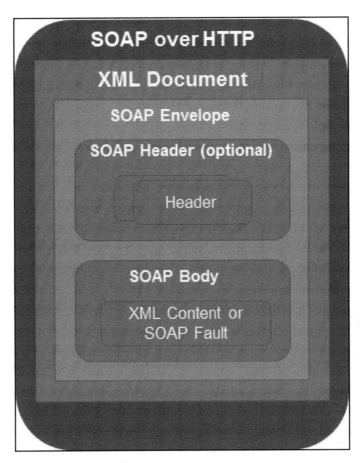

SOAP itself, also defines a small XML Envelope, which allows XML messages to be carried from one place to another without any system having to inspect the content. Compare it to sending a parcel with a courier–the courier only needs to see the information written on the box, not what is in it!

In Oracle Integration Cloud Service you can create connections based on these WSDLs. When the SOAP adapter is used in ICS you get a wizard that lets you pick one of the available operations (or select it for you if you only have one).

REST adapter

Originally an acronym for **Representational State Transfer**, REST is a software architectural style also introduced in 2000. It consists of a coordinated set of architectural constraints within distributed systems. The REST architectural style introduces certain architectural properties such as performance, scalability, simplicity, addressability, portability, and reliability. Because it is a style, there are some variations going around.

Web services or APIs that apply REST are called RESTful APIs. They are simply a collection of URIs, HTTP-based calls that use **JavaScript Object Notation (JSON)** or XML to transmit data objects, many of which will contain relational links. JSON is a human-readable text format consisting of attribute/value pairs.

RESTful APIs are usually defined with the following aspects:

- The principal of addressability is covered by the URIs, which has a base URI, such as `http://www.example.com/restfulapi/`, for all its resources.
- Each resource has its own address, also known as an URI. A resource exposes a unique piece of information that the server can provide.
- For sending the data objects, an Internet media type, often JSON, is used.
- The API uses standard HTTP methods, for example, `GET`, `PUT`, `POST`, or `DELETE`.
- Reference stat and reference-related resources use hypertext links.

RESTful APIs use common resource naming. When deciding which resources are available within your system, name the resources as nouns as opposed to verbs or actions. They should refer to a thing instead of an action. The name and structure convey meaning to those consuming the API.

Resource examples

In this example, we use our Flight API hosted on Apiary (`https://apiary.io/`).

The base URI for this API is: `http://icsflightapi.apiary-mock.com/`

To insert (create) an airline in our flight system, we can use:

```
POST http://icsflightapi.apiary-mock.com/airlines
```

To retrieve the details of the Airline with ICAO Identifier KLM, we can use the following:

```
GET http://icsflightapi.apiary-mock.com/airlines/KL
```

The same URI would be used for `PUT` and `DELETE`, to update and delete, respectively.

What about creating a new destination an airline travels to? One option is to POST to the resource URI http://icsflightapi.apiary-mock.com/destinations, but it's arguably outside the context of an airline.

Because you want to create a destination for a flight schedule, the context should be on the schedule. It can be argued that the option to POST a message to the URI http://icsflightapi.apiary-mock.com/airlines/KL/destinations better clarifies the resource. Now you know that the destination is added to the airline.

With this in mind, there is no limit on the depth of the URIs hierarchy as long as it is in the context of the parent resource.

In Oracle Integration Cloud Service you can create connections based on the base URI. When the REST adapter is used in ICS you get a wizard that lets you create the resource that you want to expose. Only one resource can be implemented per integration.

In Chapter 2, *Integrating Our First Two Applications*, both SOAP(inbound) and REST(outbound) adapters are used for our first integration.

FTP adapter

Besides web service standards of SOAP and REST, there is also a technology adapter for FTP. Originally an acronym for **File Transfer Protocol**, FTP is a protocol used to rapidly transfer files across servers originated around 1985. The FTP adapter enables you to transfer files from a source or to a target FTP server in an integration in ICS.

With this adapter you can transfer (write) files to any server that is publicly accessible through the Internet. Files can be written in either binary or ASCII format. The adapter enables you to create integrations, which will read a file from a source FTP and write it to a target FTP server. In this scenario, the integration also supports scheduling, which enables you to define the time and frequency the transfer occurs.

The adapter supports some welcome features, such as the possibility to natively translate file content and to encrypt and decrypt outbound files using **Pretty Good Privacy** (**PGP**) cryptography. With the first feature you can translate a file with comma-separated values to XML.

The adapter not only supports plain FTP, but also FTP over SSL and secure FTP (**SFTP**). FTP over SSL requires the upload of a Certificate store. SFTP requires an optional host key to ensure that you connect to the correct SFTP server and secures that your connection is not compromised.

We will use the FTP adapter when managing file transfers in `Chapter 9`, *Managed File Transfers with Scheduling*.

On-premises adapters

Of course, not all of our applications run in the cloud, for most of us it is still rather new. Most of our mission critical systems run on-premises. Oracle Integration Cloud Service provides adapters and supporting software to create a Hybrid Cloud solution.

A Hybrid Cloud is a cloud computing environment, which is a combination of on-premises, private (third-party), and public cloud services. Between the platforms we usually find an Orchestration layer. For example, an enterprise has an on-premises finance system to host critical and sensitive workloads, but want to expose this system for third-party users.

Integration Cloud Service provides adapters and the supporting software to simplify integration between cloud and on-premises applications in a secure and scalable way.

The supported adapters include technology adapters, for example, Database, File, and JMS, an adapter for Oracle E-Business Suite, Oracle Siebel and SAP, and so on.

For example, with the database adapter you can call a stored procedure in your on-premises database or execute a pure SQL statement.

The File Adapter enables file transfers between two servers that cannot talk directly with each other. **Java Message Service** (**JMS**) enables integrations with existing JEE applications.

Adapters do not indicate if it is for on-premises use only, or if it can be used with an on-premises endpoint. When creating a new connection based on the adapter it will ask for an agent to assign to the connection.

ICS includes two agents; the Connectivity and the Execution agent. An agent is a piece of software running on-premises and puts a secure bridge between the Oracle Cloud and on-premises. We will shortly describe both agents, but have dedicated `Chapter 11`, *Calling an On-Premises API* to explain them in more detail.

What is the Connectivity Agent?

The Agent is basically a gateway between cloud and on-premises, and it eliminates common security and complexity issues previously associated with integrating on-premises applications from outside the firewall. The agent can connect with on-premises applications, such as the database or ERP application, using the existing JCA adapter framework. To understand this concept we first look at the agent's architecture.

Architecture Guidelines

The Agent is developed with a few architectural guidelines in mind. The *most important guideline* is that it shouldn't be required to open inbound ports to communicate with on-premises applications. This means that there isn't a need to create firewall rules to provide access. Because of this no open ports can be abused.

The second guideline describes that it is not required to expose a private SOAP-based web service using a (reverse) proxy, for example, API Gateway or **Oracle HTTP Server (OHS)**. The third describes that no on-premises assets have to be installed in the **DeMilitarized Zone (DMZ)**. The agent is installed in the local network where the backend systems are accessible.

The fourth guideline describes that it is not required to have an existing J2EE container to deploy the agent on. The fifth and last guideline describes that it is not required to have IT personnel monitor the on-premises component. With this agent the monitoring of the component is part of monitoring UI within ICS.

Architecture

The Agent consists of two components, a Cloud Agent installed on ICS and a Client Agent installed at on-premises. The Messaging Cloud is used by the Agent for its message exchange and only allows connections established from the Oracle Cloud.

It disallows explicit inbound connections for other parties. The agent uses the existing JCA adapter framework to invoke on-premises endpoints, for example, **Database**, file, and **ERP** (Siebel/SAP):

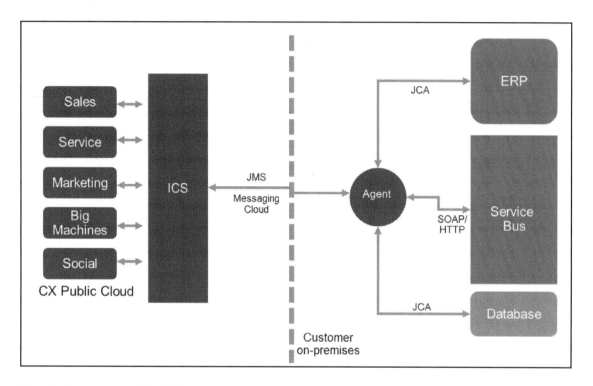

Oracle Integration Cloud Service supports multiple agents for load distribution and high availability. For example, it is possible to group multiple agents, but place each agent on a different local host/machine. Agents can be grouped on a functional, process, or organization level.

The Connectivity Agent can be downloaded from ICS and installed on demand on-premises. What you get at the end is a fully installed WebLogic server with a domain and managed server running the necessary Agent clients and JCA adapters.

Message Exchange Patterns

A **Message Exchange Pattern** (**MEP**) describes the pattern of messages required by a communication protocol for the exchange of messages between nodes. A MEP defines the sequence of messages, specifying the order, direction, and cardinality of those messages in a service call or service operation.

Two main MEPs are synchronous (request-response) and asynchronous (fire and forget).

The agent conforms to a few message exchange patterns when communicating with on-premises applications from the cloud:

- Synchronous request from cloud to on-premise to retrieve data (for example, getting the status of an order from EBS in real time)
- Cloud events triggers Async message exchange with on-premises (for example, creation of an incident in RightNow causes creation of service requests in EBS)
- On-Premises events triggers Async message exchange with the cloud (for example, service request updates event result in Async synchronization with RightNow)
- Synchronized data extracts between on-premises and Cloud applications (for example, EBS-based customer data synchronized with CRM)

What is the Execution Agent?

This Agent is a fully fledged Integration Cloud Service that you can install on-premises. When you subscribe to ICS, you also have the option to install an on-premises version in your local environment (that is, DMZ). This enables you to use ICS as a proxy server that sits between your mission critical systems protected by a firewall and the cloud version. More on this agent in Chapter 11, *Calling an On-Premises API*.

Noticeable differences

After installing the on-premises version of ICS you can create users and assign roles to these users. This is done in the provided **Users** page of the on-premises ICS. This page is not available in the Cloud version.

You also have access to the WebLogic Console, Service Console, and Fusion Middleware Control. This means that you can take a peak in the deployed applications, the Service Bus resources, and in the log files. When something goes wrong you can debug the problem without the help of Oracle Support. This is not possible in the Cloud version.

Restrictions between connectivity and execution agent

Another difference or even a restriction between the Cloud and the on-premises version is that you aren't able to configure Connectivity Agents. With this restriction in place, the adapters for connecting to the Oracle Database, MySQL Database, and Oracle SAP are not supported.

There is a default Agent group available in the Cloud version of ICS. All installed Execution Agents will be registered under this group, which restricts assigning connections to a specific Execution Agent:

We will explore both the Connectivity and Execution Agent in `Chapter 11`, *Calling an On-Premises API*.

Social and productivity adapters

Oracle Integration Cloud Service comes with a dozen of other kinds of adapters. These applications can also be categorized as SaaS applications; they're not in a traditional sense that is, enterprise applications, but offer Internet services. I'm talking about services where people can be social or collaborate with each other.

Integration Cloud Service supports social apps such as Facebook, LinkedIn, and Twitter, to post a status update. The supported productivity apps include Google, Microsoft Calendar and Mail, Google Task, MailChimp, and SurveyMonkey; and this list is updated on a monthly cycle:

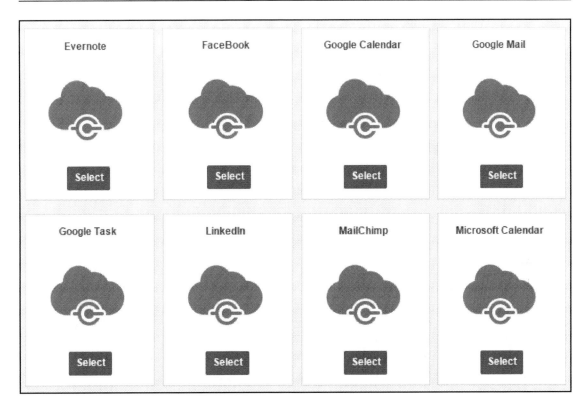

If you're looking for a full reference of all the supported adapters, please take a look at the documentation which can be found at: `https://docs.oracle.com/cloud/latest/intcs_g s/ICSUG/GUID-8BE53B5C-6436-4F81-AD20-78ECE5589BA9.htm`.

Integrations

In Oracle Integration Cloud Service, the core function is creating integrations between applications. Integrations use the created connections to connect to our applications. Integrations define how information is shared between these applications.

Integrations can be created from scratch, but can also be imported from an existing environment (that is, using an exported integration). As explained earlier, an integration always has a source and a target connection. The source and the target define the type of integration pattern that is implemented.

There are four types of integrations; point-to-point (that is, data mapping), publish messages or subscribe to messages, content-based routing, and Orchestration:

For these types of integration you can start with a blank canvas, but Oracle Integration Cloud Service provides templates to quick start your integration.

Point-to-point integration

A point-to-point integration, also known as a **Basic Map Data** integration in ICS, is the least complex integration pattern. We use a point-to-point integration when we have to send a message to a single receiver (that is, a 1:1 relationship). For example, a customer is updated in the HCM Cloud, which sends out an automatic message to the ERP, to also update the customer details. Another example is that a third-party channel calls an API, which returns flight data from an on-premises database.

This integration pattern is the most common pattern that advertises Oracle Integration Cloud Service. You create an integration and use your defined connections for the **Source** and **Target**. You also define data-mappings between the **Source** and **Target** and vice versa.

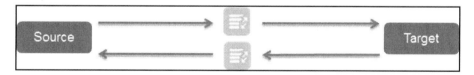

As mentioned previously, the source and target operation that is implemented, determines the kind of integration capabilities. A one-way source can only send data to a one-way target, and a synchronous source can only send data to a synchronous target. This integration does not support mixing one-way with synchronous operations:

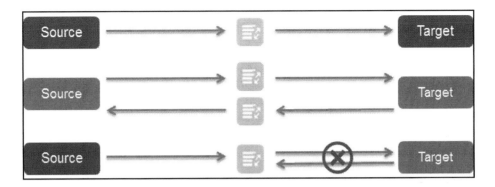

Although this pattern supports a more complex integration flow, Integration Cloud Service provides the possibility to enrich the data, by calling another service between the source and the target or vice versa. For example, the target requires more data for its input than the source provides.

By using enrichment services you are able to invoke a service operation that returns the required data. The data from the source and the data from the enrichment service can then be used for the request mapping to the target:

In a one-way integration the source data can be enriched by calling an additional service:

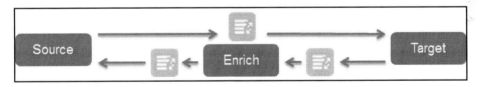

In a synchronous integration both sources as target data can be enriched by calling additional services.

Publish-subscribe integration

A publish-subscribe integration, in ICS separated in two separate integrations, implements a messaging pattern where messages are not directly sent to a specific receiver. The senders of messages are called publishers and the receivers of messages are called subscribers.

Topology

Publishers send messages, which are then published to an intermediary message broker or event bus without knowledge of which subscribers, if any, are interested in the message. On the other hand, subscribers register subscriptions on messages they are interested in, without knowledge of which publishers, if any, are sending these messages. The event bus performs a store and forward to route messages from publishers to subscribers:

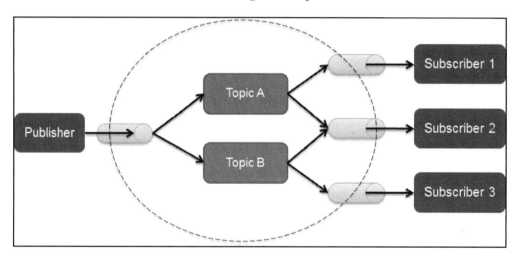

This pattern generally uses the message queue paradigm and provides greater scalability and a more dynamic network topology. Most messaging systems support this pattern in their API using **Java Message Service (JMS)**.

The publish-subscribe pattern in ICS can be implemented using its own messaging service, by using the **Oracle Messaging Cloud Service (OMCS)** adapter or the JMS adapter for on-premises connectivity. All implementations use JMS as its underlying protocol.

The ICS Messaging Service also uses the OMCS for its delivery, but these messages can't be accessed outside of ICS.

Advantages of pub-sub

The two major advantages of using this kind of pattern are scalability and loose coupling.

Scalability

This integration pattern provides the opportunity for better scalability of the message flow. Messages can be handled in parallel instead of being processed one after each other. If the amount of messages succeeds the amount the systems can process, a new system or a subscriber can be added. A subscriber can also choose to temporarily stop receiving messages to process already received messages.

Loosely coupled

When using the publish-subscribe pattern, publishers and subscribers are loosely coupled and generally don't know of each other's existence. Both can operate normally regardless of the state of the other. In a point-to-point integration, the systems are tightly coupled and can't process messages if one of the services is not running. When using ICS it is possible to even decouple the location of the publishers and subscribers by using OMCS or the on-premises JMS adapter.

Disadvantages of pub-sub

The advantage of loosely coupling also introduces side effects, which can lead to serious problems. We should also consider issues that can occur during the delivery of messages.

Inflexibility of decoupling

Because the publishers and subscribers do not need to know of each other's existence, it is important that the data is well defined. This can lead to inflexibility of the integration, because in order to change the data structure you need to notify the subscribers. This can make it difficult for the publishers to refactor their code. In ICS this should not be a problem because it can be fixed by versioning the integration and its data structure.

Issues with message delivery

Because a pub-sub system is decoupled, it should be carefully designed to assure message delivery. If it is important for the publisher to know a message is delivered to the subscriber, the receiving system can send a confirmation back to the publisher. If, for example, a message can not be delivered, it is important to log the error and notify someone to resend the failed messages. When designing an integration, keep in mind that delivery management is important to implement.

Content-based routing

An integration with content-based routing is a more advanced version of the point-to-point integration. Content-based routing essentially means that the message is routed based on a value in the message payload, rather than an explicitly specified destination:

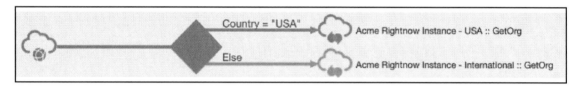

A use case for this type of routing is the possibility to retrieve data from a different application based on the country code.

Topology

Typically, a point-to-point integration receives a message and sends the message to an endpoint. This endpoint identifies the service or client that will eventually process the message. However, what if the data is not available (anymore) at that destination? For example, what if the data specific to the callers country is available at a different site and the service cannot return the requested data? Is it also possible that one destination can only process specific types of messages and no longer support the original functions.

A solution for this is content-based routing. A content-based routing is built on two components: services and routers. Services are the consumers of the messages, and like all the other integrations they decide on which messages they are interested in.

Routers, usually one per integration, route messages. When a message is received the message is inspected and a set of rules are applied to determine the destination interested in the message content. With this pattern we can provide a high degree of flexibility and can easily adapt to changes, for example, adding a destination. The sender also does not need to know everything about where the message is going to end up.

Each destination can have its own implementation, which means the router also needs to transform the message where necessary.

Simple example architecture

The following diagram illustrates a simple example of the content-based routing architecture. It shows how a message is sent to the endpoint of **Service A**. **Service A** receives the message and the **Router** routes the message to **Service B** or **Service C**, based on the content of the message:

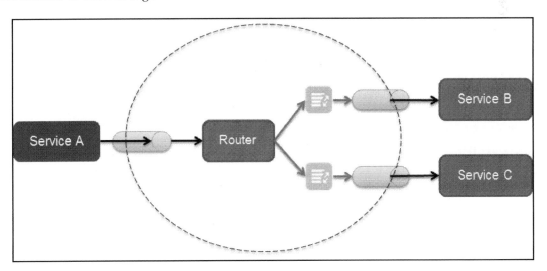

With Integration Cloud Service it is as easy as adding a filter on the request operation of the source connection. We can define multiple rules in an `if-then-else` construction and in every rule we can filter on multiple fields within the request message.

Advantages of content-based routing

The two major advantages for using this kind of pattern are efficiency and sophisticated decisions.

Very efficient

Content-based routing is very efficient. This is because the decision to route the message to one consumer or the other is kept away from the provider. The decision is based on the provider's request. There is also no risk of more systems than necessary consuming the message (when compared to the pub/sub integration), because we route to dedicated consumers.

Sophisticated routing decisions

When designing a content-based router it can become highly sophisticated. We can have multiple routing rules where one rule can filter on multiple fields of the request message. Content-based routing is easier to incorporate into a process pipeline more often than not.

Disadvantages of content-based routing

The disadvantages arise when the number of consumers grows.

Additional consumers

When we introduce an additional consumer it also means changing the router (compared to a pub-sub integration, which requires no change). We also need to add an extra routing decision.

Sequential processing

Content-based routing runs in a sequential process compared to Orchestration where we can execute in a parallel framework. Every rule is evaluated one after the other, which increases the execution runtime.

Orchestration for complex integrations

The usage of Orchestration comes into the picture when we discuss integrations in the context of service-oriented architecture. Service Orchestration is usually an automated process where two or more applications and/or services are integrated.

Topology

We have discussed point-to-point integrations and have seen that in many use cases this pattern fulfills our requirements. However, point-to-point integrations can lead to complex dependencies, if we need to integrate multiple application and/or services. The downside of this is that it is hard to manage, maintain, and possibly monitor.

An integration that implements Orchestration provides an approach that aggregates services into application processes. Orchestration has the capabilities for message routing, transformation, keeping the process state for reliability, and security through policies. The most important capability of Orchestration is centralized management, for example, resources and monitoring.

Orchestration, in a sense, is a controller, which deals with the coordination of (a)synchronous interactions and controls the flow. Usually **Business Process Execution Language** (**BPEL**) is used to write the code that is executed. This is also the case with Integration Cloud Service; however, a visual representation is used to define the process.

Practical example

To get a practical sense of service Orchestration, let us take a look at an example of a mortgage application. A mortgage broker wants to request a mortgage on behalf of a customer. The application uses API that calls an HTTP endpoint, which sends the initial request to the orchestrator through **Service A**.

The orchestrator enriches the customer data by calling **Service B**. Based on the age of the customer, **Service C** or **Service D** is called to find special mortgage quotes, but **Service E** is called for everyone. **Service E** retrieves credit scores belonging to that customer. The data from both service calls are merged and sent to **Service F** to return the best quote for that customer:

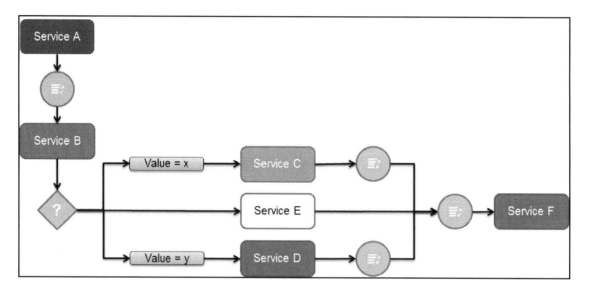

Advantages of Orchestration

The two major advantages of using this kind of pattern are loose coupling and enabling automation.

Loosely coupled

Application and business services can be designed to be process-agnostic and reusable. The business process is responsible for the management and coordination of state, which frees composite services from a number of design constraints. Additionally, the logic of the business process is centralized in one location, instead of being distributed across and embedded within multiple services.

Enables automation

In day-to-day operations, Orchestration enables us to automate processes such as insurance claims that come from medical offices. This is one process where human approval can be removed by programming parameters to accept claims. Orchestration can also automate error handling; for example, a message can be retried automatically when an endpoint is unavailable or a notification can be sent to a human when it needs to be recovered manually.

Disadvantages of Orchestration

There is one major disadvantage and that is debugging. There can be complex processes, which have multiple service interactions, nested loops, and so on. In these situations, it's not easy to debug your process if something goes wrong, because we need to know what message initiated the flow. We will touch on this topic in `Chapter 10`, *Advanced Orchestration with Branching and Asynchronous Flows.*

Transformation and lookups

When talking about integrations between application and/or services we can't escape the fact that messages need to be transformed. Most of the time the applications and/or services do not talk the same language (that is, message structure or even data types, for example, milliseconds from epoch versus date time). Besides transforming the structure, we sometimes need to convert values (that is, domain value mapping).

Transformations

Oracle Integration Cloud Service uses XML as its message format for its data objects and messages. To transform XML-based messages from one structure to another there are two main open standards that can be used to manipulate data; XQuery (more info at `https://www.w3.org/TR/xquery/`) and XSLT (`https://www.w3.org/TR/xslt`).

XQuery

XQuery is like the name suggests, a query language, but besides that it is also a functional programming language. It queries and transforms collections of data, both structured as unstructured. It can transform messages to XML, but also text and other data formats, for example, JSON and HTML.

Using XQuery we can extract and manipulate XML documents or any source that can be viewed in XML, such as office documents or database schemas. It has built-in support for XPath expressions. With XPath we can address specific nodes within the XML document. XQuery is a SQL-like query language that supplements XPath and uses **FLWOR** expressions for performing joins. A FLWOR expression is named after the five parts it is constructed of: FOR, LET, WHERE, ORDER BY, and RETURN.

XQuery has the capability to transform, and it also allows us to create new XML documents. Where normally the elements and attributes are known in advance, it can use expressions to construct dynamic nodes, including conditional expressions, list expressions, quantified expressions, and so on. A simple example of XQuery is shown as follows:

```
<html><body>
  LET $book := doc("bookstore.xml")/book
  FOR $ch in $book/chapter
  WHERE $book/chapter/num < 10
  ORDER BY $ch/pagecount DESC
  RETURN <h2>{ $ch/title }</h2>
</body></html>
```

XSLT

Originally an acronym for **Extensible Stylesheet Language Transformations**, XSLT is as the name suggests, a language for transforming XML documents and is basically a style sheet to transform XML documents into other XML documents, or other data formats such as (X)HTML, XSL Formatting Objects (such as generating PDFs), RSS, and non XML (such as CSV):

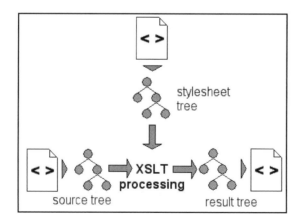

XSLT processing takes an XML source document and a XSLT style sheet, and produces a new output document. The XSLT style sheet contains static XML that is used to construct the output structure. It uses XPath expressions, just like XQuery, to get data from the XML source. The XSLT language includes logic (`if-else`) and operators (`for-each`) to process the XML source.

An XSLT style sheet is an XML document containing the root node `<xsl:stylesheet>`, which is declared by the `xsl` prefix and is mandatory. An XSLT style sheet contains one or more `<xsl:template>` elements and other XML elements defining transformation rules:

```xml
<?xml version="1.0" encoding="UTF-8"?>
<xsl:stylesheet version="1.0"
xmlns:xsl="http://www.w3.org/1999/XSL/Transform">
  <xsl:template match="/">
    <html>
      <body>
        <h2>Book Collection</h2>
        <table border="1">
          <tr>
            <th>Title</th><th>Author</th>
          </tr>
          <xsl:for-each select="bookstore/book">
            <tr>
              <td><xsl:value-of select="title"/></td>
              <td><xsl:value-of select="author"/></td>
            </tr>
          </xsl:for-each>
        </table>
      </body>
    </html>
  </xsl:template>
</xsl:stylesheet>
```

Integration Cloud Service currently only supports XSLT, because it is a transformation/mapping language, which can easily be made visually. Let's discuss XSLT in more detail.

XPath expressions

XSLT, like XQuery, uses XPath expressions to address specific nodes within the source document and perform a calculation. XSLT can use a range of functions that XPath provides to further augment itself.

Originally an acronym for **XML Path Language**, XPath is used for selecting nodes from an XML document. It models XML as a tree of nodes. XPath is named after its use of a path notation for navigating through the hierarchical structure of an XML document. XPath uses a compact, non-XML syntax to form expressions for use in **Uniform Resource Identifier (URI)** and XML attribute values.

XPath models an XML document as a tree of nodes. The following figure depicts the different types of nodes, as seen by XPath, in an XML document:

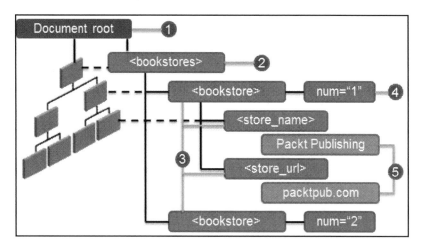

The elements in the preceding diagram are:

- A document root, which is a virtual document root that is the parent of the entire XML document containing the XML declaration, the root element and its children, comments, and processing instructions at the beginning and the end of the document.
- A root element (for example, the `<bookstores>` element).
- Element nodes (for example, the `<bookstore>`, `<store_name>`, and `<store_url>` elements). The root element is also an element node.
- Attribute nodes (for example, the `num="1"` node).
- Text nodes (for example, the nodes containing the text, **Packt Publishing**).

In the XPath model, the document root is not the same as the root element node. XPath defines a way to compute a string value for each type of node, some of which have names. Because XPath fully supports the XML Namespaces Recommendation, the node name is modeled as a pair known as the expanded name, which consists of a local part and a namespace URL, which may be null.

XPath allows various kinds of expressions to be nested with full generality (that is, using wildcards). It is a strongly typed language, such that the operands of various expressions, operators, and functions must conform to designated types. XPath is a case-sensitive expression language.

XPath Examples

The following are some examples of XPath expressions:

Get the `store_name` node of the bookstore identified with number 1:

```
/bookstores/bookstore[@num="1"]/store_name
```

Get the text value of the `store_name` node of the last bookstore:

```
/bookstores/bookstore[last()]/store_name/text()
```

Check if a bookstore exists in the source document (prefixing `//` means a wildcard search):

```
count(//bookstore[store_name="Packt Publishing"]) = 1
```

XLST constructs

With XSLT it is possible to create really dynamic output documents using XSLT constructs together with XPath expressions. XLST construct are specific elements that are defined by the XSLT standard. XSLT defines the following construct elements: `output`, `template`, `value-of`, `for-each`, `if`, and `choose`.

The xsl:output element

The output element specifies the output format of the result tree and it must be a direct child of the style sheet root element. The element has a few attributes. The `method` attribute defines which processor needs to be used, such as `xml`, `html`, or `text`, and the `media-type` attribute defines the target type, for example, `application/json`:

```
<xsl:output method="html" media-type="text/xml"/>
```

The xsl:template element

The template element defines a template rule that matches a specific node in the source document using an XPath pattern value. The output expression contains the formatting instructions to produce a result tree:

```
<xsl:template match="pattern">
  output-expressions
</xsl:template>
```

The match pattern determines the context node within the template. The most common match is on the root element of the source document tree:

```
<xsl:template match="/">
  A simple text string
</xsl:template>
```

A template can also be given a name and called by its name within another template by passing a parameter:

```
<xsl:template name="minValue">
  <xsl:param name="values"/>
  ...
</xsl:template>
<xsl:template match="/">
  <xsl:call-template name="minValue">
    <xsl:with-param name="values"
                    select="bookstore/book/year"/>
  </xsl:call-template>
</xsl:template>
```

The xsl:value-of element

The `value-of` element is used to insert the text value of the expression. This element defines a `select` attribute, which contains an expression and is used inside a template element:

```
<xsl:template match="name">
  Name:
  <xsl:value-of select="name"/>
</xsl:template>
```

The xsl:for-each element

The `for-each` element is used to loop over node-sets. This element defines a `select` attribute, which instructs the XSLT processor to loop over the node set returned by the given XPath expression:

```
<xsl:template match="/">
  <xsl:for-each select="catalog/book">
    <p><xsl:value-of select="title"/></p>
  </xsl:for-each>
</xsl:template>
```

Inside the `for-each` element, the current node in the set is the context. The `position()` function returns the index in the loop, that is, the iteration counter. It is also possible to sort the order in which the nodes are looped over using the `xsl:sort` element. It defines a `select` attribute that contains an expression whose value is sorted on:

```
<xsl:for-each select="catalog/book">
<xsl:sort select="year" data-type="number" order="descending"/>
  <p>
    <xsl:value-of select="title"/>
  </p>
</xsl:for-each>
```

To apply multiple criteria, we can use several `xsl:sort` elements after each other.

The xsl:if element

Sometimes a section of the XSLT tree should only be processed under certain conditions. With the `if` element we can build that conditionally. The `if` element defines a `test` attribute, which contains an XPath expression that should evaluate to a Boolean value:

```
<xsl:for-each select="catalog/book">
  <xsl:if test="year = 2016" >
    <p><xsl:value-of select="title"/></p>
  </xsl:if>
</xsl:for-each>
```

There is no `else` statement, but for this XSLT defines the `xsl:choose` element.

The xsl:choose element

XSLT supports multiple mutually exclusive branches with the `choose` element. The `xsl:choose` element contains `xsl:when` tags that define parallel branches, one of which is executed. The `xsl:otherwise` tag can be used to define a default branch.

We use the `choose` element for `if-the-else` constructions:

```
<xsl:for-each select="catalog/book">
  <xsl:choose>
    <xsl:when test="year = 2016" >
      <xsl:text>New Arrivals</xsl:text>
    </xsl:when>
    <xsl:when test="year < 2015" >
      <xsl:text>Our Classics</xsl:text>
    </xsl:when>
    <xsl:otherwise>
      <xsl:text>Top Picks</xsl:text>
    </xsl:otherwise>
  </xsl:choose>
</xsl:for-each>
```

When implementing integrations with ICS we will use XSLT for creating mappings between source and target connections. The major advantage of ICS is that we can build these mappings with a visual editor.

Lookups

A lookup, also known as **Domain Value Maps (DVM)**, associates values used by one application for a specific field to the values used by other applications for the same field.

They enable us to map from one vocabulary used in a given domain to another vocabulary used in a different domain. For example, one domain may represent a country with a long name (Netherlands), while another domain may represent a country with a short name (NL). In such cases, you can directly map the values by using domain value maps.

Simple example:

CountryCode	CountryName
NL	Netherlands
UK	United Kingdom
USA	United States

A lookup also supports qualifiers. A mapping may not be valid unless qualified with additional information. For example, a DVM containing a code-to-name mapping may have multiple mappings from ABE to Aberdeen because Aberdeen is a city in both UK and the USA. Therefore, this mapping requires a qualifier (UK or USA) to qualify when the mapping becomes valid.

Qualifier example:

Country (qualifier)	CityCode	CityName
United Kingdom	ABE	Aberdeen
United States	ABE	Aberdeen
Netherlands	AMS	Amsterdam

Qualifier order support

We can also specify multiple qualifiers for a lookup using a qualifier order. Using this, ICS can find the best match during lookup at runtime. Hierarchical lookups are supported. If you specify a qualifier value during a lookup and no exact match is found, then the lookup mechanism tries to find the next match using the following qualifier. It proceeds until a match is found, or until no match is found even with all qualifiers set to an empty value.

One-to-Many Mapping Support

We can map one value to multiple values in a domain value map. For example, DVM for subscription payments can contain mapping to three values such as discount percentage, discount period, and subscription period.

Summary

In this chapter, we addressed the concepts and terminology surrounding Oracle Integration Cloud Service and standards such as. XML, XSLT and XQuery used by ICS. With ICS we can create integration between cloud services and between cloud and on-premises applications. An integration consists of one trigger and one invoke called connections, and it can call multiple enrichment services. Between the trigger, enrichment services, and invoke, ICS uses XSLT mappings to transform the message structure.

We looked at the ideas and terminology around how ICS connects to the applications it can integrate with. ICS comes with a large set of out-of-the-box Cloud adapters to connect to these applications, and in upcoming chapters we will explore these connections in depth.

Integrations use the created connections to connect to our applications. Integrations define how information is shared between these applications, for example, exposed operation, message structure, and so on. We discussed the four types of integrations ICS supports and its advantages and disadvantages.

When integrating applications and/or services we can't escape the fact that messages need to be transformed, because they don't talk the same language (that is, message structure or even data types, for example, milliseconds from epoch versus date time). ICS uses the open standard XSLT for manipulating data. We discussed the language and its structure. Besides transforming the data we sometimes need to convert values (that is, domain value mapping). ICS supports lookups that we can use to convert a value provided by the source to a format the target understands.

In the next chapter, we will explain the steps to create a basic integration between two cloud services based on an SOAP and a REST interface.

2
Integrating Our First Two Applications

In the previous chapter we looked at the components that make up an integration; and introduced the concepts surrounding the different types of connections and integration patterns. This book we will demonstrate the different kinds of use cases that can be implemented with **Oracle Integration Cloud Service**.

In this chapter we will create our first integration, and experience the first practical use of Integration Cloud Service, which will be illustrated by integrating two systems together. It explains, using a step-by-step approach, the actions of creating an integration.

As we mentioned in the preface, to make our use cases available to everyone we will use services that are free-to-play and do not cost us an extra investment in terms of money. The integration we are going to build in this chapter, does not use live APIs offered on websites, such as FlightAware (`https://flightaware.com`) and UrTheCast (`https://urthecast.co m`), but it is based on the idea of integrating such services.

As shown in the following diagram, our integration will use a SOAP connection for our inbound interface and transforms the message to the format that the outbound REST connection expects:

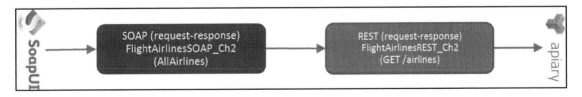

Getting ready

Before we build our first integration, let's get acquainted with the APIs we are going to use in this first service. As shown in the preceding diagram our inbound call is a SOAP request and therefore we need a WSDL definition which defines the inbound API. Our outbound call is a REST request to a service we host on apiary (`https://apiary.io`) and uses the API Blueprint standard (`https://apiblueprint.org`) to define the REST API.

Let's start with the inbound or source definition as shown in the following screenshot. The WSDL has one operation which uses an input, output, and a fault message:

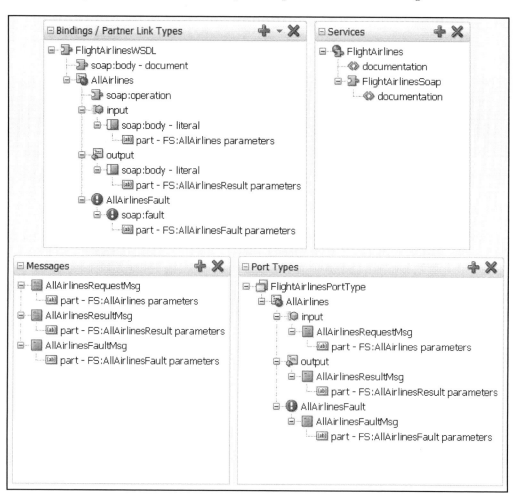

The messages reference an XSD which defines the structure for our input, output, and fault message is as follows:

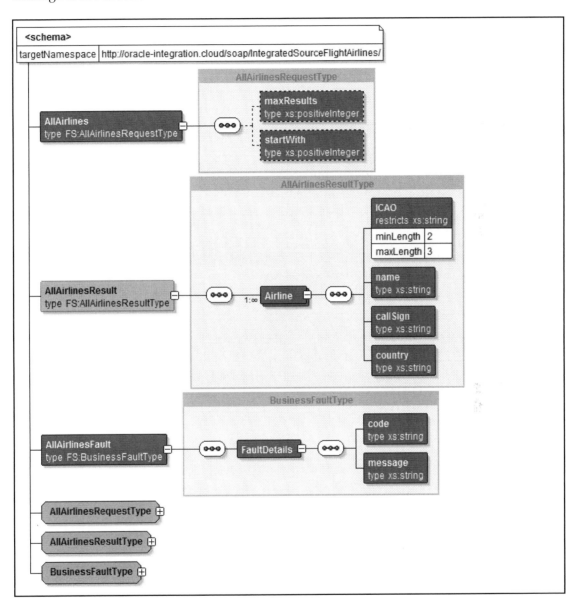

The WSDL is available in the downloads as `ICSBook-Ch2-FlightAirlines-Source.WSDL`.

As you can see the WSDL contains one synchronous operation called `AllAirlines`, which uses elements from the embedded XML schema for the input, output, and fault message. In `Chapter 1`, *Introducing the Concepts and Terminology*, we looked at a typical workflow, using this WSDL we eventually have to create mappings for the request, response, and fault flow. The request message contains two optional elements `maxResults` and `startWith`. Both elements control both the amount and which part of the set of airlines is returned. We can leave both elements from our request message in order to return the whole list.

The response message contains a list of airlines present in our backend, including their **ICAO (International Civil Aviation Organization)** code and call sign. The ICAO code is a location indicator used by air traffic control for flight planning. When an exception occurs, a WSDL fault is returned to the inbound caller, describing the fault. The backend API however, uses a different technology: Instead of SOAP it uses REST as its interface. Because REST is a software architectural style and not a hard defined standard, whereas SOAP binds directly to the use of a WSDL, there are multiple languages to define a REST API. The best known languages include RAML (`http://raml.org`), Swagger (`http://swagger.io`) and API Blueprint (`https://apiblueprint.org`). The latter two are supported by apiary, but we will use API Blueprint, because it is easier to understand. API Blueprint is a syntax to document an API in a concise yet expressive manner. We can easily design and prototype the APIs that we need to create or document. Additionally, we can test our prototype and even any already deployed APIs.

We define the data structure first and use the objects in our API endpoint. Doing this we decouple the elements of the API and enable modularity and the reuse of data. In this chapter, we are going to design and test our API first before using it in our integration. For example, we can model our data using the data description syntax used and reused in our API endpoints as follows:

```
# Data Structures

## Airline (object)
+ icao: UAL (string, required)
+ name: United Airlines (string, required)
+ callsign: UNITED (string)
+ country: United States (string)

# Airlines [/airlines]

## Retrieve Chapters [GET]
+ Response 200 (application/json)
  + Attributes (array[Airline])
```

For the full API Blueprint specification you can find a well documented specification at: `https://apiblueprint.org/documentation/specification.html`.

The resulting JSON for which we are going to create the API for will look something like as follows:

```
{
  "Airline":[
    {
      "icao": "KLM",
      "name": "KLM",
      "callsign": "KLM",
      "country": "The Netherlands"
    },
    {
      "icao": "UAL",
      "name": "United Airlines",
      "callsign": "UNITED",
      "country": "United States"
    }
  ]
}
```

Setting up apiary

Before we start creating the integration, let's set up our backend REST API with the tools needed to receive and mock our web service calls. With Apiary we can design and mock our APIs without writing a single line of code. Upon visiting `apiary.io` (`https://apiary.io`), we are welcomed with direct access to sign up for the service. If you have a GitHub account you can sign up just by logging in, but you also have the option to sign up using a Twitter account or your existing account.

Once signed up and signed in to Apiary we can create our new API by picking the default name, which is the same as your username, or choose a different one as shown in the following screenshot:

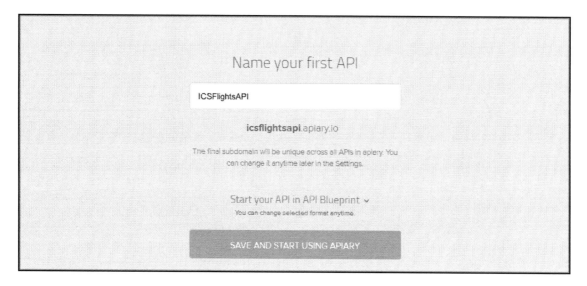

After choosing a name you will see the main editor where we can build our API. For a quick start, apiary supplies a demo API. You can look at this to get a feeling of the syntax that is used and get familiar with the UI.

Replace the contents of the editor with the ICS Flights API. The API Blueprint is available in the downloads as `ICSBook-Ch2-Apiary-Flights-API.apib`. The editor shown as follows illustrates our flights API:

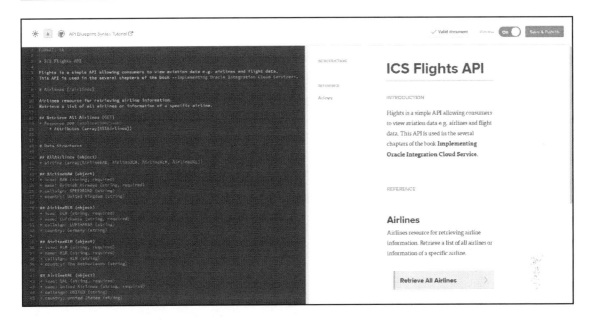

Looking at the preceding screenshot, on the left side we find our API Blueprint and on the right side the live preview of the documentation. If we look at the API in the editor, it consists of three sections: An introduction, an airlines resource and the data structures that are used in the resources.

The introduction, shown in the following screenshot, tells us that the format we are using is API Blueprint and for which purpose the API has been created:

```
1   FORMAT: 1A
2
3   # ICS Flights API
4
5   Flights is a simple API allowing consumers to view aviation data e.g. airlines and flight data.
6   This API is used in the several chapters of the book **Implementing Oracle Integration Cloud Service**.
7
```

The current API contains only one resource, the /airlines resource. On each resource one operation of each HTTP method can be defined, but in our API we only accept the GET method. The API replies with the HTTP response code 200 and returns a JSON payload of the AllAirlines object:

```
 8  # Airlines [/airlines]
 9
10  Airlines resource for retrieving airline information.
11  Retrieve a list of all airlines or information of a specific airline.
12
13  ## Retrieve All Airlines [GET]
14  + Response 200 (application/json)
15      + Attributes (array[AllAirlines])
16
```

The AllAirlines object that is referenced under Attributes is described in the Data Structures section. The AllAirlines object itself references the specific airline objects. Each airline object defines its ICAO code, name, callsign, and country of origin as shown in the following screenshot:

```
18  # Data Structures
19
20  ## AllAirlines (object)
21  + airline (array[AirlineBAW, AirlineDLH, AirlineKLM, AirlineUAL])
22
23  ## AirlineBAW (object)
24  + icao: BAW (string, required)
25  + name: British Airways (string, required)
26  + callsign: SPEEDBIRD (string)
27  + country: United Kingdom (string)
28
29  ## AirlineDLH (object)
30  + icao: DLH (string, required)
31  + name: Lufthansa (string, required)
32  + callsign: LUFTHANSA (string)
33  + country: Germany (string)
34
35  ## AirlineKLM (object)
36  + icao: KLM (string, required)
37  + name: KLM (string, required)
38  + callsign: KLM (string)
39  + country: The Netherlands (string)
40
41  ## AirlineUAL (object)
42  + icao: UAL (string, required)
43  + name: United Airlines (string, required)
44  + callsign: UNITED (string)
45  + country: United States (string)
```

Now that we have defined the API, we can test the /AllAirlines resource to see the result when the API is called. With apiary we can do this directly from the editor. On the right side of the editor, click the **Retrieve All Airlines** button to open the test console. In the test console, click the **Call Resource** button to fire a request as shown in the following screenshot:

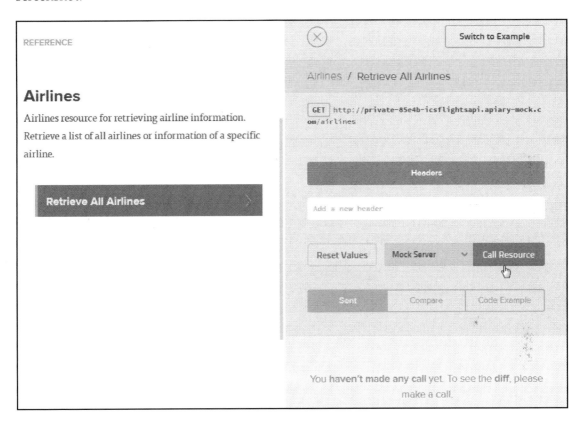

We can inspect the call when we scroll down. Both request and response are shown including the JSON payload constructed from our data objects. We can see all the incoming calls by viewing the **Inspector** page as shown in the following screenshot:

Time to switch to integration cloud

With the REST backend ready, the next step is to login for the first time during this book to your Oracle Integration Cloud Service instance. This would typically be done by a developer that is responsible for creating integrations between IT systems. Upon visiting your instance using `https://xxx-yyy.integration.zzz.oraclecloud.com/ics/` and signing in with a valid account, you will be welcomed by the colorful home page. Using this page we can navigate to the **Designer**, **Monitoring**, and **Administration** pages. The page has some quick start links and links to the documentation. It's time to create our integration.

As we said earlier in `Chapter 1`, *Introducing the Concepts and Terminology*, the next step is creating the inbound and outbound connections.

Define the necessary connections

Because creating connections is one of the core components of an integration, we can easily navigate to the designer portal and start creating connections.

On the home page, click the **Create** link of the **Connection** tile:

The **Connections** page will load; this lists all created connections, and a modal dialog automatically opens on top of the list. This pop-up shows all the adapter types we can create. As we explained in `Chapter 1`, *Introducing the Concepts and Terminology*, there are a few types of adapters. For our first integration we define two technology adapter connections: An inbound SOAP connection and an outbound REST connection.

Inbound SOAP connection

In the pop-up we can scroll down the list and find the SOAP adapter, but the modal dialog also includes a search field. Just search on `SOAP` and the list will show the adapters matching the search criteria as shown in the following screenshot:

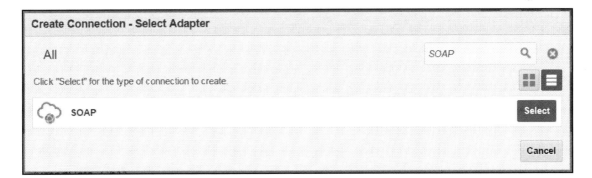

 Find your adapter by searching on the name or change the appearance from card to list view to show more adapters at once.

Click **Select** to open the **New Connection** page. Before we can setup any adapter specific configurations, every creation starts with choosing a name and an optional description as shown in the following screenshot:

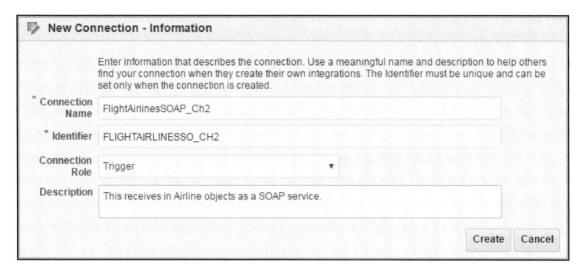

Create the connection with the details shown in the following table:

Property	Description
Connection Name	Enter your connection name as FlightAirlinesSOAP_Ch2.
Identifier	This will be proposed based on the connection name and there is no need to change unless you would like an alternate name. It is usually the name in block capitals and without spaces and has a max length of 32 characters.
Connection Role	**Trigger**, The role chosen restricts the connection to be used only in selected role(s).
Description	Enter the description such as This receives in Airline objects as a SOAP service..

Click the **Create** button to accept the details. This will bring us to the specific adapter configuration page where we can add and modify the necessary properties. The one thing all the adapters have in common is the optional **E-mail Address** under **Connection Administration**. This e-mail address is used to send notifications when problems or changes occur in the connection.

A SOAP connection consists of three sections: **Connection Properties**, **Security**, and an optional **Agent Group**. On the right side of each section we can find a button to configure its properties.

Let's configure each section using the following steps:

1. Click the **Configure Connectivity** button.
2. Instead of entering in an URL, we are uploading the WSDL file.
3. Check the box in the **Upload File** column.
4. Click the newly shown **Upload** button.
5. Upload the file `ICSBook-Ch2-FlightAirlines-Source WSDL`.

Notice the other three optional options. We do not use them, but we will explain them shortly. The first option **Target Server's TLS Version** can be set to a specific version when calling a SSL endpoint, but the default is **TLSv1.1**. The second option and third option can change the behavior when using the **Username Password Token** security policy, which you can set when configuring the connection' credentials. The option **Suppress insertion of timestamp into the req** means that you can suppress adding a timestamp to the WS-Security header sent as part of the outbound request. This timestamp normally defines the lifetime of the message in which it is placed. The option **Ignore timestamp in response message** means that, we want to ignore the timestamp of the WS-Security header in the response message. If set to **Yes**, then the timestamp is not required in the response message, but if set, and timestamp is present, it is ignored.

For more information on Secure Sockets Layer (SSL) / Transport Layer Security (TLS) refer to: https://en.wikipedia.org/wiki/Transport_Lay er_Security.

6. Click **OK** to save the properties.
7. Next click the **Configure Credentials** button.

In the pop-up that is shown we can configure the security credentials. We have the choice of **Basic Authentication, Username Password Token** (WS-Security), or **No Security Policy**. Because we use it for our inbound connection, we do not have to configure this.

 For more information on **Web Services Security (WS-Security, WSS)** refer to: https://en.wikipedia.org/wiki/WS-Security.

8. Select **No Security Policy** from the dropdown list.
9. This removes the username and password fields.

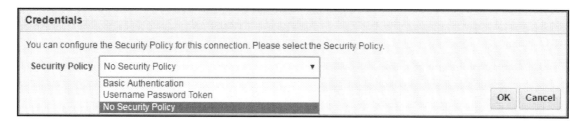

10. Click **OK** to save the properties.

We will leave the **Agent Group** section untouched. We can attach an agent group if we want to use it as an outbound connection to an on-premises web service.

11. Click **Test** to check if the connection is working (otherwise it cannot be used).

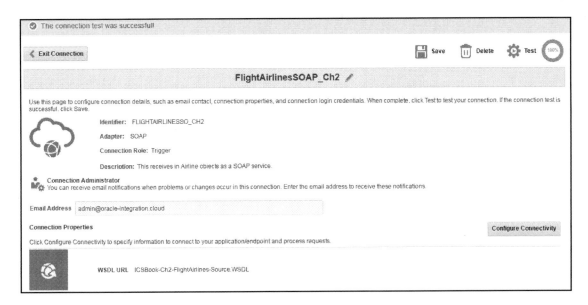

For SOAP, it simply checks if the definition is valid (that is, valid WSDL) to test the connection, but others for example, the Oracle SaaS adapters, it also authenticates and collect metadata.

12. Click the **Save** button at the top of the page to persist the changes.
13. Click **Exit Connection** to return to the list from where we started.

Outbound REST connection

Now that the inbound connection is created we can create our REST adapter. Click the **New Connection** button to show the **Create Connection** pop-up again and select the **REST** adapter as shown in the following screenshot:

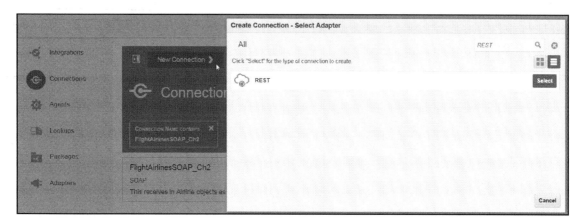

Create the connection with the details given in the following table:

Property	Description
Connection Name	Enter your connection name as `FlightAirlinesREST_Ch2`
Identifier	This will be proposed based on the connection name
Connection Role	Select **Invoke**
Description	Enter the description as `This returns the Airline objects as a REST/JSON service.`
E-mail Address	Your e-mail address to use to send notifications to

Let's configure the connection properties using the following steps:

1. Click the **Configure Connectivity** button.
2. Select **REST API Base URL** for the **Connection Type**.
3. Enter the URL were your apiary mock is running on:
   `http://private-xxxx-yourapidomain.apiary-mock.com.`

4. Click **OK** to save the values:

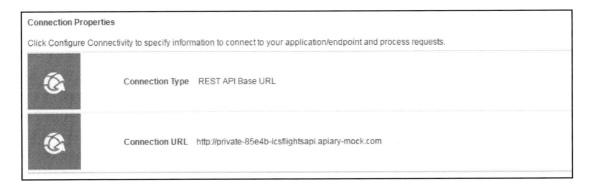

Next configure the security credentials using the following steps:

1. Click the **Configure Credentials** button.
2. Select **No Security Policy** for the **Security Policy**.
3. This removes the **Username** and **Password** fields.

Notice that we have a lot of different security policies like OAuth, which is an open standard for authorization commonly used to authorize websites or applications to access information of internet users. We will use some of them in later chapters.

4. Click the **OK** button to save:

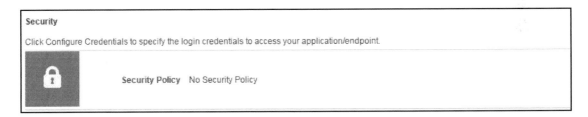

5. Click **Test** at the top to check if the connection is working.
6. Click the **Save** button at the top of the page to persist our changes.
7. Click **Exit Connection** to return to the list from where we started.

Troubleshooting

If the test fails for one of these connections, check if the correct WSDL has been used or that the connection URL for the REST adapter exists/reachable.

Integrate the two applications

Now that we have created two connections, we can integrate our applications by creating the integration. From the **Connections** page of the developer portal, we can navigate to the **Integrations** page, to create our first integration by clicking the **Integrations** link in the menu at the left side of the page, as shown in the following screenshot:

Let's click the **New Integration** button. We are presented with a pop-up that gives us multiple patterns to create an integration as shown in the next screenshot. We discussed these integration patterns in Chapter 1, *Introducing the Concepts and Terminology*:

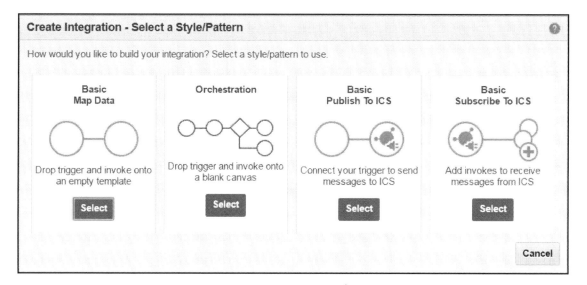

Select the **Basic Map Data** pattern for our first point-to-point integration. Before we can setup any integration, every creation starts with choosing a name, version, package name, and an optional description as shown in the following screenshot:

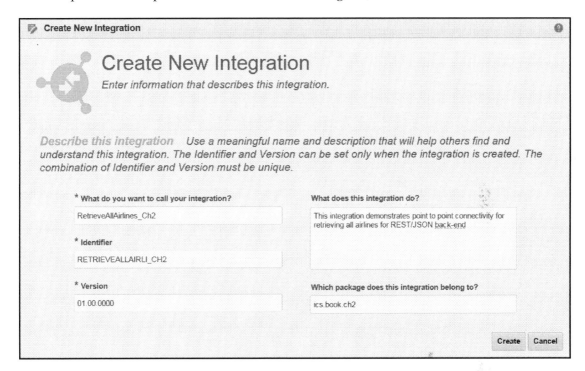

Create the integration with the details given in the following table:

Property	Description
Integration Name	Enter integration name as `RetrieveAllAirlines_Ch2`
Identifier	This will be proposed based on the integration name and there is no need to change unless you would like an alternative name
Version	Enter version as `01.00.0000`
Package Name	Enter package name as `ics.book.ch2` (this will be our pattern for each chapter)
Description	Enter description as `This integration demonstrates point-to-point connectivity for retrieving all airlines for REST/JSON back-end`

With the basic details for the integration completed we can now drag and drop our connections from the connector palette. For the **Trigger**, drag and drop the `FlightAirlinesSOAP_Ch2` connector as shown in the following screenshot:

The more connections that are created, the longer the list of items will be in the connector palette. Use the search filter to limit the amount of items.

A pop-up is shown with tabbed panels; you can navigate through the steps using the **Next** and **Back** buttons. Complete the SOAP endpoint configuration using the following steps:

1. In the **Basic Info** tab, call the endpoint: `Source`.
2. Add the description: `receives SOAP request to get list of all airlines`.
3. If there is an option to **Preview updated adapter runtime** set that to **Yes**:

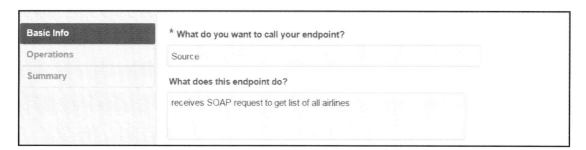

4. Click **Next** to go to the **Operations** tab.

As we only have a single operation in the WSDL, it selects this operation and its objects. If a WSDL has multiple port types and/or operations this step will give you the option to select the one you want to use. We will show this in `Chapter 5`, *Going Social with Twitter and Google*. This tab also gives you the choice **disable SoapAction validation**, which means the service can be called using a different SoapAction than defined in the WSDL, but we recommend keeping this option set to **No**, to not accept unknown actions as shown in the following screenshot:

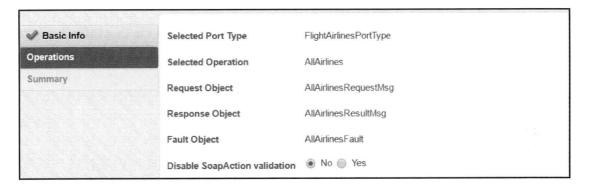

1. Click **Next** to go to the **Summary** tab.
2. This tab shows the details of the configured endpoint:

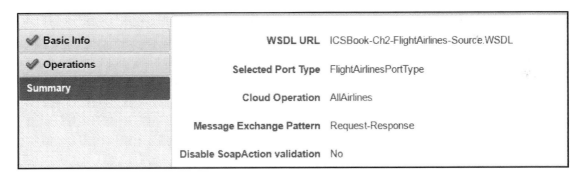

3. Click **Done** to complete our endpoint configuration.

We can now define the other end of the integration by dropping the connector `FlightAirlinesREST_Ch2` onto the **Invoke** target. A REST connector has many more options that we need to configure.

The resultant dialog can be completed with the following details (leave other fields default):

Tab	Question	Action
Basic Info	**Call your endpoint field?**	Call it: `Target`
	What does this endpoint do?	Add the description: `receives a list of all airlinse from an external REST service.`
	What is the endpoint's relative resource URI?	Enter the URI: `/airlines`
	What actions does the endpoint perform?	Select the `GET` method
	Configure request and response payload	Check option: **Configure this endpoint to receive the response**
	Configure request and response headers	Keep both options unchecked

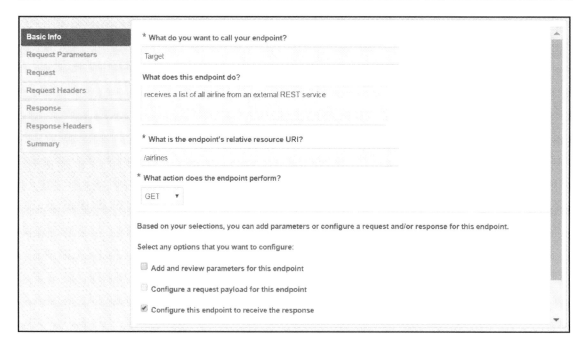

Tab	Section	Action
Response	Select Response payload	Pick: **JSON Sample**
	Enter sample JSON (click the inline link)	```json { "airline": [{ "icao": "DLH", "name": "Lufthansa", "callsign": "LUFTHANSA", "country": "Germany" }, { "icao": "KLM", "name": "KLM", "callsign": "KLM", "country": "The Netherlands" }] } ```

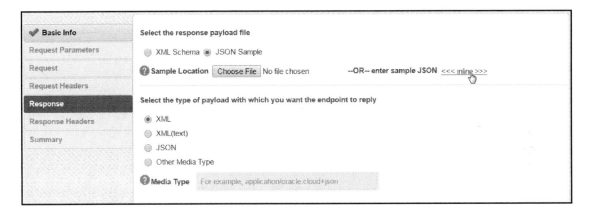

Tab	Section	Action
Summary	Description	The description we entered
	REST Service URI	http://private-xxxx-yourapidomain.apiary-mock.com/airlines
	Method	GET
	Response Media Type	application/json

Map message data

Now that we finished the initial integration between our two applications it is time to map the incoming SOAP request message to the REST outbound message. The same goes for mapping the REST response message to the SOAP outbound message.

Currently our integrations looks as follows:

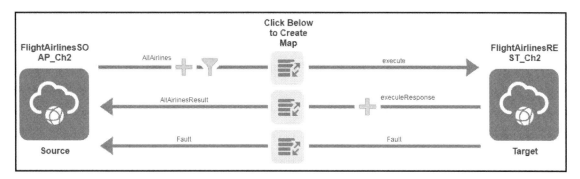

Mappings can be created or imported (from local disk) by clicking on the icon in the center of the integration. From top to bottom we will define the request, response, and fault mapping. First click on the request mapping and then on the plus sign, to create a new mapping. We are presented with a feature full mapping UI which has all capabilities that XSLT supports. In this chapter, we will not go into detail about all these capabilities, but we will touch base on them during later chapters.

The default view shows us the source message on the left and the target message on the right. The nodes to map depend on the selected adapters. Our target message doesn't have any leaf nodes, but we are still required to assign the root node. Because we cannot assign a leaf node in the default view, hence the warning, click on the **execute** node. In **Build Mapping** view drag and drop the AllAirlines node on the execute node as shown in the following screenshot:

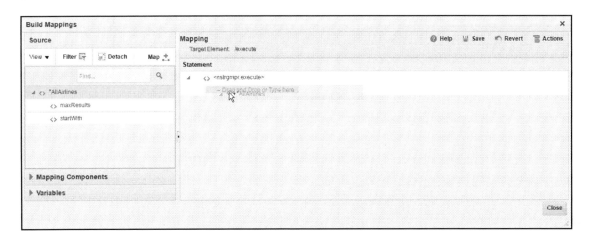

Click on **Save** and then **Close** to return to the default view. You can see that the `AllAirlines` node is mapped. Click on **Save** and **Exit Mapper** to finish our first mapping.

The next step is mapping the returning JSON message to our SOAP response message. Create a new response mapping in the same way as the request mapping. The source tree shows the returning JSON. Notice that it is displayed as an XML representation of the JSON sample we provided. First map the **Source** `airline` node to the **Target** `Airline` node. This will create a `for-each`, because it is a list and not a single node. Map the **Source** to **Target** leaf nodes which are named the same. We also have access to our request object, which contains two leaf nodes, `maxResults` and `startWith`, which can be used to minimize the search result; but for now let's keep it simple, as shown in the following screenshot:

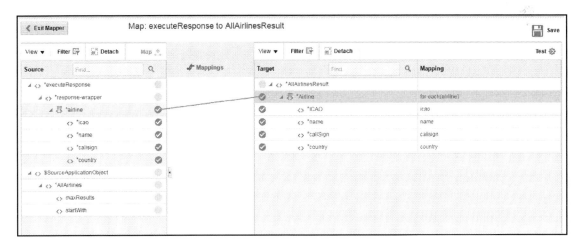

Click on **Save** and then **Exit Mapper** to finish our response mapping.

The last mapping we should create is the fault mapping. This time the process is a little different. Click the bottom mapping icon to open the **Fault Mappings** dialog. In this dialog, route the **APIInvocationException** to the **AllAirlinesFault** and click the map icon to create the mapping as shown in the following screenshot:

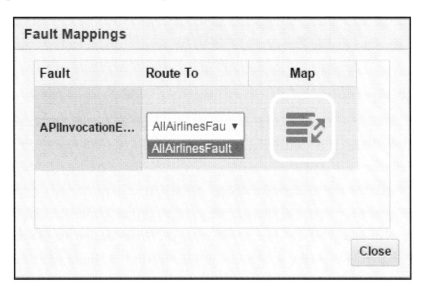

Map the **Source** nodes errorCode and details to the **Target** nodes code and message in the same way we would when mapping data from an **Invoke** and **Trigger**. To finish mapping click **Save** and **Exit Mapper**.

Completing and activating the integration

Our integration is almost finished: At the top right of the integration canvas you will see the overall completion progress which now states **87%**. Our final task is to configure the field(s) we want to track our instances on:

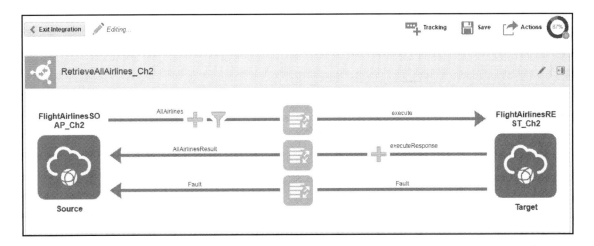

At the top right click **Tracking** to open the business identifiers dialog. Business identifiers enable runtime tracking on messages. Instance tracking is important to trace messages across integration flows. Any values selected are written into log files, so be careful not to use sensitive values as the logs are readable by anyone with access rights. We can specify up to three tracking fields, but a primary identifier is required. Drag and drop both maxResults and startWith to the list. Click **Done** to save the identifiers as shown in the following screenshot:

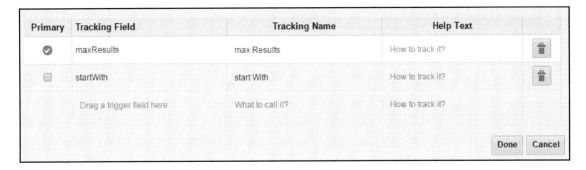

Notice at the top right corner that the completion progress states **100%**, which means our integration is done. Click **Save** and **Exit Integration** to finish our first integration. We are returned back to the list of all integrations which will include our newly created integration at the top. Integrations need to be activated first before they are available for use as shown in the following screenshot:

Click the **PENDING ACTIVATION** button, this will show a **Confirmation** dialog. In this dialog, we get the choice to enable tracing. This should be handled with care because, as as the dialog explains, this isn't recommended in a production environment, but can be used for debugging purposes. In our case keep it disabled and click **Yes** as shown in the following screenshot:

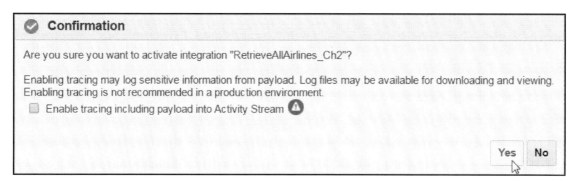

Activation checks the connectivity of the used connections and validates the integration. Activation can fail, but we will discuss this in a later chapter.

Testing the Integration

The final step of completing our first integration is testing the final result. We first need to know the web address for the endpoint our integration is running. Click the information icon on the right side of our entry, to view its activation details as shown in the following screenshot:

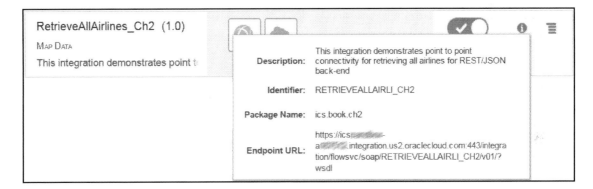

In the details we find the **Endpoint URL**, the integration can be invoked on. Copy the URL to your clipboard since we are going to use it shortly. The URL will look something like:

```
https://xxx-yyy.integration.zzz.oraclecloud.com/integration/
flowsvc/soap/RETRIEVEALLAIRLI_CH2/v01/?wsdl.
```

Invoke SOAP endpoint using SoapUI

The tool we are using for testing our SOAP endpoints, published by ICS, is SoapUI from Smartbear. We are using the open source edition of SoapUI to simulate our flight tracking and incident system that would normally call this endpoint SoapUI can be used for functional testing of SOAP and REST API, but also supports other protocols, such as JMS and JDBC. If you do not already use this tool then you can download the latest version of SoapUI open source from `https://www.soapui.org` and install the software using the installer.

Open SoapUI, by starting the application using the executable (Windows) or shell script (Linux). With our WSDL endpoint URL, we can create a new SOAP project. This can be done through the **File** menu by selecting **New SOAP Project,** or just by hitting **Ctrl + N**.

Create the SOAP project using the following information:

- **Project Name**: Enter project name as `RetrieveAllAirlines_Ch2`
- **Initial WSDL**: The WSDL endpoint URL of integration.
- **Create Requests**: Check this box
- **Create TestSuite**: Keep this box unchecked
- **Relative Paths**: Keep this box unchecked

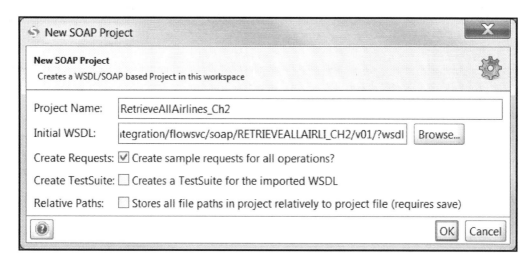

On the left side of the SoapUI window we find the projects explorer. Notice that our project `RetrieveAllAirlines_Ch2` has been added to the list. If you expand the project you will find the binding `FlightAirlinesPortType` and its operation `AllAirlines`. Double-click on the generated sample request named **Request 1**.

Remember that our integration doesn't do anything with the optional elements, so we can safely remove them. Our request will look like the following snippet:

```
<soap:Envelope
  xmlns:soap="http://schemas.xmlsoap.org/soap/envelope/"
  xmlns:int="http://oracle
integration.cloud/soap/IntegratedSourceFlightAirlines/">

  <soap:Header/>
  <soap:Body>
    <int:AllAirlines/>
  </soap:Body>
</soap:Envelope>
```

Click the green play button in the toolbar, to send this request to our integration, as shown in the following screenshot:

```
▶ ✔ ⚙ ⊠ □ ⚫  https://xxx-vvv.integration.zzz.oraclecloud.com:443/integration/flowsvc/soap/RETRIEVEALLAIRLI CH2/v01/  ▼
```

Instead of getting a valid response we receive a SOAP fault from our ICS instance. The server gives us the reason: OSB-386200: General web service security error. This means that ICS requires some authentication on the endpoint. If we look at the fault details of the message we can find a more detailed fault explanation:

```
Caused by: oracle.wsm.security.SecurityException: WSM-00069 : The security
header is missing. Ensure that there is a valid security policy attached at
the client side, and the policy is enabled.
```

We get this SOAP fault because our ICS integration doesn't expose our selected WSDL when creating the connection, but a new WSDL that only contains the selected operation when creating the trigger source. The new WSDL includes a security policy which forces us to send a valid WS-Security username token. In SoapUI it only takes a few easy steps to add the required header.

Providing a valid WS-Security header

Invoking ICS requires us to use the OASIS web services security username token specification. With WS-Security, which is a protocol, we can apply security to SOAP web services. WS-Security allows secure communication of various security token formats including the UsernameToken header. It explains that a client needs to supply a UsernameToken when calling the web service as a means of identifying the requester by using a username, and optionally by using a password. A web service that requires this type of token exposes a WSDL where the following snippet will be present.

```
<sp:SupportingTokens
  xmlns:sp=".../ws/2005/07/securitypolicy">
  <wsp:Policy xmlns:wsp=".../ws/2004/09/policy">
    <sp:UsernameToken
sp:IncludeToken="http://schemas.xmlsoap.org/ws/2005/07/securitypolicy/Inclu
deToken/AlwaysToRecipient">
      <wsp:Policy>
        <sp:WssUsernameToken10/>
      </wsp:Policy>
    </sp:UsernameToken>
  </wsp:Policy>
</sp:SupportingTokens>
```

Let's add the required header to our request in SoapUI. In the **Request 1** window you will find a tab called **Auth (Basic)** on the bottom left corner. Create a new basic authorization and supply the username and password of your ICS instance. This can be the same user that you use to login to the ICS portal as shown in the following screenshot:

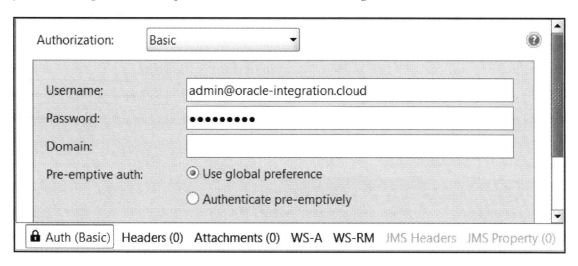

To add the username token to our **Request 1** message simply right-click in the window that contains the request message and select **Add WSS Username Token**. We are asked which type of password we want to use. ICS only supports **PasswordText** so select this option from the list. SoapUI adds the correct header to our request message. Click the green play button in the toolbar again to send this new request to our integration.

Instead of getting a valid response we receive another SOAP fault. The server gives us the reason: `OSB-386200: General web service security error`. Is this another authentication error? If we look at the fault details of the message we can find a more detailed fault explanation as `Caused by:` `oracle.wsm.security.SecurityException: WSM-00122 : Valid timestamp is not present in the message`.

We get this SOAP, fault because our ICS integration wants to check the freshness of the message, and does this by validating a timestamp to mitigate replay attacks. The `Timestamp` element is also part of the WS-Security specification. Because we didn't send a `Timestamp` element in our security header, the validation fails.

To add the timestamp to our **Request 1** message, simply right-click in the window that contains the request message and select **Add WS-Timestamp**. We are asked for the time-to-live of the message; the default is 60 seconds, but for testing purposes we will set it to 300 seconds. Notice that the Timestamp element is added to our request message.

```
<wsse:Security soapenv:mustUnderstand="1">

  <wsse:UsernameToken wsu:Id="UsernameToken-20321312">
  <wsse:Username>
    admin@oracle-integration.cloud
  </wsse:Username>
  <wsse:Password Type="...#PasswordText">
    your-password-in-plaintext
  </wsse:Password>
  <wsse:Nonce EncodingType="...#Base64Binary">
    ww0GzvB+d+Cx0VwEqEXNbw==
  </wsse:Nonce>
  <wsu:Created>
    2016-06-19T18:52:05.432Z
  </wsu:Created>
  </wsse:UsernameToken>
  <wsu:Timestamp wsu:Id="TS-328A93">
    <wsu:Created>2016-06-19T18:52:21.009Z</wsu:Created>
    <wsu:Expires>2016-06-19T18:57:21.009Z</wsu:Expires>
  </wsu:Timestamp>
</wsse:Security>
```

Invoking the integration for the first time

Now that we have got the security pre-requirements in-place, we finally get to invoke the integration for the first time. Till now the underlying message level security blocked the messages. Click the green play button in the toolbar again to send this new request to our integration.

This time we receive a valid response back from our integration. The SOAP body includes the XML response of the JSON data returned by the REST service.

```
<fas:AllAirlinesResult
xmlns:fas="http://oracle-integration.cloud/soap/IntegratedSourceFlightAirli
nes/">
  <fas:Airline>
    <fas:ICAO>BAW</fas:ICAO>
    <fas:name>British Airways</fas:name>
    <fas:callSign>SPEEDBIRD</fas:callSign>
    <fas:country>United Kingdom</fas:country>
```

```
   </fas:Airline>
   <fas:Airline>
     <fas:ICAO>DLH</fas:ICAO>
     <fas:name>Lufthansa</fas:name>
     <fas:callSign>LUFTHANSA</fas:callSign>
     <fas:country>Germany</fas:country>
   </fas:Airline>   ...
 </fas:AllAirlinesResult>
```

Monitoring the instance flow

To see the result of our labor, we can take a look at the instance flow of the request we have just sent to our integration. Use a browser to login to your integration cloud instance and, instead of navigating to the designer portal, go to the monitoring dashboard by clicking **Monitoring** in the menu on the top-right corner as shown in the following screenshot:

We will discuss the monitoring dashboard later in Chapter 12, *Are My Integrations Running Fine, and What If They Are Not?*, so for now we won't go into too much detail but we will navigate directly to the **Integrations** section. Click the corresponding menu item on the left side.

Enter the text Ch2 into the search box to filter out all other integrations, if any. For each integration this pages shows the amount of received messages, how many are processed, and for the processed messages how many where successful or had errors as shown in the following screenshot:

To see the messages processed by a specific integration, we can click on the message icon on the right side or on one of the numbers. Click the show messages icon of the `RetrieveAllAirlines_Ch2` integration.

We are routed to the **Tracking** section of the monitoring dashboard, which shows a list of messages. Since we only invoke the integration once, we see one message. Notice that the title of the message instance includes the tracking field we set when finishing the integration, as shown in the following screenshot:

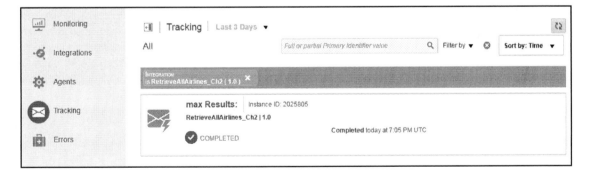

To see the message flow of a specific instance, we can click on the instance title. Click on **max Results:** to look at the instance details. The following screenshot shows the message flow using the same view as the integration canvas. Our instance completed successful so the flows show two green arrows from and to the **Source** and **Target**.

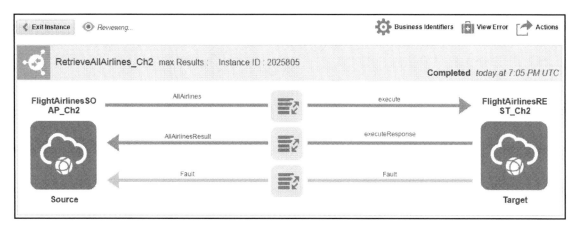

For each instance we can view the business identifiers, view any errors that occurred and execute various actions, for example view the **Audit Trail** as shown in the following screenshot:

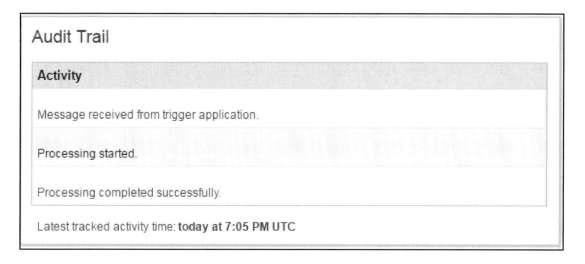

Verifying the message processed by the backend

The message sent and received by ICS to our backend REST service can be viewed in apiary. Visit `apiary.io` again and login with your account. Navigate to the **Inspector** page of your API. The **Inspector** page, as we explained earlier, shows us the received requests from ICS.

The incoming request was processed and returned with the following JSON response:

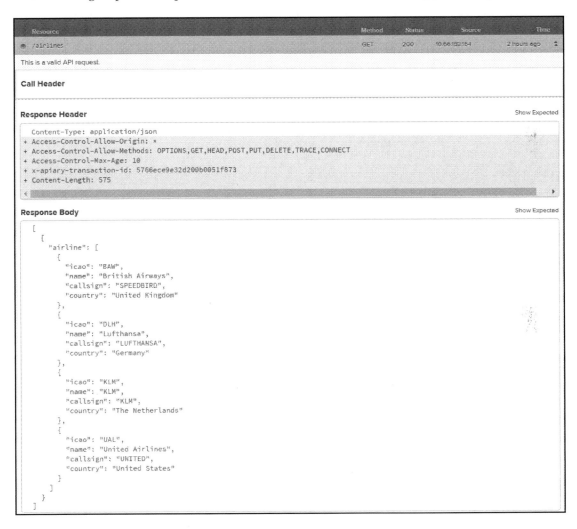

Summary

In this chapter, we have seen how easy it is to create a simple integration in ICS between two web services using different technologies. We looked at the processes of creating and testing the necessary connections and the creation of the integration itself.

In demonstrating the integration, we have seen how to use apiary to document and mock our backend REST service. We finally tested the integration using SoapUI to invoke the SOAP service, exposed by our integration, and explained the attached security policy, and the need to add a valid WS-Security `UsernameToken` header to identify the requester as a valid user of ICS.

In the next chapter, we will look at another kind of integration that we can build in ICS. We will build our first publish/subscribe integration, using the ICS Messaging Service, and bring this idea alive by creating an integration that represents a flight update being received, and then sent onto one then multiple destinations.

3
Distribute Messages Using the Pub-Sub Model

In `Chapter 1`, *Introducing the Concepts and Terminology* when we looked at some of the broader integration concepts, we introduced the idea of publish and subscribe (or pub-sub for short) such as enabling a single event to be sent to multiple interested parties. In this chapter, we are going to bring the idea alive by creating an integration that represents a flight update being received and then sent onto one then multiple destinations (which could range from websites to other aviation-related systems). The services we are going to build don not directly map to what is offered by websites such as FlightAware. But we will talk about the steps to connect sites such as FlightAware to our integrations. We will also build on the ideas around pub-sub to explain some advanced design patterns.

In this chapter, we are going to make use of Mockable.io (often just referred to as Mockable); like Apiary it can be used to define and create mocked web services. Where Apiary focuses on supporting REST and its service definition standards, Mockable focuses on the just the testing aspect of web services and provides good support for WSDL/SOAP-defined services. As this is the first time we make use of Mockable in the book we will devote some attention to it. Note that Mockable does provide its own documentation within the tool as well.

To show how we can reuse connectors, we will start with a normal integration and then convert to a pub-sub reusing the connectors, as shown in the following diagram:

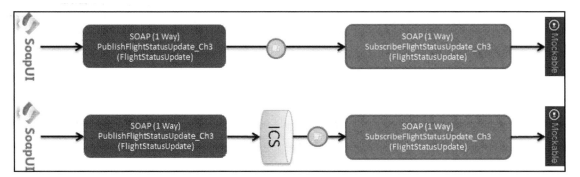

We can then extend our service so we can have multiple subscribers, like this:

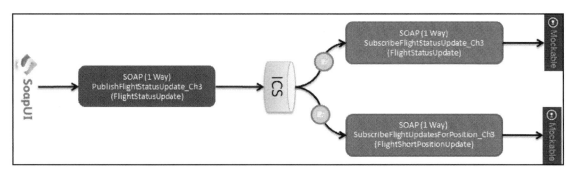

Getting ready

Before we start building the services, let's take a look at the WSDLs for the inbound and outbound calls for our first inbound and outbound definitions. Let's start with the inbound or source definition, as shown in the following illustration:

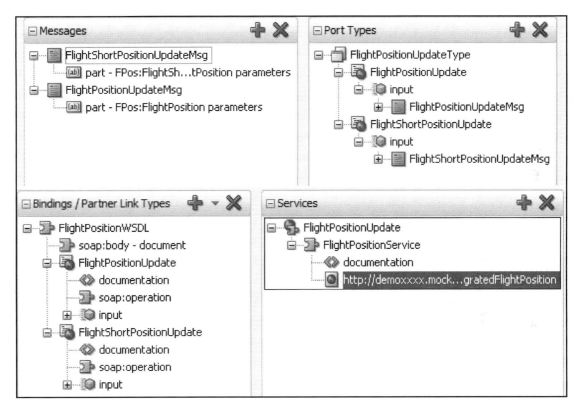

The service payload is defined by a schema within the file and is structured as follows:

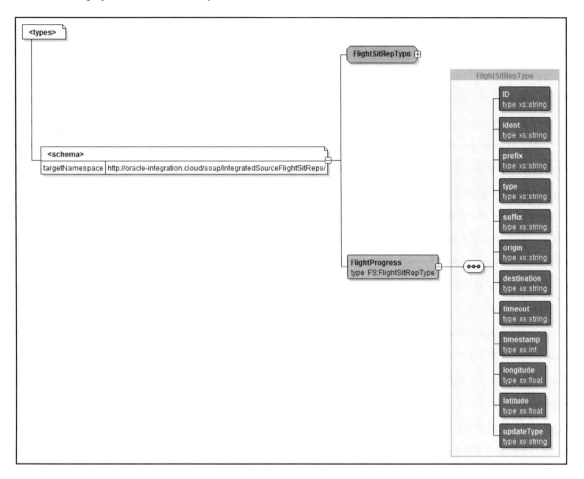

The inbound WSDL is available in the downloads as `ICSBook-Ch3-FlightProgress-Source.WSDL`.

As you can see, the idea of the message is to describe the status of a flight, including its destination and where it is. The first thing of note is that ICS has to offer the implementation URL of the service to be called, so the `SOAP:Address` location attribute is missing.

However, if you look at the destination WSDL, it has to contain the concrete target address (shown as `http://XXXX.mockable.io/FlightServices`) so that ICS knows where to call out to. When we set up Mockable, we will need to change this address to our unique account identified mock of the target web service. This target WSDL is available in the downloads as `ICSBook-Ch3-FlightProgress-Target.WSDL`:

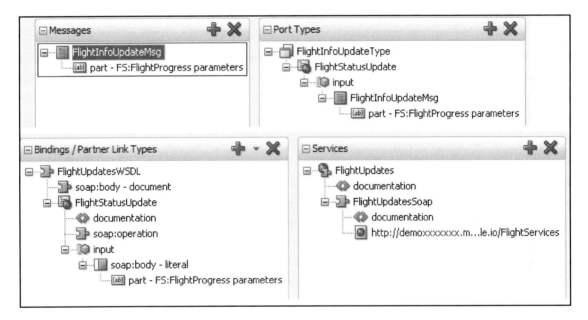

The following illustration shows the structure of the `FlightProgress` WSDL:

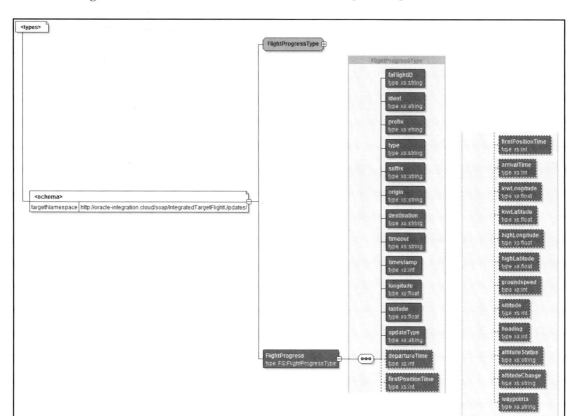

You should also note the `wsdl:service` provided, as we will need this for the mock interface (along with the `targetName` space attribute).

Setting up Mockable

So before we start on the integrations, let's get set up with the tools needed to send and receive web service calls. This is always a good development practice. Upon visiting Mockable.io (`https://mockable.io`) you will get several options to quickly establish a mock, or to log in to an account. You can work with the quick-start approach, but the mock will only remain for a limited period, so you may want to consider creating a login.

Once you are into Mockable, you will see a dashboard like that in the next screenshot, showing the number of mocks created and how many are active. At this stage, of course, you will not have any.

The preceding screenshot shows the main page of Mockable.io with a single tab and a button for **+ Add Domain**. As we are using the free version of the solution you will only be able to work with the single provided domain. It is possible to create targets against domain names, but this is a licensed feature and is not needed for our purposes.

At this stage, we need to manage our Mockable subdomain and establish our mock service, so click the **MANAGE** button. This will present us with the primary screen for controlling mocks, as shown here:

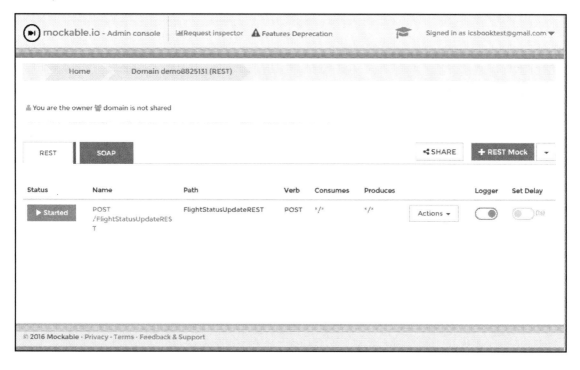

The left-hand tabs (**REST** and **SOAP**) allow you to switch between the types of mock you have. In this case, we want to create a SOAP service. Select the **SOAP** tab, and then click the **+ SOAP Mock** button. This brings us into the final screen, where we can define the mock, as you can see here:

To complete our mock, we need to provide the following information on this screen:

Property	Description
Endpoint	This forms part of the URI we need to wire into the outbound WSDL. You will probably want to use either a test name or the service name. To keep things simple, we have used the service name. In our case, we have used `FlightServices`.
SoapAction	This defines the action that should be called when the WSDL URL is addressed. This is made up of our namespace plus the service name defined. So our WSDL means this needs to be `http://oracle-integration.cloud/soap/IntegratedTargetFlightUpdates/FlightStatusUpdate`.
Headers	If we wish to pass any security tokens or special attributes, then this is where we would define what is expected. However, in this chapter we are going to keep things simple, so this can be left unmodified with no values.
Response status	As we are using the HTTP protocol to carry the SOAP object, we need to tell Mockable how to respond at the HTTP level. To start with, we want to keep this simple, which means returning a success result, that is, code 200. The full set of error codes is published as part of the standard definition. For more information on HTTP response codes, go to `https://www.w3.org/Protocols/HTTP/HTRESP.html`.
Content-encoding	When passing information around using HTTP, there should be a description of the type of content in the header elements. This provides the opportunity to define the encoding of the response. For our use cases, the default value is sufficient. For more information about header content encoding, go to `https://www.w3.org/Protocols/rfc2616/rfc2616-sec14.html`.
Response Body	Mockable offers the ability to incorporate some intelligence into the response through the use of Jinja2, a Python based templating tool, or Mustache, which has its own notation. Presently we have no need to have a dynamic response, so the option can be left unset. More information on these tools can be seen at: • Jinja2–`http://jinja.pocoo.org/` • Mustache–`https://mustache.github.io/` If the service was a request and response (bidirectional) communication, then we would provide the HTTP body content to return here. As we are actually performing a one-way call, we only need to worry about the HTTP response code, and this field can be cleared.

Display Name	When looking at the mock dashboard, this is the name that will be used for this mock. The best thing to do here is to align it to the endpoint name for simplicity, for example, `FlightUpdateStatus`.
Enable Request Logger	When requests are received, you can control whether the information is logged. For our benefit, we want to see what has been received. So you want to click on the icon so it turns green.
Set response delay	You might want to simulate the effect of a delay in responding, to reflect the typical real execution time. This is good if you need to manage the risk of timeouts on target systems, or you want to prove the integration will time out a connection rather than leaving things hanging. For basic testing we can leave this unchanged.

With all this information provided, we then can save the configuration with the **Save** button. Note that, having provided the details, you will now have a banner at the top of the page showing what the URLs are for invoking the mock service. The HTTP URL needs to be incorporated into the outbound schema's SOAP Address Location attribute, as mentioned before.

The last step is to enable the mock. We can use the URL path indication near the top of the page to navigate back to the test domain level, for example, `http://xxxx.mockable.io/`. The mock needs to be enabled to capture the calls. This can be done with the button on the left of the line for each mock, which will toggle between **Stopped** and **Started**, as shown here:

The alternative is via the **Actions** dropdown and the **Stop** and **Start** options, as you can see in the following screenshot:

Setting up SoapUI

With the mock ready, the next step is to prepare the part in SoapUI that will simulate the source of the web service call. As we have already used SoapUI in the previous chapter, we will not go into too much depth here. But the steps needed are as follows: open SoapUI, load the WSDL file that defines the integration trigger, and use SoapUI to help generate some test values to send to the integration.

Note we will need to revisit SoapUI to apply a couple of revisions when we are ready to test, specifically:

- Set the URL for the service once it has been created, so SoapUI knows where to make the invocation
- Set the credentials and the time to live for that information with respect to the connection to ICS, as we did in the previous setup for SoapUI

Stage 1 – creating the direct connection integration

With the preparation complete, we can focus on the creation of the integration, which means defining the connections to receive the test call from SoapUI and to call Mockable, for the outbound service as well as the integration itself.

Defining the connections in ICS

Like in the previous chapter, we need to create SOAP connectors; this time we will create two: one that will be called by SoapUI, and a second to call Mockable.io.

As before, navigate into the **Connections** part of the **Designer** and create a SOAP connection with the following details:

Property	Value
Connection Name	`FlightSitRep_Ch3`
Identifier	This will be proposed based on the connection name and there is no need to change it unless you would like an alternate name
Connection Role	Accept the defaults of **Trigger and Invoke**
Description	This receives `FlightStatusUpdate` objects as a SOAP service.
Email Address	Your e-mail address
WSDL URL | Connection Properties	Tick **Upload File**, then use the **File** selection to upload the `ICSBook-FlightProgress-Source` WSDL. Close with the **OK** button
Security Policy | Credentials	Set **Security Policy** to **No Security Policy**. Close the dialog with the **OK** button

Once the fields are complete, use the **Test** button at the top of the page to validate the connection configuration; the percentage complete should reach 100% at this point. Click the **Save** and **Exit Connection** button.

Now we repeat this to create the second connector with the following details:

Property	Value
Connection Name	`ReceiveFlightStatusUpdate_Ch3`
Identifier	This will be proposed based on the connection name and there is no need to change it unless you would like an alternate name.
Connection Role	Accept the defaults of **Trigger and Invoke**
Description	Receive flight status update information within the integration and pass it to the Mockable.io target
Email Address	Your e-mail address.
WSDL URL | Connection Properties	Tick **Upload File**, then use the **File** selection to upload the `ICSBook-FlightProgress-Target` WSDL. Close with the **OK** button
Security Policy | Credentials	Set **Security Policy** to **No Security Policy**. Close the dialog with the **OK** Button

We should now have two connections successfully created. So now we can navigate to the **Integrations** part of the **Designer** and create the integration. This process is very similar to the integration created in `Chapter 2`, *Integrating Our First Two Applications*, with one key difference–as we have defined both SOAP connections in the WSDL to be one-way (so no return result or fault definition), we will only see a one-directional flow. Click the **Create New Integration** button, and select the **Basic Map Data** pattern. Now we can complete the creation of the integration with the following details:

Property	Value
Integration name	`FlightStatusUpdateDirect_Ch3`
Identifier	This will be proposed based on the connection name and there is no need to change it unless you would like an alternate name.
Connection Role	Accept the defaults of **Trigger and Invoke**
Version	01.00.0000
Package Name	`ics.book.ch3`
Description	`This integration demonstrates point-to-point connectivity for the FlightStatusUpdate.`

With the basic details for the integration completed, we can now drag and drop our connections from the connector palette. For the **Source** side, we want to drop the `FlightSitRep_Ch3` connector. With the icon displayed, we can then proceed to edit the details of the connector to use. The **Source** and **Trigger** spots are as you may remember tabbed panels, and can be navigated through using the **Next** and **Back** buttons. But we need to complete the following information:

Tab	Question	Action
Basic Info	**Call your endpoint field?**	To keep it simple, call it `Source`.
	What does this end point do?	Add the description: `receives the flight status update from an external service.`
Operations	**Selected Port Type**	As we only have a single operation in the WSDL, this tab will not offer any options.
	Selected Operation	
	Request Object	
Summary	**WSDL URL**	As we only have a single operation in the WSDL, this tab will not offer any options. But should reflect the selected connector information.
	Selected Port Type	
	Cloud Operation	
	Message Exchange Pattern	

We can now define the other end of the integration by dropping the connector
`ReceiveFlightStatus_Ch3` onto the **Invoke** target. The resultant dialog can be completed
with the following information:

Tab	Question	Action
Basic Info	**Call your endpoint field?**	To keep it simple, call it `Target`.
	What does this end point do?	Add the description: `receives the flight status update from an internal source to then call out.`
Operations	**Selected Port Type**	As we only have a single operation in the WSDL, this tab will not offer any options.
	Selected Operation	
	Request Object	
Summary	**WSDL URL**	As we only have a single operation in the WSDL, this tab will not offer any options. But should reflect the selected connector information.
	Selected Port Type	
	Cloud Operation	
	Message Exchange Pattern	

Now we need to complete the mapping. This will be a little more complex than in the previous chapter. But we start in the same way by selecting the mapping icon in the middle of the flow. Then we link the source and target elements by clicking and dragging the dot symbol using the following table to define the mapping:

Source	Target
id	FaFlightID
ident	ident
prefix	prefix
type	type
suffix	suffix
origin	origin
destination	destination
timeout	timeout
timeout	firstPositionTime
timestamp	timestamp
longitude	longitude
latitude	latitude
updateType	updateType

You will note we have deliberately mapped a source element to a destination element twice, as illustrated in the following screenshot, so the outbound data will have the same value in both elements:

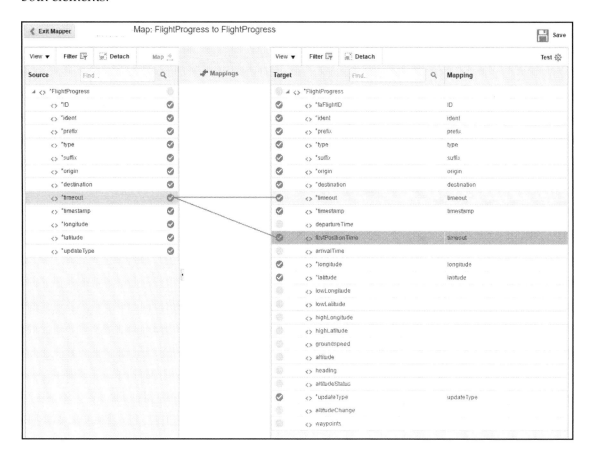

The diagram and table also show that we can map a single element of the source to more than one element on the target. To help differentiate the multiple integrations without bound endpoints, we are going to illustrate how to hardwire a target value.

The first step is to open up the specific mapping by clicking on `ident` in the target, which will show us the **Build Mappings** screen:

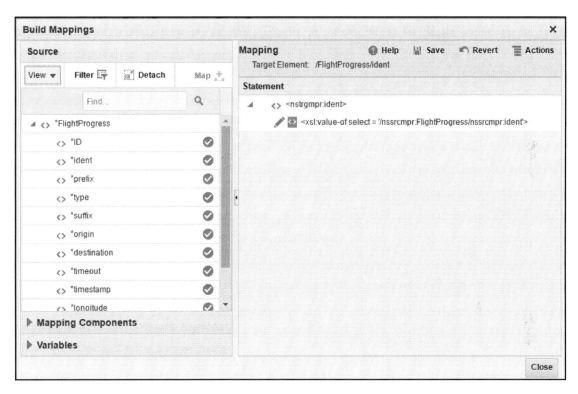

To do this, we are going to modify the `ident` target field to have a prefixed string. You may recognize the expression in the statement; this shows the selected element from the source by providing an XSLT (XSL Transform). We are going to extend this to have a prefix of `Direct-`; to do this, select the edit statement (pencil) icon on the right. We will now be able to edit the schema.

On the right-hand side is the **Source**, and so on. Select the **Mapping Components** menu and open the **String** option in the collapsed tree. Scroll through the list until you see **concat**, then select this and drag and drop it onto the editor icon on the right-hand side.

Doing this will trigger a popup called **Select Parameter**. Now select the string1 field and click on **OK**. This will set the path into the position for the string1 field. To set the literal value, simply double-click on the string2 parameter and then change the value to the literal Direct-. Your statement should look like the following screenshot:

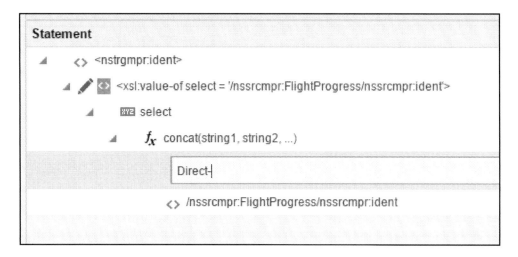

As you can see, the expression inside the select clause looks vaguely Excel-like. Once done, select the **Save** button and close the dialog with the **Close** button. Back at the main mapper page, you want to press the **Save** button to be safe.

You may also note that some of the elements are prefixed with an asterisk. This denotes whether the element is declared as mandatory or not (indicated in the schemas within our WSDL files by the minimum number of occurrences attribute on an element definition) as you can see here:

```
<xs:element maxOccurs="1" minOccurs="0" name="heading" type="xs:int"/>
```

We can confirm the mapping is as expected using the test option which can be accessed by the **Test** button. When you open the **Test Mapper** screen, you are presented with two large fields representing the input and output. As we have a WSDL and a schema, we can have some test values generated for us, by selecting the **Generate Inputs** button, which will populate the **Inputs** field. Alternatively, it is possible to paste in some input XML. Then by selecting the **Execute** button, the mapping process is performed and the **Outputs** field is populated. When you do this, you should notice the ident output is the input combined with the literal string. The following screenshot shows the outcome of generating and testing a mapping:

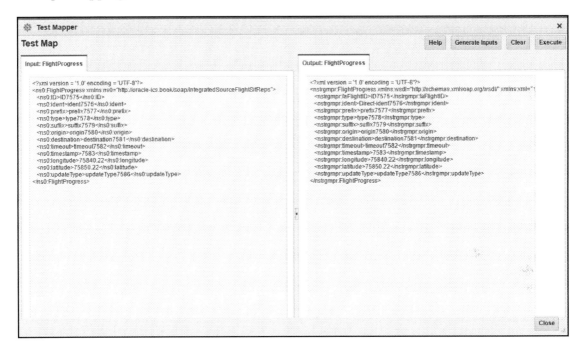

If the input is not suitable, then you will see an error message in the output panel, such as:

```
There has been an error executing this map:
<Line 10, Column 1>: XML-20210: (Fatal Error) Unexpected EOF.
```

With the mapping complete, we can exit the mapper and set the **Tracking**. For this test case we would recommend tracking the Id element of the source.

Testing the integration

Having saved and tested the integration within the editor, we can make it **Active** using the button on the **Integrations** page. Once this process has completed, then we can get the URL for the service via the information icon. It will include the endpoint URL along the lines of `https://icssandbox-xxxx.integration.us2.oraclecloud.com:443/integration/flowsvc /soap/TEST_SOAP_CH3/v01/?wsdl`.

If you paste the URL into the toolbar of your browser, you will see the actual WSDL rather than invoke the service. To actually trigger the service you will need to remove `?wsdl` from the URL (as this parameter is a common way to ask for the WSDL description to be returned). This path can be added to Mockable. Before running, also ensure that SoapUI includes the appropriate credentials, as you will have seen in the previous chapter. Once the service has been triggered, we can check the **Monitoring** page is showing when the service was triggered. But, most importantly, we can examine what has been received in Mockable. By selecting **Request Inspector** at the top of the screen, we will be presented with a screen showing what events have occurred, as follows:

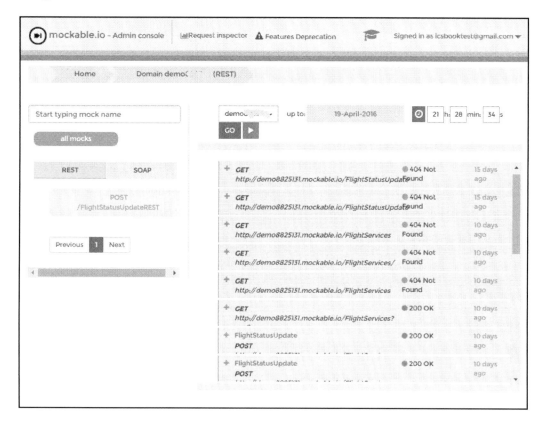

Within the **Request Inspector** , we can open up any of the requests and examine the content, which will show us the XML payload, as can be seen here:

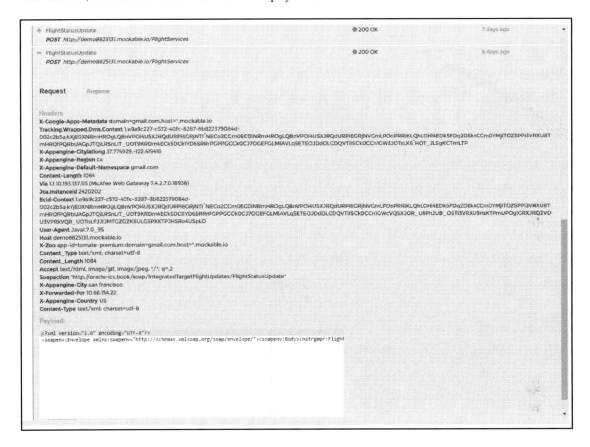

To see the XML payload, you will need to use the scroll bars, but you should be able observe their information.

Stage 2 – reworking to use the pub-sub approach

With the point-to-point integration proven to be working, we can now create a version of the same integration using the pub-sub pattern provided by ICS. We can re-use the existing connectors, and we can jump straight into creating the integrations.

Defining the publication service

So, in the integrations view we can select **Create New Integration**; however, when the pattern popup is presented, this time we want to select **Publish To ICS**.

The following table, as before, will guide you through setting up the integration description:

Property	Value
Integration Name	PublishFlightStatusUpdate_Ch3
Identifier	Take default
Version	01.00.0000
Package Name	ics.book.ch3
Description	Makes available flight status update information available to any subscribers.

With the basic integration stuff defined we can now apply the connector. As with the original source, locate the `FlightSitRep_Ch3` connector, apply it to the source, and complete the source configuration with the following information:

Tab	Question	Action
Basic Info	Call your endpoint field?	To keep it simple, call it `Source`.
	What does this end point do?	Add the description: `receives the flight status update from an external service`.
Operations	Selected Port Type	As we only have a single operation in the WSDL, this tab will not offer any options.
	Selected Operation	
	Request Object	
Summary	WSDL URL	As we only have a single operation in the WSDL, this tab will not offer any options. But should reflect the selected connector information.
	Selected Port Type	
	Cloud Operation	
	Message Exchange Pattern	

As the target is the ICS Message service, we do not need to do any configuration for this end of the integration as the section of the pattern has told ICS how the target should work and it can derive all the necessary information from the rest of the integration. The last step to configure the tracking is to test and save the integration, which also follows same the values for the source in our `FlightStatusUpdateDirect_Ch3` integration.

Defining the subscription service

Having created the publication service it is now possible to implement the subscription. So we go through the **Create New Integration** process, but this time select the **Subscribe To ICS** pattern.

The following table, as before, will guide you through setting up the integration description:

Property	Value
Integration Name	`SubscribeFlightUpdate_Ch3`
Identifier	Go with the proposed value.
Version	01.00.0000
Package Name	`ics.book.ch3`
Description	`Subscribes to the publication of FlightStatusUpdate events created within ICS.`

To start with, we need to drag the ICS Messaging Service onto the **Invoke** part of the template. When this is done, a list of possible publish services to connect to will be displayed. For example:

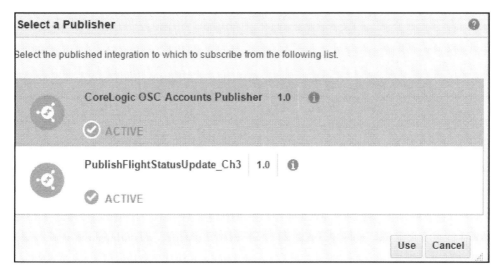

We can select our `PublishFlightStatusUpdate_Ch3` service and click on the **Use** button. Note that the version information is available, so if going forward we have two versions of the same interface, you can choose between the versions to pick up a subscription.

With the basic integration stuff defined, we can now apply the connector that will send the SOAP event to Mockable. Locate the `ReceiveFlightStatusUpdate_Ch3` connector and drop it onto the target. Complete the wizard using the following information:

Tab	Question	Action
Basic Info	**Call your endpoint field?**	To keep it simple, call it `Target`.
	What does this end point do?	Passes `FlightStatusUpdates` to the Mockable service.
	Preview updated SOAP adaptor runtime	This should be set to **No**
Operations	**Selected Port Type**	As we only have a single operation in the WSDL, this tab will not offer any options.
	Selected Operation	
	Request Object	
Summary	**WSDL URL**	As we only have a single operation in the WSDL, this tab will not offer any options. But should reflect the selected connector information.
	Selected Port Type	
	Cloud Operation	
	Message Exchange Pattern	

So at this stage, we have a service looking like this:

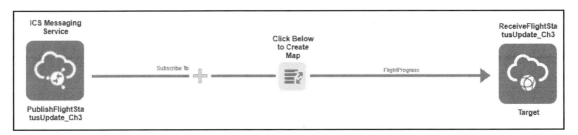

Running the test again

Having created these new integrations, we need to get them activated. Once activated, use the info icon to get the target URI for the service. The new URI can be inserted into the destination address of the original SoapUI test. Before you trigger the SoapUI test again, you probably want to refresh the user credentials to ensure the username and password are still correct, to avoid problems from the timestamp element of the security details having expired.

When you fire the trigger service now you should be able to see in the **Monitoring** view (more on this in `Chapter 12`, *Are My Integrations Running Fine, and What if They Are Not?*) that the publish and subscribe integrations have been triggered. We can see the monitoring information by navigating to the integration list page and clicking on the **Monitoring** tab, then on the monitoring dashboard by clicking on **Activity Stream**, which will list integrations that have been executed. We can also go to Mockable and look at the events list again. As before, Mockable should show the service being invoked.

Stage 3 – adding a second subscriber

So now let's extend the service by adding a new second integration that subscribes to `PublishFlightStatusUIpdate_Ch3`, with both subscribers calling their respective Mockable endpoints. To keep things simple the second target will be a variation on the theme of the existing services. This time the consumer represents a system that is only interested in the last reported position of the aircraft.

Setting up a second Mockable.io service

Rather than taking you through the process of setting up a new mock interface screen by screen, since you have already done this, we will highlight the steps and the values you need to complete the new mock interface:

Log back into Mockable.io. Once logged in, on the Home screen, select the **Manage** button.

You should now be able to click on the **SOAP** tab. Now you should be able to click on the **+ SOAP Mock** button.

With that, a new **SOAP Mock** screen should be displayed, which can be configured with the following values:

Field	Value
Endpoint	`FlightShortPositionUpdate`
SoapAction	`http://oracle-integration.cloud/soap/` `IntegratedFlightPositions/FlightShortPositionUpdate`
Headers	Leave blank
Response Status	200–OK
Content-Type	`Text/xml`
Content-Encoding	UTF-8
Response Body	Leave the **Dynamic Response** switch unset. Clear the content as we are unconcerned about the response body
Display Name	`FlightPositions`
Enable Request Logger	Click on the toggle switch so it goes green
Set Response Delay	Leave this set to off

Take note of the URL provided by Mockable for this endpoint. Click on the **Save** button. Click on the **Stopped** button under the **Status** heading so it toggles to show **Started**. With that, we now have another mock ready to be used.

Setting up the subscriber integration

To illustrate the difference in the UI when a WSDL has more than one service described, we have deliberately included two WSDL services, a short position report and a slightly longer one. As you can see within the `ICSBook-Ch3-FlightProgress-Target2.wsdl` file, in the schema definition you will see that we have also exploited the means to extend definitions within schemas. So the more advanced service extends the basic one at the schema level, but the WSDL definitions are completely separate. The following illustration shows this WSDL:

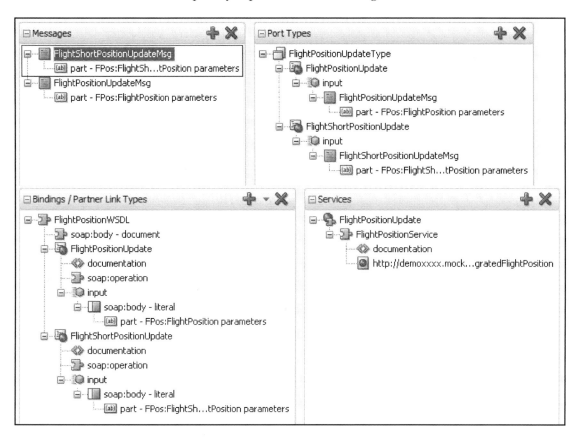

The following diagram illustrates the more advanced structure of the schema we will now use:

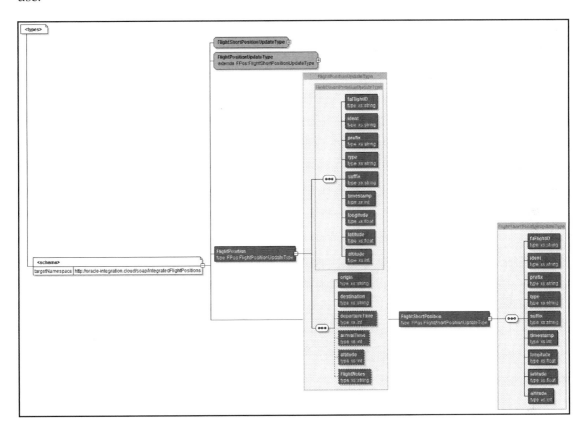

Taking this definition, we start by creating a new connection by navigating to the **Connections** part of the **Designer**. Click on the **Create New Connection** button. Locate the **SOAP** connection type from the dialog of connection types and select it. Complete the **New Connection** information, with the following details:

Field	Value
Connection Name	FlightPositionUpdates_Ch3
Identifier	Accept the default value
Connection Role	Accept the defaults of **Trigger and Invoke**
Description	Defines the interface to Mockable for handling flight position updates

With these provided values, click on the **Create** button. Add the e-mail address of the connection administrator–that is, you. Click **Configure Connectivity**. In the **Connection Properties** popup, select **Upload File**, select the file, and then click the **Upload** button that will be displayed. Select the file holding the WSDL provided earlier (`ICSBook-Ch3-FlightProgress-Target2.wsdl`). Close the dialog by clicking the **OK** button.

Click the **Configure Credentials** button, in the **Credential** dialog, set the **Security Policy** to **No Security Policy**. Close the dialog by clicking the **OK** button.

Click the **Test** button at the top of the page–this should transform the progress to 100% complete and green. Click the **Save** button. At the top of the page. Click **Exit Connection** to return to the list of defined connections.

We now have the connection complete, so we can go into the service design now. As with the connection we will keep the steps short and focused as you will have done this by now a couple of times.

So now we can create a new integration by navigating to the **Integrations** part of the **Designer**. Click on the **Create New Integration** button. Locate the **Subscribe To ICS** pattern and click on **Select**. This will launch the screen to define the initial integration details, which can be populated with:

Property	Value
Integration Name	`SubscribeFlightUpdatesForPosition_Ch3`
Identifier	Take the default
Version	01.00.0000
Package Name	`ics.book.ch3`
Description	`Extract just the position information from the FlightUpdate and send it to our position reporting mock.`

Complete the creation by clicking the **Create** button. Select the **Publisher** `PublishFlightStatusUpdate_Ch3` and click the **Use** button. In the right-hand list of connections, locate `FlightPositionUpdates_Ch3` and drag it to the **Invoke** target.

In the **Configure SOAP Endpoint** dialog, configure the following values:

Tab	Question	Action
Basic Info	Call your endpoint field?	To keep it simple, call it `Target`.
	What does this end point do?	Sends the position updates to Mockable.
Operations	Selected Port Type	Select `FlightShortPositionUpdate` from the **Select the service** dropdown.
	Selected Operation	
	Request Object	
Summary	WSDL URL	This will reflect the filename uploaded.
	Selected Port Type	
	Cloud Operation	
	Message Exchange Pattern	

You will have noticed that the **Operations** tab is a little more complex, as you have the choice of two operations here, reflecting that we represented a `FlightPositionShort` service and a normal service in the WSDL:

Select the mapping icon to open the mapping editor. Link the source and target, as shown in the following table:

Source	Target
id	FaFlightID
ident	ident
prefix	prefix
type	type
suffix	suffix
timestamp	timestamp
longitude	longitude
latitude	latitude

You will note that we have not mapped the source attributes such as origin, destination, and timeout, as for this message we are only interested in the flight's current location. Select the **Save** button, then leave the mapper by selecting **Exit Mapper**.

Open the **Tracking** screen–you should see that the tracking is set to tack against the Id. Leave the tracking screen without making any changes. Use the **Save** button on the integration and leave by clicking **Exit Integration**.

With the integration complete, we can activate it using the **Active** button.

Running the test with two subscribers

We do not have to do any further setup when it comes to SoapUI, as the same event we sent previously should not trigger both subscriber integrations. So, if you trigger the SOAP message in SoapUI, do not forget to ensure that the security credentials and timestamp are current. Then navigate to Mockable's **Request Inspector** page and use the green play icon to start refreshing updates. You will soon see something like this appearing:

As you can see, both mocks have been triggered and you can inspect the payload content to confirm the same values are being passed through as expected.

You can also see what is happening through the **Monitoring** screens. By navigating into the **Monitoring** part of ICS and then selecting **Integrations** from the left menu, it is possible to see which integrations have fired, along with the tracking element (for our services, this has been set to Id). As you can see in the following screenshot, we have not run the integrations recently, so no errors are being reported. If a service does fail, for example, if the destination URI to Mockable.io was wrong, then the **Errors** count will show an error. The warning symbol for that integration will be clickable, and will present you with more information about the error. The following screenshot shows the **Integrations** part of the **Monitoing** in ICS:

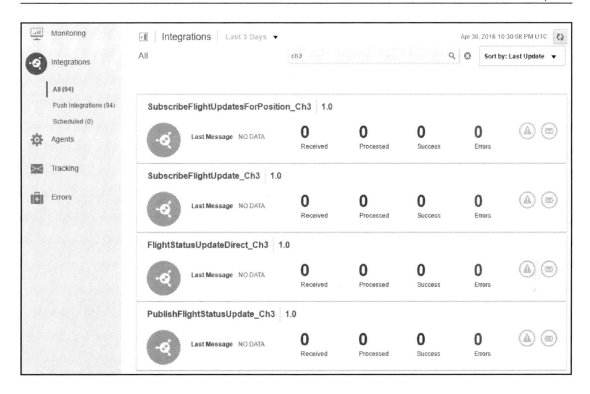

You can also drill into the integration by clicking on the integration name to see more detail on the error. We will go into troubleshooting in a lot more depth in Chapter 12, *Are My Integrations Running Fine, and What if They Are Not?*

Enhanced techniques

We have covered the simplest and most common use cases of publish and subscribe, but we should understand some of the more advanced approaches. Let's explore them in this section.

Multiple sources

We may wish to extend our integration to accommodate multiple source systems with the source data differing a little bit, so the same source connection cannot be reused. Thus, the goal would be to achieve something along these lines:

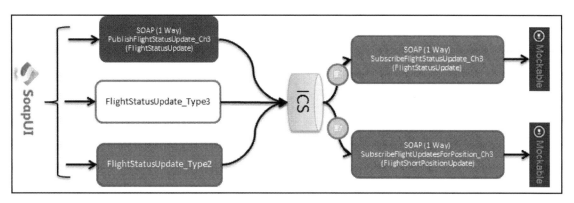

However, the problem we have here is that the publish integration has no way to transform the payload so it is consistent, and the process of creating a subscription relates to the publish integration not a connection description for the ICS messaging solution. So the question is: How we can solve this? There is an architectural concept we will introduce shortly to help here, but from an integration creation process, we would implement things in the following way:

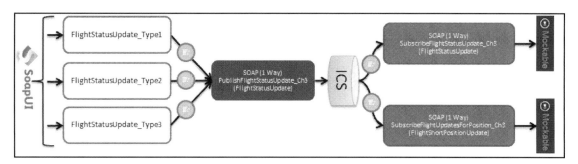

Canonical data model pattern and normalizers

In `Chapter 1`, *Introducing the Concepts and Terminology*, we introduced the idea of design patterns. This scenario leads us to a couple of integration design patterns that can make thing a lot easier, specifically the canonical model and, to an extent, a normalizer.

 The commonly accepted definitions of these patterns can be found here: Canonical Data Model–`http://www.enterpriseintegrationpatterns.com/patterns/messaging/CanonicalDataModel.html`
Normalizer–`http://www.enterpriseintegrationpatterns.com/patterns/messaging/Normalizer.html`

The essence of a canonical model is a standardized message structure and definition for the data. The benefit of this is that, if all the systems being integrated understand the canonical model, then the integrations need only determine who receives what, and you do not have to convert data back and forth between different representations. In practical terms, our examples have included location values as latitude and longitude. Both values could be expressed as a decimal representation with accuracy to a number of decimal places, but also could be expressed as degrees, minutes, and seconds. If you have integrations chained or orchestrated you could easily end up converting back and forth, each time introducing rounding errors or even simply losing precision by reducing the number of decimal places. By applying a canonical model, we can apply the transform at worst twice (once to the canonical form, and again to the target system representation). Typically, the canonical form will offer a level of precision of detail equal to, or greater than, that needed by any of the associated systems.

The value of a canonical form goes further than the definition of any one element but can extend to describing whole structures of related items, such as an address. This can start to sound like a lot of work to define the canonical form, but it need not be. There are a number of organizations that have allowed different companies with a common interest in an area of industry (for example, retail, shipping, and logistics) to get together to agree a common means to describe significant pieces of data, often in a manner that allows a degree of customization. For example, one of the major agreed standards for retail is known as ARTS; a very broad overarching organization covering a range of industries is known as OASIS. By adopting parts of the entirety of these standards, the chances of the integrations becoming very easy will increase as many suppliers support these organizations and standards, including Oracle.

More information on the sources of canonical definition be obtained from:
ARTS–`https://nrf.com/arts-operational-data-model-70`
OASIS–`https://www.oasis-open.org/`
OAGIS–`http://www.oagi.org/`

So, going back to our examples again, if the connector for the publisher represented the canonical form for the flight data, then everything else is likely to get easier (and definitely more maintainable). Those outer integrations shown become effectively part of a normalizer pattern.

Summary

In this chapter we have seen how to take a simple integration and convert it into a publish and subscribe pair of integrations, and then extend it with additional subscriber integrations. In demonstrating the integrations, we have seen how to use Mockable to capture the inbound events and examine the content of the SOAP service calls in Mockable. We then looked at a couple of design ideas that allow the publish and subscribe framework to be taken forward using enterprise patterns.

In the next chapter, we will take the basics from the last couple of chapters and examine how ICS can be used to perform integrations between known SaaS solutions, such as those provided by Oracle.

4
Integrations between SaaS Applications

In the previous chapters, we looked at basic integration patterns. In Chapter 2, *Integrating Our First Two Applications*, we created a point-to-point integration, integrating a SOAP inbound service and a REST outbound service, and in Chapter 3, *Distribute Messages Using the Pub-Sub Model*, we converted a simple integration into a publish and subscribe pair of integrations and extended it with multiple subscribers.

So far we have demonstrated the use of our own service definitions for the trigger services and online tooling to document and mock our back-end services. In this chapter we're going to demonstrate the integration between existing **SaaS (Software as a Service)** applications. Integrating with SaaS applications is getting more and more important now that companies are moving away from on-premises application to Cloud hosted solutions. Where we have the need to share data between on-premises applications, for example integrating our CRM with our ERP application, this requirement will still exist when using Cloud hosted versions of these solutions. As we do not have direct access to where these applications are hosted, we need some kind of integration platform like Oracle Integration Cloud Service to connect these applications with each other.

As SaaS solutions are created to provide economies of scale, are exposed to the unrestricted internet and need to support many variations in capability this can lead to complex APIs. To address this, we will often see adapters being provided to ease these challenges as we will see in this chapter.

We are going to bring the idea alive by introducing you to our aircraft maintenance department. This department uses Salesforce for CRM purposes and other SaaS applications for collaboration and messaging. The maintenance department has the requirement to interact these applications with each other, but they did not have an integration component and decided to use ICS. The first thing the department want to create is an integration that represents a scheduled aircraft maintenance that gets escalated which triggers sending a notification to the mobile phone of the case owner by **SMS (Short Message Service)**.

Both service providers are SaaS applications. For the case management we are going to use Service Cloud from Salesforce (`http://salesforce.com`), and for sending SMS messages we will use Twilio (`https://twilio.com`). This chapter not only shows the steps to create the integration in ICS using simplified adapters, but also the configuration in both SaaS applications. The integration we are building in this chapter is shown here:

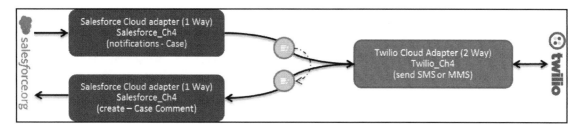

In this chapter, we will cover the following topics:

- How to set up the SaaS application
- Defining the necessary SaaS connections
- Differences in creating the integration with cloud adapters
- Simplifying the mapping of complex message structures
- How to test and troubleshoot the SaaS integration

Getting ready

Before we can build our integration, let's get acquainted with the SaaS applications we are going to integrate with. As shown in the previous diagram our inbound call is a notification send by Salesforce, this is in itself an asynchronous call. The notification is triggered when a Case in Service Cloud is escalated. Oracle ICS supports an **out-of-the-box (OOTB)** adapter that supports inbound interactions from Salesforce to ICS. Without a lot of extra configuration in Salesforce the adapter in ICS is capable of receiving notifications.

Our outbound call is also using an OOTB Cloud adapter, but Twilio. Twilio provides a Cloud service to send messages using SMS, MMS and voice messaging to mobile phones. The response of the message will create a new comment for the case that is escalated, mentioning the case owner received a SMS.

Setting up Salesforce

For this integration, we are going to use Service Cloud. Service Cloud is a customer service application. One major component is for creating cases around issues that are reported by customers. To complete our setup of Salesforce to send escalated cases to Integration Cloud, we need to execute the following steps:

1. Get access to a Salesforce (Service Cloud) Enterprise or Developer instance.
2. Generate the enterprise service definition (WSDL).
3. Obtain or reset your security token.
4. Create a workflow rule that triggers on escalated cases.
5. Create an outbound message format and generate message WSDL.

Step 1 – get access to a Salesforce instance

If your organization already uses Salesforce (Service Cloud) request a user account with system administration rights or check if your existing account has these rights. If your organization doesn't have access to a Salesforce instance, like we encountered, or you want an environment for testing solutions, obtain a Salesforce Developer Edition instance. Go to `https://developer.salesforce.com/signup`and follow the instructions.

Step 2 – generate the Enterprise service definition

To integrate Salesforce with ICS we need the Enterprise Web Service definition. This is a WSDL file we need to generate in order to get access to the API. You can generate it yourself or obtain it from your organization's Salesforce administrator.

In our case, since we are using a developer instance we can generate the WSDL file ourselves. Log in to your Salesforce account. You must log in as a user who had the **Modify All Data** permission. After logging in, navigate to the **Setup** page. On the top right corner of each page you will find a set of icons as shown here:

Click on the setup icon, which is the third icon from the right in the menu in the top-right corner of the screen, and select the **Setup Home** item.

On the **Setup** page, we find a **Quick Find** box; enter API and select **API** under **Custom Code** to navigate to the download page. ICS uses the Force.com Enterprise WSDL in its communication. Scroll down to the **WSDL and Client Certificates** section and generate the **Enterprise WSDL** and save it as SForce-Enterprise.wsdl.

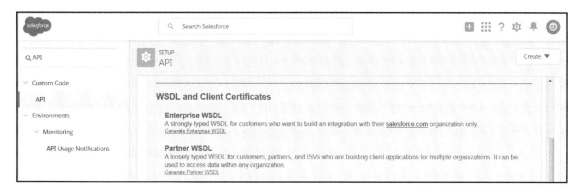

Step 3 – obtain or reset your security token

Because we access Salesforce from an IP address that isn't likely to be trusted for our instance, and because we use the API from ICS, we need a security token to log in. The security token is a case-sensitive alphanumeric code that we need to append to our password. Whenever your password is reset, your security token is also reset.

If you have already obtained the security token or can obtain it from your administrator, then the next step can be skipped, but in our case, we don't know it yet.

Click on the view profile icon, which is the last icon on the right, of the menu in the top-right corner of the screen and select the **Settings**. Enter `Reset` in the **Quick Find** box and select **Reset My Security Token** under **My Personal Information**.

On this page, click the **Reset Security Token** button, which will send out an e-mail with your new token. Be warned that after a reset, you can't use your old token anymore, and clients that use it will stop working:

Step 4 – create workflow rule for escalated cases

Now that we have retrieved the WSDL and security token that we can use in ICS to create our connection, we need to define the actual workflow rule. Workflow rules are triggered when its conditions are met. In our scenario, we want the case owner to be notified when one of their cases is escalated, which happens when the **Case Status** is changed to **Escalated**.

Again, we need to navigate to the **Setup Home** page. In the **Quick Find** box, enter `Workflow` and select **Workflow Rules** under **Process Automation** to navigate to the rules page.

This page lists all workflow rules that are created for your organization. When starting with a clean environment, this list will be empty. On this page, we will find some quick tips and links to sample workflow rules and video tutorials.

Click the **New Rule** button to open the wizard for creating a new workflow rule:

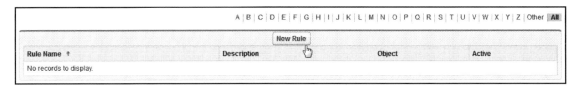

In our case, we want to trigger the case object. In the first step, select **Case** in the **Object** drop-down list and click the **Next** button to proceed:

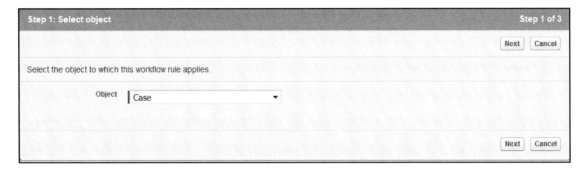

In the second step, we configure the workflow rule. In this step, we enter the name, description and criteria to trigger our workflow rule. Complete the configuration with the following details:

Criteria	Property	Action
Edit Rule	**Rule Name**	Call it `Escalated Case`
	Description	Add the description: `Trigger when case is escalated.`
Evaluation Criteria	**Evaluate then rule when a record is?**	Choose the (default) option, created, and any time it's edited to subsequently meet criteria
Rule Criteria	**Run this rule if the following?**	Choose **criteria are met**
	Field	Select the Case: **Status field**
	Operator	Select the equals: **operator**
	Value	Click the lookup icon and check the **Escalated** option

Click the **Save** and **Next** buttons to proceed. In the third step we can specify workflow actions that are executed when the criteria are met. You have the option to create a new task, send an email alert, automatically update a field, send an outbound message or select an existing action you created earlier. In our case let's choose to create a new outbound message. If this workflow action is triggered it sends a message to an external endpoint. Which is exactly what we want. The **New Task** and **Field Update** actions are internal actions whereas the **New Email Alert** sends an e-mail to given recipients.

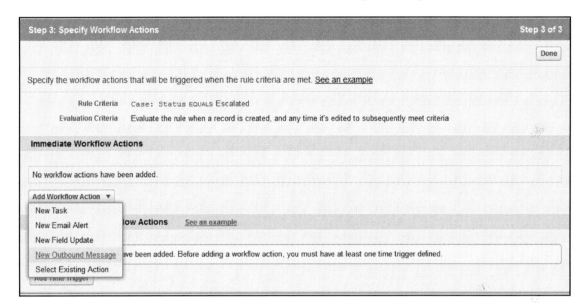

Step 5 – define outbound message and generate message WSDL

The **Outbound** Messages page is where we can configure our new outbound message. Complete the configuration with the following details:

Property	Value
Name	Case_OM
Unique Name	This will be proposed based on the rule name and there is no need to change unless you'd like an alternate name.
Description	Send escalated case information to Integration Cloud.

Endpoint URL	Because we don't know endpoint from ICS yet, since we still need to create our integration, enter: `https://url-to-ics-integration.oraclecloud.com`
User to send as	Choose the account that is the owner of the sent message, for example, your own account.
Protected Component	Keep unchecked.
Send Session ID	Keep unchecked.
Case fields to send	Select the following available fields: `CaseNumber OwnerId Product_cc Subject`

Click the **Save** button to accept the configuration. This will bring us back to the last step of creating the workflow rule. Click **Done** to complete the process.

Before we can activate our workflow rule, we need to complete our integration in ICS first. To complete the integration we need to generate the WSDL that we use to let ICS know what the message format is that it will receive from Salesforce.

On the **Workflow Rule Detail** page, click on the outbound message **Case_OM**:

We are navigated to the **Workflow Outbound Message Detail** page. To generate and download the WSDL, click the link after the field **Endpoint URL**. Save the WSDL file as `SForce-CaseEscalated.wsdl`:

Outbound Message: Case			
Name	Case_OM	User to send as	Robert van Mölken
Unique Name	Case_OM	API Version	37,0
Description	Send escalated case information to Integration Cloud Service		
Object	Case		
Endpoint URL	http://dummy.com	Modified By	Robert van Mölken
Endpoint WSDL	Click for WSDL		
Send Session ID			
Fields to Send	CaseNumber Id OwnerId Product__c Subject		
Created By	Robert van Mölken		

At this point we have configured Salesforce as much as we can right now. We will return to Salesforce when the integration is done to edit the Endpoint URL and to activate our workflow rule.

Setting up Twilio

For this integration we are going to invoke Twilio. Twilio allows software developers to send and receive SMS, MMS, and voice messages using web service APIs. In our integration, we are using Twilio to send out an SMS message to the mobile phone of the case owner. To complete our setup of Twilio to send escalated cases to the mobile phone, we need to execute the following steps:

1. Get access to a Twilio account.
2. Create or port a phone number for sending messages.
3. Add verified caller IDs.
4. Obtain live and/or test API credentials.

Step 1 – get access to a Twilio account

If your organization already uses Twilio, you can skip right to the *Step 3 - add verified callers IDs* section. If your organization doesn't have access to a Twilio account, as we found, or you want an account for testing solutions, obtain a free Twilio account. Go to `https://www.twilio.com/try-twilio` and follow the instructions. For the question **WHICH PRODUCT DO YOU PLAN TO USE FIRST?**, select the option **SMS**. For **WHAT ARE YOU BUILDING?**, select the option **Other types of SMS Alerts** and for **CHOOSE YOUR LANGUAGE**, select **Java** (because ICS adapters are built with Java).

Step 2 – create phone number for sending messages

This step is not necessary if you want to create a test solution. Each Twilio account comes with a live and test credentials when using the API. In our case, we can use the test credentials, but if you want to create (buy) or port a phone number, there are a few steps to complete.

To create or port a phone number navigate to the **Phone Numbers** service. Click the all products and services icon, which is always the bottom icon, in the menu on the left.

For easy access, pin the **Phone Numbers** and **Programmable SMS** services to the menu by clicking on the pin icon next to the service.

Click on the **Phone Numbers** service to manage the phone numbers of your account. In our case, we do not yet have a phone number for sending out SMS messages. In the submenu, click the item **Manage Numbers** and get a new number:

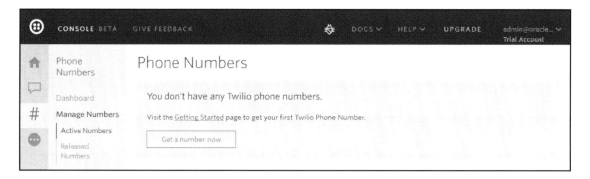

Use the **Get a number now** button to navigate to the **Get** Started page and subsequently click **Get your first Twilio phone number**. This will show a dialog box where you can pick your first phone number. Pick a phone number that can send SMS messages. An available number is assigned to you, but it isn't the default that will support SMS, just like in our case:

Search for a different number supports SMS. Your first number is part of the trial:

You can always go back to the chosen number on the **Manage Number** page where we started to create our first phone number:

Step 3 – add verified callers IDs

To send messages to mobile phones, we first need to verify them so Twilio knows we are not spamming the number without their knowledge. In the **Phone Number** service, click on **Verified Caller IDs** and add the numbers you want to send messages to.

Step 4 – obtain live and/or test API credentials

Like we mentioned in the previous step, we don't necessary need a phone number to send messages to a real device. We can use the test credentials, which uses a default phone number, +15005550006, to virtually send messages from.

To obtain the API credentials navigate to your account settings. Click the console home icon, which is always the top icon in the menu on the left. In the submenu, click the item **Account** and view the **API Credentials**. We will start building our integration with the **TEST Credentials**, but will use the **LIVE Credentials** during the final step. To see the Auth token, click on the lock icon. We need both values to create our connection in ICS shown as follows:

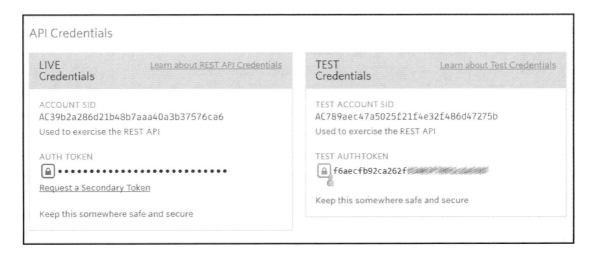

Define the necessary connections

For this integration, we use both SaaS applications. For each application, we'll create a connection, one will be triggered by our Salesforce instance and one will invoke Twilio.

As before, log back into ICS and navigate to the **Connections** part of the **Designer** and create a Salesforce connection by selecting the **Salesforce** adapter.

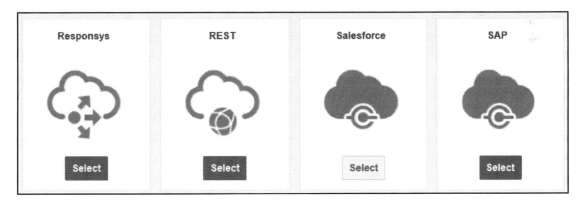

Create the connection with the following details:

Property	Value
Connection Name	`Salesforce_Ch4`
Identifier	This will be proposed based on the connection name, and there is no need to change unless you'd like an alternate name.
Connection Role	**Trigger and Invoke.**
Description	`This connection interacts with the Salesforce instance, for example, to receive outgoing messages.`

After creation, configure the connection with the following details:

Property	Description
Email Address	Your e-mail address.
Configure connectivity | Enterprise WSDL location	Tick the **Upload File**, and then use the **File** selection to upload the `SForce-Enterprise` WSDL. Close with the **OK** button.
Configure Security | Credentials	Set **Security Policy** to **Salesforce Custom Policy**. Enter **Username** of valid system admin account. Enter and confirm a **Password**. The value is the password of the user and attached to that the security token, for example, `passwordSecurityToken`. Close the dialog with the **OK** button.

The following screenshot shows our security configuration:

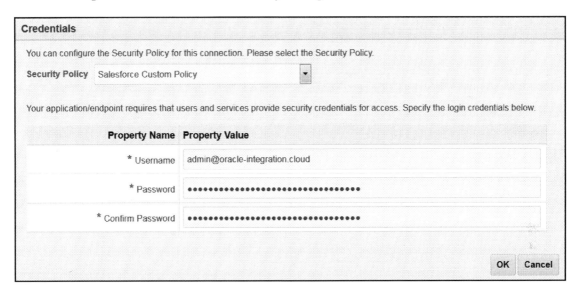

Once the fields are complete, use the **Test** button at the top of the page to validate the connection configuration; the percentage completion should reach 100% at this point. Click the **Save and Exit Connection** button.

Now we repeat this to create the Twilio connector with the following details:

Property	Value
Connection Name	Twilio_Ch4
Identifier	This will be proposed based on the integration name, and there is no need to change unless you'd like an alternate name.
Connection Role	**Invoke** (the only option)
Description	This connection can send SMS, MMS, or voice messages through Twilio to mobile phones.

After creation, configure the connection with the following details:

Property	Value
Email Address	Your e-mail address
Configure Security | Credential	Set **Security Policy** to **Twilio Security Policy**. Enter **AccountSID** of test credentials (see the Twilio account). Enter and confirm `AuthToken` (see the Twilio account). Close the dialog with the **OK** button.

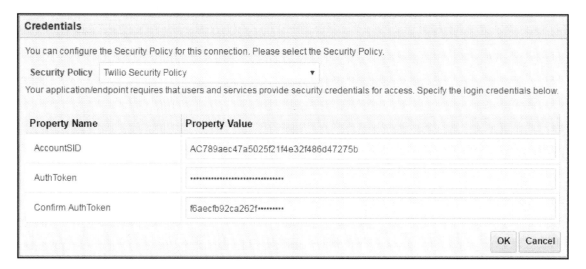

Click **Test** at the top of the page to validate the connection configuration. After validating the connection, click the **Save and Exit Connection** button. We should now have two connections successfully created.

Troubleshooting

If the test fails for one of these connections, check if the correct credentials where used. When connecting to Salesforce, remember that the password is a combination of the users' password and their security token. When the failure is from Twilio, check to see whether you mixed up the live and test credentials.

Integrate the SaaS applications

Now that we have created the connections we can integrate our SaaS applications by creating the integration. Let's navigate to the **Integrations** page, click **Create New Integration**, and select the **Basic Map Data** pattern. Now we can complete the creation of the integration with the following details:

Property	Value
Integration Name	`EscalateAircraftMaintenance_Ch4`
Identifier	This will be proposed based on the connection name, and there is no need to change unless you'd like an alternate name.
Version	01.00.0000
Package Name	`ics.book.ch4`
Description	`This integration demonstrates escalated cases in Salesforce being reported via SMS to the case owner.`

With the basic details for the integration completed, we can now drag and drop our connections from the connector palette. For the **Trigger** side, we want to drop the `Salesforce_Ch4` connector. With the icon displayed, we can then proceed to edit the details of the connector to use. The **Configure Salesforce Endpoint** dialog is shown, as you may remember it uses tabbed panels, and can be navigated through using the **Next** and **Back** buttons.

We can complete the configuration using the following information:

Tab	Question	Action
Basic Info	**Call your endpoint field?**	Use something more meaningful; call it `ReceiveEscalatedCases`.
	What does this end point do?	Add the following description: `receives a notification when a case gets escalated.`
Outbound Messaging	**Prerequisite**	Read the prerequisite notes and learn that we executed these steps when we set up Salesforce.
	Select the Outbound Messaging WSDL	Tick the **Upload File**, and then use the **File** selection to upload the `SForce-CaseEscalated` WSDL.

The next step in the configuration is slightly more complex so we will look at this in more detail. In the **Response t**ab, keep the checkbox for **Send a response** checked. The notification that we receive will be a one-way interaction, but we can configure a callback for a successful and a failure response. The scenario here is that we want to have clear visibility of the SMS notification delivery in Salesforce (has it, or has it not been delivered yet). To do this we are configuring both a successful and failure callback. Click the successful callback **Configure** button.

When a SMS message is sent to the case owner with success, we want to create a new comment for the specific case telling the SMS was sent. Use the following information:

Section	Sub-section	Action
Successful Callback	**Select and Operation Type**	Select **CRUD** in the operations list. Select create in the types list.
	Select Business Objects	Select the **CaseComment** object and click on the single arrow. You case use the filter to quickly find the object. Accept the configuration with the **OK** button

The result of entering the configuration is shown in the following screenshot:

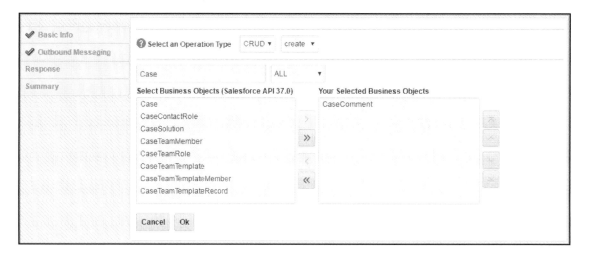

When a SMS message could not be delivered, we want to create a new comment on the personal feed of the case owner informing about the failure. Click the failure callback **Configure** button and use the following information:

Section	Sub-section	Value
Failure Callback	**Select and Operation Type**	Select **CRUD** in the operations list. Select create in the types list.
	Select Business Objects	Select **FeedItem** and tick the single arrow. You case use the filter to quickly find the object. Accept the configuration with the **OK** button.

Back on the **Response tab**, we can see the configured successful and failure callbacks. For each callback, we can also configure more advanced automated action by configuring headers, for example, e-mail alerts, but we will leave that for another time. The following screenshot shows the result of the callback configuration:

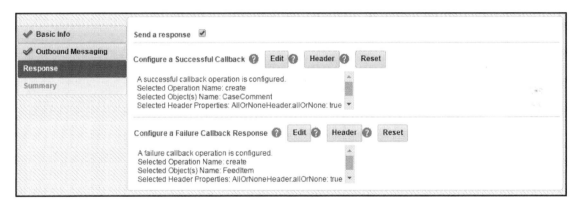

Click the **Next** button to proceed. In the **Summary** tab, read the next steps and see that after we complete the integration we need to update the dummy URL, entered in Salesforce when creating the outbound message, to the ICS **Endpoint URL**. The **Summary** view also shows the **Notification Object for Outbound Messaging** we choose in Salesforce and the configuration for the success and failure callbacks.

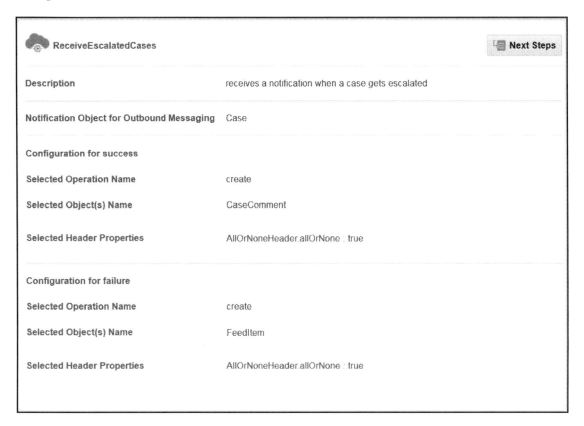

Click **Done**, and subsequently the **Save** button to secure our progress. We can now define the other end of the integration by dropping the `Twilio_Ch4` connector onto the **Invoke** target. The resultant dialog can be completed with the following:

Tab	Question	Action
Basic Info	**Call your endpoint field?**	Call it **SendMessage**.
	What does this end point do?	Add the description: `sends a SMS message to the owner of the escalated case.`
Operations	Select Operation	Select **Send SMS or MMS**.
Summary	Description	The Endpoint URI shows the URL of the Twilio API: `https://api.twilio.com/2010-04-01/Accounts/{accountId}/ Messages.json` This endpoint could also be used for sending a plain REST/JSON `POST` call.
	Endpoint URI	
	Method	

The integration looks a little different than before:

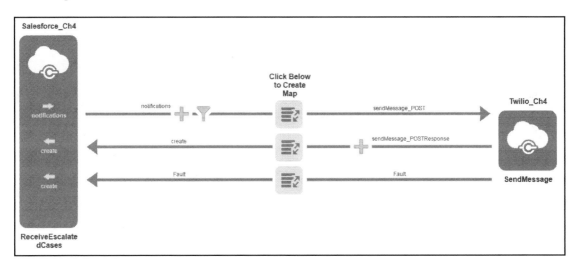

Because we configured two callbacks, we see three operations on the trigger side of the integration. One notifications operations coming inbound and two create operation going outbound.

Map message data

To complete our integration we need to map the messages between Salesforce and Twilio and vice versa. The inbound notification from Salesforce maps to the request of the synchronous call to Twilio, the response of Twilio is mapped to the create `CaseComment` callback, and a fault response from Twilio is mapped to the create `FeedItem` callback.

Map Salesforce notifications to Twilio requests

Let's create the request mapping. First, click the mapping icon, in the middle of the flow, and then on the plus sign to create a new mapping. This will be a little more complex than in the previous chapter. In this test, we are going to send the SMS message to our own phone.

Since we don't receive this phone number in our notification, we need to assign the value manually or retrieve it in a separate service call. In this first iteration, we manually assign the **From** and **To** phone number and concatenate some nodes of the notification to compose the body node of the SMS message.

In the mapping UI, click on the target's `From` node, which shows the **Build Mappings** screen, and lets us type the value itself instead of mapping a source node to it. Since we used the test credentials for setting up our connection, we enter the only valid phone number, for example, `+15005550006`:

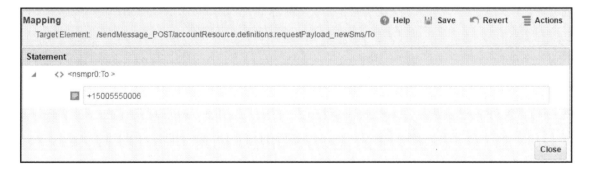

Click **Save** and **Close** to return and do the same for the target's `To` node. Enter a phone number that you want to receive the message, that is, our own. This phone number should be a verified caller ID in Twilio, like we did in the *Step 3 – add verified callers IDs* section of our Twilio setup.

Click **Save** and Close to return and click on the target's `Body` node. Because we want to send the values of multiple nodes in our message, it is composed of three string labels and three source nodes: `CaseNumber,` `Product__c,` and `Subject.`

On the **Build Mappings** screen you find a sub-section called **Mapping Components**. Click on **Mapping Components** to open this section. Drag and drop the `concat` function, under **Functions | Strings**, to the target's `Body` node. This will add the function to the node:

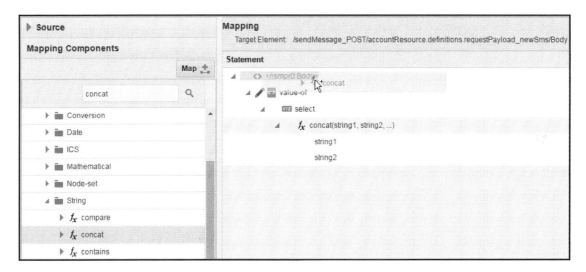

Notice that we have two string value fields. In total we want six fields, but it's not possible to create the empty fields first, because the UI restricts this to two empty values, so we need to have a value first. To get access to the source nodes, open the **Source** section by clicking on it.

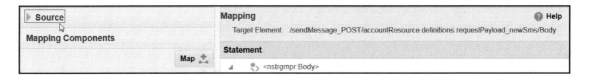

 To only see a specific node, for example, Case, with its children, right-click on the node and select the **Show as Top** option.

[153]

Complete the following mapping:

Source / Text value	Target
Case #:	string1
CaseNumber	string2

To add the other four values we need to create a new sibling after the last value, right-click on the last field, CaseNumber, and select **Insert Sibling After**. This will add a new field that we can drag and drop a source node to or enter a text value in. We can complete the mapping for the next four fields using the following table:

Source/text value	Target
, Product:	string3
*Case / Product__c	string4
, Case Subject:	string5
*Case / Subject	string6

The mapping of the **Body** node should look like the following statement:

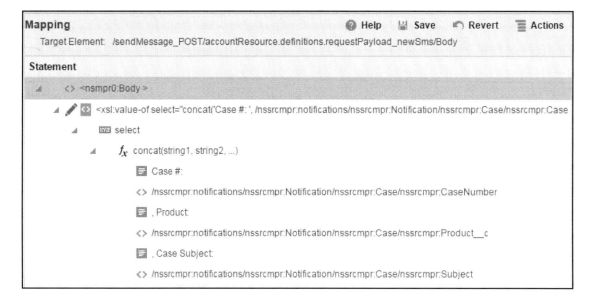

Click **Save** and Close to return to the mapping UI. We will now have mapped the `To`, `From`, and `Body` nodes of the target. The target message had many more nodes, but we can leave them unassigned:

Save the mapping and click on **Exit Mapper**.

Map Twilio's response to Salesforce's case comment

Next, we will create the response mapping of the synchronous response of Twilio and map it to the create a `CaseComment` request message to Salesforce. Click the mapping icon and create a new response mapping. When the mapping UI opens, it displays an error: **can't display all available nodes for the target message**. This is because it uses the same large object for receiving and updating `CaseComments`. Luckily for us, we only need to map three nodes. Define the mapping using the following table:

Source/text value	Target
The Case owner is notified about the escalation.	`ContentBody`
`True (Boolean)`	`IsPublished`
`$SourceApplicationObject// Case/Id`	`ParentId`

To set a Boolean value, click on the target node and open the **Mapping Components**. Search for Boolean and drag and drop the true or false function to the target statement.

Notice that we don't map any nodes from the response of the invoke to Twilio for our integration as it doesn't include any useful information:

 A list of nodes can be very long. You can detach the source or target to see the full list in a separate window. To know which nodes are mapped, use the filter option of the mapping UI to only show mapped fields.

Save the mapping and click on **Exit Mapper**.

Map Twilio's fault to Salesforce's feed comment

Finally, we will create the fault mapping of the fault response of Twilio and map it to the create `FeedItem` request message to Salesforce. Click the mapping icon and create a new fault mapping for `APIInvocationError`.

Notice that we only have access to the fault variable and not to our original request message. To create a `FeedItem`, we need a `ParentId`, for example, our profile feed. It's not that difficult to retrieve; just follow these steps:

1. Open a new tab, log into Salesforce, and visit your profile page.
2. Investigate the URL of the page; it will include the following pattern:
   `/sObject/00558000001NCwhAAG/view`.
3. Copy the value after `sObject`, for example, `00558000001NCwhAAG`
4. Return to your mapping in ICS.

Now we can define the mapping using the following table:

Source/text value	Target
concat SMS notification failed to send to case owner. Reason: fault/reason	`Body`
`TextPost`	`Type`
Value you collected in previous steps	`ParentId`

To find out more of what the Salesforce API can do, visit the following URL:
`https://developer.salesforce.com/docs/atlas.en-us.api.meta/api/sforce_api_objects_list.html`

Save the mapping and click on **Exit Mapper**.

Completing and activating the integration

Now that the mappings of our integration are finished, we only need to add the tracking fields before we can complete and activate the integration.

At the top-right, click **Tracking** to open the **Business identifiers** dialog. In this case, we are going to set two tracking fields: `CaseNumber` and `Product__c`. Drag and drop both trigger fields to the list and use `CaseNumber` as the primary identifier. Change the **Tracking Name** of the `Product__c` field to **Product Number**:

Primary	Tracking Field	Tracking Name	Help Text	
✔	CaseNumber	Case Number	How to track it?	🗑
☐	Product__c	Product Number	How to track it?	🗑
	Drag a trigger field here	What to call it?	How to track it?	

Done   Cancel

Click **Done** to save the identifiers, and in the integration canvas, **Save** and **Exit Integration** to finish our integration. We are returned again to the list of all integrations. Use the **PENDING ACTIVATION** button of the integration we just created to make it active. This time, in the **Confirmation** screen, enable tracing so we can inspect payloads later:

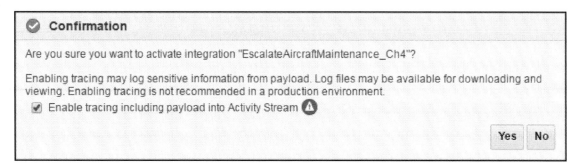

Before testing our solution, we need to change the endpoint URL in Salesforce that our outbound message is send to. Remember that we set it to `http://url-to-ics-integration.oraclecloud.com` when creating the outbound message. Find the **Endpoint URL** within the integration details and copy the address to your clipboard.

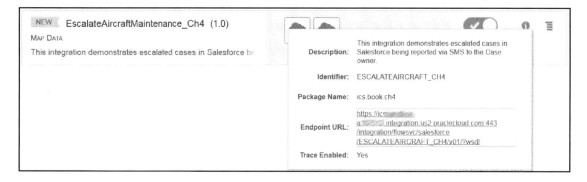

Now head over to Salesforce where we will configure this endpoint for our outbound message. In Salesforce, navigate to **Setup Home** and find the **Workflow Outbound Message** named **Case_OM** in the **Most Recently Used** section.

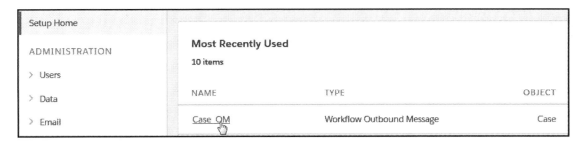

Click on the name to open the details and edit the configuration of the endpoint URL. Paste the URL we copied from ICS into the corresponding field, but remove the `?wsdl` part, and **Save** the configuration.

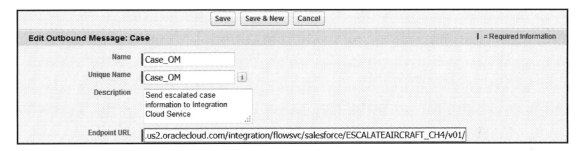

Finally, in the **Workflow Rules Using This Outbound Message** section, click the **Activate** link in front of our rule. When the workflow rule is triggered, a notification will now be sent to our endpoint.

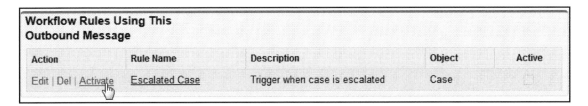

Testing the integration

To test the integration, we're going to escalate a case in Salesforce. In our scenario, we escalate high-priority cases that still have the status **New** after an hour. To notify the assigned case owner, we're going to change the **STATUS** of a case to **Escalated**:

In our Salesforce, we have one case that meets our criteria, but the trigger works with every case where the status is changed to **Escalated**. Click on the case number that we want to escalate to inform the case owner to take a closer look. The page shows the case details, which also includes the interaction feed and its related items, for example, case comments.

To change the status of a case, click on the pencil next to the status field to edit it. It will change the form from text to input fields. Select the **Escalated** status from the list:

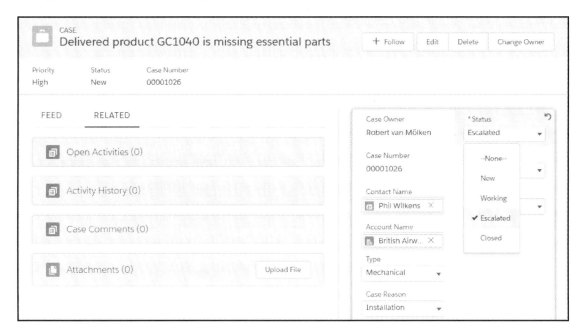

After changing the status we can save the new value. Click **Save** on the bottom of the form to accept the change. This will instantly trigger our workflow rule, and when the message is successfully sent through Twilio, we will see a new case comment added to the related case items:

We see that the case comment is created, which means that the outbound message was sent to ICS and delivered to Twilio. Because we are using the test credentials, the SMS is not yet delivered to our mobile phone.

Let's investigate the instance in ICS itself. Log into ICS and navigate to the monitoring page. Click on **Tracking** in the left-hand menu to see all instances that have recently run. If you have a lot of instances, you can use the primary tracking field value to find the instance. Enter your case number in the search field to filter out the other messages, in our case, it's `00001026`. You can also limit the timeframe by changing it to the last hour or day:

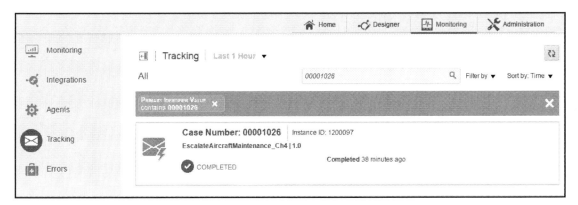

If we look at the details of the instance, we see that the notification was received and the successful callback was called:

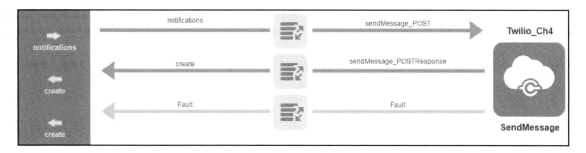

Despite all the details about the instance given, we won't find the message payload that was sent to Twilio and back to Salesforce on this page. Remember that we enabled tracing when activating the integration. This stated that the message payloads were also going to be saved. The payloads are saved to the ICS diagnostic log files. To retrieve these log files, navigate to the **Monitoring** page and find the **Download Logs** link on the right side of the page. Click on the link and select the **Download Diagnostic Logs** option.

This will download a ZIP file with all the log files of our instance. Unzip the downloaded file and take a look in either `ics_server1-diagnostic.log` or `ics_server2-diagnostic.log`. It can be a long file, so scroll to the end to find our instance tracing details. In our case, we can see the payload of the request message from Salesforce, a compressed request to Twilio, the response from Twilio, and the request to Salesforce.

Here we can see the message we sent to the mobile phone as part of the response:

```
<accountResource.definitions.newSms_response>
  <to>+31645100000</to>
  <from>+15005550006</from>
  <body>Sent from your Twilio trial account - Case #: 00001026, Product:
GC1040, Case Subject: Delivered product GC1040 is missing essential
parts</body>
</accountResource.definitions.newSms_response>
```

We also see the request message to Salesforce that ultimately creates the comment:

```
<nstrgmpr:create
xmlns:ens="urn:sobject.enterprise.soap.sforce.com"
xmlns:nstrgmpr="http://xmlns.oracle.com/cloud/adapter/salesforce/ReceiveEsc
alatedCases_CALLBACK_SUC">
  <nstrgmpr:CaseComment>
  <ens:CommentBody>The Case owner is notified about the
escalation.</ens:CommentBody>
```

```
    <ens:IsPublished>true</ens:IsPublished>
    <ens:ParentId>500580000023G7aAAE</ens:ParentId>
    </nstrgmpr:CaseComment>
</nstrgmpr:create>
```

Troubleshooting

In this scenario, everything went as planned for us, but in the real world it is possible we will run into problems with one of the applications we are integrating. For example, the phone number given is not verified or the number we are sending from is not one that is capable of sending SMS messages.

To simulate this and test if the fault callback will create a new `FeedItem`, we are going to change the Twilio connection settings and change the configuration so it uses the live credentials.

Log into ICS and navigate to the **Connections** page of the **Developer Portal**. Search for the `Twillio_Ch4` connection and click the name to open the configuration. Reconfigure the **Security** settings and change the `AccountSID` and `AuthToken` values to represent the **LIVE credentials** of your account. **Test** and **Save** the connection. Notice the warning popping up mentioning that it might affect our integration. Click **Yes** and **Exit Connection**.

Navigate to the integrations page and see if our integration is still active; it should be, but if it is inactive, re-activate the integration. Now that we have set up the connection in ICS with the new credentials, we can come back to Salesforce and escalate the case again.

We can change the case status to **Working** first and subsequently change it back to **Escalated**. Instead of a new case comment being created, a new feed item is created in our personal feed. We can access our feed by clicking the feed icon in the menu on the left. In our feed, we see that a new item has been created, letting us know that the given phone number is not capable of sending SMS messages. The reason is that we are still using the number we can only use with our test credentials:

Let's investigate the instance in ICS itself. In ICS, navigate to the **Tracking** page. Again, search for the case number, for example, `00001026`, to find our instance and to filter out the other messages. This time, ICS also reports that the instance has failed with a business fault:

If we look at the details of the instance, we see that the notification was received, an error occurred when invoking Twilio, and that the fault callback was called:

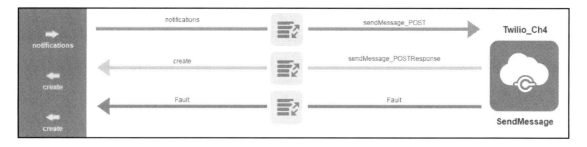

To see the fault details, we download the **Diagnostic Logs**. Again, look in the `ics_server*-diagnostic.log` file. We see the same error as is shown in our Salesforce feed:

```
{"code": 21606, "message": "The From phone number +15005550006 is not a
valid, SMS-capable inbound phone number or short code for your account.",
"more_info": "https://www.twilio.com/docs/errors/21606", "status": 400}
```

Next steps

Now that we know we are using the wrong phone number in combination with the live credentials, we need to change it. Navigate to the list of active integrations, and before we can edit the integration, we need to deactivate it. Deactivate the integration using the actions menu (the hamburger icon) and edit the request mapping. Change the target's from value in the request mapping to represent the phone number you assigned when setting up Twilio. Subsequently save and exit the mapper and integration.

Now that we are using a real phone number to send our messages from we can re-activate the integration. You can enable tracing again, but it is not necessary.

Retest the process of escalating a case in Salesforce and test whether you receive a SMS message on the phone number mapped to the target's `To` node:

If you want to experiment with this scenario, it is possible to create an enrichment service to call Salesforce to retrieve the phone number from the case owner instead of assigning a hardcoded phone number to send the message to, as we did. For example, we can use the `ownerId` to retrieve a `People` object.

Summary

In this chapter, we have integrated two SaaS applications that are generally available to everybody and are widely used are enterprise businesses. We started the chapter showing how to configure these two SaaS applications, Salesforce and Twilio.

In Salesforce, we created a workflow rule and outbound message that get triggered when a case is escalated by changing its status. The outbound message holds the message structure and the endpoint of ICS.

We then created a Twilio account and set up the SMS messaging service and required phone numbers. Twilio offers both live and test credentials, which we used in our solution.

With both SaaS applications set up, we then created the connections and the integration. The integration consists of a notification that it receives from Salesforce and sends to Twilio and the response or fault from Twilio, which creates a case comment or feed item in Salesforce.

After creating the mappings and completing the integration, we tested the solution a few times with both test and live credentials by escalating a specific case in Salesforce. We looked at the instance flows and the tracing in the log files to troubleshoot problems.

At the end of the chapter, we showed that by using the live credentials and right phone numbers we receive a SMS on our phone.

In the next chapter, we will look into the social integrations we can achieve with ICS.

5
Going Social with Twitter and Google

In the previous chapter, we built upon the ideas presented so far, and explored how to integrate SaaS solutions and how you can test your integration without impacting a live system. We continue this road and look at how connecting social applications differ. As social capabilities become ever more important, we explore how to connect and authenticate against such services.

To demonstrate the different social interaction we are going to use Twitter and Google. ICS provides out-of-the-box cloud adapters for connecting to these services. While one adapter provides all Twitter services there is one adapter per supported Google service, for example, Mail, Calendar, and Tasks.

Tweet changes in flight schedules

The first social integration we are demonstrating is when a flight schedule is changed and the flight is delayed or is arriving early, a tweet is sent out to inform passengers about the change, as you can see here:

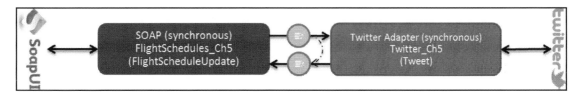

To demonstrate the scenario, we start by showing how to set up a Twitter account and the necessary application. Then we define the necessary social connection and show how to give consent to ICS to use our social account. We then use it in our integration. This time, we create a mapping and use XSL Elements to make the tweet text dynamic based on the request. We conclude the scenario by showing how to test and troubleshoot the social integration.

Getting ready

As with `Chapter 4`, *Integrations between SaaS Applications*, before we can build the integration we need to set up the social application we are integrating with. As shown in the preceding diagram, our inbound call receives the notification of the flight schedule update. Our outbound call is a synchronous call to Twitter. To call Twitter from ICS, we need to authorize ICS as an application that is allowed to tweet to our account.

Setting up Twitter

In our case, we are going to invoke Twitter to post a message on the timeline of our corporate account. Besides tweeting a message, Twitter also allows applications to search tweets; get trends, followers, and subscribers; look up statuses, and more. To complete our setup of Twitter so ICS can interact with our account, we need to follow these steps:

1. Get access to a Twitter account.
2. Register a new application.
3. Create access token and obtain API credentials.

Step 1 – get access to a Twitter account

For this integration we can use any Twitter account you can get access to. If you do not have an account yet, or want to have an extra account for testing purposes, go to `https://twitter.com/signup` and follow the instructions.

Step 2 – register a new application

To allow ICS to interact with your Twitter account, we need to create an application and set its permissions. Go to `https://apps.twitter.com/` and click the **Create New App** button.

Complete the form with following information:

Section	Field	Value
Application Details	**Name**	Your application name, for example, `IntegrationCloud`.
	Description	Application for connecting Oracle Integration Cloud Service.
	Website	URL to your application's website, for example, `http://example.com`.
	Callback URL	Leave blank. This is only necessary for OAuth 1.0 authentication, and ICS uses OAuth 2.0.
Developer Agreement	**Twitter Developer Agreement**	Read the agreement and tick the **Yes, I agree box**.

Application Details

Name *

IntegrationCloud

Your application name. This is used to attribute the source of a tweet and in user-facing authorization screens. 32 characters max.

Description *

Application for connecting Oracle Integration Cloud Service

Your application description, which will be shown in user-facing authorization screens. Between 10 and 200 characters max.

Website *

https://oracle-integration.cloud

Your application's publicly accessible home page, where users can go to download, make use of, or find out more information about your application. This fully-qualified URL is used in the source attribution for tweets created by your application and will be shown in user-facing authorization screens. (If you don't have a URL yet, just put a placeholder here but remember to change it later.)

Callback URL

Where should we return after successfully authenticating? OAuth 1.0a applications should explicitly specify their oauth_callback URL on the request token step, regardless of the value given here. To restrict your application from using callbacks, leave this field blank.

Once the application is created, you can go to the **Settings** page and update the settings if you want. You can also set an application icon and info about your organization.

Step 3 – create access token and obtain API credentials

Finally, we need to create our access token and obtain the API credentials. Go to the **Keys and Access Tokens** page. On this page, you find the **Consumer Key** and **Consumer Secret**.

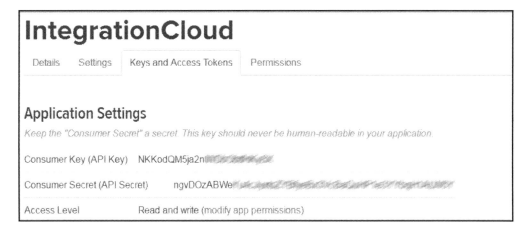

Obtain the values and save them somewhere you can retrieve when we create the connection. At the bottom of the page, click **Create my access token** to obtain your token and save the values of **Access Token** and the **Access Token Secret**.

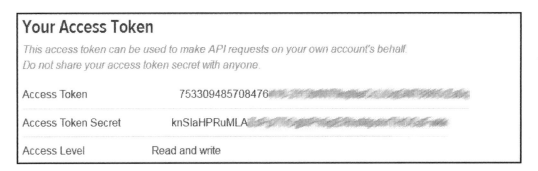

Inbound WSDL with multiple operations

For our inbound call, this time we use a WSDL with multiple operations. The operations define the use of a SOAP header for both the request and the response. The WSDL definition used is shown here:

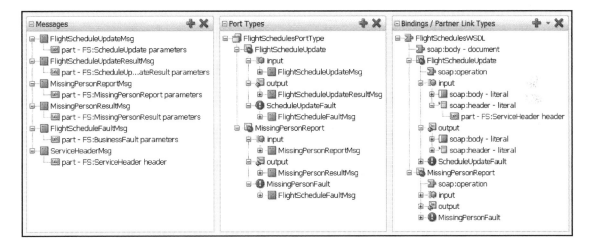

The WSDL consists of two operations, `FlightScheduleUpdate` and `MissingPersonReport`. Both operations define an input, output, and fault message, and the input and output binding includes a SOAP header and a SOAP body. For this integration, we are going to use the first operation. We have made the WSDL available in the downloads as `ICSBook-Ch5-FlightSchedules-Source.WSDL`.

Define the necessary connections

For this integration, we are going to create a connection for our inbound SOAP service and a Twitter connection for integrating with our `IntegrationCloud` application.

Let's first create the client connection using `ICSBook-Ch5-FlightSchedules-Source.WSDL`. The steps to create the connection are the same as in Chapter 2, *Integrating Our First Two Applications*, and Chapter 3, *Distribute Messages Using the Pub-Sub Model*, so if you need the detailed steps, you should refer back to those chapters. Use the following configuration to create the connection:

Property	Value
Connection name	`FlightSchedules_Ch5`
Identifier	This will be proposed based on the Connection name, and there is no need to change it unless you would like an alternate name.
Description	`This receives changes to Flight Schedules as a SOAP service.`
Email Address	Your e-mail address.
WSDL URL | Connection Properties	Tick the **Upload File**, and then use the **File** selection to upload the `ICSBook-Ch5-FlightSchedules-Source.WSDL`. Close with the **OK** button.
Security Policy | Credentials	Set **Security Policy** to **No Security Policy**. Close the dialog with the **OK** button.

Test the connection to validate the configuration and subsequently click the **Save** and **Exit Connection** button. Now we take a look at the interesting part of the integration, which is the connection to Twitter.

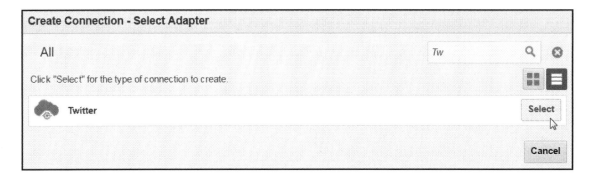

Create a Twitter connection with the following details:

Property	Value
Connection name	Twitter_Ch5
Identifier	This will be proposed based on the Connection name and there is no need to change it unless you would like an alternate name.
Connection Role	**Invoke** (social adapter cannot be used as triggers)
Description	This connection interacts with the Twitter application, for example to send out or search for tweets.

After creation configure the connection with the following details:

Property	Value
Email Address	Your e-mail address
Configure Security | Credentials	Set Security Policy to Custom Security Policy. Enter the four values we collected in third step of the setup for consumer key and consumer secret, and for the access token and access secret. Close the dialog with the **OK** button.

Never share your consumer secret and access secret with anymore unauthorized. Keep in mind the values are visible within ICS, so be careful if you use a shared environment. The finished configuration is shown as follows:

Test the connection to validate the configuration. After validating the connection, click the **Save** and **Exit Connection** button. We should have created two connections.

Tweet when a flight schedule has changed

With the connectors established, we can start the process of creating the integration. Because we have already done this many times before, we only provide the details to create the integration. Create an integration with the **Basic Map Data** pattern using the following details:

Property	Value
Integration name	`TweetFlightScheduleChanges_Ch5`
Identifier	This will be proposed based on the integration name and there is no need to change it unless you would like an alternate name.
Version	`01.00.0000`
Package Name	`ics.book.ch5`
Description	`This integration will take the ScheduleUpdate request and send out a tweet returning a result or fault as response.`

With the basic integration created, we can now drag and drop our connections from the connector palette. For the **Trigger** side, we drag and drop the `FlightSchedules_Ch5` connector. This is a SOAP connection, but because we now have a WSDL with multiple operations and the operations support SOAP headers, the process is slightly different:

Tab	Question	Action
Basic Info	**Call your endpoint field?**	Because of multiple operations, call it `ScheduleUpdate`.
	What does this end point do?	Add the following description: `provides the parameters to request a schedule update for the identified flight.`

The **Operations** tab is different in this case; it lets us select the operation to expose:

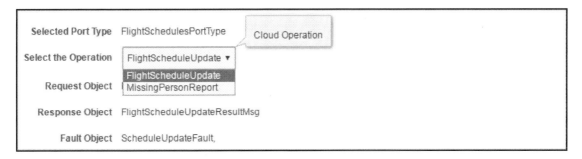

Complete the wizard using the following details:

Tab	Section	Action
Operations	**Selected Port Type**	This is automatically selected because only one is defined in WSDL, `FlightSchedulesPortType`.
	Select the Operation	Select `FlightScheduleUpdate`.
	Request Object	The objects that are assigned to the operation are displayed. These values change when a different operation is selected.
	Response Object	
	Fault Object	
Request-Headers	**Header Object**	The object that is assigned to the operation as a request header is displayed, that is, `ServiceHeader`.
Response-Headers	**Header Object**	The object that is assigned to the operation as a response header is displayed, that is, `ServiceHeader`
Summary	**WSDL URL**	The **Summary** tab, as always, shows the selected connector information. The Cloud Operation matches the operation we selected in the **Operations** tab, that is, `FlightScheduleUpdate`.
	Selected Port Type	
	Cloud Operation	
	Message Exchange Pattern	

Click **Done** and the Save button to secure our progress. The next step is to configure the invoke to Twitter. Drag and drop the `Twitter_Ch5` connector to the invoke drop zone. The resultant dialog can be completed with the following information:

Tab	Question	Action
Basic Info	**Call your endpoint field?**	Call it `TweetUpdate`.
	What does this end point do?	Add the following description: `sends a Tweet to the corporate Twitter timeline.`
Operation	**Select Operation**	Select **Tweet**.
Summary	**Description**	This tab shows the connector settings. The Twitter URI shows the URL of the Twitter API: `https://api.twitter.com/1.1/ statuses/update.json` It also lists the query parameters we can provide to send out a more advanced tweet, such as geo-location information.
	Twitter Resource URI	
	Method	
	Query Parameters	

We mentioned earlier there are more options to interact with Twitter, as shown here:

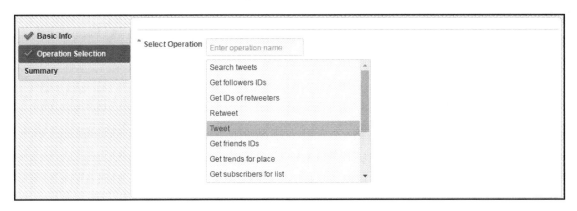

Complete configuring the trigger and invoke operation and **Save** the integration.

Map message data

Because both connectors are synchronous operations, that is request-response, and the operation defined a WSDL fault we need to define three mappings.

Map FlightScheduleUpdate to Twitter's request

We start with the request mapping. Click the mapping icon, and then on the plus sign to create a new mapping. Notice that the target message contains nine parameters we can assign, but the most important one is `status`. We will assign one of four different messages to the `status` node depending on the request message, but first assign the optional source's latitude and longitude to the target's lat and long nodes.

As we said, we want to send out a dynamic tweet. In total, we want to send out four different messages. The four message types will be similar to this:

1. Flight #KL1350 en route from #AMS to #PRG is 23 minutes delayed
2. Flight #KL1350 en route from #AMS to #PRG is 10 minutes early
3. Flight #KL1350 arrival to #PRG from #AMS is 1 hour and 2 minutes delayed
4. Flight #KL1350 arrival to #PRG from #AMS is 6 minutes early

In the mapper, click on the `status` node to create these dynamic messages. First, drag and drop the `choose` element to the status node statement, which can be found under **Mapping Components | XSL Elements**. The reason we are doing this is because we want to determine whether a flight is en route, at its origin, or is in flight to destination.

Notice that a `choose` statement is built and a `when` element is added as a child. The `when` element has a test attribute we need to configure with an expression. The result of the expression should be a Boolean.

Instead of creating the expression from scratch by dragging and dropping the different parts, it is also possible to enter the expression itself. To check if a flight has departed, we can use the following expression:

```
xsd:duration(fn:current-dateTime() -
xsd:dateTime(/nssrcmpr:ScheduleUpdate/nssrcmpr:departureTime)) >
xsd:duration('PT0S')
```

We check whether the duration between the `current-dateTime` and `departureTime`, which is also a `dateTime`, is greater than zero seconds. If this is true, then it means the flight has arrived; otherwise, the flight is en route. Click **Type here... for 'test'** and enter the preceding expression.

Next, we create the `otherwise` clause. We can do this by creating a new **Sibling After** the `xsl:when` element using the right-click contextual menu. Drag the element `otherwise` from the **Mapping components | XSL Elements** to the new created sibling. The statement should now look similar to the following screenshot:

Statement
◢ `<> <nsmpr0:status>`
◢ `◪ <xsl:choose />`
✎ ◪ `<xsl:when test = "xsd:duration(fn:current-dateTime() - xsd:dateTime(/nssrcmpr:ScheduleUpdate/nssrcmpr:departureTime)) > xsd:duration('PT0S')">`
◪ `<xsl:otherwise />`

Now that the main XSL construction is in place, we add a child to both the `xsl:when` and `xsl:otherwise` elements. Right-click the element and select **Insert Child**. Each child is a concatenated string of source nodes and literal text phrases.

 Remember that we talked about XSLT constructs in `Chapter 1`, *Introducing the Concepts and Terminology*. You can always refer to this to get more context about specific XSL elements.

For our own convenience, we will not drag and drop with functions and source nodes. We are going to use the `value-of` XSL element. Using this element, we can add an expression that represents the same outcome as when we would have used the mapper UI in the same way we have demonstrated in past chapters.

Drag the `value-of` element from **Mapping components | XSL Elements** to the child of `xsl:when`. This will create a `value-of` element with a `select` attribute. Click **Type here... for 'select'** and enter the following expression. This expression concatenates source nodes to create the message that will be tweeted if an airplane is on its way. We use the double slashes, which is a wildcard, to shorten the expression.

```
concat('Flight #', //nssrcmpr:ident, ' arrival to #',
//nssrcmpr:destination, ' from #', //nssrcmpr:origin, ' is ',
//nssrcmpr:durationString, ' ', //nssrcmpr:updateType)
```

Save your progress and do the same process for the otherwise, but instead use the following expression:

```
concat('Flight #', //nssrcmpr:ident, ' en route from #', //nssrcmpr:origin,
' to #', //nssrcmpr:destination, ' is ', //nssrcmpr:durationString, ' ',
//nssrcmpr:updateType)
```

Again, save your progress, and we should now have a complete mapping for the target's status node. The statement should now look similar to the following screenshot:

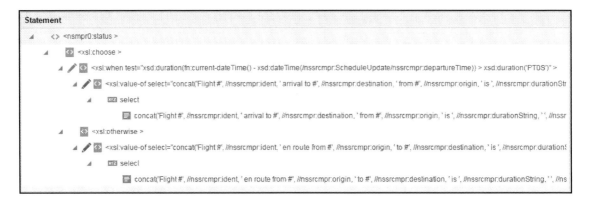

Close the mapping of the `status` node to return to the mapper. Notice that all the used elements we mapped using the wildcard expression are visually mapped in the UI:

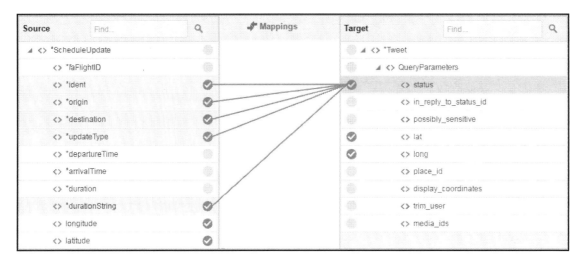

To test our mapping, we can click the **Test** button below the **Save** button. This will open the **Test Mapper**. Generate inputs and execute the test to see the result. Play around with `destinationTime` to the see different messages. Close the **Test Mapper** and subsequently click **Save** and **Exit Mapper** to return to our integration.

Map Twitter's response to ScheduleUpdateResult

For the response mapping, we are mapping the result from Twitter to the result of our SOAP service. Create the response mapping and map the nodes as follows:

Source	Target
ScheduleUpdate/faFlightID	parentID
True (Boolean)	processed
TweetResponse/text	message

Save the mapping and click on **Exit Mapper**.

Mapping Twitter's fault to BusinessFault

For the fault mapping, we are mapping APIInvocationError from Twitter to the BusinessFault of our SOAP service. Create the fault mapping and map the nodes as follows:

Source	Target
errorCode	code
details	message

Save the mapping and click on **Exit Mapper**.

Completing and activating the integration

Now that we have mapped all the data of our integration, we again need to add the tracking fields before we can complete and activate the integration.

At the top-right, click **Tracking** to open the business identifiers dialog. In this case, we are going to set three tracking fields: ident, updateType, and duration. Drag and drop the trigger fields to the list and use ident as primary identifier. Change the **Tracking Names** to Flight Number, Status, and Duration.

Click **Done** to save the identifiers, and in the integration canvas click on **Save** and **Exit Integration** to finish our Integration. Use the **PENDING ACTIVATION** button of the integration to make it active.

Testing the integration

Now that the integration is done, the final step is testing the SOAP service. Again, we first need to know the web address for the endpoint our integration is running. Click the info icon on the right side of our entry to view its activation details.

In the details, we find the **Endpoint URL** the integration can be invoked on. Copy the URL to your clipboard since we are going to use it shortly.

Invoke cloud endpoint using SoapUI

For testing our cloud endpoint, we are going to use SoapUI again to simulate our Flight Tracking and Incident system. With our WSDL endpoint URL, create a new SOAP project. This can be done through the **File** menu and selecting **New SOAP Project**.

Create the SOAP project using the following information:

Property	Value
Project name	`TweetFlightScheduleChanges_Ch5`
Initials WSDL	The WSDL endpoint URL of integration
Create Requests	Check this box
Create TestSuite	Keep this box unchecked
Relative Paths	Keep this box unchecked

On the left side of the SoapUI window, expand the project and find the binding `FlightSchedulesPortType` and its `FlightScheduleUpdate` operation. Double-click on the generated sample request, named `Request 1`.

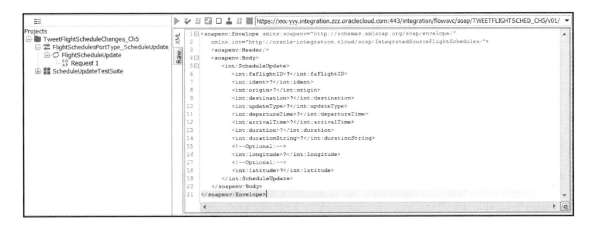

The request will represent a flight update sent from our Flight Tracking system. To test our integration, we are going to send different updates to test all possible conditions. Our first update represents flight KL2016, whose its departure is delayed by 10 minutes.

We can use the following example snippet for our request:

```
<FS:ScheduleUpdate
xmlns:FS="http://oracle-integration.cloud/soap/IntegratedSourceFlightSchedu
les/">
  <FS:faFlightID>102</FS:faFlightID>
  <FS:ident>KL2016</FS:ident>
  <FS:origin>AMS</FS:origin>
  <FS:destination>SFO</FS:destination>
  <!-- delayed, early, on time -->
  <FS:updateType>delayed</FS:updateType>
  <FS:departureTime>
   2016-07-01T07:50:00
  </FS:departureTime>
  <FS:arrivalTime>
   2016-07-01T18:25:00
  </FS:arrivalTime>
  <FS:duration>PT10M</FS:duration>
  <FS:durationString>10 minutes</FS:durationString>
  <FS:longitude>52.3105419</FS:longitude>
  <FS:latitude>4.7660857</FS:latitude>
</FS:ScheduleUpdate>
```

The departureTime, updateType, and durationString elements in the preceding snippet are the drivers for different outcomes we send to Twitter, and the longitude and latitude elements are optional. If the departureTime is before the current date and time, the flight has departed; otherwise, the plane is still at its origin. The departureTime and the arrivalTime can include time zones, but to keep it simple we do not specify one that is using the UTC time zone. The current date and time is determined by ICS, which also uses the UTC time zone. So to fully test your integration you should check on which time your instance runs, which can be determined when you test the mapping in ICS.

Before executing any requests, add the required WS-Security header and WS-Timestamp header, as we demonstrated in past chapters, for example, Chapter 2, *Integrating Our First Two Applications*.

Let's play around with these fields and look at the results when we execute the request. When a tweet is sent successfully, we get a response from ICS that includes the text message that was generated based on the values of the request message:

```
<FS:ScheduleUpdateResult xmlns:FS="..."
  <FS:parentID>101</nstrgmpr:parentID>
  <FS:processed>true</nstrgmpr:processed>
  <FS:message>Flight #KL2016 en route from #AMS to #SFO is 10 minutes
delayed</FS:message>
</FS:ScheduleUpdateResult>
```

Let's have a look at the following messages and how we can trigger them:

- Flight #KL1350 en route from #AMS to #PRG is 23 minutes delayed. This is triggered when departureTime is after the current date and time and updateType is delayed.
- Flight #KL1350 en route from #AMS to #PRG is 10 minutes early. This is triggered when departureTime is after the current date and time and updateType is early.
- Flight #KL1350 arrival to #PRG from #AMS is 1 hour and 2 minutes delayed. This is triggered when departureTime is before the current date and time and updateType is delayed.
- Flight #KL1350 arrival to #PRG from #AMS is 6 minutes early. This is triggered when departureTime is before the current date and time and updateType is early.
- Flight #KL1350 arrival to #PRG from #AMS is on time. This is triggered when departureTime is before the current date and time and updateType is on time.

Execute these requests to the cloud endpoint of your integration to see the results in Twitter. If all goes successfully, you will see five new tweets on the timeline of your account:

 The resources of this chapter include a SoapUI project that includes these requests. Follow the project instructions to configure your instance.

If we take a look in the **Tracking** section of the monitoring page, we also see the same five instances. The monitoring information will be examined in more depth in Chapter 12, *Are My Instances Running Fine, and What if They Are Not?*:

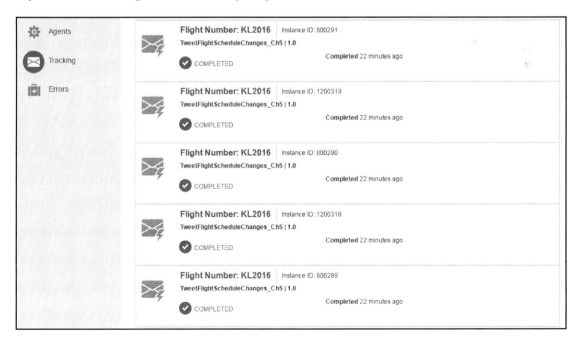

Troubleshooting

During testing, it may happen that you run into errors/exceptions returned by ICS to the client. In this short section, we will look into a few of them:

- Twitter rejects duplicate messages
- No valid authentication token
- No rights to write a tweet on the timeline

Another obvious one is a missing or incorrect `WS-Security` or `WS-Timestamp` header, but since we already covered that one in previous chapters, we will focus on the first three.

Twitter rejects duplicate messages

When an identical message is sent within a period of time, Twitter can reject the message because it is categorized as a duplicate message. This can easily be reproduced by sending the requests twice, immediately after each other.

This will result in the following exception visible at the client, that is, SoapUI:

```
{"errors": [
  {
   "code":187,
   "message":"Status is a duplicate."
  }]
}
```

Try not to send multiple source events with the same values so that the call to Twitter will have different messages and prevent this error.

No valid authentication token

If one of the authentication settings, such as consumer key/secret and access token/secret, is invalid, Twitter will reject the message because it can not authenticate the caller. This can be reproduced by editing the security settings in ICS or by revoking the access token of the Twitter application.

When invoking the integration, the following exception will result:

```
{"errors": [
 {
  "code":32,
  "message":"Could not authenticate you."
 }]
}
```

No rights to write a tweet on the timeline

The owner of the Twitter account can set the access the Twitter application requires. To post a tweet, the application needs read and write access at a minimum. This can be reproduced by changing the access token to read only within the Twitter configuration.

When invoking the integration, the following exception will result:

```
{
 "request":"\/1.1\/statuses\/update.json",
 "error":"Read-only application cannot POST."
}
```

Send missing person report by e-mail

In this second social integration we are demonstrating the use of Gmail when a passenger is missing and is delaying the flight. Our Flight Tracking and Incident system will send out a missing person report, which is send by e-mail to the front desk with the request to call for the passenger through the public announcement system, as you can see in the following diagram:

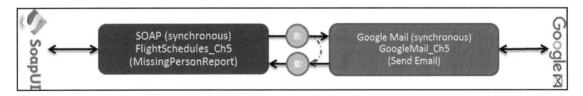

In this scenario, we will cover how to set up a Google account and application. We define the necessary social connection and show how to give consent to ICS to use our Google account. With the connection, we create a simple e-mail integration and finally show how to test and troubleshoot the integration.

Getting ready

In the same way as our first social integration, before we can build the integration we need to set up our social application. As shown in the diagram, our inbound call uses the same adapter as with the Twitter integration. It receives the notification of the missing person from our simulated Flight Tracking and Incident system through SOAP. Our outbound call, on the other hand, is a synchronous call to the Google Mail API.

Setting up Google

In our case, we are going to invoke the Gmail API to send an e-mail to the front desk. Besides the Gmail API, Google offers a many more APIs, but ICS only supports the most popular ones, for example, Mail, Calendar, and Tasks. They all use the same process to set up, as described here:

1. Get access to a Google account.
2. Register a new project and enable the necessary API.
3. Create an access token and obtain API credentials.

Step 1 – get access to a Google account

For this integration we can use any Google account you can get access to. If you do not have an account yet, or want to have an extra account for testing purposes, go to `https://accounts.google.com/signup` and follow the instructions.

Step 2 – register a new project and enable API

To allow ICS to interact with your Twitter account, we need to create an application and set its permissions. Go to `https://console.developers.google.com/`, and in the Library section search for the **Gmail API** or find it under the **popular APIs**:

Click on **Gmail API** to navigate to the API details. Before enabling an API you need a project. In our case we do not have any projects created so we receive a message that we need to create a project. If you already have projects, create a new one for this scenario. To create your first project, click the **Create project** button:

You are navigated to the project creation wizard. Enter the name `AircraftCX` and optionally show the advanced options and change the App Engine location to your preferred data center. Click **Create** and wait a few moments until the process completes:

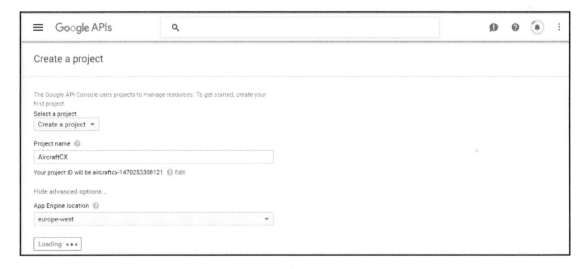

After creating the project, we return to the **Gmail API** page, but if you redirected to somewhere else, just search for the API again in the **Library** section. Click **ENABLE** to activate the API for your application:

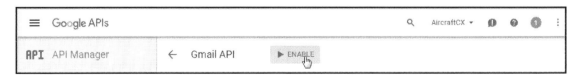

Step 3 – create access token and obtain API credentials

Finally, we need to create our access token and obtain the API credentials. Because we have not set this up yet for our project, we get a warning after enabling the API to set up our credentials. It is strongly advised to do it right away. Click the **Go to** Credentials button to proceed:

We are taken to the page where we can add credentials to our project. We are presented with a four-step wizard. Walk through the wizard using the following details:

Section	Field	Action
What credentials you need	**Which API are you using?**	Select **Gmail API** (if not already selected)
	Where will you be calling the API from?	Select **Web browser** (JavaScript)
	What data will you be accessing?	Choose **User data**
Create OAuth 2.0 client ID	**Name**	Enter `IntegrationCloud`
	Authorized redirect URIs	Enter the following callback URI: `https://xxx-yyy.integration.zzz.oraclecloud.com/icsapis/agent/oauth/callback` Note that core domain name is that of your ICS instance.

The following screenshot shows the **Create OAuth 2.0 client ID** step of the wizard:

Click the **Create client ID** button so we can create the consent screen. This screen is shown when an application wants to get consent to use Google APIs using an OAuth client. OAuth is an authorization framework. It enables applications to obtain (limited) access to user accounts on an HTTP service. It delegates the user authentication to the service, and authorizes applications to access the user account.

Select the e-mail address you want to assign to the project and enter the product name, for example, `AircraftCX Google Integration`:

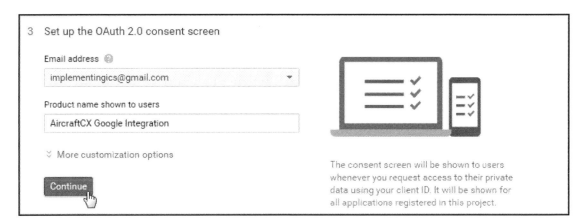

Click **Continue**, and in the last step you get the option to download the credentials, but we will retrieve these in a moment. Click the **Save** button to create the credentials. You will return to the **Credentials** sections, where all the OAuth 2.0 client IDs are listed, including ours:

Click on the name of the **Client ID** to retrieve the client ID and secret we need when we create the connection in ICS:

Copy the client ID and secret to a convenient location so that you can copy them when needed when we create the connection.

Define the necessary connections

For this second integration we only need to create the connection to Google. For the inbound SOAP service, we are going to reuse the one we created for our Twitter integration, that is, `FlightSchedules_Ch5`.

In ICS, navigate to the **Connections** page and create a connection using the Google Mail adapter. Notice that when you search on Google in the **Create Connection** dialog you will see adapters of all supported Google APIs, for example, Calendar, Mail, and Tasks:

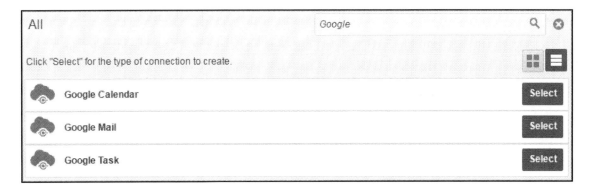

Select the Google Mail adapter and create the connection with the following details:

Property	Value
Connection name	GoogleMail_Ch5
Identifier	This will be proposed based on the **Connection name** and there is no need to change it unless you would like an alternate name.
Connection Role	**Invoke**
Description	This connection interacts with the Gmail API of the AirportCX application, for example to send out emails.

After creation, configure the connection with the following details:

Section	Action
Email Address	Your e-mail address
Configure Security | Credentials	Set **Security Policy** to **Google OAuth Authorization**. Enter the values we collected in third step of the setup for **Client ID** and **Client Secret**.
	We also need to provide the access scope for this connection. The Gmail API supports different levels of access, which are documented on the developers portal: https://developers.google.com/gmail/api/auth/scopes For this connection use: https://www.googleapis.com/auth/gmail.compose

Before we can accept the values, we need to give ICS consent to use our Google Client ID. Click the **Provide Consent** button:

A new window/tab is opened in the browser, which redirects us to Google. If you are logged in with multiple accounts, select the account your project is registered under. In the consent screen, click **Allow** to accept the access rules:

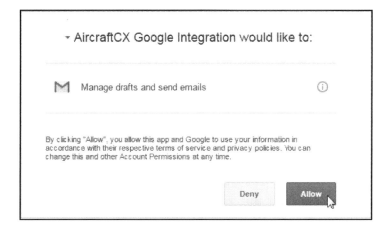

Return to the browser tab with ICS and notice that the credentials are accepted. Test the connection to validate the configuration. After validating the connection, click the **Save** and **Exit Connection** button.

E-mail the front desk to report a missing person

With the necessary connections created, we can create the integration. Again, navigate to the **Integrations** page and create a new integration. Select the **Map My Data** pattern using the following details:

Property	Value
Integration name	`EmailMissingPersonReport_Ch5`
Identifier	This will be proposed based on the integration name and there is no need to change it unless you would like an alternate name.
Version	01.00.0000
Package Name	`ics.book.ch5`
Description	`This integration will take the MissingPersonReport request and send out an email to the front desk.`

With the basic integration created, drag and drop our connections from the connector palette. For the **Trigger** side, we drag and drop the `FlightSchedules_Ch5` connector. This is the same SOAP connection as the previous integration, but this time we will use the other operation:

Tab	Question	Action
Basic Info	**Call your endpoint field?**	Because of multiple operations, call it `MissingPersonReport`.
	What does this end point do?	Add the following description: `provides the parameters to request a missing person report for the identified flight.`
Operations	**Selected Port Type**	This is automatically selected because only one is defined in WSDL, that is, `FlightSchedulesPortType`.
	Select the Operation	Select `MissingPersonReport`.
	Request Object	The objects that are assigned to the operation are displayed. This value changes when a different operation is selected.
	Response Object	
	Fault Object	

Summary	WSDL URL	The **Summary** tab as always shows the selected connector information. The Cloud Operation matches the operation we selected in the **Operations** tab, that is, `FlightScheduleUpdate`.
	Selected Port Type	
	Cloud Operation	
	Message Exchange Pattern	

Click **Done** and the **Save** button to secure our progress. Next, configure the invoke to Google. Drag and drop the `GoogleMail_Ch5` connector on the invoke drop zone. The resultant dialog can be completed with the following information:

Tab	Question	Action
Basic Info	**Call your endpoint field?**	Call it `SendEmail`.
	What does this end point do?	Add the following description: `sends an email to the front desk so they search for the missing person.`
Operations	**Select Operation**	Select **Send Message**
Parameters	**Query Parameters**	Leave the required `uploadType` selected
Summary	**Description**	This tab shows the connector settings. The Google Mail URI shows the URL of the Gmail API: `https://www.googleapis.com/upload/gmail/v1/users/me/messages/send` It also lists the query parameter we need to provide.
	Gmail Resource URI	
	Method	
	Query Parameters	

Like we mentioned earlier, there are more options to interact with Gmail shown as follows:

Complete configuring the trigger and invoke operations and **Save** the integration.

Map message data

Because both connectors are synchronous operations, that is request-response, and the operation defined a WSDL fault, we need to define three mappings again, just like our first integration in this chapter.

Map MissingPersonReport to Google's sendMsg request

Create a request mapping, just as we have before. Notice that the target message contains only a few fields. The most important one is raw, but mediaType also needs to be set. The raw node is a special field as well, the assigned content can be in the MIME e-mail format, which is what we will use as it is the common approach to e-mail content. With the available source nodes we can construct this, but it isn't a small task:

Multipurpose Internet Mail Extensions (**MIME**) and is a standard to extend the format in which an e-mail is described to support multipart messages; non-text attachments as audio, video, and images; and text in different character sets than ASCII.
There's more info at `https://en.wikipedia.org/wiki/MIME`.

The final e-mail format should look like this:

```
From: <from>
To: <to>
Subject: Missing Person Report
MIME-Version: 1.0
Content-Type: text/plain; charset=utf-8

New missing person report:

<title> <initials> (<firstname>) <lastname> is late for flight #<ident>
Luggage Tag #<luggageTag>
```

Instead of creating this e-mail transformation step by step, we have created a XSL already for convenience. In this chapter's resources you find a mapping file called `ICSBook-MissingPerson-to-Gmail-req.xsl`, which we will use instead. You can have a look in the file to see how the e-mail is constructed. The other required field is `uploadType`, which can hold the values `media`, `multipart`, or `resumable`. The difference is explained at the

Gmail

API reference website, `https://developers.google.com/gmail/api/v1/reference`, but in this case, we choose `media`. Media is used when the e-mail does not contain attachments.

Instead of mapping the field using the UI, we want to show you how you can export and import XSLT mappings. Map the literal value `media` to the `uploadType`. We need to map at least one field to create the request mapping and to be able to export it.

Save and exit the mapper and save and exit the integration. We need to export the full integration to make local changes to the XSLT file. In the list of integrations, click the actions icon on the right side of our `EmailMissingPersonReport_Ch5` integration and select **Export**. This will download an IAR file, which is basically a zip file but with its own extension; just rename the IAR file extension to ZIP and unzip the file to a folder:

Take a look into the folder and navigate to `\icspackage\project\EMAILMISSINGPERS_CH5*\resources\processor_*\resourcegroup_*`.

The request can usually be found in the lowest processor. We are going to add some mappings before importing the XSL again. Open the `req_*.xsl` file in your favorite text editor and notice it includes the mapping of the `uploadType` node, but most importantly it includes the paths to WSDL files containing the XSD schemas. Because these paths are different every time, it is not possible to reuse XSLT files created by other integrations.

In the chapter's resources, find the `ICSBook-MissingPerson-to-Gmail-req-tpl.xsl` file and then open it in a text editor. Notice the completed template for this integration. Its first creates an XSL variable with the exact mapping to create the MIME mail. To do a CRLF, we use `&#xa;`. These special characters should always be parsed by the `xsl:text` element.

This variable is later used in the mapping of the raw message node with a `xsl:value-of` element, which selects the variable:

```xml
<!--User Editing allowed BELOW this line - DO NOT DELETE THIS LINE-->
<xsl:template match="/" xml:id="id_11">
   <xsl:variable name="email" xml:id="id_12">
      <xsl:value-of select="'concat('To: ',
      concat(/nssrcmpr:MissingPersonReport/nssrcmpr:mailSettings/nssrcmpr:to)" xml:id="id_13"/>
      <xsl:text xml:id="id_14">&#xa;</xsl:text>
      <xsl:value-of select="'concat('From: ',
      concat(/nssrcmpr:MissingPersonReport/nssrcmpr:mailSettings/nssrcmpr:from)" xml:id="id_15"/>
      <xsl:text xml:id="id_16">&#xa;</xsl:text>
      <xsl:value-of select="'Subject: Missing Person Report'" xml:id="id_17"/>
      <xsl:text xml:id="id_18">&#xa;</xsl:text>
      <xsl:value-of select="'Content-Type: text/plain; charset=utf-8'" xml:id="id_19"/>
      <xsl:text xml:id="id_20">&#xa;</xsl:text>
      <xsl:value-of select="'MIME-Version: 1.0'" xml:id="id_21"/>
      <xsl:text xml:id="id_22">&#xa;</xsl:text>
      <xsl:text xml:id="id_23">&#xa;</xsl:text>
      <xsl:value-of select="'New missing person report:'" xml:id="id_24"/>
      <xsl:text xml:id="id_25">&#xa;</xsl:text>
      <xsl:text xml:id="id_26">&#xa;</xsl:text>
      <xsl:value-of xml:id="id_27"
            select="concat(/nssrcmpr:MissingPersonReport/nssrcmpr:missingPerson/nssrcmpr:title, ' ',
            /nssrcmpr:MissingPersonReport/nssrcmpr:missingPerson/nssrcmpr:initials, ' (',
            /nssrcmpr:MissingPersonReport/nssrcmpr:missingPerson/nssrcmpr:firstName, ') ',
            /nssrcmpr:MissingPersonReport/nssrcmpr:missingPerson/nssrcmpr:lastName, ' is late for
            flight #', /nssrcmpr:MissingPersonReport/nssrcmpr:ident)"/>
      <xsl:text xml:id="id_28">&#xa;</xsl:text>
      <xsl:value-of xml:id="id_29"
            select='concat ("Luggage Tag #",
            /nssrcmpr:MissingPersonReport/nssrcmpr:missingPerson/nssrcmpr:luggageTag )'/>
   </xsl:variable>
   <nstrgmpr:sendMsg xml:id="id_30">
      <nstrgmpr:Messages.definitions.requestPayLoadForSendMsg xml:id="id_31">
         <nsmpr0:raw xml:id="id_32">
            <xsl:value-of select="$email" xml:id="id_33"/>
         </nsmpr0:raw>
      </nstrgmpr:Messages.definitions.requestPayLoadForSendMsg>
      <nstrgmpr:QueryParameters xml:id="id_34">
         <nsmpr0:uploadType xml:id="id_35">media</nsmpr0:uploadType>
      </nstrgmpr:QueryParameters>
   </nstrgmpr:sendMsg>
</xsl:template>
```

Copy the template code and replace the template code of the XSL file of the exported integration. Save the new integration; you can choose to save it as a new file, for example, `ICSBook-MissingPerson-to-Gmail-req.xsl`.

Now we can return to our integration in ICS. This time, instead of creating the request message, import the XSL file. Click the mapping icon and then on the import sign to import a new mapping. In the dialog, choose the renewed XSL file you created:

If the template is copied correctly the integration will show a green notification showing that the import was successful. If not, and you get an error, then repeat the previous steps and take a look at the full example in the chapter's resource for comparison. The mapping icon also changes to one with a lock. Import mappings cannot be changed through the mapping UI because it can include unsupported XSL features. In `Chapter 13`, *Where Can I Go From Here?* we will look in more detail at the concepts around importing and exporting integrations.

Map Google's response to MissingPersonResult

For the response mapping, we are mapping the result from GMail to the result of our SOAP service. Create the response mapping and map the nodes as follows:

Source	Target
`MissingPersonReport/faFlightID`	`parentID`
`True (Boolean)`	`processed`

`concat`
`-"Email successful send for the missing person: "`
`-MissingPersonReport/missingPerson/title`
`" "`
`-MissingPersonReport/missingPerson/lastName`
	`message`

Save the mapping and click on **Exit Mapper**.

Map Twitter's fault to BusinessFault

For the fault mapping, we are mapping the `APIInvocationError` from Twitter to the `BusinessFault` of our SOAP service. Create the fault mapping and map the nodes as follows:

Source	Target
errorCode	code
details	message

Save the mapping and click on **Exit Mapper**.

Completing and activating the integration

Just like before, to complete our integration we need to add a minimum of one tracking field before we can complete and activate the integration.

At the top-right, click **Tracking** to open the business identifiers dialog. In this case, we are going to set two tracking fields, **lastName** and **ident**. Drag and drop the **trigger** fields and use `lastName` as the primary identifier. Change the **Tracking Names** to `Last Name` and `Flight Number`.

Click on **Done** to save the identifiers, and in the integration canvas **Save** and **Exit Integration** to finish our integration. Use the **PENDING ACTIVATION** button of the integration to make it active.

Testing the integration

Now that the integration is done, we can test the endpoint again through the SOAP service. Collect the web address of the endpoint to our integration by clicking on the info icon on the right side of our entry to view its activation details. In the details, we find the **Endpoint URL** and copy the URL to your clipboard.

Invoking the Cloud endpoint using SoapUI

To test our Cloud endpoint, we are going to use SoapUI again to simulate our Flight Tracking and Incident system. With our WSDL endpoint URL, create a new SOAP project with the name `EmailMissingPersonReport_Ch5` and base it on the WSDL endpoint of the integration.

On the left side of the SoapUI window, expand the project and find the `FlightSchedulesPortType` binding and its `MissingPersonReport` operation. Double-click on the generated sample request named `Request 1`.

The request represents a notification about a missing person from our Flight Tracking system. This integration only has one possible scenario, and to test our integration we just need one message; the values determine the outcome of the e-mail's contents.

We can use the following example snippet for our request:

```
<int:MissingPersonReport
xmlns:int="http://oracle-integration.cloud/soap/
IntegratedSourceFlightSchedules/">

  <int:faFlightID>201</int:faFlightID>
  <int:ident>KL2016</int:ident>
  <int:origin>AMS</int:origin>
  <int:destination>VLC</int:destination>
  <int:missingPerson>
    <int:idNumber>MG642RCC9</int:idNumber>
    <int:idType>passport</int:idType>
    <!-- Mr, Ms, Mrs or Mx -->
    <int:title>Mr</int:title>
    <!-- Optional: -->
    <int:firstName>John</int:firstName>
    <!-- Optional: -->
    <int:initials>JJ</int:initials>
    <int:lastName>Smith</int:lastName>
    <int:luggageTag>
      4b510c52-96f3-4854-a680-41dfefef2075
    </int:luggageTag>
  </int:missingPerson>
  <int:mailSettings>
    <int:from>implementingics@gmail.com</int:from>
    <int:to>test@oracle-integration.cloud</int:to>
  </int:mailSettings>
</int:MissingPersonReport>
```

There are some special elements in this snippet. The `title` element only accepts the values `Mr`, `Mrs`, `Ms`, or `Mx`; the `luggageTag` element only accept GUIDs; and the from e-mail address should be the account assigned to the Google application.

Do not forget to add the required `WS-Security` header and `WS-Timestamp` header to the request before executing, as we demonstrated in previous chapters.

Execute the request to the cloud endpoint of your integration and take a look in the **Inbox** of the receiver or in the sent mail of the account assigned to the Google application. You should see the message in the **Inbox**:

It should be the same as in the **Sent Mail**:

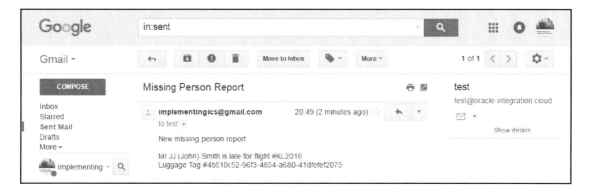

Troubleshooting

During testing, it may be that you run into errors/exceptions returned by ICS to the client. In this short section, we will look into a few of them:

- No valid `client ID` found
- Use of Gmail API is disabled in Google's API Manager
- Wrong scope defined for chosen operation

No valid client ID found

When a message is sent to any Google API, OAuth is used to log in. That is why you need to create credentials and give consent to the application. But if the given client ID is not known for the account that is used, the request is rejected. This can easily be reproduced by renewing the credentials or removing the consent for the application.

This will result in the following exception visible at the client, that is, SoapUI:

```
{"errors": [
 {
  "code":400,
  "message":" Could not determine client ID from request."
 }]
}
```

If this happens, check whether the client ID and secret the connection is using are still valid.

Use of Gmail API is disabled in Google's API Manager

If the use of the Gmail API is disabled, it is not possible to send messages through the API and the request is rejected. This can be reproduced by disabling the API in the API Manager.

When invoking the integration, the following exception will result:

```
{"errors": [
 {
  "code":403,
  "message":"Access Not Configured. Please use Google Developers Console to
activate the API for your project."
 }]
}
```

If this happens, check whether the API is disabled or notify the admin of the account to check the status.

Wrong scope defined for chosen operation

When the connection in ICS has the wrong scope configured for the action defined in the integration, the request will be rejected when calling the API. This can be reproduced by setting an insufficient scope when creating the connection in ICS, for example, read-only, or you can remove parts of the already given consent.

When invoking the integration, the following exception will result:

```
{"errors": [
 {
  "code":403,
  "message":"Insufficient Permission."
 }]
}
```

Summary

In this chapter, we looked at the social integration capabilities that ICS provides out-of-the box. We integrated with Twitter in our first integration and with Google in our second integration.

In the integration with Twitter, we set up a new application on Twitter that uses the assigned account to post tweets by creating the application and creating the necessary API credentials. With these credentials we created a connection from ICS to Twitter by configuring the API credentials to use.

The inbound connection of the integration used a WSDL with multiple operations, which we used for both the Twitter and the Google integration. For the Twitter integration, the `FlightScheduleUpate` operation was used.

In the integration, we showed that, based on the incoming request message, we constructed a dynamic message, a tweet, and sent it to Twitter. In the request mapping, we constructed the tweet dynamically using XSL elements such as `choose`, `when`, and `otherwise`.

After finishing the integration, we tested with five different request messages and showed that the tweets were posting on our timeline. We concluded by looking at troubleshooting.

In the second integration, with Google, we showed how to set up a new project in the Google developer console, create the necessary credentials, and enable the Gmail API in the API Manager. With the credentials, we created the connection from ICS to Google Mail by configuring the API credentials, but also by providing the required security scope and giving consent to ICS to interact with the API.

The integration used the same WSDL, but in this case the `MissingPersonReport` operation was used. In the integration, we showed how the export and import functionality of the XSL mapper works, but also how to reuse an existing XSL template.

The XSL mapping constructed a MIME e-mail format based on the values in the request message. This message was then sent through the Gmail API.

After finishing the integration, we tested with one request, which sent an e-mail from the assigned account to the defined receiver. We concluded this integration by also looking at troubleshooting.

In the next chapter, and the third part of the book, we are going to go a step further and look at creating more complex transformations. We are going to incorporate an enrichment service and see how we can exploit the additional variables that hold the data. In this chapter, we will also look at the concepts of lookups to substitute domain values.

6
Creating Complex Transformations

So far, this book has focused on relatively straightforward mapping and simple transforms. As introduced in Chapter 1, *Introducing the Concepts and Terminology*, the tooling for transformation is built on industry standards around XML such as XSLT. We are not going to go in depth into these standards here, as to do the subject justice you would have to devote a whole book to it. There are plenty of texts on the subject, although we will show a bit more on the application of these standards within ICS as we go. Additionally, it is also worth noting that ICS will provide links to the relevant standards documentation within the mapping editor. The challenge this chapter is going to focus on is how we get additional information that you may need to complete a transformation, including activities such as variable use, lookups, and calling enrichment services.

Using variables to enrich messages

Certain integration patterns have both in and out flows, and it is possible for ICS to enrich the response message with information in the request message. This can be achieved because the request message is held as a variable in the integration. Currently, the use of variables only appears in the **Basic Map Data** pattern, but we will see the capability appear in other patterns where appropriate, soon enough.

We can use this capability to enrich the response with part of the request. This makes it possible to address situations where the requester wants to work in a stateless manner (that is, does not keep track of what was requested between the call and the response. As is the case in the REST architectural style).

To demonstrate this, we will create a scenario where a web service is offered and allows a status request for the position information of a flight, but assumes the caller is context-aware. But we want to return to the originator sufficient information in such a way that they do not need to be context-aware. The application will be mocked with Mockable and we will use the ability to define a return value here. So, the integration will look like this:

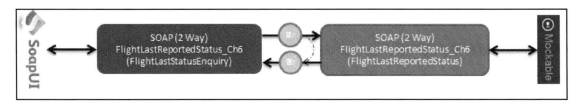

Preparation

To start with, we need two connections and WSDLs to go with them. As we have created a number of connections and integrations, we will provide the details in the following tables. The steps to create the content are the same as in previous chapters, such as Chapter 3, *Distribute Messages Using the Pub-Sub Model*, if you need to refer back to the detailed steps.

Client connection

The following details describe the client end, in terms of WSDL. In the downloadable resources, we have called this schema ICSBook-Ch6-FlightLocationRequest-Client.WSDL and the connection configuration is as follows:

Property	Value
Connection name	FlightLastStatusEnquiry_Ch6
Identifier	This will be proposed based on the connection name and there is no need to change it unless you would like an alternate name.
Description	Use this page to configure connection details, such as e-mail contact, connection properties, and connection login credentials.

Email Address	Your e-mail address
WSDL URL | Connection Properties	Tick **Upload File**, then use the **File** selection to upload the `ICSBook-Ch6-FlightLocationRequest-Client.WSDL` (provided previously). Close with the **OK** button.
Security Policy | Credentials	Set **Security Policy** to **No Security Policy**. Close the dialog with the **OK** button.

For the target end, which will be handled by Mockable, we need the following WSDL (which is in the download pack is called `ICSBook-Ch6-FlightLocationRequest-Target.WSDL`) and an ICS connector defined as follows:

Property	Value
Connection name	`FlightLastStatusEnquiry_Ch6`
Identifier	A call and response service to get the last update information for an identified flight.
Description	This receives in `FlightStatusUpdate` objects as a SOAP service.
Email Address	Your e-mail address
WSDL URL | Connection Properties	Tick **Upload File**, then use the **File** selection to upload the `ICSBook-Ch6-FlightLocationRequest-Target.WSDL` (provided previously). Close with the **OK** button.
Security Policy | Credentials	Set **Security Policy** to **No Security Policy**. Close the dialog with the **OK** button.

With the connectors established, we can start the processing of creating the integration. By this point, the process of creating integrations should be pretty straightforward, so here are the details to create the integration

Property	Value
Integration name	`FlightStatusEnquiry_Ch6`
Identifier	This will be proposed based on the integration name and there is no need to change it unless you would like an alternate name.
Version	01.00.0000
Package Name	`ics.book.ch6`
Description	`This service will take the request and communicate with a backend system, returning the fully filled out response.`

Drop the `FlightLastStatusEnquiry_Ch6` connector on the **Trigger** spot, and complete the dialog with the following values:

Tab	Question	Action
Basic Info	**Call your endpoint field?**	To keep it simple, call it `Source`.
	What does this endpoint do?	Add the following description: `provides the parameters to request the last status report for the identified flight.`
Operations	**Selected Port Type**	As we only have a single operation in the WSDL, this tab will not offer any options.
	Selected Operation	
	Request Object	
Summary	**WSDL URL**	As we only have a single operation in the WSDL this tab will not offer any options. But should reflect the selected connector information
	Selected Port Type	
	Cloud Operation	
	Message Exchange Pattern	

Now drop the `FlightLastReportedStatus_Ch6` connection on the invocation spot and complete the connection wizard with the following values:

Tab	Question	Action
Basic Info	**Call your endpoint field?**	To keep it simple, call it `Target`.
	What does this endpoint do?	Add the following description: `We retrieve from the mocked back end the last reported flight information for the requested flight.`
Operations	**Selected Port Type**	As we only have a single operation in the WSDL this tab will not offer any options.
	Selected Operation	
	Request Object	
Summary	**WSDL URL**	As we only have a single operation in the WSDL this tab will not offer any options. But should reflect the selected connector information.
	Selected Port Type	
	Cloud Operation	
	Message Exchange Pattern	

As with previous integrations, we can create the source to target mapping with the following details:

Source	Target
`faFlightID`	`faFlightID`
`ident`	`ident`
`prefix`	`prefix`
`type`	`type`
`suffix`	`suffix`

With the source to target mapping completed and saved we can start on the response flow (target to source) which is where we can use a variable.

Creating the enriched mapping

This means we are now in a position to work on the response mapping. Opening up the mapping for the response, we should see something like the following screenshot:

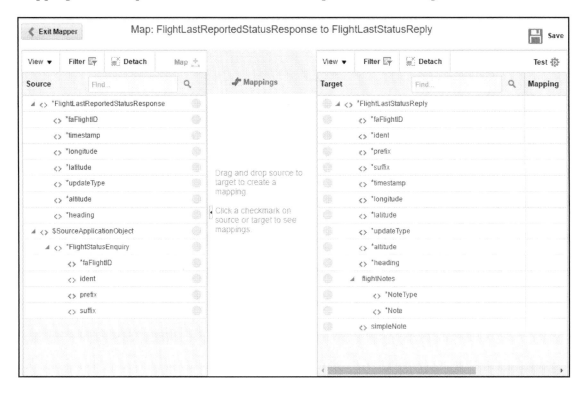

Note on the source side you have a variable with attributes below it. We recognize the variable by the $ prefix. This variable represents our trigger message and makes use of the name of the data flow in the source request. As a result, it is possible to reference and map these values into the target. So complete the mapping as follows:

Source	Target
`faFlightID` (from `$SourceApplicationObject`)	`faFlightID`
`ident` (from `$SourceApplicationObject`)	`ident`
`prefix`	`prefix`
`type`	`type`
`suffix`	`suffix`
`timestamp`	`timestamp`
`longitude`	`longitude`
`latitude`	`latitude`
`updateType`	`updateType`
`altitude`	`altitude`
`heading`	`heading`
`prefix` (from `$SourceApplicationObject`)	`prefix`
`suffix` (from `$SourceApplicationObject`)	`suffix`

In the mapping you will note that we are returning some of the original triggering call values; this is a reflection of the fact that we are supporting the idea that ideally systems are stateless using the REST architectural style.

With the mappings complete, it is worth saving and using the mapping test functionality to confirm the mapping produced the expected results. Once into the mapper, the source side will have two tabs now, one for the response payload and one with the variable holding the request payload. Use the **Generate Values** and **Execute** buttons to test the outcomes. The following screenshot illustrates the test:

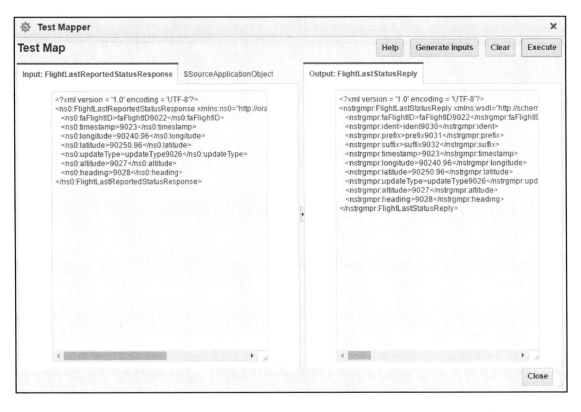

Let's close the **Test Mapper** and complete the integration. The last step within the integration is to set up the tracking, so select the **Tracking** button. We want to track against the `faFlightId`, so drag it from the available **Trigger** fields on the left on to the first row on the right-hand side of the screen. With that, we can complete the process by pressing the **Done** button. Let's save the integration using the **Save** button, and we should see the percentage completion rise to 100%. Click **Exit Integration**, and then activate the integration by clicking on the **Activate** button.

Setting up SoapUI and Mockable

We will need to create some test data to initiate the service call with, and Mockable needs to have a payload to respond with. To help create the Mockable response, we can use SoapUI to create some test data–this is done in a similar manner to building the request representation.

Once a project is named, you can right-click on the project name and click on **Generate SOAP Mock Service**. This will launch the following dialog, in which you need to select the target WSDL provided and tick **Create MockService** as shown here:

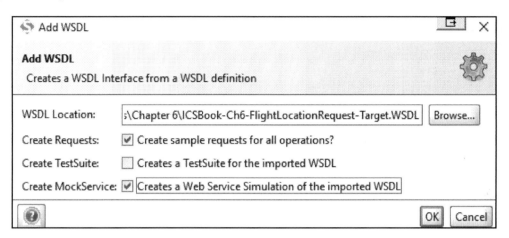

Complete the dialog by clicking on the **OK** button. This will then result in a series of popups through which you will determine which service to mock, although our WSDL does only have one service that can be mocked. At the end of this sequence you will have a SOAP Response object in the project tree–if you open it, you will see some XML along the lines of:

```
<soapenv:Envelope xmlns:soapenv="http://schemas.xmlsoap.org/soap/envelope/"
xmlns:flig="http://oracle-integration.cloud/soap/FlightStatusEnquiry">
    <soapenv:Header/>
    <soapenv:Body>
        <flig:FlightLastReportedStatusResponse>
            <flig:faFlightID>?</flig:faFlightID>
            <flig:timestamp>?</flig:timestamp>
            <flig:longitude>?</flig:longitude>
            <flig:latitude>?</flig:latitude>
            <flig:updateType>?</flig:updateType>
            <flig:altitude>?</flig:altitude>
            <flig:heading>?</flig:heading>
        </flig:FlightLastReportedStatusResponse>
    </soapenv:Body>
</soapenv:Envelope>
```

We can then tailor the values to be returned. The values ideally should make some sort of sense with the request object as well, as you can see in the recommended configuration shown in the next section.

Mockable

We need to configure Mockable to provide a suitable endpoint with a return construct as well. Complete the Mockable configuration with the following values:

Property	Description
Endpoint	`FlightStatusEnquiry`
SoapAction	`http://oracle-integration.cloud/soap/` `FlightStatusEnquiry/GetLastReportedPos`
Headers	This can be left blank
Response Status	200-OK
Content-Type	`Text/XML`
Content-Encoding	UTF-8
Response	`<soapenv:Envelope xmlns:soapenv="http://schemas.xmlsoap.org/soap/envelope/" xmlns:flig="http://oracle-integration.cloud/soap/FlightStatusEnquiry">` `<soapenv:Header/>` `<soapenv:Body>` `<flig:FlightLastReportedStatusResponse>` `<flig:faFlightID>1</flig:faFlightID>` `<flig:timestamp>1463266075432</flig:timestamp>` `<flig:longitude>01.27</flig:longitude>` `<flig:latitude>51.50</flig:latitude>` `<flig:updateType>POS</flig:updateType>` `<flig:altitude>25000</flig:altitude>` `<flig:heading>90</flig:heading>` `</flig:FlightLastReportedStatusResponse>` `</soapenv:Body>` `</soapenv:Envelope>`
Display Name	`FlightStatusEnquiry`
Enable Request Logger	Toggle this to on
Set Response Delay	Do not set

SoapUI

With SoapUI, we can use the schema as before to generate the XML to send; remember that we need to also obtain the URL to invoke by looking at the information popup on the active integration. For the integration to make sense, the request and response value setup should have some commonality in their values.

SoapUI should display a result body along the lines of this:

```
<soapenv:Body
xmlns:flig="http://oracle-integration.cloud/soap/FlightStatusEnquiry">
    <nstrgmpr:FlightLastStatusReply
xmlns:wsdl="http://schemas.xmlsoap.org/wsdl/"
xmlns:nstrgmpr="http://oracle-integration.cloud/soap/FlightStatusInfoSystem
" xmlns:soapenc="http://schemas.xmlsoap.org/soap/encoding/"
xmlns:http="http://schemas.xmlsoap.org/wsdl/http/"
xmlns:mime="http://schemas.xmlsoap.org/wsdl/mime/"
xmlns:soap="http://schemas.xmlsoap.org/wsdl/soap/">
        <nstrgmpr:faFlightID>510</nstrgmpr:faFlightID>
        <nstrgmpr:ident>1</nstrgmpr:ident>
        <nstrgmpr:prefix>BA</nstrgmpr:prefix>
        <nstrgmpr:suffix>1</nstrgmpr:suffix>
        <nstrgmpr:timestamp>1</nstrgmpr:timestamp>
        <nstrgmpr:longitude>1</nstrgmpr:longitude>
        <nstrgmpr:latitude>1</nstrgmpr:latitude>
        <nstrgmpr:updateType>1</nstrgmpr:updateType>
        <nstrgmpr:altitude>1</nstrgmpr:altitude>
        <nstrgmpr:heading>1</nstrgmpr:heading>
    </nstrgmpr:FlightLastStatusReply>
  </soapenv:Body>
</soapenv:Envelope>
```

Note which values match the original input values and which values correspond to the dummy return values.

As with previous integration creation, we would suggest you provide the following values:

Property	Value
Integration name	`FlightStatusEnquiry_Ch6_2`
Identifier	This will be proposed based on the integration name and there is no need to change it unless you would like an alternate name.
Version	01.00.0000
Package Name	`ics.book.ch6`
Description	`This integration extends upon FlightStatusEnquiry_Ch6 to use lookups. It will take the request and communicate to a backend system returning the fully filled out response`

Unlike a normal creation process, the pattern details are all defined and copied from the integration cloned. We could, if we wanted, activate the clone and run it, with the only difference being the target URL to use in SoapUI.

Enrichment services

An enrichment point within an integration is intended to provide a means to add information to the integration through the invocation of another integration or web service. With an enrichment operation, there is one key requirement: the enrichment works in a two-way manner so that the response can be used to enrich our integration.

For our example, we are going extend our current integration and utilize a genuine external service rather than Apiary or Mockable. The service we are introducing is a REST-based service (although the response is provided in the form of XML) from TimeZoneDB (`https://timezonedb.com/api`). Of course, it is also possible to mock this service if you prefer. Using TimeZoneDB allows us to introduce a common idea used by many public web services, that of the API Key, sometimes referred to as an API token. The integration will ultimately look like this:

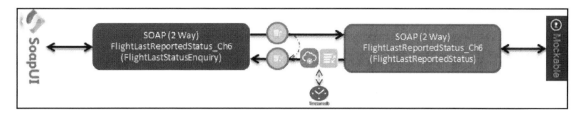

As you can see, we have incorporated the enrichment step on the response leg from Mockable, which will take the latitude and longitude values in the dummy payload and retrieve the country code and name of the region (or zone) in which that country resides.

Web services will often use a token as a proxy to providing personal credentials as it anonymizes the account details; this means that the identifier can be included as a URL parameter without raising issues about the implications of personal information being recorded by network infrastructure as it tracks traffic across the Internet. Additionally, it removes all the issues of having to handle characters that are not allowed in a URI. The token approach is also a lot easier to implement when the service is being incorporated into application code in comparison to more sophisticated credential mechanisms such as OAuth. Typically, to get a token you will need to register with the web service provider and provide them with some details. At the basic end of the scale, this will be sufficient to contact the service user, and at the other end there will be information about collecting service charges and so on. For services such as TimeZoneDB, the credentials are only really needed to understand service usage, and most importantly a means to contact you if the provider believes you are abusing the service.

Preparation

The first thing that needs to be done is to register with TimeZoneDB (`https://timezonedb.com/api`) by following the link and accessing the registration page. As part of the registration process you will be provided with your API key–keep the information handy as we will need to include that.

Creating the connector

To use TimeZoneDB we obviously need a suitable REST connection created. So from the **Connections** page, click on **Create New Connection**, select a REST adapter, and then use the following values to create a new connection:

Property	Value
Connection name	TimeDB_Ch6
Identifier	This will be proposed based on the connection name and there is no need to change it unless you would like an alternate name.
Description	Add the following description: This exposes TimeZoneDB API
Email Address	Your e-mail address
Configure Connectivity | Connection Properties	Set the **Connection Type** to **This exposes TimeZoneDB API**. Set the **Connection URL** to http://api.timezonedb.com. Close with the **OK** button.
Security Policy | Credentials	Set **Security Policy** to **No Security Policy**. Close the dialog with the **OK** button.

As before, click on the **Test** and **Save** buttons before clicking on **Exit Connection**.

Creating the integration

Rather than creating a new integration from scratch, we can short-circuit the process by cloning our previous integration, FlightStatusEnquiry_Ch6, and creating a service called FlightStatusEnquiry_Ch6_1. The **Clone** option is part of the popup menu on the right of the integration information in the **Integration** view of the **Designer**.

Rather than change this integration, we can start by using the clone function on the action menu of the integrations, as can be seen here:

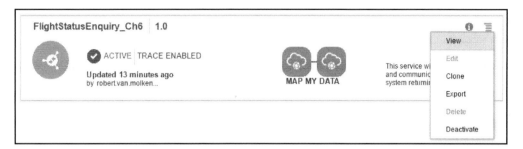

Once the **Clone** option has been clicked on, a dialog very much like the **Creation Integration** dialog will be displayed, as shown here:

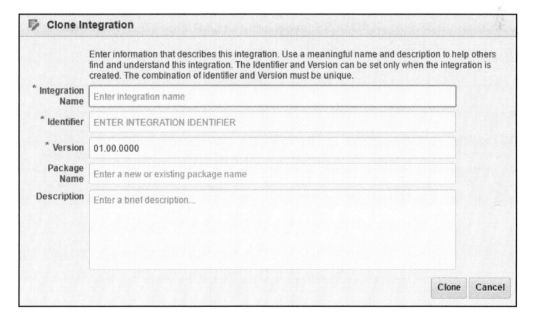

We should complete the dialog with the following details:

Property	Value
Integration name	FlightStatusEnquiry_Ch6_1
Identifier	This will be proposed based on the connection name and there is no need to change it unless you would like an alternate name.
Version	01.00.0000
Package Name	ics.book.ch6
Description	This service will take the request and communicate to a backend system, returning the fully filled out response.

With the integration ready, we can add the enrichment; the process is very much like creating the main integration but, rather than dropping the connection onto the trigger spot, we drop it on top of the enrichment icon in the flows, as you can see here:

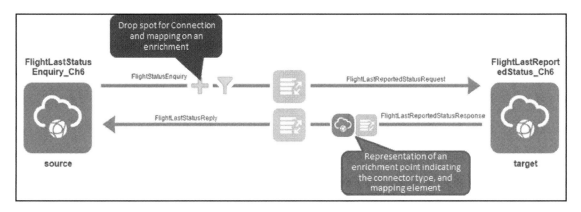

To implement the enrichment, the first step is to find the previously set up REST connector that we called `TimeDB_Ch6`. Dropping the connection on the plus symbol will trigger the presentation of a **Configure Oracle REST Endpoint** dialog. As previous chapters have illustrated the configuration of a REST endpoint, we can just use the following table to define the values needed:

Property	Question	Action
Basic Info	**Call your endpoint field?**	`TimeZoneEnrichment`
	What does this endpoint do?	Add the following description: `Gets TimeZone information using the Lat & Long parameters.`
	What is the endpoint's relative resource URI?	The base URL we have defined in the connector. This field is used to describe how any HTTP parameters should be included in the complete URI, for example: `http://www.mydomain.com/service ?param1=a_value&param2=b_value)` It can also be used to describe how to compose the full URL path in line with proper REST pattern, for example: `http://www.mydomain.com/service /entity/{entityId})`. In our case the API definition requires three parameters, so enter this: `/?lat=1&lng=1&key=1` The curly bracketed elements define the value substitutions that need to be performed. In our case the API definition does not have a path just three parameters, so enter: We will define the query parameters in a moment.
	What action does the endpoint perform?	As this is a request, then the HTTP operations should be a `GET`.
	Select any options that you want to configure:	The `Add` and `review` parameters for this endpoint and configure this endpoint to receive the response checkboxes should both be ticked. This allows us to ensure that parameters are correctly defined, along with the result payload.
	Configure Request Headers?	These can remain unticked. Sometimes, services look for additional information beyond standards such as OAuth to help accelerate initial processing of service calls or carry additional credential information.
	Configure Response Headers?	These can remain unticked. This also exists for the same reason as the request headers.

Request Parameters	Specify Query Parameters	Add to the table the URI's query parameters and define the expected data types. Defining values other than string should help prevent calling the enrichment service with bad values (for example, a letter instead of a number). The table needs to contain the following:

lat	string
lng	string
key	string

		The names in the table need to also correspond to the parameter names in the URI. Whilst the latitude and longitude are actually numeric values, we can simplify here as we know the numeric types are enforced by the schema for the data source.
	Template Parameters	None will be defined as the URI uses query parameters.
Request & Request Headers		As we have not chosen to define the header information, these tabs are skipped.
Response	Select the response payload file	As the TimeZoneDB response defaults to use XML, we can use that, so select the **XML Schema** option. We need to provide a schema so that ICS can understand the response data structure for the mapping mechanisms. As TimeZoneDB presently does not provide a schema for its response, we have taken the example and created a schema that you can download and use (this is not an unusual requirement). Use **Choose file** to upload the provided `TimeZoneDB.xsd` file.
	Select the type of payload with which you want the endpoint to reply	Click on the **XML** option.
Response Headers		As we are not manipulating any of the headers, this panel will be skipped.
Summary		This simply provides what you have provided in the previous tabs–you need only verify it reflects the values correctly.

Although the displayed URL on the summary path does not show the query parameters (which may be a little misleading to look at, particularly if you compare the summary with an illustration of the service API being called), they will be added.

This is shown in the following screenshot:

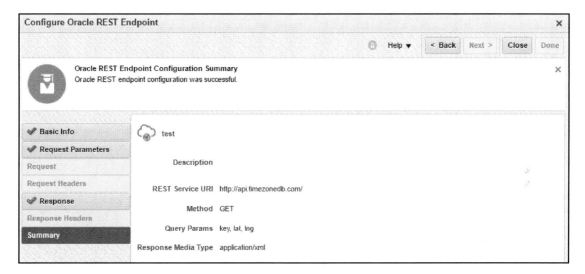

Complete the endpoint configuration by pressing the **Done** button, which will close this dialog. As our service needs to be given three parameters, the latitude, longitude, and API key, we need to map into the enrichment call the appropriate values to call.

> The information included into URLs either as part of the path or as a query parameter should be given consideration and treated with care. This is because, when the URL is being communicated across the network, unlike the body of a call it is never encrypted and will be seen and recorded by the servers that are part of the message routing, so any credentials could be easily picked up.

The mapping works like the previous use of mappings we implemented previously, with the source showing all the variables and the target (that is, query parameters) on the right. The mapping should be as follows:

Source	Target
latitude (from *FlightLastReportStatusResponse)	lat

Longitude (from *FlightLastReportStatusResponse)	lng
key	Literal string that represents the key from TimeZoneDB

As a result, the mapping should look like this:

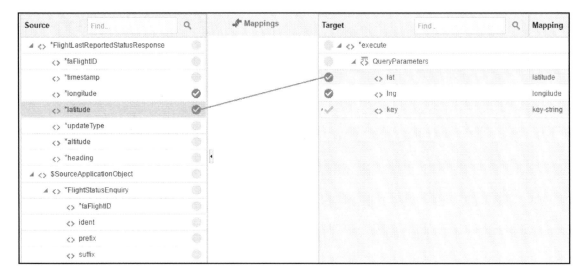

If you use this connection in more than one place, you might consider using a lookup (which we will explore in detail shortly) to define the key string and then use the lookup in the target expression. This way, if you need to change the key, you need only update the lookup rather than deactivating, changing each hardwired use, and then re-activating the integration.

As we have already defined a mapping between our source and target SOAP objects, you will get a warning displayed that introducing an enrichment point may invalidate mappings (as the enrichment point may impact variables and naming within the transform). As we are introducing new values to the integration this should not be an issue, so we can close the warning using the **OK** button. We can now extend the main mapping to exploit the enrichment data.

In the mapping, an additional variable will now appear on the left-hand side (`$ResponseEnrichmentApplicationObject`) and will contain the response data provided by the enrichment service. We can therefore exploit this data by adding the following mappings:

Source	Target
countryCode (from $ ResponseEnrichmentApplicationObject)	Note
ZoneName (from *FlightLastReportStatusResponse)	lng

This completes the incorporation of the enrichment data, so click on the **Save** button, then the **Exit Mapper** button (unless you want to first test the mapping; note that this will not test the enrichment service but will use the response definition to create test values). Now save the integration, return the list of integrations, and activate the integration ready for use.

Testing the enriched integration

As this integration been developed as an extension of `FlightStatusEnquiry_Ch6`, we can actually tweak the target URL (which can be retrieved from the information popup on the integration, once activated) in SoapUI to execute the integration (do not forget to reset the security timestamp as well).

The only difference should be that the response will now have the `flightNotes` element populated. Given the latitude and longitude provided in the test data, you should expect `NoteType` to reflect a value of `Europe/London` with `GB` for the `Note` element. We have included the following example of the core of the response body expected in SoapUI:

```
<flig:FlightLastStatusReply>
    <flig:faFlightID>530</nstrgmpr:faFlightID>
    <flig:ident>1</nstrgmpr:ident>
    <flig:prefix>BA</nstrgmpr:prefix>
    <flig:suffix>1</nstrgmpr:suffix>
    <flig:timestamp>1463266075432</flig:timestamp>
    <flig:longitude>01.27</nstrgmpr:longitude>
    <flig:latitude>51.50</nstrgmpr:latitude>
    <flig:updateType>POS</nstrgmpr:updateType>
    <flig:altitude>25000</nstrgmpr:altitude>
    <flig:heading>90</nstrgmpr:heading>
    <flig:flightNotes>
        <flig:NoteType>Europe/London</flig:NoteType>
```

```
        <flig:Note>GB</flig:Note>
    </flig:flightNotes>
/flig:FlightLastStatusReply>
```

Using lookups

Lookups provide a means to map a value used in one system to how that value is presented in another. For example, our flight data may refer to BA, but if we wanted to incorporate the details into an e-mail, we may want to refer to British Airways. Sometimes, these lookups are referred to as **Domain Value Mappings** (as the mapping is from one the value represented in one domain or application to another); this is something of a hangover from one of Oracle's other integration products (SOA Suite and Service Bus). The lookup scenario we will be implementing can be shown as follows:

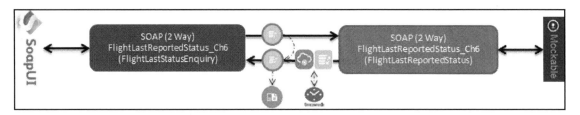

As with the previous enrichment integration, we are going to shortcut the development process by using the **Clone** option, but this time cloning integration FlightStatusEnquiry_Ch6_1. Complete the clone dialog with the following details:

Property	Description
Integration name	FlightStatusEnquiry_Ch6_2
Identifier	This will be proposed based on the integration name and there is no need to change it unless you would like an alternate name.
Version	01.00.0000
Package Name	ics.book.ch6
Description	This integration extends FlightStatusEnquiry_Ch6_1 to use lookups. It will take the request and communicate to a backend system, returning the fully filled out response

Creating a lookup

Before we can use a lookup, we first need to create a lookup to use. Navigate to the **Lookups** part of the **Designer**, and you will see a screen like this:

Select the **Create New Lookup** button, which will launch a dialog, as shown here:

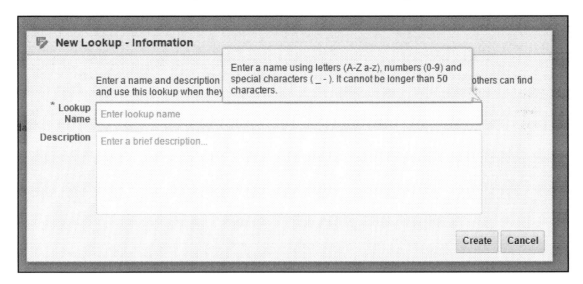

We can complete this form with the following information:

Property	Value
Lookup Name	`AirlineCodesNameCallsign_Ch6`
Description	`Maps the IATA, ICAO, name, and flight call sign names`

Complete the form by pressing the **Create** button. Now we are presented with a screen that is used for building out a table of values. Use the following screenshot to help populate the table for us to use. The plus symbol at the top of the right-hand columns will add the columns needed, and the plus symbol at the bottom of the table will add rows as you can see here:

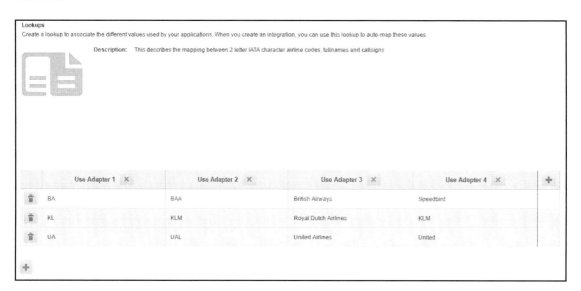

With the data setup, we need to link to each column an adapter or a name space. When using a name space, you would typically use the name space used by the system related to the column. For this example, we are just going to concentrate on adapters. The adapter can then be used to index against that column for its key values. For our example we want to link the adapters as follows:

Adapter Type	Column
SOAP	1
File	2

REST	3
FTP	4

These adapter mappings may seem counter-intuitive, but when we apply the lookup, you will see how the adapter is being applied. With the adapters allocated we can save the lookup using the top **Save** button, and **Exit Lookup** to start incorporating the lookup in the integration.

Alternate lookup creation

It is also possible to create a lookup by importing a CSV file. This is done by clicking on the **Import** button on the colored banner which will launch a standard file selection dialog. When you click the **Import** button on the dialog then import process will start. For this to work the CSV file needs two lines providing information before the data. This looks like the following:

- Line 1
- Fixed value of DVM
- Lookup name, for example, FlightData
- Lookup description within double quotes, for example, `Aircraft information`
- Line 2; each cell has the name of the data in that column
- Line 3; the first row of data values

Within the resources we have provided an example file called `AircraftData_Ch6.csv` which you can use to see the structure and try the import process.

Incorporating a lookup into a mapping

So, let's start editing the lookup; in the Integration view, click on `FlightStatusEnquiry_Ch6_2` so we can start to edit it. Open up the target to source mapping view and we are going to add a mapping to the `simpleNote` element that takes the suffix that we are going to use to represent the two-letter IATA airline code and retrieves the airline's full name. So, select `simpleNote` field on the right side of the mapping, which will take us to the **Build Mapping** view. On the left side of the panel, select **Mapping Components**, and then open up the folder tree beneath it so the tree reveals **Functions | ICS** and the **lookupValue** option with in. You should see part of the **Build Mappings** screen shown as follows.

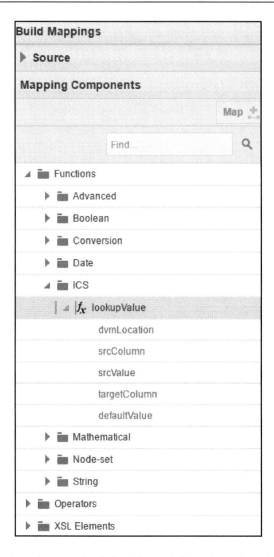

Select the **lookupValue** function on the left side and drag it to the right-hand side and release it where it says: **Drag and Drop or Type here...** The right-hand statement area will expand to show all the parameters of the lookup function. At the same time, a dialog will also pop up to help us to select the relevant lookups. The dialog displayed is very much like the dialogs used when defining the trigger and invoke information for a connection in an integration and will allow us to select the correct lookup and retained details, as you can see:

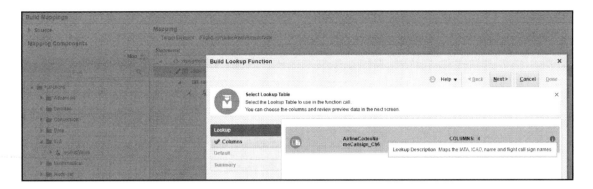

Note that in the previous screenshot, we have also clicked on the information icon, which will display the lookup description. The first step in the wizard is to select our lookup; as we only have one lookup we can select this and move on using the **Next** button. This will then present us with a view of the lookup. By clicking on the **Source** and **Target** column names we get a popup that will allow us to choose which column to use in the lookup. Once selected, values from that column are displayed as you can see:

For our scenario we want to set the columns to be SOAP and REST in this order. By clicking on the **Next** button now, we get to define what the default value should be. In our case this should be Not Known, as follows:

Again, we can move on with the **Next** button to see a **Summary** of our lookup. The summary shows the details of our chosen lookup and its settings, along with the XSLT. This can be seen here:

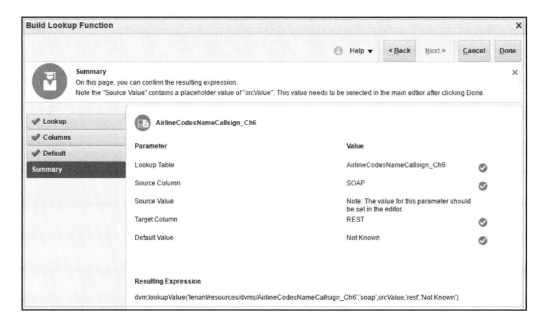

With this we can click on the **Done** button. We can now see the lookup displayed as an expression, but note that the value to put into the lookup is still represented as `srcValue`, as shown next.

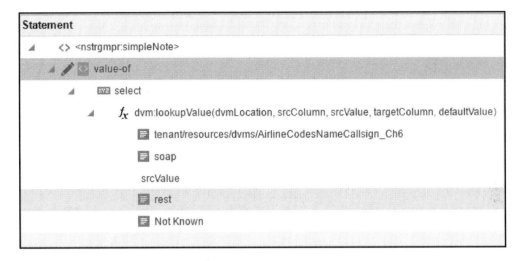

We need to select the `suffix` field from our source and list on the left and drag it over to replace that value. This result in the screen looks something like this:

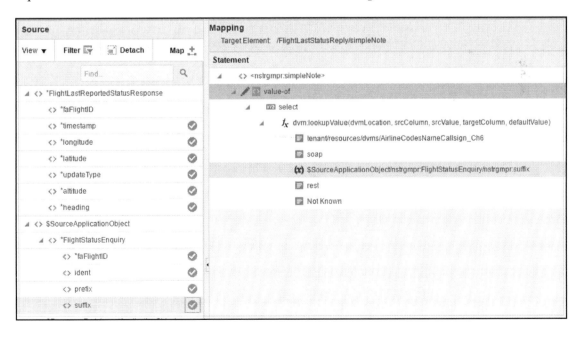

It is also possible to configure a lookup without needing the dialogs, but it is a lot easier to define the lookup using them. We can **Save** and **Close** this dialog. Likewise, we can save and close the **Build Mapping** screen.

Before we go too far, we can test the mapping within the editor; it is worth using the facility to test the mapping. So select the **Test** button, which will launch the **Test Mapper** screen. We can use the tool to generate some initial XML values for us with the **Generate Inputs** button, which will populate the left-hand side of the panel. Note the value in the `suffix` field on the input side. Given the value, we should see `simpleNote` element with the value of `Not Known`. Now if you edit the suffix on the source as a value of `BA` and **Execute** again, the `simpleNote` element will reflect the expected value of British Airways, as you can see next:

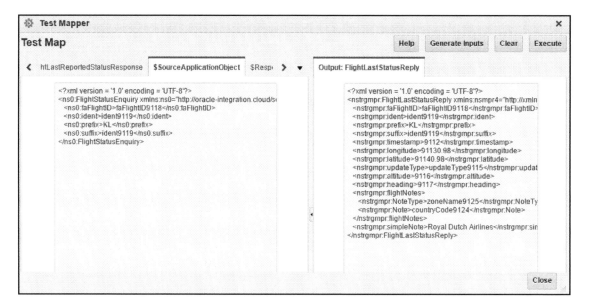

It is worth remembering that this capability is case-sensitive.

How to get function documentation

As you can see in the following screenshot, by double-clicking on the function listed, we get a little popup that will provide a brief description and a **Learn More** link. Clicking that link will launch a browser page explaining the industry standard definition of that function as you can see here:

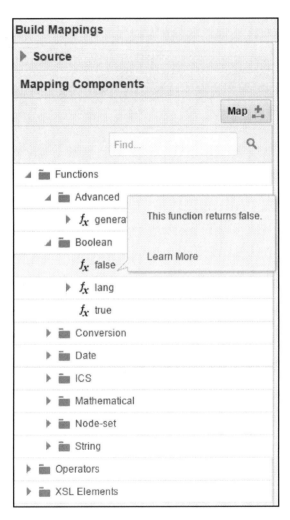

You will note that the list of **Mapping Components** in the previous image includes a folder for ICS. This is where ICS' extensions are held.

Executing the integration with a lookup

With this complete, let's follow what we did in Chapter 3, *Distribute Messages Using the Pub-Sub Model*, by setting the **Tracking**. Then **Save**, **Exit Integration**, and **Activate** the integration.

We can repeat the previous process of adjusting the invocation of FlightStatusEnquiry_Ch6 with the trigger URL for this integration (remember, the security timestamp will need resetting). The response should look like this:

```
<soapenv:Body
xmlns:flig="http://oracle-integration.cloud/soap/FlightStatusEnquiry">
    <flig:FlightLastStatusReply>
        <flig:faFlightID>530</flig:faFlightID>
        <flig:ident>1</flig:ident>
        <flig:prefix>BA</flig:prefix>
        <flig:suffix>1</flig:suffix>
        <flig:timestamp>1463266075432</flig:timestamp>
        <flig:longitude>01.27</flig:longitude>
        <flig:latitude>51.50</flig:latitude>
        <flig:updateType>POS</flig:updateType>
        <flig:altitude>25000</flig:altitude>
        <flig:heading>90</flig:heading>
        <flig:flightNotes>
            <flig:NoteType>Europe/London</flig:NoteType>
            <flig:Note>GB</flig:Note>
        </flig:flightNotes>
        <flig:simpleNote>British Airways</flig:simpleNote>
    </flig:FlightLastStatusReply>
</soapenv:Body>
```

Note that, the value in the simpleNote element should reflect the lookup values configured.

Summary

In this chapter, we created a request and response integration and then used the request to enrich the response with the original request values. This was then cloned and extended to incorporate an enrichment service that was implemented using a REST-based web service. We then looked at how mapping exploits an additional variable that holds the enrichment data. All forms of enrichment will follow these basic patterns.

Although we used an external web service to perform the enrichment, it would be equally possible to perform the enrichment using another ICS integration, as long as it met the need for a synchronous request and response.

We then enhanced the integration after cloning it again, this time utilizing a lookup mechanism to retrieve additional values related to one of the response object's values to populate another element. We used the lookup to simply enrich our service (so it was possible to see both the original value and the lookup result). But often, the lookup would be doing value substitutions, for example, replacing UK with GB, and so on.

A natural step on from this would be to explore using more advanced XSLT and XQuery operations to complete sophisticated enrichment and data mapping.

In the next chapter, we continue working with **Basic Map Data** pattern, but to filter events, so that only specific message types can reach a destination based upon the data in the integration. This also leads to routing events to different endpoints, subject to message content.

7
Routing and Filtering

There are times when you need to decide whether destinations should receive data depending upon the information in the message, or invoke different endpoints depending upon the content. In terms of integration patterns, these are described as filtering and routing, respectively. In this chapter, we are going to look at ICS capabilities outside the orchestration pattern.

To illustrate routing and filtering we are going to build on an idea first seen in Chapter 3, *Distribute Messages Using the Pub-Sub Model*, where we received a flight status update and then distributed it onward. As part of a publish and subscribe model, you assume everyone subscribing wants to know about every event. For this chapter, we are going to take the idea of receiving the status updates, but filter out updates based on the update type, so our mock consumer will only get position reports, not events representing departures and arrivals. Having established the ability to implement a filter, we will extend the scenario to separate out position status messages so that they go to one endpoint and all other events are routed to a different endpoint.

With routing, the different endpoints can easily be different adapters, different services within a connection, or even actually the same service within the same connector, but with different data mappings. Given this, within our examples we are going to focus on using a single target and show the routing by changing the mapping. By doing so it will be a lot simpler to track the actions to confirm that the routing is working.

In this chapter, we will cover the following topics:

- Explanation of conditional/content-based routing
- Create initial filters on an existing target instance
- Reuse existing mappings
- Define alternative routes to another instance

Preparation

Before we start you will need to download the book's resources for this chapter as they contain the inbound (trigger) WSDL called `ICSBook-Ch7-FlightProgress-Source.WSDL` and the outbound WSDL definition file called `ICSBook-Ch7-FlightProgress-Target.WSDL`, along with a response payload to use with `Mockable.io` called `ICSBook-Ch7-MockResponse.txt`.

Before the outbound WSDL definition can be used, it will need to be edited as before so that the `soap:address` element has its `location` attribute referencing your instance of `Mockable.io` (that is, replace the `xxxx.mockable.io` part of the URL). With this saved and ready to use, we can get started.

Creating connections

We need to build two SOAP connections. As we have done this a number of times in previous chapters, now we can just provide you with the necessary details. The first connection can be created with the following details:

Properties	Description
Connection Name	`FlightStatusReport_Ch7`
Identifier	This will be proposed based on the connection name and there is no need to change unless you would like an alternate name
Connection Role	**Trigger**
Description	The description should be: `receives flight status report information and returns relevant update information based on the update type`

With that the connection can be created and the connection details can be defined with the following details:

Properties	Description
Email Address	Your e-mail address
Connection Properties | Upload File	Set the checkbox, so that we can use the file selector provided to upload `ICSBook-Ch7-FlightProgress-Source.WSDL`

Credentials | Security Policy	Select **No Security Policy**

With these values set, the connection can be tested by clicking **Test** at the top of the page, which will set the progress to **100%** and we can click on **Save** and then **Exit Connection**. We now need to repeat this with the modified outbound WSDL. From the **Connections** screen create a new connection with the following values:

Properties	Description
Connection Name	`FilteredFlightProgressReport_Ch7`
Identifier	This will be proposed based on the connection name and there is no need to change unless you would like an alternate name
Connection Role	Invoke
Description	Description will be `This sends the progress report to the mocked end system. The schema used for this connection includes elements that are intended to be hard-coded by the integration`

With the connection created we need to configure it with the following information:

Properties	Description
Email Address	Your e-mail address
Connection Properties | Upload File	Set the checkbox, so that we can use the file selector provided to upload `ICSBook-Ch7-FlightProgress-Target.WSDL`
Credentials| Security Policy	Select **No Security Policy**

With those details provided we can repeat the process of testing and saving the connection.

Creating a filtered integration

With the connections defined we can start to create the filtered connection, which will look like:

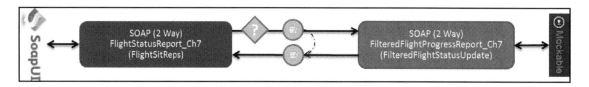

It is worth noting that the integration is two-way; this is because we want to show a return value that clearly represents an outcome: having succeeded or failing to pass through the filter. But additionally, ICS will not allow one-way integrations to have a filter. You can verify this by creating a version of our source connection with a modified WSDL where, `wsdl:message name="FlightInfoUpdateResponseMsg"` and `<wsdl:output>` elements are removed, and then trying to construct the integration we are about to describe; you will then see that the option to incorporate a filter is not available.

This constraint is based on the possibility that, when filters are used for routes, one endpoint may return a result and the other does not, in which case what do you do? Enforcing a return solves the problem in terms of consistency, even if you then define the return value to be completely optional within the definition of the trigger endpoint.

As we have done in previous chapters, we need to create an integration using the **Basic Map Data** pattern. We can complete the creation process with the following details:

Properties	Description
Integration Name	`FilteredStatusReporting_Ch7`
Identifier	This will be proposed based on the connection name and there is no need to change unless you would like an alternate name
Version	`01.00.0000`
Package Name	`ics.book.ch7`
Description	The description should be: `This service will take the request and communicate to a backend system, returning the fully filled out response if the message type is accepted`

Completing these details by clicking on the **Create** button means that we now have the usual integration canvas to populate. We can start this by locating `FlightStatusReport_Ch7` and dropping it on the **Trigger** pad on the canvas. We can then complete the configuration of the connection with the following details:

Tab	Question	Action
Basic Info	**Call your endpoint field?**	To keep it simple call it `Source`.
	What does this end point do?	Add the description: `receives flight status information`.
	Preview updated SOAP Adapter Runtime	Click on **Yes**.
Operations	**Selected Port Type**	As we only have a single operation in the WSDL this tab will not offer any options.
	Selected Operation	
	Request Object	
	Disable SOAP Action Validation	Set to **Yes**. Given what we want to achieve in this integration let's keep things simple.
Summary	**WSDL URL**	As we only have a single operation in the WSDL this tab will not offer any options. But should reflect the selected connector information.

Complete the wizard by clicking on the **Done** button. We can now set up the target side of the integration by dropping the `FlightFlightProgressReport_Ch7` connection onto the **Invoke** pad on the canvas. Again we need to complete the wizard to define all the attributes of the connection, as shown in the following table:

Tab	Question	Action
Basic Info	**Call your endpoint field?**	To keep it simple call it `target`.
	What does this end point do?	Add the description: `passes the position updates to a downstream system`.
	Preview updated SOAP Adapter Runtime	Click on **Yes**.
Operations	**Selected Port Type**	As we only have a single operation in the WSDL this tab will not offer any options.

	Selected Operation	
	Request Object	
	Disable SOAP Action Validation	Set to **Yes**. Given what we want to achieve in this integration let's keep things simple.
Summary	**WSDL URL**	As we only have a single operation in the WSDL this tab will not offer any options. But should reflect the selected connector information.

Complete the wizard by clicking on the **Done** button. With that we will have the basic integration defined. The next step is to define the mappings. Click on the mapping icon for the source to target flow to enter the **Mapper** screen. We can drag and drop to define the following mappings:

Source (FlightProgress)	Target (FilteredFlightProgress)
ID	ID
ident	ident
prefix	prefix
type	type
ICAORef	suffix
origin	origin
destination	destination
timeout	Timeout
timestamp	timestamp
longitude	longitude
latitude	latitude
updateType	updateType

The last value on the target is called notes. We want to hard-code the value for this in the integration. Click on **Notes** and the **Build Mappings** screen will be displayed. In the **Statement** part of the screen, click where it says – **Drag and drop or type here**; we want to add the text, `pos filtered`. Then click on **Save** and **Close**. The text should now appear in the mapping for the target. We can now click on **Save** and then **Exit Mapper**.

We can now set up the response mapping (target to source) in the same way using the following mappings:

Source (FilteredFlightProgressResponse) and $SourceApplicationObject	Target (FlightProgressResponse)
ID (from $SourceApplicationObject)	ID
ident (from $SourceApplicationObject)	ident
prefix (from $SourceApplicationObject)	updateType
notified (from FilteredFlightProgressResponse)	notified

The majority of the mapped values come from $SourceApplicationObject, so that they reflects the values sent rather than the hard-coded values in the mock. With the exception of notified, which will come from the Mockable endpoint as we are happy with this being hard wired and it will reflect that the invocation passed through the filter and reached the Mockable.io stub. As before, complete the mapping by clicking on **Save** and **Exit Mapper**. We now have an integration that could be executed, although no filtration would be applied. So let's now define the filter.

Applying a filter

The filter point within the integration is represented by a funnel style icon on the request flow, as shown in the following icon:

Clicking on the **Filter** icon where no filter already exists will offer you an option to create the filter (if a filter exists then you would have the options to modify or delete the filter). The full set of filter editing options is shown in the following as follows:

The left icon represented edit, the middle icon represents clear expression – this is where the filter will remain, but the expression as you will see when we create it can be removed, and finally the filter can be completely removed.

As we have not yet created the filter we can click on the **Filter** icon. This will present us with the expression editor screen, which structurally looks a lot like the mappings editor, as you can see in the following screenshot:

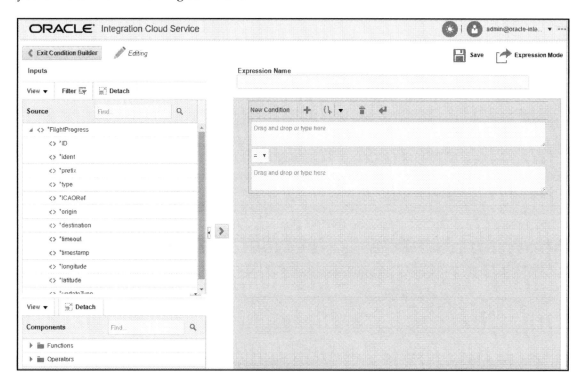

As we can see, the left-hand side represents the available inputs and functions, and the right-hand side represents the means to describe the expression, which will be used to define the expression. The outcome of any expression represented, as we can see, needs to be Boolean in nature, that is True or False. We can start by defining whether the type value is POS.

To do this, we need to select the **type** input from the left and drag and drop it into the top field of the condition. Between the fields is a drop-down list of Boolean operators (equals, greater than, and so on); for this expression we need the drop-down to have equals selected (=). The last step in defining the filter expression is to provide the value to match against; if we want to have the lower field, we need to define the value we want a match to. Thus, add "POS" (including the quotes). Finally, we also need to provide the expression with a simple name in the **Expression Name** field, so enter isPosReport.

The expression side of the **Condition Builder** should now look like:

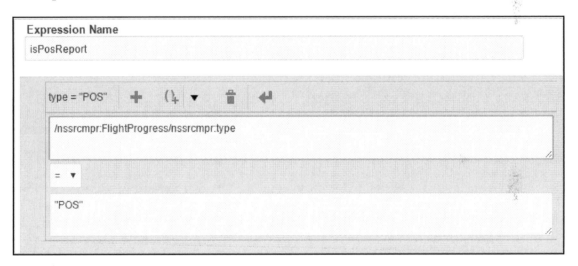

Click the **Save** button. Before we leave the expression editor let's look at some of the other aspects of it. We can work with the raw XQuery expression by clicking on the **Expression Mode** button. Note in this view that the expression also has a simple summary shown. The expression mode is shown in the following screenshot:

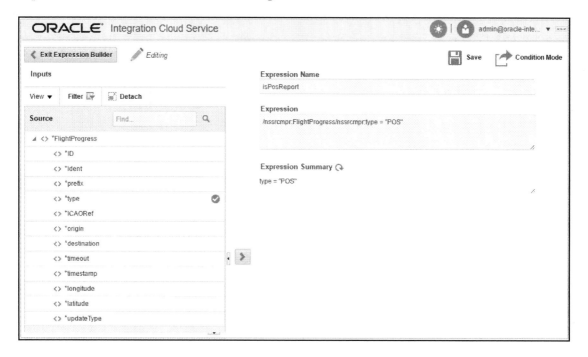

Returning to the original condition view is done by clicking on the **Condition Mode** button. Upon returning to the condition view, you will see that it has collapsed our expression to the summary of the expression. Click on **Expression Summary** and the view will open up to the full expression. The reason for the collapse is that it is possible to build a series of expressions using the plus symbol (+), including the grouping of expressions using the (()+) symbol. Given we do not want the expression to be any more complex at this stage, we can click on the **Exit Condition Builder** button.

With the condition built back on the main integration screen, the top of the canvas area now shows the existence of the filter, as you can see in the following screenshot:

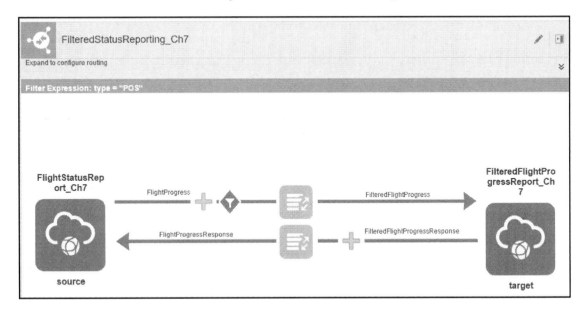

We can expand this view using the double down arrow above the expression bar on the right to view the filter, as shown in the following screenshot:

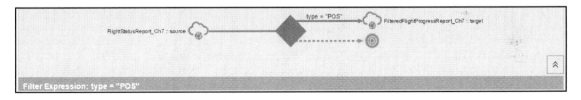

You can also hide the filter view with the up arrow as well. We now have to set the tracking details as we did with the previous integrations. We would recommend that you set the tracking fields to ID, ident, and type. With this completed, we can save the integration, exit, and, once back at the integrations view, activate the integration.

Setting up Mockable

The last step before we can exercise the integration is to configure `Mockable.io` to consume and respond accordingly. Log back into your Mockable account and navigate to the list of SOAP mocks. We need to add a new mock endpoint by clicking on the **+ SOAP Mock** button. We can then complete the details of the mock, as shown in the following table:

Properties	Description
Endpoint	Add `FilteredFlightServices` to the prefixed endpoint path; this will need to match up with the URL we modified in the WSDL at the beginning of this chapter
Headers	No header information is required
Response status	This can be left with **200 – OK**
Content-Type	`text/xml`
Content-Encoding	Should be the default, `UTF-8`
Response body	In this field paste the contents of the `ICSBook-Ch7-MockResponse.txt` file; as you can see, this is a hard-wired XML response matching the schema definition
Display Name	This can be anything you like, but we have used `FilteredFlightStatusUpdate`
Enable Request Logger	This needs to be toggled on
Set response delay	This can be left with the `1` second default value

With these values set, the mock should be saved and started using the buttons at the bottom of the mock setup. With that completed, we can go to the **Request Inspector** view by clicking on the button at the top of the page. The following screenshot reflects the configurations described in the preceding table:

Testing the integration

With the integration complete and activated, the mock is ready and we can set up SoapUI and test the integration. To do this, we can use the **Add WSDL** function and supply the `ICSBook-Ch7-FlightProgress-Source.WSDL` file. With the WSDL added, a request will be created. You can either edit the values in the generated sample or paste the contents of `ICSBook-Ch7-FlightProgress-SourceTestSample.xml` into the value. Aside from using the correct data types, the crucial thing is the value provided for the `type` element.

For the first execution, this should be `POS`, which should allow the integration to pass through the filter. The path to the service is needed, which as you may recall can be retrieved from the information popup on the **Integrations** view once the integration has been activated. It should look something like:
`https://XXXX.oraclecloud.com/integration/flowsvc/soap/FILTEREDSTATUSRE_CH7/v01/` where `XXXX` is the domain and data center part of the URL for your instance of ICS.

The final step is to set up the basic authentication in SoapUI as done previously and apply both the authentication and timeout into the payload. With this done, we can fire the integration test. The results returned should appear in the XML tab along the lines of:

```
<env:Envelope xmlns:env="http://schemas.xmlsoap.org/soap/envelope/">
    <env:Header/>
    <env:Body>
        <nstrgmpr:FlightProgressResponse
        xmlns:wsdl="http://schemas.xmlsoap.org/wsdl/"
        xmlns:nstrgmpr="http://oracle-integration.cloud/soap/IntegratedSourceFlightSit
        xmlns:soapenc="http://schemas.xmlsoap.org/soap/encoding/"
        xmlns:http="http://schemas.xmlsoap.org/wsdl/http/"
        xmlns:mime="http://schemas.xmlsoap.org/wsdl/mime/"
        xmlns:soap="http://schemas.xmlsoap.org/wsdl/soap/">
            <nstrgmpr:ID>994</nstrgmpr:ID>
            <nstrgmpr:ident>110</nstrgmpr:ident>
            <nstrgmpr:updateType>POS</nstrgmpr:updateType>
            <nstrgmpr:notified>success</nstrgmpr:notified>
        </nstrgmpr:FlightProgressResponse>
    </env:Body>
</env:Envelope>
```

Note how the values returned except the `notified` element correspond to what was sent, but the `notified` element is the same as to the mock. You can verify this by changing that part of the mock and executing the integration again. You can also verify what is going on by viewing the contents of the **Request Inspector** (make sure you have the view refreshed). We would recommend you change the `ID` each time you trigger the test so that in the monitoring it is easy to separate each execution. We will look at monitoring in depth in `Chapter 12`, *Are My Integrations Running Fine, and What If They Are Not?*

The next test we should do is for the filter to block the invocation of the mock. To do this, change the `type` element in the XML to have a value such as `DEP` (for departure) and then invoke the web call again. This time the response back to you will be a reflection of the request sent because the value was not what was wanted by the filter.

Routing by Message Content

We have seen how a filter works in an integration; in doing so you may have recognized how conditional routing can be introduced, but let's step through an example by extending our `FilteredStatusReporting_Ch7` integration, so it looks as follows:

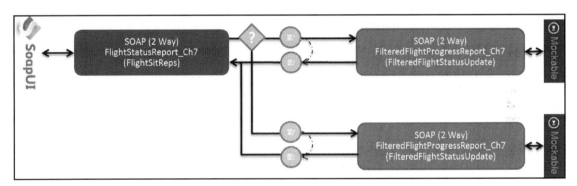

In the introduction, we mentioned that actually beyond the filter the different paths could call the same endpoint with different values or very different endpoints (different in terms of adapter, connection, and payload). As you can see, in our example we are going to only differentiate by mapping and use the same endpoint; in doing so we can focus on the integration, not the setting up of more connections and mocks.

Creating the Routing Integration

We can accelerate the process by cloning `FilteredStatusReporting_Ch7` (use the **Clone** option on the menu for the integration in the **Integrations** view). Use the following details to create the new integration:

Properties	Description
Integration Name	`RoutedStatusReporting_Ch7`
Identifier	This will be proposed based on the connection name and there is no need to change unless you would like an alternate name
Version	`01.00.0000`
Package Name	`ics.book.ch7`
Description	The description should be: `This service will take the request and communicate to a backend system returning the filled out response. The returned details will depend upon the message type element`

This should give us a new integration. We can now change this filter into a routed integration by clicking on the double down arrow (on the right-hand side below the integration name details) to show the filter information. In this view, you can click on the right-hand endpoints (as the upper half of the following screenshot shows). Currently in the filtered view, this shows a SOAP endpoint and a null or empty endpoint beneath the SOAP icon. Click on the lower endpoint, and you will be presented with the canvas with a source, but there is now an invoke connection on the canvas as you can see in the following screenshot:

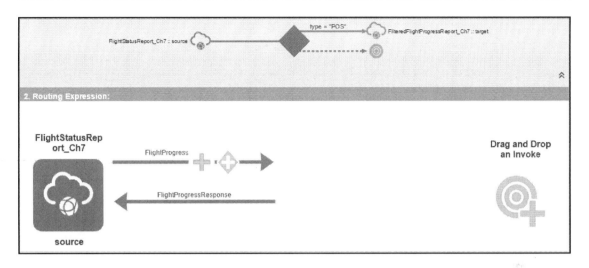

You can tell which branch you are looking at any time based on the upper part of the preceding screenshot having the selected route shown in color rather than gray, not to mention in the color separator is the relevant filter expression (or **Routing Expression**) when no endpoint exists. You might want to switch back and forth to see.

To create the alternate route, we can add the `FilteredFlightProgressReport_Ch7` connection to the invoke point on the canvas, and complete the configuration wizard with the following values given in the table:

Tab	Question	Action
Basic Info	**Call your endpoint field?**	To keep it simple call it `AlternateTarget`.
	What does this end point do?	Add the description: `non positional progress reports on`.
	Preview updated SOAP Adapter Runtime	Click on **Yes**.
Operations	**Selected Port Type**	As we only have a single operation in the WSDL this tab will not offer any options.
	Selected Operation	
	Request Object	
	Disable SOAP Action Validation	Set to **Yes**. Given what we want to achieve in this integration let's keep things simple.

Summary	WSDL URL	As we only have a single operation in the WSDL this tab will not offer any options. But should reflect the selected connector information.

Mapping the alternate route

With the endpoint defined, we can now apply the mapping. For the
`FilteredFlightProgress` bound flow, we can reuse the same mapping when we
configured the filter mapping, but with one exception: to differentiate the calls we need to
use a different literal (hard-coded) `notes` string. Thus, using the same technique as before,
set the `notes` to have the value of a `Not POS` based position report. With that the mapping
can be saved and exited.

For the `FlightProgressResponse` bound mapping we can apply the same mapping
values with one distinct difference. So we can see the response has come through the
alternate path we will concatenate the response with a literal prefix string (of `Alternate Path`). As we have walked through the process of creating a more complex expression,
rather than repeating the steps, you need to construct the mapping for the `notified`
element, as given in the following screenshot:

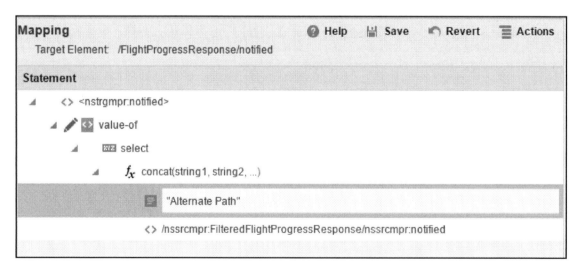

 An XQuery expression will appear as something like:
```
<xsl:value-of select = 'concat("Alternate Path",
/nssrcmpr:FilteredFlightProgressResponse/nssrcmp.
```

With the endpoint and mapping established, the last step is to configure the routing condition itself. As with the filter this is expressed on the `FilteredFlightProgress` bound flow after the enrichment option. But rather than the funnel icon we get symbols indicating the addition of an expression (the branch) or define this as the path for everything excluded by the previous filter (**E**). The following image shows the appropriate icon and buttons associated with it:

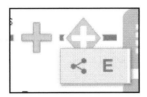

For this example, we want to just set the path to be the **Else** route, so click on the **E** symbol. We should now have an integration that looks as follows:

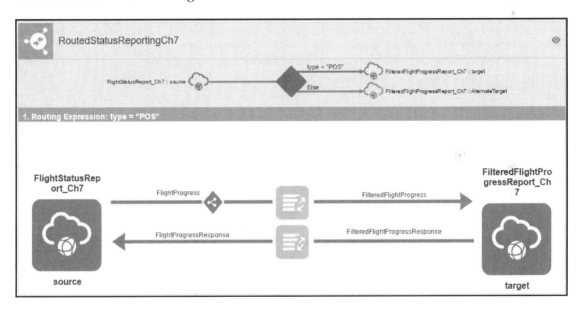

Note in the previous screenshot that the **Else** branch is marked in the upper part of the screenshot, now with its endpoint.

We can now click on **Save** and exit this integration. Once back in the **Integrations** view, activate the integration, so we can test it.

Testing the routing

Returning to SoapUI, we can use the **Clone Request** option to make a slightly modified integration call. We need to modify the call as we are triggering a different integration; therefore we need to correct the URL to point to this new integration, but all the values can remain the same.

By sending this integration a message with the `type` set to `POS`, the response should remain the same as the filtered integration. But this time if we set `type` to be `DEP` again, we can see a similar result to the `POS` response, except the `notified` element reflects the constructed string. This is illustrated in the following screenshot:

```
<env:Envelope xmlns:env="http://schemas.xmlsoap.org/soap/envelope/">
    <env:Header/>
    <env:Body>
        <nstrgmpr:FlightProgressResponse
        xmlns:wsdl="http://schemas.xmlsoap.org/wsdl/"
        xmlns:nstrgmpr="http://oracle-integration.cloud/soap/IntegratedSourceFlightSit
        xmlns:soapenc="http://schemas.xmlsoap.org/soap/encoding/"
        xmlns:http="http://schemas.xmlsoap.org/wsdl/http/"
        xmlns:mime="http://schemas.xmlsoap.org/wsdl/mime/"
        xmlns:soap="http://schemas.xmlsoap.org/wsdl/soap/">
            <nstrgmpr:ID>989</nstrgmpr:ID>
            <nstrgmpr:ident>hardwired ident</nstrgmpr:ident>
            <nstrgmpr:updateType>updateType38</nstrgmpr:updateType>
            <nstrgmpr:notified>Alternative Path success</nstrgmpr:notified>
        </nstrgmpr:FlightProgressResponse>
    </env:Body>
</env:Envelope>
```

Extending the filter integration to use a REST source

We have seen how to use WSDL based endpoints for filtering and routing integrations, but how would the filter integration look and behave if we replaced the trigger with a REST connector and a JSON payload? While it should be possible to achieve the same integration, what does a REST connector look like that provides the two-way behavior we mentioned on the WSDL source? Is the mapping impacted at all by the fact we are receiving a JSON payload now? Our filter condition has also been a lot simpler, so we should try a more complex filter.

While we look at these points, we also have the opportunity to examine a couple of other important ideas such as CORS, which we have not yet seen in previous example integrations. This integration should look as follows:

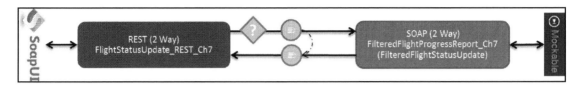

Creating the trigger REST connection

So we need to create a new REST connection. This process is started the same way as any other connector from within the connections part of the designer, except we choose the REST connector type. We can then provide the creation dialog with the following values:

Properties	Description
Connection Name	`FlightStatusReport_REST_Ch7`
Identifier	This will be proposed based on the connection name and there is no need to change unless you would like an alternate name
Connection Role	**Trigger**
Description	The description should be: `Receives flight status report information and returns relevant update information based on the update type`

With the connection description provided we can complete the remaining configuration of the REST endpoint with the details given in the following table:

Properties	Description
Email Address	Your e-mail address
Security I Security Policy	Select **Basic Authentication** as this is the only option available

As you can see, the REST endpoint connector is extremely simple; the majority of the REST details come into the equation when defining the use of the connection within the integration. We should have a REST connection configuration that looks something like the following screenshot:

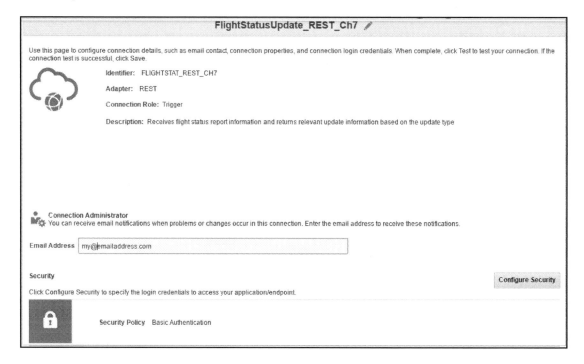

To complete the configuration, click on the **Test** and then **Save** button, and finally click on **Exit Connection**.

Cloning the filter integration

To shortcut some of the setup, we are going to use the clone facility again to reduce the amount of work. In the **Integrations** view use the **Clone** option on the `FilteredStatusReport_Ch7` integration and complete the clone creation process with the information given in the following table:

Properties	Description
Integration Name	`FilteredStatusReport_REST_Ch7`
Identifier	This will be proposed based on the connection name and there is no need to change unless you would like an alternate name
Version	`01.00.0000`
Package Name	`ics.book.ch7`
Description	The description should be: `This service will take the request and communicate to a backend system, returning the fully filled out response if the message type is accepted. The source will be represented in JSON format`

With this we have a completed integration. However, we need to replace the source, so select the source on the canvas and this will present the menu of options; click on the dustbin icon to delete the source. This will provide you with a warning, which we want to accept, so click on **Yes**.

Changing the invoke connector

In the list of connections, locate our newly created `FlightStatusReport_REST_Ch7` connection from the connections list to the right of the canvas and drag and drop it onto the **Trigger** pad. This will then display the endpoint configuration wizard. We can start to complete the wizard with the details given in the following table:

Tab	Properties	Description
Basic Info	**Call your endpoint field?**	To keep it simple call it `RESTSource`.
	What does this end point do?	Add the description: receives JSON formatted progress status messages.

	What is the endpoint's relative resource URI?	We want to add to the server URL the name `/FlightStatusUpdate/` for this service.
	What action does the endpoint perform?	As we are providing data we should be using `PUT` or `POST`, as we want a response it is better to use POST.
	Add and review parameters for this end point	As we are not going to use any parameters in the URL this should be unset.
	Configure a request payload for this endpoint	We do need to define the message payload, so this needs to set.
	Configure this endpoint to receive the response	We do need to define the response body, so this needs to be set.
	Configure request Headers	We do not want to modify any aspect of the HTTP request header so leave these unset.
	Configure Response Headers	We do not want to modify any aspect of the HTTP response header so leave these unset.
	Configure CORS	We can leave this unset.

Parameters

Classic REST will make use of URI to define object values in the path and/or query parameters as well. This means that ICS has to provide a means by which the URI can be processed to extract values; for example, `https://mywebService.com/products/101/` could be used to refer to products identified by an ID of `101`. In proper REST service terms this would return the details of `product 101`, but if we want to query all products for those containing `oil` you might have a URI like `https://mywebService.com/products/?contains=oil`, so you need to be able to link possible query values. In our case, we do not need any parameters or attribute related details in the URI.

HTTP Headers and CORS

Before we move onto the next tab, let's address two considerations that you may wish to use in the future – the use of headers and CORS. The use of HTTP headers was referenced in `Chapter 1`, *Introducing the Concepts and Terminology* and `Chapter 2`, *Integrating Our First Two Applications*. The HTTP header normally carries a number of standard parameters that describe the nature of the HTTP payload and its delivery as name value pairs. Best practice points to using custom header attributes for informational purposes only; for example, the data in a HTTP body originates from a web cache. Many of the additional header attributes have become de-facto standards, for example, pingback addresses for WordPress.

 More information on the HTTP standard and the header attributes can be found at the **Internet Engineering Task Force (IETF)** site – `https://www.ietf.org/rfc/rfc2616.txt` The IETF have taken over the task of managing the HTTP standard from the World Wide Web Consortium (W3C) – `https://www.w3.org/`.

Cross-Origin Resource Sharing (CORS), like HTTP, CORS has originated from the W3C to help address the problem where if a website then wants to exploit resources from a different website where these websites have different domains, (for example, `www.myWebsite.com` and `www.google.com`) as many of the HTTP API functions used by things such as JavaScript (for example, `XMLHttpRequest`, which is used by AJAX calls) are restricted calls within their own domain – for example, my web application provided by `www.MyWebsite.com` would not be allowed to call `www.google.com/API/GetSomeData`. This restriction is to mitigate against **Cross Site Scripting** attacks. The CORS standard, which is now realized by all recent browser versions, addresses this by working through an agreed set of types of interaction or through an agreed handshake protocol. The use of CORS when the handshake approach is used is done primarily through header attributes. The tick box provided by ICS provides the means to configure these headers.

 More information on CORS can be found at the W3C site – `https://www.w3.org/TR/cors/`. A working example of CORS in use can be seen at `http://www.html5rocks.com/en/tutorials/cors/`.

Having explored these other areas a bit more, we can move to the next tab using the **Next** button.

Configuring the Request

Having provided the details of the first tab, which informs how the remaining tabs will appear, we can start on the request information by completing the details as shown in the following table:

Tab	Section	Action
Request	**Accept attachments from Select the type of payload with which you want the endpoint to receive request**	If your REST service was taking an attachment – for example an upload service, then you would need to set this. As we do not want attachments leave unset.
	Request is HTML form	If the integration service is being invoked from a web form – then select as you will need to examine part of the HTML structure. Not so in this case, so leave the checkbox unchecked.
	Select the request payload file – XML Schema/JSON Sample radio buttons	Select the **JSON Sample**. We will complete this in next section.
	Element	This will appear once we have provided the JSON sample. The drop-down menu should be set to **request-wrapper** as this is the only option available.
	Select the type of payload with which you want the endpoint to receive	Within the HTTP header information is provided that describes the payload body. This toggle sets that attribute. In our case we simply want to pass JSON so our prior selections should have defaulted JSON, but confirm or force the selection of JSON.

Coming back to the payload request, we can provide our payload sample by using the file selector or paste it in for ICS to see. The file selection is no different to selecting a WSDL or any other file we have seen so far. We are going to choose the **<<< inline >>>** option. Click on **<<< inline >>>** to get a new screen displayed, as you can see in the following screenshot:

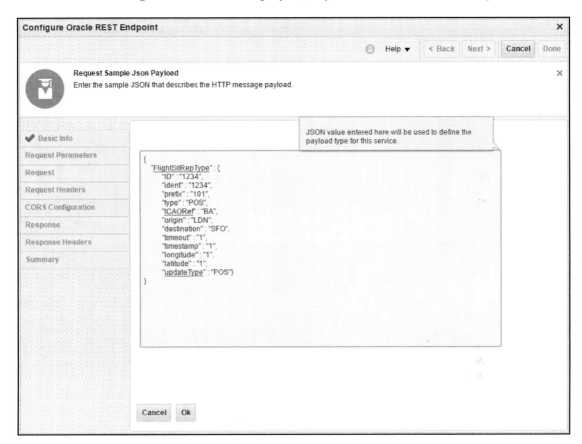

The JSON payload for the request has already been created and can be found with the other chapter resources, in a file called `ICSBook-Ch7-FlightProgress-Source-request.json`. The content of this file needs to be just pasted into the form. If the JSON within the form is incorrect, Oracle will alert you to this fact. The JSON content provided is valid, but by editing it you can see the validation fail the payload easily. With the valid JSON loaded, we can complete the dialog by clicking on the **OK** button. Then we need to move on to the next part of the configuration by clicking on the **Next** button. As we have chosen not to do anything with regards to the Request Header or CORS, this will take us into completing the details defining the response payload. The following table provides the details to complete this:

Tab	Section	Action
Response	**Select the response payload file – XML Schema/JSON Sample radio buttons**	Set the checkbox to be **JSON Sample**. You can complete this as we did with the **Request** or simply choose the file as we have done with the WSDL files. The file containing the JSON is called `ICSBook-Ch7-RoutedFlightStatusEnquiryResponse.json`.
	Element	This will appear once we have provided the **JSON Sample**. The drop-down menu should be set to **response-wrapper** as this is the only option available.
	Select the type of payload with which you want the endpoint to receive	Within the HTTP header information is provided that describes the payload body. This toggle sets that attribute. In our case we simply want to pass JSON so our prior selections should have defaulted JSON, but confirm or force the selection of JSON.

Reapplying mappings

Once the response details have been provided we can move on again with a click of the **Next** button. As we are not changing the Response Headers either, we will move onto the summary stage. The REST endpoint summary is like any other endpoint summary, so we can complete the process by clicking on the **Done** button.

As we have replaced the source, we will need to reapply the mappings; the details are given in the following table:

Source (execute | request wrapper | FlightSitRepType)	Target (FilteredFlightProgress)
`ID`	`ID`
`ident`	`ident`
`prefix`	`prefix`
`type`	`type`
`ICAORef`	`suffix`
`origin`	`origin`
`destination`	`destination`
`timeout`	`Timeout`
`timestamp`	`timestamp`
`longitude`	`longitude`
`latitude`	`latitude`
`updateType`	`updateType`

As with our original filter, we want to set the `notes` field on the target side to be a literal value, but this time the value should be JSON source. This will mean we can differentiate the call between the two integrations to the common `Mockable.io` endpoint. With that, the flow to `FilteredFlightProgress` mapping is complete and we can use the **Save** and **Exit Mapper** buttons.

We also need to reapply the `executeResponse` flow, with the mapping values given in the following table:

Source (FilteredFlightProgressResponse) and $SourceApplicationObject | execute | request wrapper	Target (FlightProgressResponse)
`ID` (from `$SourceApplicationObject`)	`ID`
`ident` (from `$SourceApplicationObject`)	`ident`
`prefix` (from `$SourceApplicationObject`)	`updateType`

We should also apply the same approach to the value for the target `notified` element where the `notified` element from `FilteredFlightProgressResponse` is prefixed using the string `concat` function with the literal value of `JSON response is`. The mapping should look something like:

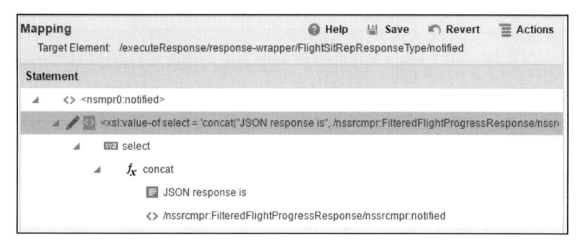

Again, save the mapping and exit. This just leaves applying the filter again.

Defining a multipart filter

When we first introduced filter capabilities, we highlighted the possibility of creating multipart filters. Unlike last time where we wanted POS messages, we are going to extend the expression to be allowed a POS report for only flights that have the `ICAORef` values for British Airways (BA) or KLM Royal Dutch Airlines (KLM).

The first step is to recreate the filter, as we explained earlier in the chapter. Once that is complete, click on the **()+** button; this will provide a menu with the **All of** and **Any of** values. As we want `ICAORef` to be accepted with a value of either `BA` or `KL` we should click on **Any of**.

This will display a new expression block where we can drag and drop `ICAORef` from the inputs side into the top field and set the bottom field to `BA`. To add the second condition as part of the **Any Of** list we click on the **+** symbol while the `BA` entry is still in the view, and then repeat this to define the KLM option. At the end of the process, the expression should appear as follows:

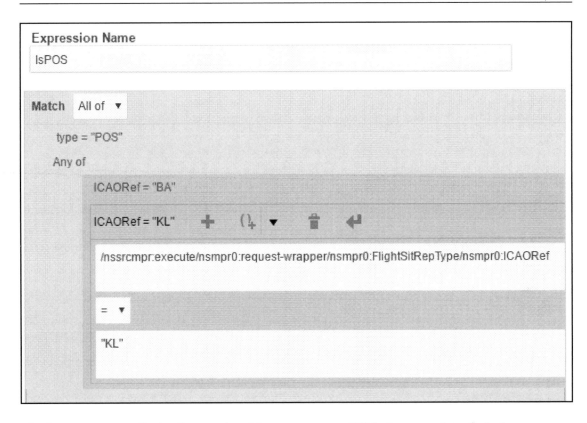

The last step is to edit the **Expression Name** to IsPOS. With that complete, as before we can save the condition and exit the **Condition Builder**. The integration is also complete, so we can save the entire integration and return from the integration editor back to the integrations list view, where we can activate the completed integration.

Running the REST filter service

We now need to add a new test call into SoapUI. Before we can do this we need to get the URL that will trigger the service. To get this information we should click on the integration's information icon and then click on the metadata URL included in the information. This will launch a new browser window with the metadata information; depending on how you have your browser set up, you may have to provide your normal ICS credentials as part of the process. The metadata screen will look something like the following:

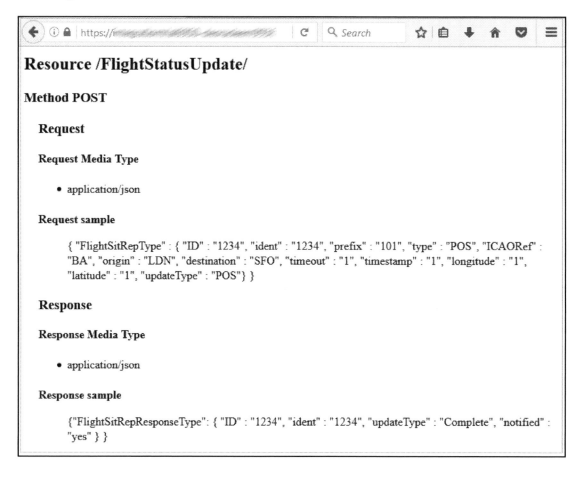

This can be done by selecting a project to hold the test call in, and then right-click on the project in the left-hand tree. In the presented menu of options, click on the **New RESTService from URL** option. This will pop up a new dialog where we can provide the REST service's URL (this can be derived from the browser's URL by swapping the reference to metadata to the resource name), for example: `https://XXXX.oraclecloud.com/integration/flowapi/rest/FILTEREDST_REST_CH7/v01/FlightStatusUpdate/` where XXX represents the domain name and data center of the ICS instance being used. With the URL provided, clicking on the **OK** button will result in a partially complete test request being displayed.

The request will need to be configured with the security credentials for the service call. The method needs to be set to `POST`, and we also need a test JSON payload to use. For a test payload we can copy in the sample JSON used while defining the endpoint (that is, the `ICSBook-Ch7-FlightProgress-Source-request.json` file in the chapter's resources). With that applied, the test call to the integration can be made. With the initial data value type being `POS`, and `ICAORef` being `BA` we get a successful result, as you can see here:

```
1  "FlightSitRepResponseType": {
2      "ID": "54321",
3      "ident": "1234",
4      "updateType": "POS",
5      "notified": "JSON response is success"
6  }}
```

However, if you call the integration with a type changed to `DPA`, for example, or swap the `ICAORef` to something that is not `BA` or `KL`, then you will receive an error back as the filter has blocked the call.

Summary

In this chapter, we started out looking at a very simple filter determining whether to allow a message to be sent to `Mockable.io`. We then extended this and turned the filter into a routing where, if the condition was not satisfied, it would be handled by an alternate route with a different mapping; we saw this in action. We then took the filter integration, swapping the source to a REST call, and extended the filtering conditions; in doing so we got to see a more complex filter being defined, but also explored some of the more advanced REST endpoint properties.

In the next chapter, we will look at how integrations can be connected to the Oracle Messaging Cloud Service for publishing and subscribing messages to third-party applications.

8
Publish and Subscribe with External Applications

In Chapter 3, *Distribute Messages Using the Pub-Sub Model,* we introduced the idea of publishing and subscribing within ICS and looked at the benefits of using such a framework. However, the ICS publish and subscribe mechanism only works within ICS and cannot be accessed directly from external applications. Oracle does, however, offer a service known as **Oracle Messaging Cloud Service** (**OMCS**) as part of its platform as a service group of services (`https://cloud.oracle.com/messaging`). This provides all the benefits of publish and subscribe, as well as a provider-consumer pattern.

OMCS is an enterprise messaging solution built using WebLogic Messaging at its heart, but it extends this to provide a framework, which means clients can utilize the messaging infrastructure through web services and have the means to mitigate against certain types of security attacks.

For developers, OMCS is a powerful tool, as it implements the mature industry standard API known as **Java Messaging Service** (**JMS**). This means that it can be very simple to integrate messaging into third-party solutions. In addition to this, ICS has an adapter dedicated to supporting OMCS.

In this chapter, we are going to demonstrate how OMCS can be easily connected to ICS; both as a triggering system and as a target for ICS to invoke.

Throughout this chapter, we will demonstrate a simple integration where we send aircraft updates into OMCS to then be consumed by ICS and placed in another OMCS message queue. The second message queue will be consumed by another part of the application that creates the events. Our application will preclude the need to use SoapUI in this chapter or any of the other mocking frameworks. This means that the integration will look like the following diagram:

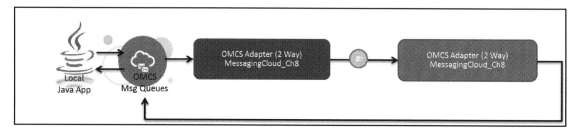

We are going to run the Java application locally, but there should not be any reason why it could not be executed from Oracle's Java Standard Edition Cloud Service if you wanted.

Preparation

First and foremost, we need an account that provides access to OMCS; this can be a trial account. We are not going to walk you through the process of applying for an OMCS trial service, as many of Oracle's services are straightforward and the chances are you may have used a trial account to get started with ICS. OMCS can be found at `https://cloud.oracle.com/messaging`. Additional information on setting up OMCS can be found at `https://oracle-integration.cloud`.

 For some Oracle PaaS solutions to work together, they are required to work within the same domain (that is, the domain ID provided when commissioning the service). Note that this is not the case for web services using WSDL and SOAP, but for other connections it is necessary. If in doubt, talk with Oracle before commissioning the services.

Once the service has been activated, no additional preparation with OMCS is needed, as our Java application will create the queues.

As you can see in the preceding diagram, we will need a small Java application. We could of course use SoapUI to load the message queue, but by using a Java application you get to see how you can communicate with OMCS via a JMS API. The Java application is available as source code, along with a JAR from the book's download site. With it are some configuration files you will need to modify to connect to your instance of ICS. This doe means you do not need to have any Java development skills, but you do need to have a JRE or JDK installed wherever you want to run the application from. Of course, if you are a developer, you will understand by looking at the code how to exploit the Java library provided.

We are going to assume you have successfully installed Java or have had it installed for you, and that it is available to you in the system PATH. This can be confirmed using the java -version command. If Java is installed and set up as needed, then you will see the Java version installed. If not, then either Java is not installed or not on your path. A solution for the latter can be found at https://www.java.com/en/download/help/path.xml.

Overview of our Java application

As previously mentioned, the Java application makes it easy to demonstrate the use of OMCS. By utilizing the OMCS library, our application is able to exploit the full capabilities of the JMS standard. As a result, when executing the application, it will read a .properties file, which will contain your OMCS credentials, and then connect to the server. It will check for the existence of two queues:

- TrackerQueue
- ProcessedQueue

If the queues do not already exist, then the application will create them. Once created, two threads are launched; one will read a file of position updates and add one every 30 seconds to the TrackerQueue. The messages (XML defined by a schema in the JAR file) in this queue are then passed to ICS, transformed and placed in the ProcessedQueue. A second thread in our application then consumes the messages in this queue. As each message is consumed, the application logs what is consumed, so you can see what is happening.

The dataset provided is large enough for you to see this happening for a couple of hours, giving you time to view the activity via the ICS monitoring views if you wish.

The application has been built in such a manner that, by adding some additional configuration information to the JAR file, it can be deployed and run in the Oracle Java Cloud `https://docs.oracle.com/cloud/latest/jcs_gs/` (WebLogic server in the cloud for hosting apps), or the Application Container Cloud `https://cloud.oracle.com/acc`, which can run Java SE style applications (along with other things such as Node.js), although we will not be using these services here.

Within the download resources are the resources necessary to enable you to rebuild the application, so it can be used as the basis for other experiments if desired.

Configuring ready to go

Once you have downloaded the JAR file, if you open the file (a JAR file is just a special zip file), you will see your preferred zip file tool in the various folders:

- Configuration attributes for OMCS–`\resources\instance.properties`
- Test data–`\resources\KL605_AMS_SFO.csv`
- Source code
- OMCS library
- Class files–`\ics\book\tracker`

We do need to do a little bit of configuring, as mentioned, so we need to extract and modify the OMCS connection–we need to tell the application which instance of the OMCS service to use and provide the authenticating credentials to allow a messaging connection to be established. The PROPERTIES file is called `instance.properties` and can be found in the `\resources` folder.

All the other changes are entirely up to you, such as the data to be played into the system, but in case you do want to change this, then the data is located at `\resources\`.

With all of this prepared, we can start the application up to ensure there are not any problems. To do this, you need to open a Command Prompt and issue the following command in a shell console:

```
java -jar "FlightPositionTracker.jar"
```

If everything has been successful, you should see something like the following screenshot:

You will note that the messages are being slowly added to one queue, but nothing is being retrieved from the output because the ICS integration is not running yet.

With our connectivity established and proven, let's stop the application and start setting up the ICS side of things.

The last piece of preparation is getting the `FlightPathOMCS.xsd`, which is provided. This schema is needed to allow us to define structure to the message payload for the inbound and outbound messages being put onto the OMCS provided queue.

OMCS connection

Using ICS with OMCS is just the same as any other integration; we need to establish appropriate connectors using the correct adapter, then create the integration applying the connectors and the relevant mappings and any desired enrichment. So, in the **Connections** list page, click on the **Create Connection** button and we get the usual popup, but we want to choose the **Oracle Messaging Cloud Service** option this time. The relevant connector is shown on the right-side, middle row, in the following screenshot:

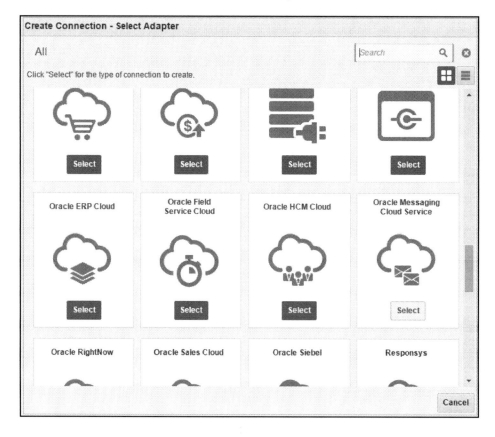

As usual, this results in a screen being displayed to define the connection name and other properties. We can complete this with the following details:

Property	Description
Connection Name	MessagingCloud_Ch8
Identifier	This will be proposed based on the connection name and there is no need to change unless you would like an alternate name.
Connection Role	**Trigger and Invoke**–as we are sending a message back on a different queue to the one received, we need to be able to trigger, but also invoke, through the same connection.
Description	Publish and subscribe to a Queue or Topic on the Messaging Cloud

Completing this screen by clicking on the **Done** button will then display the full connection dialog, as shown in the following screenshot:

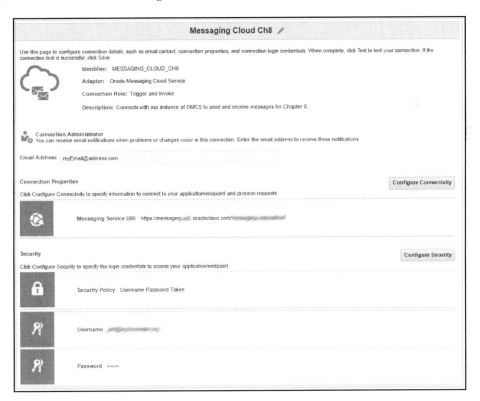

As you can see, the details needed relate to the instance and permissions to connect with OMCS. We can complete the connection details with the following:

Property	Description
Email Address	Your e-mail address.
Connection Properties | Messaging Service URI	Here you need to provide the URI of the OMCS service, which will have been identified when you created the service.
Credentials | Security Policy	Select **Username Password Token**.
Credentials | Username	Username that will be accepted by the OMCS service. You might want to create a separate set of credentials in OMCS for this.
Credentials | Password	This matches the provided OMCS credentials.

With these details provided, it just remains for us to click **Test** to ensure connectivity can be established, click **Save** and **Exit Connection**.

Creating the integration

With the connection successfully created and tested, we can start creating the integration. So, once we have navigated to the **Integrations** of the designer, we need to click on **New Integration** and select the **Basic Map Data** pattern. We can then define the integration as follows:

Property	Description
Integration Name	PositionMessaging_Ch8
Identifier	This will be proposed based on the connection name, and there is no need to change it unless you would like an alternate name.
Version	01.00.0000
Package Name	ics.book.ch8
Description	This will receive a position message on an OMCS queue and send a response message on another OMCS queue

Configuring Trigger and Invoke

With this complete, we can see the integration canvas. Locate the `MessagingCloud_Ch8` connection and drag and drop it on to the **Trigger** pad. This will launch the wizard for defining the message queue to receive messages on. The wizard, in many ways, will be a lot like the REST definition, as we need to describe the queue to receive from and the message payload, so that structure can be applied.

We can use the following details to complete the configuration:

Tab	Question	Action
Basic Info	**Call your endpoint field?**	To keep it simple, call it `source`.
	What does this end point do?	Add the description: `configure OMCS outbound`

You should have a screen that looks something like the following:

Click on the **Next** button, so we can configure the next **Operations** tab, which will look something like the following screenshot:

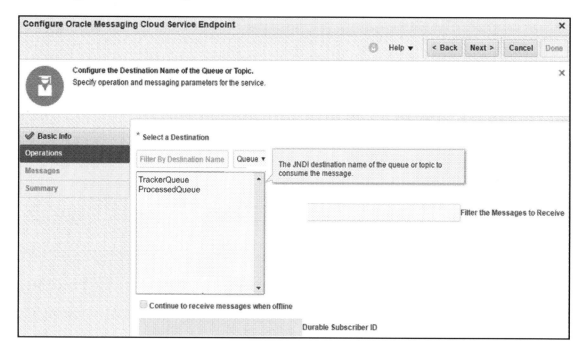

We can complete this tab using the following details:

Tab	Field	Action
Oracle Messaging Cloud Service	Destination Name Filter	A messaging service can be significantly populated with both queues and topics, therefore we can filter this down using the connection type (select **Queue**) and then by part of the name.
	Select Destination	With the list of options reduced, the option of our inbound queue (TrackerQueue) should be easier to select. The content of the list is derived from part of the naming service (JNDI) information provided by the underlying application server. This does mean that other unexpected services might appear here.

	Filter the Messages to Receive	This provides the means to filter messages down using elements in the JMS header. As we have elected not to use this we can leave this empty. In complex environments with a shared queue it is possible to filter down what is received–for example, by the header containing a recipient Id. So each recipient connected to the queue could then apply a filter for just their IDs. Information on the syntax of a selector can be found at `http://docs.oracle.com/javaee/6/api/javax/jms/Message.html`
	Continue to receive messages when offline	This is only applicable to **Topics**, as it declares the subscription as durable, so if we lose contact with OMCS then it will hold messages for ICS when connectivity is recovered. For this to work, OMCS needs an identifier for each subscriber so it can determine which messages need to still be consumed once connectivity is re-established.
	SubscriberID	If we want a durable subscription this value needs to be set. As durability is not an issue in our example this can be left unmodified.

Additional information about selectors can be obtained from the following.

The syntax for message selector criteria is aligned to SQL 92 specification, which can be found at: `http://www.contrib.andrew.cmu.edu/~shadow/sql/sql1992.txt,`

More information on JMS selectors can be seen at: `http://docs.oracle.com/javaee/6/api/javax/jms/Message.html`

The expressions limited to 255 characters and standard JMS header attributes are defined at: `https://docs.oracle.com/cd/E19798-01/821-1841/bnces/index.html`

Once this is complete, we have completed all the connectivity information and we can move on as usual by clicking the **Next** button. The next tab describes how to handle the messages, and looks like the following screenshot:

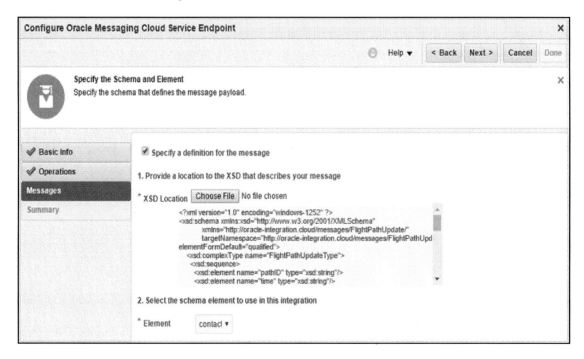

For our use case, we should configure the tab using the following details:

Tab	Field	Action
Oracle Messaging Cloud Service Message	Specify a definition for the message	We want to use a schema to provide structure to the message–so set this as ticked.
	Provide a location to the XSD that describes your message	Select **Choose File** and browse to where the chapter resources are and select the FlightPathOMCS.xsd file. By providing a schema, we are telling ICS that we expect the message payload to comply to this structure.

	Select the schema element to use in this integration	For the trigger, we want to use `FlightPathUpdate`, so select this value.

With these details provided, we can click the **Next** button to see the **Summary** tab. The **Summary** tab should represent the details provided. With that we can complete the wizard by clicking on the **Done** button.

With this, we can now define the invoke end of the integration. As we have defined our connection as both **Trigger** and **Invoke**, we can drag and drop the `MessageCloud_Ch8` connection onto the **Invoke** pad. We can then complete the definition with the following details:

Property	Sub-property	Description
Basic Info	**Call your endpoint field?**	To keep it simple, call it `target`.
	What does this end point do?	Add the description: `sends receipt confirmation messages back through OMCS`
Oracle Messaging Cloud Service	**Destination Name Filter**	A messaging service can be significantly populated with different queues and topics, therefore we can filter this down using the connection type (select **Queue**) and then by part of the name.
	Select Destination	With the list of options reduced, the option of our inbound queue should be easy to select–so select `ProcessedQueue`.
	Remove Message after 0 seconds	It is possible to limit the amount of time that a message may reside on OMCS before the message is then removed from the queue. This can be used if the message has a limited period of meaning and is not transactionally sensitive. In our case, we do not want messages lingering on the queue for the maximum 14 days. So set the value to 600 seconds (10 minutes).

This section, once complete, should look like the following screenshot:

With the connectivity aspects complete on the wizard, click on **Done** to define the payload aspects, using the following values:

Property	Sub-property	Description
Oracle Messaging Cloud Service	Specify a definition for the message	We want to use a schema to provide structure to the message–so set this checkbox.
	Provide a location to the XSD that describes your message	Select the **Upload File** and browse to where the chapter resources are and select the `FlightPathOMCS.xsd` file.
	Select the schema element to use in this integration	For the invoke, we want to use `ProcessedResult`, so select this value.

With these values applied, we can click on the **Next** button that will move us to the **Summary** tab, which should reflect the values provided. We can click on the **Done** button to conclude configuring the target connection.

Connecting endpoints and tracking

With the endpoints defined, we have two remaining steps–mapping the data so that the source and target data is manipulated and passed on, and configuring the tracking so that the information can be recorded during testing.

Select the mapping icon on the canvas, and use the following table to configure the mapping, as follows:

Source	Target
pathID	pathID

As the target only has one element that allows us to identify the update, we can provide simple linking and then close the mapper by clicking on **Save** and **Exit Mapper**.

To set up the tracking, click on the **Tracking** button and set the tracking to just use the pathID element. With that done, click on **Done**. On returning back to the integration, we should see something like the following screenshot:

Click on **Save** and then **Exit Integration**. We can activate this integration ready for testing.

Testing the integration

As we have already run the Java application, there may well be messages already in OMCS. We are not being definitive here, as a key element of this is the amount of time between testing the application and activating this integration–messages have a defined retention period within OMCS. With the integration activated and ready, we can start up the application, just as we did at the start of the chapter and watch the logs. After a brief period, depending upon timings of processes, we will see the response messages being consumed by the `SubscribeToCloud` thread from the OMCS `ProcessedQueue`.

The messages that we will be looking for in our test client are:

```
Oct 17, 2016 10:38:42 AM ics.book.tracker.subscribe.SubscribeToCloud run
INFO: ProcessedQueue: Response received for KL1620-2
```

Summary

In this chapter, we explored a simple application that allowed us to send and consume messages using the JMS standard implemented by OMCS. We then connected ICS and OMCS together by defining a connector. Finally, we created a simple integration that received a message with an XSD structure, mapped it, and pushed it out into another OMCS queue.

Although this is relatively simple, as an example, it is representative of the kinds of things that can be done to link ICS with other Oracle PaaS solutions that work in a more event-driven way. In Chapter 9, *Managed File Transfer with Scheduling*, we will look at the use of managed file transfers, which is a more technical connection technique that has some characteristics that are special to it. However, as file-based integration, it is typically a bulk model.

9
Managed File Transfer with Scheduling

While much of this book has focused on web services, some systems–both legacy and current, use file-based integrations. Legacy services may use them because integration technologies have been limited to file transfer. While contemporary solutions still choose file transfer as it is an effective way to move large volumes of data without exposing backend data stores as you might with **Extract Transform Load** (ETL)–the way Oracle describes and implements it. Oracle technologies perform the movement of data and then transform it within the destination data store (typically a database).

The movement of bulk data is often schedule driven and referred to as batch processing. As the need for data to be moved in a timely manner is increasing, we now come across the idea of micro-batching. This is simply the act of executing the batch process more frequently, with the batch being smaller. So, what used to be a nightly batch, may now be addressed by running it a couple of times per hour.

When file transfer is used as an integration approach, it is often used with some form of character delimiter. Most commonly, a comma is used as the delimiter (**Comma Separated Value**), although we do see the use of files with XML and JSON payloads, as they have the benefit of being self-describing.

ICS' support for files includes processing character-delimited files and mapping each line into an XML structure. Mapping the data into a defined structure makes using the contents structurally a lot easier. The need to include mapping will depend upon where you are using the connection within the different integration patterns that ICS offers. Presently, the **Basic Map Data** pattern is purely a scheduled file transfer framework, but within an Orchestration integration it becomes important as the **Orchestration** pattern has the ability to do a lot more. If you elect not to apply a schema to define the columns to the source or target file, then ICS file and FTP adapters might not behave quiet as you might expect. This is due to the way the underlying technologies used to implement the connectors work. We will talk a little more about this later in the chapter.

In this chapter, we will look at an FTP example using a **Basic Map Data** integration, then explore some of the possibilities available when using an FTP adapter within an Orchestration class of integration flow. We will not actually develop such an integration, as Chapter 10, *Advanced Orchestration with Branching and Asynchronous Flows*, will introduce Orchestration capabilities and its differences (for example, the way the canvas works differs, not to mention some of the capabilities). But combining Chapter 10, *Advanced Orchestration with Branching and Asynchronous Flows*, with what is shown here will enable you to build more advanced FTP based integrations. Before we get into a lot of the details, you may have already discovered ICS talks about FTP and File adapters, so let's start by looking at the differences between these two very similar adapters.

Differences between File and FTP connectors

ICS offers two adaptors geared up to handle flat files: one is called **File**, and the other is referred to as **File Transfer Protocol** (**FTP**). The difference between the two connectors comes down to how the file is accessed. We most often associate interaction with files in a remote location with FTP. To make files available using FTP you need an FTP server, which receives the client's calls and then interacts with the file system accordingly. So, how do you interact with a file that could be stored on a local machine where an FTP server does not exist or has network restrictions preventing direct access? This is where the File connector comes in. The File connector utilizes the connectivity agent as a sort of FTP server, allowing remote access without needing to instantiate a proper FTP server. As a result, if you look at the File adapter the configuration is focused on knowing which agent to interact with, whereas the FTP server needs connectivity details relating to the host and access credentials, much like a web service connector does.

As we cover the use of on-premises adapters in `Chapter 11`, *Calling an On-Premises API*, we have chosen to concentrate on using the FTP connection, as the steps for both connectors is exactly the same within the integration.

Scenario

Before we can create the prerequisites for our example, we first need to understand what the scenario is. As mentioned in the introduction, we will look at all the details of establishing a **Basic Map Data** FTP to FTP scenario before discussing how Orchestration can be used to realize some common FTP use cases, such as web service to FTP and FTP to web service. So, our example looks like:

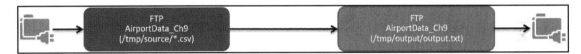

As you can see in the example, the process is extremely easy in so far as we will move data on the same server (purely for the convenience of not needing access to multiple servers).

Prerequisites

To work with the FTP connector, we will need some prerequisites. Firstly, we are going to need a web location that can be used for holding files and supports the **Secure FTP (SFTP)** standard. For the examples in the book, we will be using our book domain `https://oracle-integration.cloud/`. To implement these integrations you will need your own FTP service. If you have your own website, your hosting provider may well offer such a facility. If you do not, then there are a number of providers you could use for the purposes of the exercises in this book. To make life really easy, rather than fill the pages of this book with suggestions, we have shared some suggestions through the book's website.

We are going to need an FTP client. If you do not have one, then we would recommend the free cross-platform FileZilla client (`https://filezilla-project.org`). We will need this to load files in the source location and examine the target.

Finally, we will need some data. Within the resources for this chapter are a number of test files ready to be used.

Setting up FTP locations

Before we can do anything, the FTP locations need to be set up. Assuming you want to use FileZilla, we need to access the **Site Manager** screen (it can be found in the **File** menu). Within the **Site Manager**, as shown in the following screenshot, click on the **New Site** button. This will create an entry in the left-hand tree of sites and the name will be highlighted ready for you to key over the default. You might want to give it a meaningful name.

Then we complete the **General** tab on the right with the details based on the service being used. The **Host** field will be the domain name. You will need to set the **Logon Type** to **Normal** and provide the credentials necessary. Click on **OK**. This will save your configuration so that, in future, you can just click on the site name to connect to it:

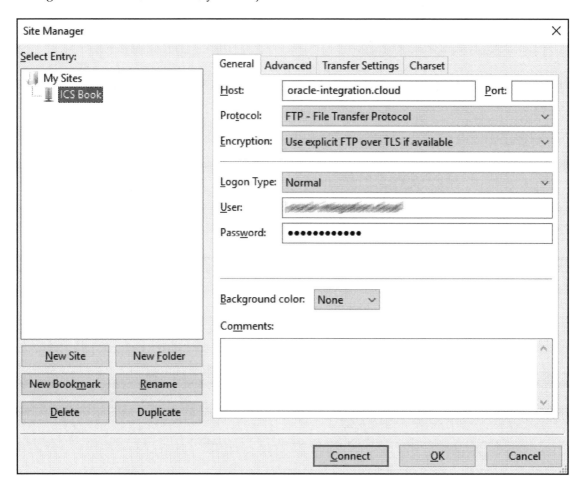

With the connection saved, re-enter the **Site Manager**, this time selecting the newly created connection. Then, click on the **Connect** button. Assuming all the configuration details are correct, you will get a connection to the FTP server. You will see information about the connection in the **Status** field. With a connection created, you need to populate the **Remote site** with a couple folders ready for us to use. In the **Remote site** panel, right-click and select the **Create Directory** option. Like any sort of file explorer/manager, a folder will be added ready for you to provide a name. To keep all of our content together, let's create a folder called `tmp` in which we will put everything we need on the FTP server. Then double-click on the `tmp` folder and repeat the process to create folders called `source`, `output`, and `output2`.

Creating the FTP connector

In ICS, we should go into the **Connections** part of the **Designer** and start creating the necessary connections. Select the **Create New Connections** button to launch the list of possible connections and select the **FTP** option. As usual, the **New Connection** dialog will be displayed, using the following values in the dialog:

Property	Value
Connection Name	`AirportData_Ch9`
Identifier	This will be proposed based on the connection name and there is no need to change it unless you would like an alternate name.
Connection Role	**Trigger** and **Invoke** (so that in a later scenario we can use this connection as the triggering source).
Description	`This connection will provide access to the secure FTP site for handling Airport description data.`

Click on the **Create** button. The **Connection Properties** process is very much the same as the process for a SOAP or REST connection. Populate the details as follows:

Property	Value
Email Address	Your e-mail address.
FTP Server Host Address	This is the domain part of your FTP URL. For this book we have used `https://oracle-integration.cloud/`. Your hosting provider will typically tell you what to use.

FTP Server Port	FTP and SFTP use standard server ports in most cases (typically port 22 for SFTP and 21 for FTP). As with the domain address, your hosting provider will confirm this; if not stated, it always tries port 21 first.
SFTP Connection	This indicates whether to use FTP or SFTP–we want to keep things simple, so select **No**. In a real-world application, it is best to work with the assumption that FTP must be secured.
Host Key	Leave blank–we are not going to use a host key.
SSL Certificate	Leave blank–we are not going to hold a local SSH certificate.
FTP Server Time Zone	Taking your local time and the timestamp of the file on the FTP server, you can deduce the probable time zone of the server.

It is worth exploring why we need to provide a time zone for our source FTP server. The FTP process can be configured to run against a schedule. After several minutes or hours, ICS will check the FTP server for new content. To be able to do that, it needs to know the time zone so it can determine the relative time difference to spot which files have changed or been added. Often, servers will run on what is often referred to as **Universal Time Code** (**UTC**). UTC is the same as GMT. The important thing is that the time zone being used by the server does not shift to compensate for daylight savings. If the server does do that, then you risk duplicate changes being detected as system clocks shift for daylight savings, or miss data accordingly (moving clocks back will mean timestamped events will come back into the scope of the next query).

 You will have noticed that both FTPS and SFTP can be supported–these are different approaches to securing FTP communications. To understand more about the differences, go to `https://en.wikipedia.org/wiki/FTPS`.

With the connection properties set, we can click on **OK** to continue. We need to complete the **Security** details for the FTP site; these details will match those entered into your FTP client (that is, FileZilla):

Property	Value
Security Policy	As we have elected to use FTP, the drop-down option is only **FTP Server Access Policy**.
User name	The username for the FTP site–the same as used in the FTP client to connect.

Password	This is the FTP site password, which was also used in the FTP client.
SSL Certificate Password	Leave blank.

With these values complete, we can close the dialog with the **OK** button. Test the connection (using the **Test** button). Assuming the test is successful, **Save** and press the **Exit Connection** button. Then navigate to the **Integration** part of the ICS tool.

The result should look something like the following:

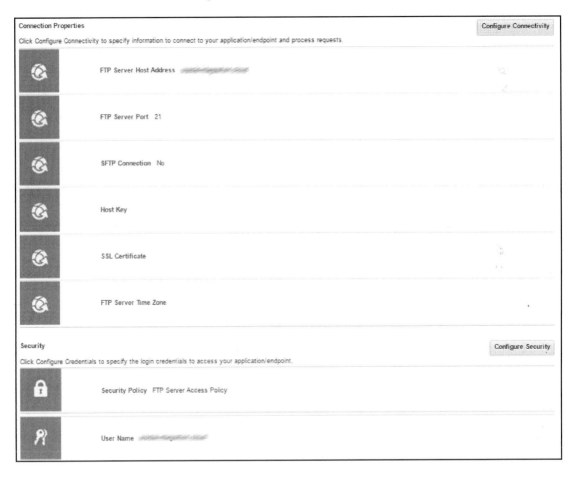

With the FTP connector in place, we need a second connector to send the data to the integration with. As we have created services like this before, we are going to provide you with just the details. Locate the WSDL file called `ICSBook-Ch9-AirportData-Client.WSDL`, which you will need to help establish the connector.

Property	Value
Connection Name	`AirportsUpdate_Ch9`
Identifier	As provided by ICS.
Connection Role	**Trigger**
Description	Provides an airport update.
Email Address	Your e-mail address.
WSDL URL | Connection Properties	Tick the **Upload File**, then use the **File** selection to upload the `ICSBook-Ch9-AirportData-Client.WSDL` Close with the **OK** button.
Security Policy | Credentials	Set **Security Policy** to **No Security Policy**. Close the dialog with the **OK** button.

With the information provided, click on the **Test** button, followed by the **Save** button, and then the **Exit Connector** button. With this done, we now have our connections ready.

Creating the FTP to FTP integration

With the connections defined, we can start with the integration. Let's create a new integration with the **Basic Map Data** pattern. Complete the creation dialog with the following values:

Property	Value
Integration Name	`MoveAirportsFiles_Ch9`
Identifier	This will be proposed based on the connection name and there is no need to change it unless you would like an alternative name.
Version	01.00.0000
Package Name	`ics.book.ch9`
Description	`This relocates files, ready for another service to consume.`

With the integration details provided, we can complete the dialog with the **Create** button, as normal. With this, we will be presented with the normal canvas. Locate the `AirportData_Ch9` connection and drop it onto the **Trigger** pad on the canvas. We can then configure the wizard with the details:

Tab	Question	Action
Basic Info	**What do you want to call your endpoint?**	As with all our other examples–we are keeping things simple with `source`
	What does this endpoint do?	`locate files to be moved`
	Do you want to define a schema for this end point?	As we are only moving files from one location to another we can set this to **No**.

This will result in a screen looking like:

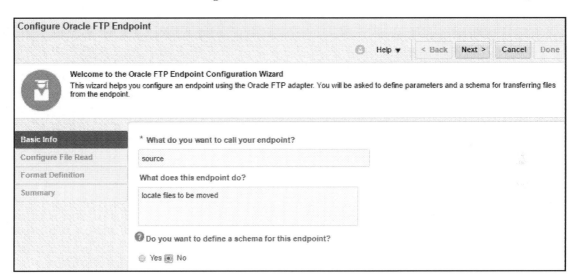

How to describe FTP file structure

Before we move on to the next section using the usual **Next** button, let's quickly explore the meaning of the schema option. In the **Orchestration** pattern of integrations, you need to define a structure to the file content if you want to process it in a manner beyond simply moving the file around. We will look at how this works in more detail later in this chapter.

The next panel captures the information about what files to process. So let's complete the dialog with the following details:

Section	Field	Value
Configure File Read	**Select a Transfer Mode**	The files we have provided as my may have noticed are textual. Ensure the **ASCII** option is selected
	Specify an Input Directory	This needs to reflect the path once you have connected to the FTP server. In our example you need to define it as `/tmp/source` (be careful about the capitalization)
	Specify a Filename Pattern	We want to be able to pick-up any CSV file, so use the pattern `*.csv`
	Maximum Files	This defines how many files can be processed in any single execution of the integration. You might wish to consider reducing this is the workload is going to be significant as depending on your processing you might experience subsequent problems for example, a slow processing cycle might result in connection timeouts with downstream processes. In this case we are not going to be using large files, and unlikely to actually create 100 files for transfer at once. We can leave the figure unchanged.
	Chunk size	This is the smallest number of files to process in one go. When processing by downstream processes carries a very large overhead, then you may choose to let the number of files build up before executing. As we want things to happen immediately–then we should leave this unchanged at 1.
	Processing Delay	The amount of time between each file processing that is required expressed in seconds. We can leave this with the default value of 0.
	Delete files after successful retrieval?	This setting is self-explanatory. To make it easy for us to see when things have triggered properly, ensure this is set to **Yes**.

The configuration should look something like this:

The final step is complete and clicking the **Next** button will take us to the **Summary** view, which should look something like this:

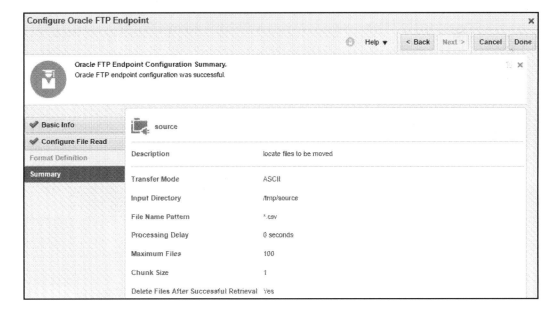

We can complete this phase with the **Done** button. We can now configure the target file system by dropping the same connection onto the **Trigger** pad on the canvas, so that the integration will look like this:

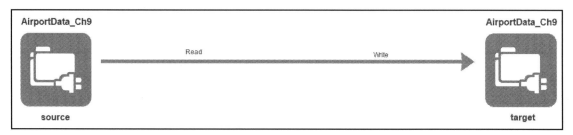

As with the trigger, the invoke goes through a similar sequence of screens.

Tab	Question	Action
Basic Info	**What do you want to call your endpoint?**	As with all our other examples–we are keeping things simple with `target`
	What does this endpoint do?	`Writes files to the target location`
	Do you want to define a schema for this end point?	As we are only moving files from one location to another we can set this to **No**.
	Do you want to enable PGP security?	We can encrypt the file using **PGP (Pretty Good Privacy)**. We will look a bit at PGP later in the chapter, so for now let's set this to **No**.
Configure File Write	**Select a Transfer Mode**	Set this to **ASCII** as we will be moving CSV files.
	Specify an Output Directory	Set the target to `/tmp/output` so we can see file being relocated.
	Specify a File Name Pattern	It is possible to define a file naming pattern, so that the name can include information such as a sequence number, or a timestamp. To illustrate this we can change the filename to be `moved%SEQ%.csv` so that the filename will contain a sequence number.
	Append to Existing File	Leave unticked as we want to have the same number of files in the target location as in the original source–it will make spotting the changes working.

We should see a **Summary** screen that should match the following image:

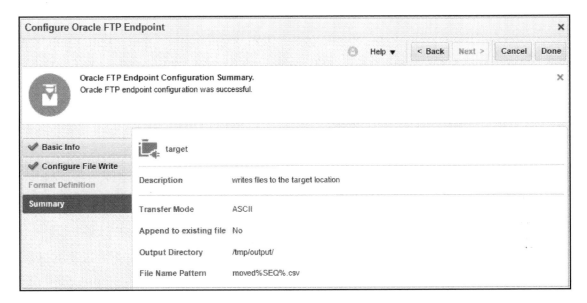

We can complete this configuration with the **Done** button, as normal. With this, we have an integration defined that should detect and move the files. Note the completion status of the integration. At this stage, the tracking values need to be set. However, the only tracking attribute that can be used is the file name. If you open the **Tracking** screen, you will see the details defined, and the options to modify this are greyed out.

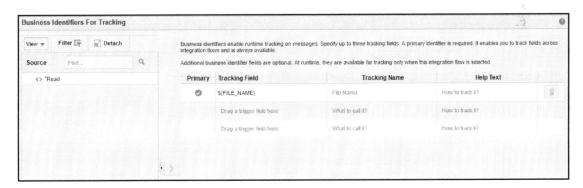

Close the **Tracking** screen, **Save** and click on the **Exit Integration** to take us back to the integrations list screen. Note how, next to the integration icon, is a schedule symbol reflecting the status of the schedule for detecting files in the source location.

Scheduling the integration

Click on the calendar icon and a new screen will be displayed that will allow us to set when a scheduler will trigger to execute the integration. It is possible to define a one-off event or a reoccurring event, as shown in the following screenshot:

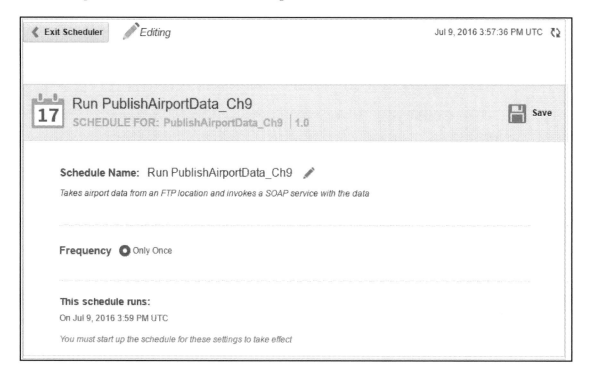

To set the schedule as reoccurring, deselect the **Frequency** toggle. This will result in a drop-down menu being presented beside the **Frequency** toggle. Select one of the **Days** or **Weeks** menus; you will then be presented with the means to select a number of weeks or months. Return back to the menu by clicking on the cross button at the end of the **Frequency** details, as can be seen in the following image:

Select **Hours and Minutes** and set the minutes to 11 minutes. To see the integration working easily, we want the integration to fire regularly. However, ICS will prevent the scheduler from running a schedule any more often than once every 10 minutes. With the frequency settings below, we can configure when to start the schedule from, whether the scheduler should run indefinitely, or until when it reaches a specific end date. We should limit the run of the integration by defining an end event date, so select a date and time and close with the **OK** button.

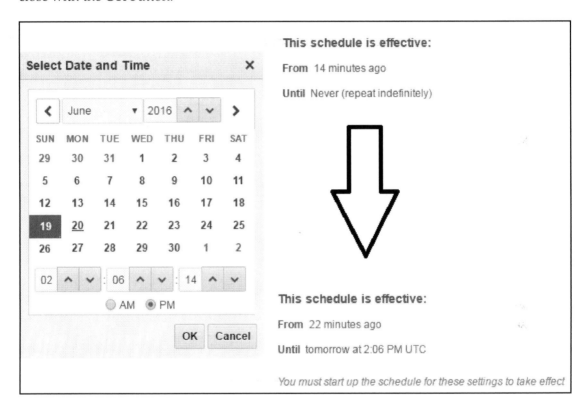

With the scheduler configured, we can click on the **Save** button and then the **Exit Scheduler** button, which takes us back to the screen to review and start the scheduler if the integration has been activated.

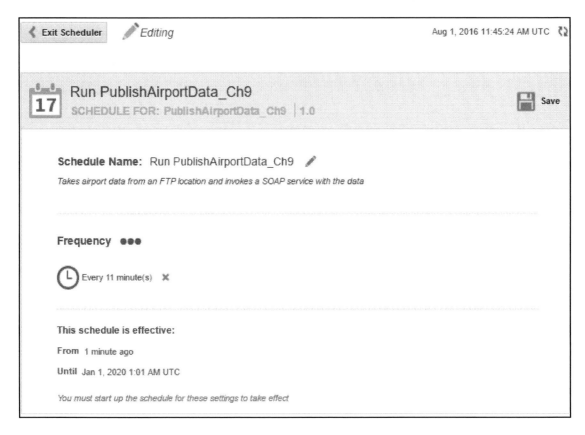

Once the schedule has been defined, we start it by clicking on the **Start Schedule**. The screen will now change to show when the schedule will be triggered. From this view, you also have several other possible operations, including reviewing previous executions with the **View Past Runs** button, pausing the schedule (**Pause** button), along with stopping the scheduled task with the **Stop Schedule** button. We are, however, going to let the schedule run.

With the scheduler running, if we reconnect to the FTP server with our FTP tool and look at the /tmp/source folder, we will see the number of files decreasing over time.

Once we have returned to the main integrations list, we can also trigger the integration manually whilst the integration is active. This can be done via the integration's drop-down menu on the main integrations list, which includes the option **Submit Now**. When clicked upon, it will trigger the integration with a confirmation message, displayed as follows:

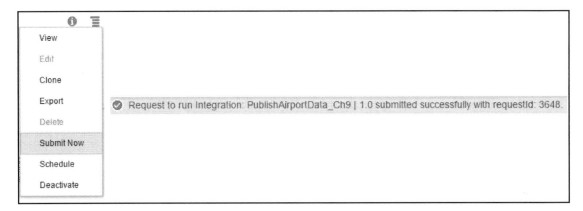

The same **Submit Now** option is presented as a button on the scheduler screen.

If we choose to deactivate the integration, the scheduler associated with it will be automatically stopped and will need reactivating with the integration again.

Using encryption

Before we can undertake the use of any encryption and/or decryption, we need a tool that can generate public and private keys and perform the appropriate encryption or decryption of the file. We have made use of the Java based open source tool Portable PGP (`http://ppgp.sourceforge.net/`), but there are plenty of other tools available. Once you have chosen the tool, we need a public and private key. The tool you select should provide guidance on how to create the keys if you need any help.

With the key files ready, to make the process quick let's clone `MoveAirportsFiles_Ch9`, as we have done in previous chapters, using the following details:

Property	Value
Integration Name	`MoveAirportsFiles_Ch9_2`
Identifier	This will be proposed based on the connection name and there is no need to change unless you would like an alternate name.

Version	01.00.0000
Package Name	`ics.book.ch9`
Description	`This builds upon MoveAirportsFiles_Ch9 this time` `encrypting the file's content.`

With the integration cloned, we can edit the target (**Invoke**) FTP adapter. On the first tab, we have a tick box available for encryption; this needs to be set now. This will then display an additional tick box asking **What security mode do you want to employ?** As our content is presently unencrypted, select **Encrypt**. If we try to move to the next page now, using the **Next** button, we will be presented with the following error:

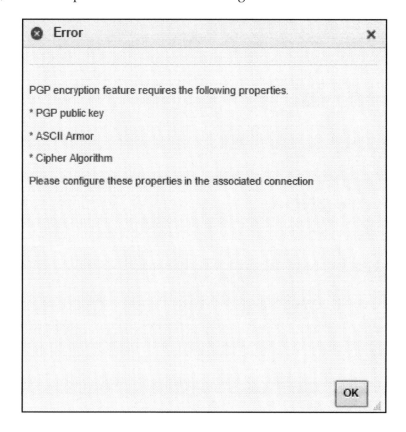

This means we need to go back to our connections to provide additional information, so close the dialog with the **OK** button, then leave the dialog with the **Cancel** button, leaving the integration unchanged.

Navigate over to the connections list. Rather than changing the connection that is working with our first integration, we should do the same thing as the integration and, using the menu, **Clone** the connection, using the following details:

Property	Value
Connection Name	AirportData_Ch9_2
Identifier	This will be proposed based on the connection name and there is no need to change unless you would like an alternate name.
Description	This is a variation on AirportData_Ch9 which supports the use of encryption.

This time, click on the **Configure Security** button and use the following values to complete the form:

Property	Value
Security Policy	As we have elected to use FTP then the only drop-down option is **FTP Server Access Policy**.
User name	The username for the FTP site–the same as used in the FTP client to connect.
Password	This is the FTP site password, which was also used in the FTP client.
Confirm Password	Repeat the password provided in the **Password** field.
SSL Certificate Password	Leave blank.
Confirm SSL Certificate Password	Leave blank.
PGP Public Key	Set this check box. This will provide an **Upload** button. Click on this and in the **File Section** dialog supply the public key created earlier.
Encryption Format	Set this to **True**.

Cipher algorithm	This field allows you to define on several encryption algorithms including CAST5, 3DES, AES128, AES192 and AES256. Provide the value `AES128`.
PGP Private Key	Leave unset.
Confirm PGP Private Key Password	Leave unset.

The screen will look like the following:

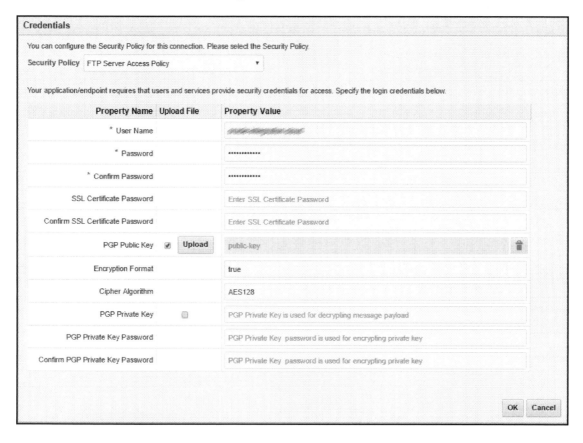

We can complete the dialog by clicking on the **OK** button, then using the **Test** and **Save** buttons on the connection. Finally, exit the connection.

With these details provided, we should return to the **Integrations** view and edit the `MoveAirportsFiles_Ch9_2` integration again. Within the integration, we should delete the invoke end of the integration from the palette and add the new connection (`AirportData_Ch9_2`) instead.

Tab	Question	Action
Basic Info	**What do you want to call your endpoint?**	As with all our other examples–we are keeping things simple with `target`
	What does this endpoint do?	`Writes files to the target location`
	Do you want to define a schema for this end point?	As we are only moving files from one location to another we can set this to **No**.
	Do you want to enable PGP security?	We can encrypt the file using **PGP** (**Pretty Good Privacy**). We will look a bit at PGP later in the chapter, so for now let's set this to **Yes**.
	What security mode do you want to employ?	As a result of saying yes, to the prior question, this option is then displayed. Select **Encrypt**
Configure File Write	**Select a Transfer Mode**	Set this to **ASCII** as we will be moving CSV files.
	Specify an Output Directory	Set the target to `/tmp/output` so we can see file being relocated.
	Specify a File Name Pattern	It is possible to define a file naming pattern, so that the name can include information such as a sequence number, or a timestamp. To illustrate this we can change the filename to be `movedEncrypted%SEQ%.csv` so that the filename will contain a sequence number.
	Append to Existing File	Leave unticked as we want to have the same number of files in the target location as in the original source–it will make spotting the changes working.

By clicking the **Done** button, this time we have successfully established the FTP invoke which will encrypt the files.

You may remember the earlier error mentioning details such as **ASCII Armor**–this comes into play when handling binary files using Base64 encoding.

ASCII-Armor means that the encrypted outcome can be represented using Base64. This means care needs to be taken when retrieving the file to decrypt, as the content will be binary. More information about PGP encryption and ASCII Armor can be seen at
`https://tools.ietf.org/html/rfc4880`

When the integration executes, using our FTP tool we should be able to find a new `movedEncrypted%SEQ%.csv` file in the target folder (you may need to force it to refresh it view of the server file system). If you examine the innards of the file, the content will be completely garbled as it is now encrypted. Retrieve the file from the FTP server and use a PGP decryption tool to decode the content (depending on the tool, you may need to provide the keys generated). When the file is decrypted, you should now be able to see the contents as a CSV file representing the information from the original CSV file used. We will not go through the process of creating an integration that uses the decrypt, as the process will essentially be the same–providing the appropriate key file and related credentials. Priming the test would mean encrypting a CSV file and then uploading it.

Common FTP use cases with Orchestration

Having provided a simple illustration, we should explore some of the richer use cases that are likely to be needed. The most likely scenarios are for integrating legacy environments with patterns such as:

- **Web service to FTP**: most likely to occur when wanting to create a file record of things happening for purposes of audit or where we have a contemporary system needing to send data to a legacy platform. The integration (or part of it) might look like:

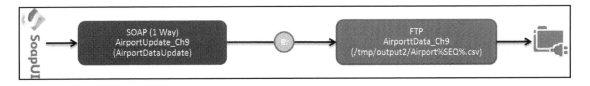

- **FTP to web service**: a case where legacy applications can only expose their data using files, so the only way to gather the data is to read the file in and process from there. For example, you might wish for your Orchestration to include:

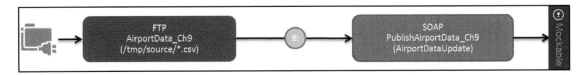

Extra steps to define structure for file content

To process a file in a meaningful way within an Orchestration, you need to be able to define some structure and meaning for the content. This can be done during the configuration of the connection within the Orchestration through the use of some additional screens within the wizard when the option **Do you want to define a schema or select an existing one? Is** set to **Yes**.

We can look at what these steps look like without needing to get involved in the details of the integration pattern, and we have also provided some files that you may wish to try using within the code files of this chapter. To continue the air flight based theme, our scenario is based on the idea of submitting airport data to a legacy system. You can source this data from several locations including `http://ourairports.com/data/`. Within the files provided, there is a full dataset (rather large) and a file called `airports_subset_Ch9.csv` which is a subset that we can to illustrate these additional steps. To configure the structural information, having confirmed we want to apply a schema, select that file (`airports_subset_Ch9.csv`). You might want to have a quick look inside the file first–you will note that the first row contains all the column names.

Having selected the file, we should complete the remaining values to be:

Section	Field	Action
Format Definition	**Selected Filename**	This should reflect the file provided–`airports_subset_Ch9.csv`
	Enter the record name	This is the name to use for a single line that is, `airport` (this is used in the definition of the schema)
	Enter the Recordset Name	`allAirports`
	Select the Field Delimiter	This provides a list of commonly used delimiters–our file uses Comma(,)
	Character Set	This allows us to define the characters being used so that languages with different characters can be supported for example Chinese. For our file we can leave this with **ASCII**

As the details are completed, the bottom of the screen will be populated to show the columns and some of the values of the file loaded, as you can see in the next screenshot. Note how the first row reflects the column names and the second row reflects the defaulted data types (for example, String).

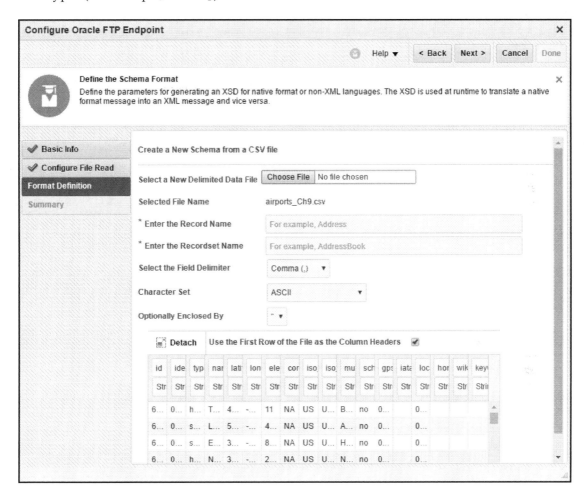

We can examine the mapping more closely and, if required it is possible to manipulate the data types. Click on the **Detach** button so we can examine the mapping more closely, as this will pop up the file view into a separate screen (as shown in the next figure). The top row of column names is derived from the information in the file and the tick box indicates that we have included into the file the first row which provides column names (you could override this if you wanted). It is also possible to manipulate both the column name and data type by selecting the field.

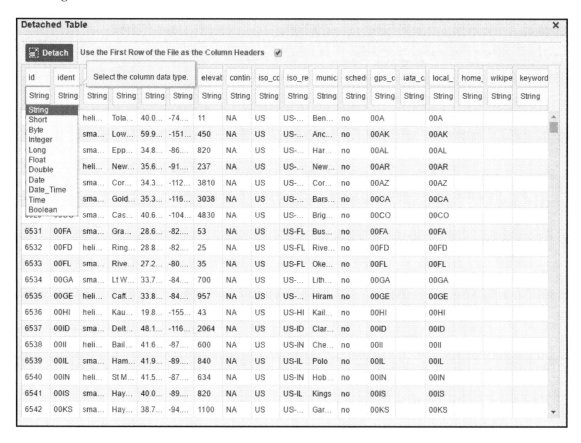

We can close the detached view just by using the cross in the top right corner (although we would always recommend using an **OK** or **Cancel** button). With the detached view closed, you can move onto the next panel.

On the **Summary** panel, when you complete the configuration of the endpoint, it will provide a means of showing the schema as a hyperlink. Click the link. This will result in a XSD representation being displayed.

With the completed mapping, it now becomes possible to realize a column by column mapping of the file's contents in any mapping operations.

Calculated filenames

We can also configure the integration to name the file or target folder based on the integration payload. Within a mapping view, you will be able to see an entry called `OutboundFTPHeaderType`, within this are elements called `fileName` and `directory`. By manipulating these values, we can dynamically set the filename and location of the output.

For example, if we are going to set the filename to be the test `Id` followed by the actual `Id` element from the source and set to be a `.txt` file, we can get a result such as `Id9001.txt` for a file. To do this we need to concatenate the literal values with `Id` element from the source. Click on the value `filename` on the target side of the tree to access the **Build Mappings** screen. Once in the **Mapping** screen, we need to drop the **concat** function onto the statement side of the editor (**concat** can be found by navigating the left menu to **Mapping Components** | **Functions** | **String**).

FTP integrations with interesting behaviors

Now we have looked at how to use the FTP connector with the use of mapping capabilities. However, as mentioned in the introduction to this chapter, things are a bit different when we do not use mapping capabilities. In the following section, we will look at these scenarios.

Using FTP without a schema mapping in Orchestration

To understand what happens without mapping, we need to understand a bit more about how the connector has been created. The connector builds upon a Java standard called the **Java Connector Architecture (JCA)**. When we use the mapping feature, the JCA connector is extended with additional intelligence to handle the schema definition and mapping. However, without this, ICS uses the basic File/FTP implementation of JCA.

The JCA implementation does not work with normal string types, but uses a data type called Base64. As files could be binary in nature (from executables to images), as well as textual, a consistent framework is needed that means the data is handled regardless of the hardware involved, and this leads to Base64. Base64 represents chunks of data (binary or strings) in a manner that allows the use of standard alphanumeric characters in its representation (if you look at a Base64 value, it will look like meaningless text). Given Base64's flexibility, it is a natural format to use with File and FTP handling.

The basic JCA implementation of a File or FTP adapter just supports Base64. Therefore, if you try to pass a normal string into a Base64 implementation, if you are lucky, it will just come up with a garbled result, but more likely it will cause an error as the conversion of the string to binary for storage is likely to fail with an error because the formatting requires specific numbers of characters, so the values need to be in Base64 format.

This creates something of a challenge as, out-of-the-box, there are not any conversion functions today that you can use within ICS. But there are several means of overcoming this; some more appealing than others:

- Export the transform and write into the exported artifact XSLT Base64 conversion mechanism and then reimport the transform. This approach can then be realized in two ways:
    - Locate the Base64 functions that Oracle must have to perform the mapping capability and exploit the XSLT–Java interface capability (more information can be seen at `https://docs.oracle.com/cd/B 19306_01/appdev.102/b14252/adx_j_xslt.htm#i1023310`).
    - Take advantage of an XSLT-only mapping solution. There are several available, such as https://github.com/ilyakharlamov/xslt_base64.
- Use the schema mapping mechanism in an intelligent way and describe a whole line as a single schema value (so you do not impose any structure beyond having one value for each line in a CSV).

Whilst the import/export approach may be more technically correct, it does require a good understanding of how to manipulate the expressions outside of ICS. It also relies on ICS' implementation not changing, to an extent (if the Base64 libraries were changed, for example, then the transform would break). Finally, it also raises the question of what happens if someone wants to come along later and modify the transformation, whether they know you need to manipulate the transform outside of ICS, and whether they know how.

As for the second option, while inelegant and subject to a couple of limitations, it does mean that all the work can remain within ICS.

 For more information on Base64, visit `https://www.base64decode.org/`.
To learn more about JCA, visit
`http://docs.oracle.com/javaee/5/tutorial/doc/bncjx.html`

Implementing the single value mapping technique

We have already illustrated how to create FTP sources and targets. To apply the idea described, we simply need to change the example CSV file that gets imported. We achieve this with a fake CSV that we have created, which contains a row that gets picked up as the output name and a second line simply containing a blank space character. Importing this has the following result:

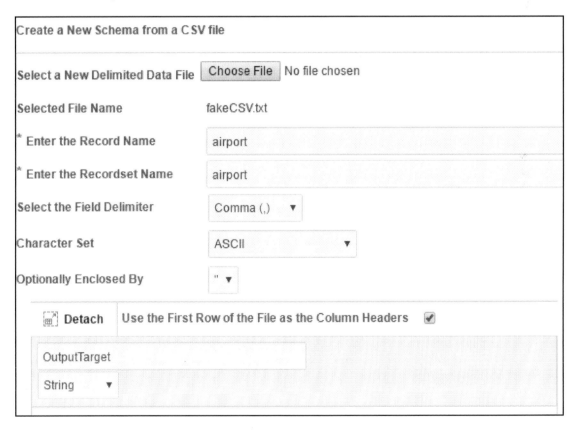

With this endpoint defined, the final step is to map the output values using the mapper to form the appropriate string structure–for example, XML or JSON forms. This approach will admittedly look ungainly in the mapper.

Summary

In this chapter, we have examined a range of capabilities of FTP and the File connector will behave the same way when using the connectivity agent (which is covered in Chapter 11, *Calling an On-Premises API*). We have looked at the use of the scheduler to trigger an integration, along with the manual trigger of the integration. We have explored some more advanced strategies for data transformation. We have also examined file encryption and decryption. Finally, we looked at how ICS is evolving in this area and how it is likely to become significantly more feature rich.

The next chapter introduces how ICS provides a means of performing a level of Orchestration in the integration.

10
Advanced Orchestration with Branching and Asynchronous Flows

In the previous chapters we built integrations that primarily had one source (trigger) and one target (invoke) service connection. Within some of our integrations we extended this by introducing enrichment services and chaining integrations using the publish/subscribe pattern. This kind of service could be called after the message was received by the source connection or after receiving the response from the target connection, just before sending the response back to the caller of the source connection. Between these service calls we transformed the message so that the message was in the correct form to be understood by the receiver of the message.

In the previous chapters you might have noticed that we were restricted in making different decisions based on the message content and the limited possibility of chaining service calls.

In this chapter we want to introduce you to orchestration. In Chapter 1, *Introducing the Concepts and Terminology*, we discussed the basic concepts of orchestration. Orchestration is another pattern that ICS supports and with it we can make more intelligent decisions based on the result of a previous activity. With orchestration we can chain activities (for example, services) to automate certain tasks, perform specific activities based on an expression (branching), and the combine results of multiple activities. In upcoming releases of ICS we will see a huge growth in functionality for this type of integration.

If you are familiar with orchestration in the context of **Business Process Execution Language** (**BPEL**) then you will notice some similarities. For example, building the actual orchestration uses a similar UI to JDeveloper's BPEL Designer for SOA Suite and will include, as time goes by, more and more activities we know of from the on-premises SOA suite.

To demonstrate this integration pattern we will revisit some of the connections and integrations we built in previous chapters and reuse them in our orchestration to perform multiple activities based on one incoming event. The following diagram shows the final state of the orchestration as we work through the chapter:

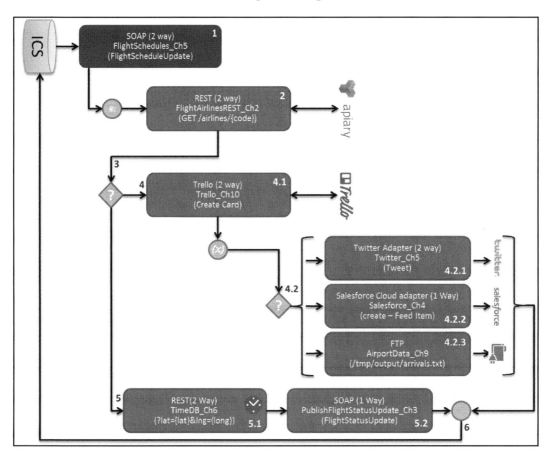

The orchestration will cover to following scenario:

1. The orchestration triggers when it receives a call about a flight schedule change from the ICS integration.
2. The process calls the `FlightAirlineREST` endpoint used in `Chapter 2`, *Integrating Our First Two Applications* to get additional information about the airline.
3. Depending on the flight status, the request is branched. There is a branch for flights that have arrived at the gate and one for other updates.
4. When a flight has arrived at the gate then the following flow will be executed:
   - The Trello API is called to create a new card/task for the ground personnel to unload the cargo from the plane.
   - Based on the social preference received from the `FlightAPI` call, the request is branched for a second time. A message announcing the arrival is either sent to:
     - Twitter: `Chapter 5`, *Going Social with Twitter and Google.*
     - Salesforce: `Chapter 4`, *Integrations between SaaS Applications.*
     - File: `Chapter 9`, *Managed File Transfer with Scheduling.*
5. When the orchestration receives a different status update the message is:
   - Enriched by calling the `TimeService` endpoint used in `Chapter 6`, *Creating Complex Transformations.*
   - Sent to our existing `PublishFlightStatusUpdate` integration used in `Chapter 3`, *Distribute Messages Using the Pub-Sub Model.*
6. Both branches return with a synchronous reply back to the caller.

Getting ready

Before we get started we need to have all connections ready for use in our orchestration. As we mentioned we are going to reuse some already existing connections, but we also have some new connections that we are going to use. The new connections include `Trello` and an updated version of the `FlightAirlineREST` API (used in `Chapter 2`, *Integrating Our First Two Applications*) which we need to set up.

For Trello, we are using another OOTB Cloud adapter. With this cloud adapter it is possible to, for example, retrieve a list of all tasks, update a task list, and create new tasks. Depending on the operation you choose you get a different response. Within the orchestration we are free to use it elsewhere in the process. For the `Flight` API, we are reusing the already existing connection, but we will update the API definition in apiary to include a new resource to have airline details include social preferences.

Setting up Trello

For this orchestration, we are going to use Trello. This is a collaboration tool that organizes projects and tasks into boards and lists. It can tell what is being worked on, who is working on what, and where something is in a process. The Trello API with the adapter offers operations to let you search, read, create, and update the board, task content, and metadata. In our case we are creating a new task for ground personnel when a flight has arrived at the gate. To complete our setup of Trello, we need to execute the following steps:

1. Get access to a Trello account.
2. Create a new Board and Tasks list.
3. Obtain list identification.
4. Obtain API credentials.

Step 1 – Getting access to a Trello account

For this integration, we can use any Trello account you can get access to. If you do not have an account yet, or want to have an extra account for testing purposes, go to `trello.com/signup` and follow the instructions.

Step 2 – Creating a new board and tasks list

To allow ICS to interact with your Trello account we need to create a board and a list to add tasks to. Once logged in to Trello with the account, you are presented with the start page, which shows all boards. Notice that by default one board is already created, but we are not going to use this board. For our orchestration we are going to create a new board called `AirlineCX`. Click on the gray box containing the text **Create new board...** Enter the title `AirlineCX` and click on **Create**.

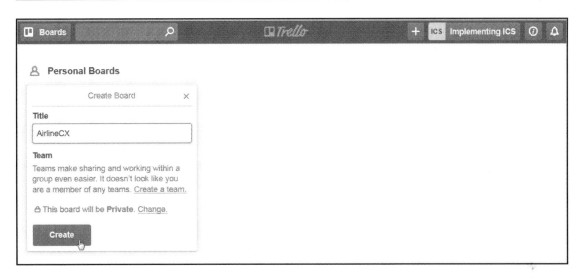

After creating the board, we are automatically redirected to its content. On this page we can create a new list. Before we continue, let's open the browser developer console so we can see what API calls are being executed. We will need the value of the id field in the response JSON of the call creating the list. In Firefox and Chrome it's available when pressing *F12*. In Firefox click on the **NET** tab and in Chrome click on the **Network** tab. We are doing it this way, because Trello is a single-page application and can not retrieve it by looking at the URL when looking at the list. Click on the dark blue area with the text **Add a list...** This will show a small dialog. Call the list FlightArrivals and create the list by pressing *Enter* or click on **Save**.

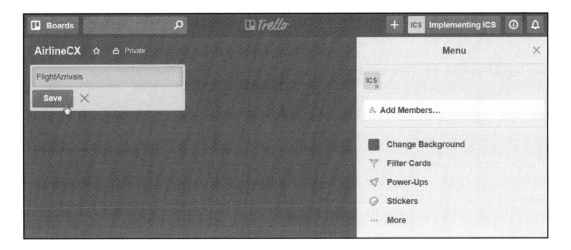

Step 3 – Obtaining a list identification

To create tasks or cards in this case we need the ID of the list that was just created. If we look in the developer console we can see that a `POST` method is called to one of the Tello APIs (that is, lists). Click on the API call and view the **Response** of the call. The response is a JSON message which has an attribute `id`. Write the value down since we will need to use it when mapping the request message. The following screenshot shows an example from Chrome:

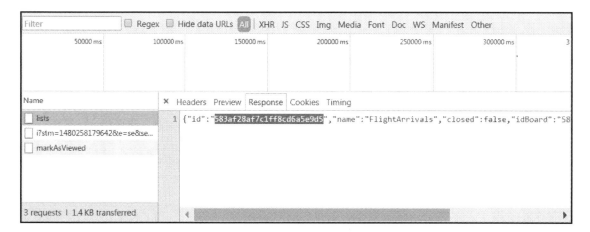

Step 4 – Obtaining API credentials

The last step of the configuration phase is to collect the API credentials. We can collect the necessary credentials from the developer console of Trello. Open a new browser tab and navigate to `https://trello.com/app-key`. We can obtain the developer API key at the top of the page and the OAuth secret further down the page. Keep a note of both values so we have them at hand later on.

Updating the apiary Flight API

For this orchestration, we are reusing the Flight API built using apiary in `Chapter 2`, *Integrating Our First Two Applications*. In the current state the Flight API only has one resource, providing a list of all airlines and the details of each airline in the list. We are going to add two more resources to get a specific airline based on a flight airline code (two characters).

To update the Flight API in apiary we need to execute these steps:

1. Log in into apiary and switch to the Flight API endpoint.
2. Change the source of the API Blueprint.

Step 1 – Log in to apiary and switch the API

To allow ICS to retrieve specific airline information we need to change the blueprint of the API. Go to `login.apiary.io`, and log in with your credentials. If you have only one API on your account you are redirected to the **ICS Flights API**; otherwise you can click on the name of the current selected API and switch to the **ICS Flights API** as shown in the following screenshot:

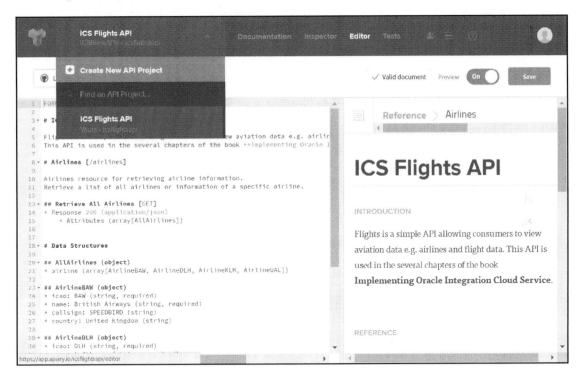

Step 2 – Change the source of the API Blueprint

We want to add two new resources that ICS can call to get specific airline information based on the first two letters of the flight identification. For example, `Flight KL1606` will result in the `Flight Code KL`.

We are going to add the resource `/airlines/BA` and the resource `/airlines/KL`. The first resource will return the `AirlineBAW` object and the second resource will return the `AirlineKLM` object defined in our API blueprint as follows:

```
18  # Airline By Code BA [/airlines/BA]
19
20  Airline resource for retrieving specific British Airways information.
21  Retrieve an airline by its *2-char code*.
22
23  ## Retrieve Airline [GET]
24  + Response 200 (application/json)
25      + Attributes (AirlineBAW)
```

For our purpose, in the orchestration we also need to edit these objects to include a new `social` property. The `AirlineBAW` object will get the value `Salesforce` and the `AirlineKLM` object will get the value `Twitter` as shown in the following screenshot:

```
56  ## AirlineKLM (object)
57  + icao: KLM (string, required)
58  + name: KLM (string, required)
59  + callsign: KLM (string)
60  + country: The Netherlands (string)
61  + social: Twitter
```

For convenience the new API blueprint is included in the source files of the book for this chapter. Just copy the content of the file `ICSBook-Ch10-Apiary-Flights-API.apib` into the editor of your Flight API in apiary and save it. If you want, you can test the new resources as explained in `Chapter 2`, *Integrating Our First Two Applications*.

Defining the necessary connections

In this chapter, we will reuse most of the inbound and outbound connections from previous chapters. The only connection that we need to create is the one to the Trello API. You should have created all the other connections in past chapters, but we will need to update one to also work as an invoke connection.

In ICS, navigate to the connections page and create a connection using the Trello adapter. Create a connection to Trello with the following details:

Property	Value
Connection Name	Trello_Ch10
Identifier	This will be proposed based on the connection name and there is no need to change it unless you would like an alternative name
Connection Role	**Invoke**
Description	The description should be: This connection interacts with the Trello API to for example create or list tasks

After creation, configure the connection with the following details:

Property	Value
Email Address	Your e-mail address
Configure Security | Credentials	Set **Security Policy** to **Custom Security Policy**. Enter the values we collected in the fourth step of the setup for API Key and Oauth Secret.
	We also need to provide the access scope for this connection. Enter: read, write

Before we can save the values we need to give ICS consent to use our Trello API key. Click the **Provide Consent** button. A new window/tab (depending on your browser) is opened in the browser and redirects us to Trello. If you are not already logged in, do so. In the consent screen, click **Allow** to accept the access rules as shown in the following screenshot:

Return to the browser tab with ICS and notice that the credentials are accepted. Test the connection to validate the configuration. After validating the connection, click the **Save** and **Exit Connection** button.

We mentioned earlier that we need to update one connection to work as an invoke. We need to edit the connection `FlightSitRep_Ch3` and change the WSDL that's being used. The WSDL structure itself is not changed, only the endpoint we are calling; this, we can use it as an invoke in our orchestration. In the book's resources for this chapter, you will find a copy of the definition `ICSBook-Ch3-FlightProgress-Source.WSDL` used in chapter 3, *Distribute Messages Using Pub-Sub Model*. Edit this file and change the attribute `wsdl:service/soap:address/@location` to represent the URL location of the `PublishFlightStatusUpdate_Ch3` integration. Next, edit the connection `FlightSitRep_Ch3` and upload the new WSDL. When saving the connection you are presented with a warning, which you can safely accept.

Checking if all connections are created

In addition to the connections added and modified, we want to reuse several other connections that are part of the previous chapters and we assume these connection are available now. For the orchestration we need the following connections to exist:

Connection	Created in
FlightAirlinesREST_Ch2	Chapter 2, *Integrating Our First Two Applications*
FlightSitRep_Ch3	Chapter 3, *Distribute Messages Using the Pub-Sub Model*
Salesforce_Ch4	Chapter 4, *Integrations between SaaS Applications*
Twitter_Ch5	Chapter 5, *Going Social with Twitter and Google*
TimeDB_Ch6	Chapter 6, *Creating Complex Transformations*
AirportData_Ch9	Chapter 9, *Managing File Transfers with Scheduling*

If the connections are unavailable, then you are going to need to return to these chapters to create the connections to complete the preparation needed.

Building the orchestration

With the connectors established we can create the orchestration. Instead of creating an integration with the **Basic Map Data** pattern, we are doing something different this time. Create an integration with the **Orchestration** pattern as shown in the following screenshot:

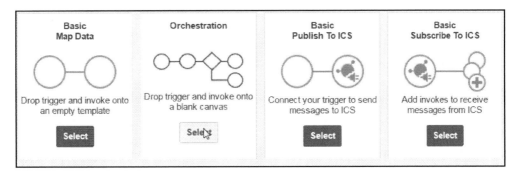

Create the orchestration using the following details:

Property	Value
Integration Name	`FlightScheduleUpdateProcess_Ch10`
Identifier	This will be proposed based on the connection name and there is no need to change it unless you would like an alternate name
Version	`01.00.0000`
Package Name	`ics.book.ch10`
Description	The description should be: `This orchestration will take the ScheduleUpdate request and will call different services based on the flight identification`

With the empty orchestration created you can immediately see that the UI is different from a basic map data pattern of integration. The UI and functionalities offered will progressively change based on the completeness of the orchestration.

It uses a different UI and workflow

The most important difference between UI and workflow The most important difference between a basic map database integration and an orchestration-based integration is that orchestrations can invoke an unlimited number of services instead of only one. The other difference lies in the way it is visually structured. Basic integrations are presented as horizontally structured, whereas orchestrations are vertically structured. When creating a new orchestration the UI shows an empty start point and an arrow pointing to the end. On the left-side you see a panel called **TRIGGERS**, which when expanded lists the adapter types for which you created one or more trigger connections. The trigger creates the inbound connection into our integration, as shown next:

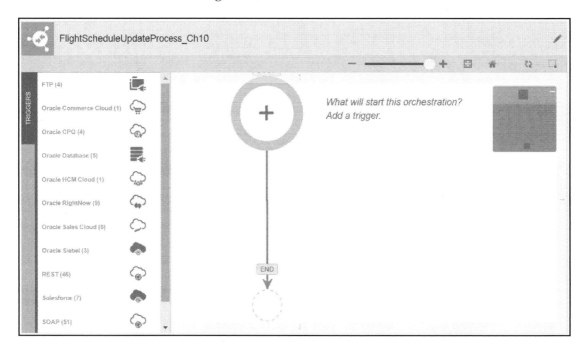

To display the configured adapters for the specific adapter type, click the adapter type and the appropriate adapters will be shown. The triggers that are supported can be synchronous, asynchronous, and fire-and-forget (one-way without response). For our orchestration we going to use the SOAP connection named FlightSchedules_Ch5, which we created in Chapter 5, *Going Social with Twitter and Google* as our start point. Expand the adapter type for SOAP connections and drag and drop FlightSchedules_Ch5 to the start point/trigger spot indicated by the large plus (**+**) symbol as shown in the following screenshot:

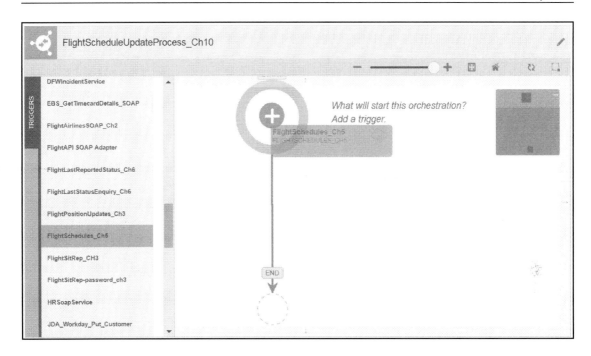

 You can start an orchestration with a REST service (or any other service) just as easily if you want.

Dropping a connection onto the canvas will result in the same wizard being displayed as we would see in a basic map data integration for that kind of connection; this will allow us to define the exact behavior wanted. Complete the endpoint configuration wizard with the following values:

Tab	Question	Action
Basic Info	Call your endpoint field?	Because of multiple operations call it ScheduleUpdate
	What does this end point do?	Add the description: provides the parameters to request a schedule update for the identified flight which triggers the orchestration
Operations	Selected Port Type	This is automatically selected because only one is defined that is, FlightSchedulesPortType

	Select the Operation	Select `FlightScheduleUpdate`
	Request Object	The objects that are assigned to the operation are displayed. These values change when a different operation is selected.
	Response Object	
	Fault Object	
	Disable validation	Select **No**.
Summary	**WSDL URL**	The Summary tab as always shows the selected connector information: The Cloud Operation matches the operation we selected in the Operations tab that is, `FlightScheduleUpdate`.
	Selected Port Type	
	Cloud Operation	
	Message Exchange Pattern	

After completing the dialog, the orchestration is updated. Because we chose a synchronous operation in the endpoint configuration, ICS automatically creates several elements, specifically:

1. A trigger.
2. An unconfigured map.
3. And a return action.

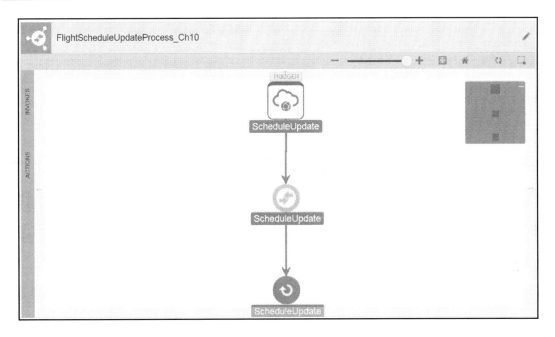

If the trigger connection has a fire-and-forget behavior then a stop action is created. If the connection was asynchronous it automatically creates an unconfigured map action and a callback action based on the one you selected when creating the trigger.

Before we go further with building our orchestration process, we want to go through the UI and the available building blocks (activities), for implementing our orchestration. At the top-right several icons are provided for adjusting the size of the integration canvas. The integration can be zoomed out (decrease size), zoomed in (increase size), and zoomed to fit the page. With the home icon we can align the integration to a normal size in the upper left corner of the page. The reset icon resets integration back to the normal size.

Activities can be moved separately on the integration canvas, but it is also possible to move multiple activities by enabling multiple select, which is the last icon on the right. Drag the cursor around parts of the integration you want to select. Below the icons you will find a box that shows the scale of the integration we are building. You can place your cursor within the box or on the canvas to move the view of your integration, as shown in the following screenshot:

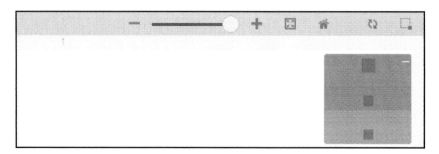

From simple to more advanced actions

On the left you will find two collapsed panels holding the available activities: **invokes** and **actions**. If you click on the **invokes** panel it expands and lists the types of adapter, for which you created one or more invoke connections. The invoke adapters that are supported can be synchronous, and fire-and-forget. If you click on **action** the panel expands and lists the available building blocks to complete your orchestration. Let us look at these actions first.

Action	Purpose
Assign	Enables you to assign variables from data that is available in the integration or assign literal values to variables. Variables you create can be used in mappers and in expressions. The variables are only available to this integration.
Callback	Enables you to end a process and return to the trigger. The callback action is only available if the trigger supports callbacks.
Map	Enables you to add ad hoc mappers to the integration. A map action is normally placed before an invoke action. The target element of the map is the source element of the invoke. The source elements of the map are the variables that are available at that time in the process.

Return	Enables you to return an immediate response. The return action is only available when the trigger is synchronous. A synchronous operation always has a return, usually at the end, but for example in a branch (of a switch) we can send a response earlier when another branch is executed.
Stop	Enables you to terminate the integration. This action is available when we are dealing with a fire-and-forget trigger or a trigger that supports callbacks. With this action no response message is returned to the trigger.
Switch	Enables you to add a switch activity for defining branches based on the routing expression in the integration. For example, if x=y execute the first branch, otherwise execute the other branch.

ICS is being regularly enhanced with additional capabilities; a number of these will resemble those provided by the SOA suite as both products look to address orchestration requirements. It is important to remember that, while SOA is guaranteed to align to the BPEL standard, ICS is not bound to these standards. Let's have a look at these more advanced actions:

Action	Purpose
Callout	Enables you to invoke callout functions to execute logic that is not possible with the standard available functionality. The callout functions are JavaScript-based, but can be compared with custom XPath functions in XSLT.
For each	Enables you to loop on files (batches) and on records (array of elements) in a message or file. The logic within the for each is executed for all files/records. A for each can run records in parallel; they are automatically split over clusters to reduce to cost.
Schedule	Enables you to trigger the integration based on a scheduled timer instead of a configured connection. This can be useful for file/batch integrations.
Stage File	Enables you to optimize the processing for file operations. It is very useful for managed file transfers. This action offers an extraction of the file system; it can read, write, or create files. You can compare it with a staging area for files. This action can extend normal file operations using callout for example, encrypt/decrypt and zip/unzip.
Wait	Enables you to put in a wait period to pause the execution before continuing with the next activity. This can be useful when executing a loop and between files or records, there needs to be a wait period because an invoking connection requires it.
While	Enables you to loop through a block of activities as long as the specified condition/expression is true.

In this chapter, we are only using the basic functionality to explain the concept around orchestration. On our website `oracle-integration.cloud`, we will explain the more advanced orchestrations.

Let's continue with our process. The first thing we are going to add is an invoke to the `FlightAirlinesREST` connection created in Chapter 2, *Integrating Our First Two Applications*. We are going to call the `/airline/{code}` resource to get additional information about the airline. Expand the **INVOKES** panel and click on **REST** to display all configured connections. Drag and drop the connection `FlightAirlinesREST_Ch2` to the plus symbol (+) above the **ScheduleUpdate** map activity as shown in the following screenshot:

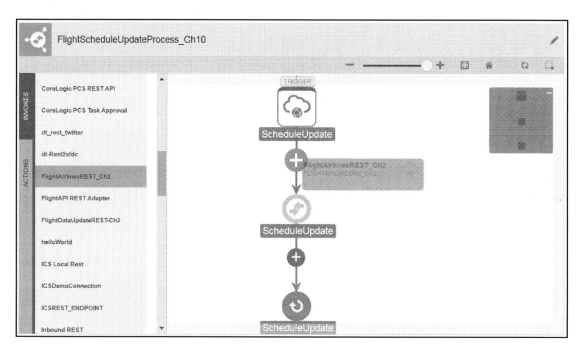

The endpoint configuration is displayed. Finish the dialog with the following details:

Tab	Question	Action
Basic Info	**Call your endpoint field?**	Call it: `GetAirlineDetails`
	What does this end point do?	Add the description: `receives the details of an airline based on its 2-character code`
	What is the endpoint's relative resource URI?	Enter the URI: `/airlines/{code}`.
	What actions does the endpoint perform?	Select the `GET` method.
	Select any options that you want to configure:	The option **Add** and **review endpoint parameters** is checked and can not be unchecked because of path parameter in URL Check option: **Configure this endpoint to receive the response**
Request Parameters	**Template parameters**	Our URL consists of the path parameter code. Select **string** to use as its type.
Response	**Select Response payload**	Pick: **JSON Sample**
	Enter **sample JSON** (click the inline link)	``` { "icao": "BAW", "name": "British Airways", "callsign": "SPEEDBIRD", "country": "United Kingdom", "social": "Salesforce" } ```
Summary	**Description**	The description we entered
	REST Service URI	`http://private-xxxx-yourapidomain.apiary-mock.com/airlines/{code}`
	Method	`GET`
	Response Media Type	`application/json`

In our process the invoke activity is added and an unconfigured map activity is added to give us a value to the code parameter that the request URL requires, as shown next:

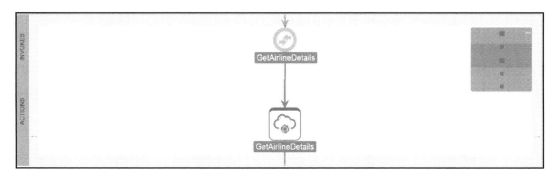

Click on the map activity and then the edit icon to configure the mapping. This will open the mapper UI, which is the same as when creating basic integrations. To determine the value of the template parameter `code`, we need to substring the first two characters from the value of the `ident` source element. Click on the target parameter `code` to open the expression builder.

In the expression builder, drag and drop the **string** function `substring` from **Mapping Components** to the `code` parameter of the selected mapping statement on the right. The function requires two arguments, the string to `substring` from and the starting location, but it can also handle an optional third argument for the length of the substring. Drag and drop the element `ident` from the **Source** to the first argument, for the second argument set the literal value 1. Right-click on the second argument and create a sibling after it. For this third argument set the literal value 2. The expression should result in: `substring(/nssrcmpr:ScheduleUpdate/nssrcmpr:ident, 1, 2)`. Click on **Save** and then **Close** to close the expression builder and then click on **Save** and then **Exit Mapper**. Notice that the `GetAirlineDetails` map activity has turned green. This means it is configured.

Extracting data into simple variables

Our main goal in the process is to act on the flight status and on the social preference of the airline. Based on these values we branch the flow, but instead of using the available data from the variables created by the trigger and the invoke, we can use the assign action to simply our own variable and make the expressions used to branch on.

Expand the **ACTIONS** panel and drag and drop the Assign action below the `GetAirlineDetails` invoke activity as shown in the following screenshot:

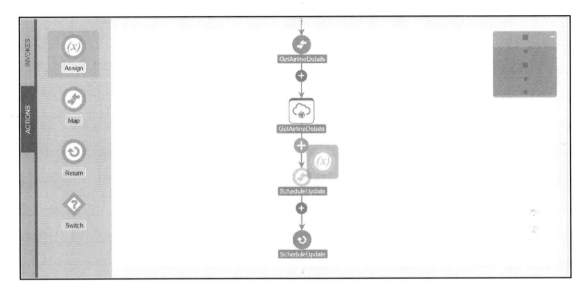

A dialog opens where you can create a set of assignments. A set requires a name and an optional description. In our case, name the set `AssignExprVariables` and give the set the description `Assign activity for set of expression variables`. Click on **OK** to create a new empty set as shown in the following screenshot:

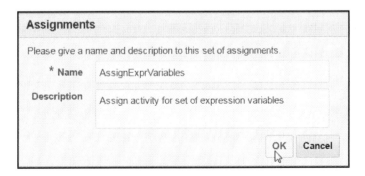

After creating the set we are presented with a page where we can create the variable assignments. A variable assignment requires a name, description, and an expression to retrieve the value as shown in the following screenshot:

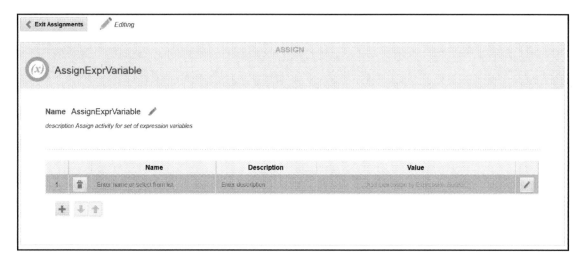

In our case, we are going to add two variable assignments. Click on the first column **Name** and enter the value `FlightStatus`. This name will be the name of the variable. For the column **Description** enter the value `Status of Flight update`. To assign the value we need to add an expression. Click on the pencil to open the expression builder. For this first variable drag and drop the source node `updateType` to the expression area on the right as shown as follows:

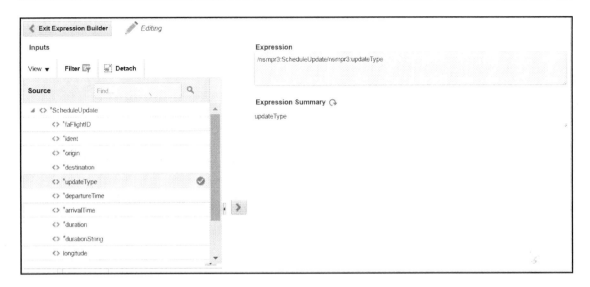

Exit the expression builder to accept the expression. Add a second assignment by clicking on the plus (+) button with the following details:

Name	Description	Value
SocialPreference	Social preference of Airline	$GetAirlineDetails /nssrcmpr:executeResponse/ nsmpr2:response-wrapper/nsmpr2:social

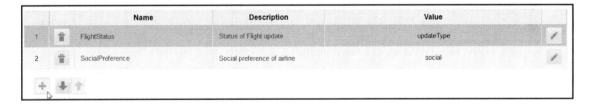

		Name	Description	Value	
1	🗑	FlightStatus	Status of Flight update	updateType	✎
2	🗑	SocialPreference	Social preference of airline	social	✎

You can add as many variable assignments as you want, but we would advise limiting one set to a maximum five assignments to keep it manageable.

Click on **Exit Assignment** to return to the orchestration canvas. The activity will turn green, which means it is configured and has one or more complete variable assignments. Now that we have those variables available in the orchestration we can use them in other assign, map, and switch actions. The next step in our process is to branch on the status of the flight update. Based on the status a different route in the process is taken if the value equals on time. Other statuses are routed to the **Otherwise** branch.

Branching the integration into multiple routes

In the orchestration canvas expand the **ACTIONS** panel and drag and drop the **Switch** action to the plus (+) symbol below the **AssignExprVariables** activity. It will add the switch (?) activity and two cases; one is **Undefined** and one is **Otherwise**, as shown in the following screenshot:

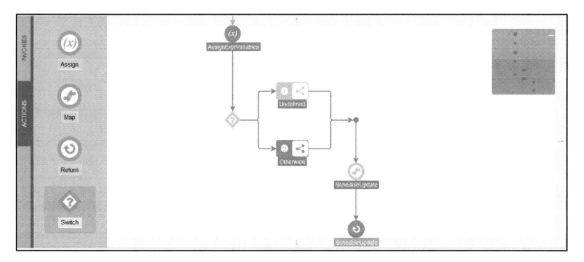

To define the expression for the flights that are on time click on the **Undefined** branch and subsequently the edit icon. The condition builder is displayed where we can enter the condition to branch on. Start by naming the expression `FlightAtGate`. For this branch we are using the `FlightStatus` variable. Find the variable in the **Source** panel and drag and drop it to the first part of the expression. In the second part enter the literal value `"at gate"` (including the quotes) as shown in the following screenshot:

Exit the condition builder and return to the orchestration canvas. Both branches are now configured and we can continue expanding our process. Let's start with the `FlightAtGate` branch, because this will include most of our process logic. Drag and drop the `Trello_Ch10` invoke from the **Invokes | Trello** panel to the plus (+) symbol behind the `FlightAtGate` condition. Complete the endpoint configuration wizard using the following details:

Tab	Question	Action
Basic Info	**Call your endpoint field?**	Call it: `CreateNewTask`.
	What does this end point do?	Add the description: `create a new task for the ground personnel to unload the aircraft`.
Operation Selection	**Select Operation**	Find and select Create a Card .
Summary	Description	The description we entered.
	Task Resource URI	`https://www.trello.com/1/cards`
	Method	**Create a Card**.

After closing the dialog a new map activity is created and then an invoke activity is created. Configure the map activity and complete the mapping using the following details:

Source Element	Target Element
The literal value of your List Id which you collected when you created the `FlightArrivals` list using Trello	`Resource. definitions.requestCreateCard/ idList`
`concat("Flight ", /nsmpr1:ScheduleUpdate/nsmpr1:ident, " has arrived at gate A", /nsmpr1:ScheduleUpdate/nsmpr1:faFlightID, ", please unload cargo and deliver on belt ", fn:day-from-date(fn:current-date()))`	`Resource.definitions. requestCreateCard/ name`

After creating these mappings exit the mapper and remember to periodically save the orchestration. Before we continue let's look at the process which should look similar to the following screenshot:

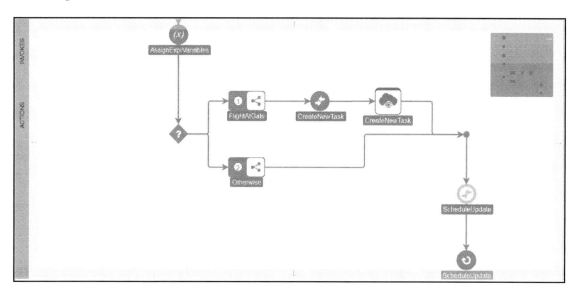

Currently there is a limitation: we cannot put a switch activity as a child of a branch. We will finish the **Otherwise** branch, which will return a response at the end so the `FlightAtGate` path can continue. In the **Otherwise** branch, we will call two services to process other flight updates. We will first retrieve the current date and time based on the longitude and latitude of the current flight position using `TimeDB_Ch6` and enrich our request. Secondly, we will publish the message to our existing integration `PublishFlightStatusUpdate_Ch3`.

Drag and drop the `TimeDB_Ch6` connection from the **INVOKES | REST** panel to the plus symbol within the **Otherwise** branch. Complete the endpoint configuration using the following details:

Tab	Question	Action
Basic Info	**Call your endpoint field?**	`EnrichTimeZone`
	What does this end point do?	Add the description: `gets TimeZone information using the Lat & Long parameters`
	What is the endpoint's relative resource URI?	Enter the URI: `/`
	What action does the endpoint perform?	Select the `GET` method.
	Select any options that you want to configure:	The options `Add` and `review endpoint parameters` and **Configure this endpoint to receive the response** should both be ticked.
	Configure Headers?	These can remain unticked.
Request Parameters	**Specify Query Parameters**	Add the URI's query parameters into the table and define the expected data types. <table><tr><td>Lat</td><td>String</td></tr><tr><td>Lng</td><td>String</td></tr><tr><td>Key</td><td>string</td></tr></table>
	Template Parameters	None will be defined as the URI uses query parameters.

Response	Select the response payload file	As the TimeZoneDB response defaults to use XML we can use that, so select the XML Schema option. We need to provide a schema so use the **Choose file** to upload the provided `TimeZoneDB.xsd`
	Select the type of payload	Click on the **XML** option.
Summary		This simply provides what you have provided in the previous tabs – you need only verify that it reflects the values correctly.

Next drag and drop the `FlightSitRep_Ch3` connection from the **INVOKES SOAP** panel to the plus (+) symbol after the `EnrichTimeZone` invoke activity. Complete the endpoint configuration using the following details:

Tab	Question	Action
Basic Info	**Call your endpoint field?**	`PublishFlightUpdate`
	What does this end point do?	Add the description: `publish flight status update information to separate integration`
Operations	**Selected Port Type**	As we only have a single operation in the WSDL this tab will not offer any options.
	Selected Operation	
	Request Object	
Callback Operation	**Choose the type of response**	Because we have selected a one-way operation, we need to choose the type of response expected for the `FlightStatusUpdate` operation. Select the option: **No Response**
Summary		This simply provides what you have provided in the previous tabs–you need only verify that it reflects the values correctly.

Lastly before we start configuring the needed mappings, for which activities are automatically created, the **Otherwise** branch will return an answer to the caller of the integration. This means that the process will complete its work and everything after this won't be executed. Drag and drop the return activity from the **ACTIONS** panel after the `PublishFlightUpdate` invoke activity. Your branches should look like what is shown in the following screenshot:

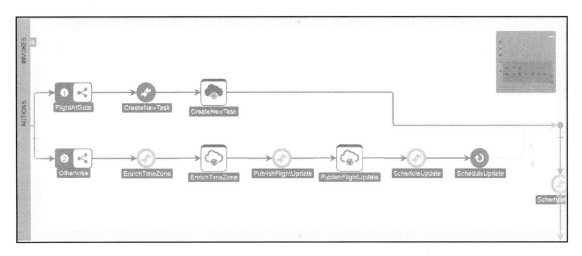

Notice that the **Otherwise** and the **FlightAtGate** branch are now two completely separate flows. Because of this we can add a second switch activity to the **FligthAtGate** branch. We will do this after completing the mapping for each of the map activities in the **Otherwise** branch. Click on the **EnrichTimeZone** map activity and configure it using these details:

Source Element	Target Element
*ScheduleUpdate / latitude	QueryParameters / lat
*ScheduleUpdate / longitude	QueryParameters / lng
Literal string that represents the key from `TimeZoneDB` (same as Chapter 6, *Creating Complex Transformations*)	QueryParameters / key

Save and exit the mapper to return to the orchestration canvas. Next click on the **PublishFlightUpdate** map activity and configure it using these details:

Source Element	Target Element
`*ScheduleUpdate / faFlightID`	`*FlightProgress / ID`
`*ScheduleUpdate / ident`	`*FlightProgress / ident`
Empty literal string	`*FlightProgress / prefix`
Empty literal string	`*FlightProgress / type`
Empty literal string	`*FlightProgress / suffix`
`*ScheduleUpdate / origin`	`*FlightProgress / origin`
`*ScheduleUpdate / destination`	`*FlightProgress / destination`
String function `translate (3 args) -` `*ScheduleUpdate / duration - HPTM` `- : (colon)`	`*FlightProgress / timeout PT1H30M` `-> 1:30`
`$EnrichTimeZone / timestamp`	`*FlightProgress / timestamp`
`*ScheduleUpdate / longitude`	`*FlightProgress / longitude`
`*ScheduleUpdate / latitude`	`*FlightProgress / latitude`
`*ScheduleUpdate / updateType`	`* FlightProgress / updateType`

Save and exit the mapper to return and lastly click on the **ScheduleUpdate** map activity and configure it using these details:

Source Element	Target Element
`*ScheduleUpdate / faFlightID`	`*ScheduleUpdateResult / parentID`
Literal string with value 1	`*ScheduleUpdateResult / processed`
`"Message published to subscribers"`	`*ScheduleUpdateResult / message`

For the final time in the **Otherwise** branch, save and exit the mapper. We have finished this branch and it may be a good time to save the orchestration. With this part behind us we can continue to complete the FlightAtGate route. Drag and drop a switch activity from the ACTIONS panel after the **CreateNewTask** invoke activity and just before the **ScheduleUpdate** map activity. This switch activity is going to have three branches and we will branch based on the social preference of the airline. By default, we have one **unconfigured** branch and one **Otherwise** branch. For our orchestration we want a branch when the airline's preference is Twitter, a branch when the preference is Salesforce, and an **Otherwise** branch. We need to add a second branch that we can configure. Click on the switch activity represented by the question mark icon and subsequently click on the plus (+) icon to add a new branch.

Click on the first branch and click the pencil icon to edit the condition. Name the expression SocialPrefTwitter. For this condition we are going to match the SocialPreference variable with the literal value Twitter. Drag and drop the variable from the **Source** panel to the first part of the expression and type the literal value into the second part. Save the condition and exit the condition builder. Do the same for the second branch, but this time call the expression Salesforce and configure the condition to match SocialPreference against the literal value Salesforce. This part of the process should look similar to the following screenshot:

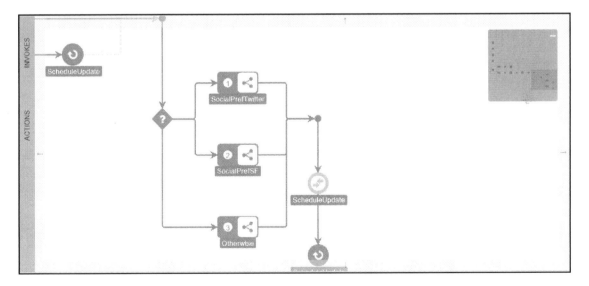

Now the three branches are configured, we can complete each branch with the correct invocation. The first branch will send an update to Twitter, the second branch will create a `FeedUpdate` in Salesforce, and the third otherwise branch will write the update to a FTP target. Drag and drop the `Twitter_Ch5` connection from the **INVOKES** panel under the **Twitter** category to the plus (+) symbol within the **SocialPrefTwitter** branch. Complete the endpoint configuration using the following details:

Tab	Question	Action
Basic Info	**Call your endpoint field?**	Call it `TweetUpdate`
	What does this end point do?	Add the description: `sends a Tweet to the corporate Twitter timeline`
Operation	**Select Operation**	Select **Tweet**
Summary	**Description**	This tab shows the connector settings. The Twitter URI shows the URL of the Twitter API. `https://api.twitter.com/1.1/ statuses/update.json` It also lists the query parameters we can provide to send out a more advanced tweet, like geo-location information.
	Twitter Resource URI	
	Method	
	Query Parameters	

After closing the dialog the invoke activity and featured map activity are created. Complete the mapper configuration with the following source-to-target mappings:

Source Element	Target Element
`concat("Flight #", /nsmpr1:ScheduleUpdate/nsmpr1:ident, " from #", /nsmpr1:ScheduleUpdate/nsmpr1:origin, " has arrived at gate A", /nsmpr1:ScheduleUpdate/nsmpr1:faFlightID)`	`QueryParameters / status`
`*ScheduleUpdate / latitude`	`QueryParameters / lat`

ScheduleUpdate / longitude	QueryParameters / long

After creating the mapping click on **Save** and **Exit Mapper** to return to the orchestration canvas. We mentioned that we keep these branches simple, so this branch is now completed and we can continue with the **SocialPrefSF** branch. Drag and drop the `Salesforce_Ch4` connection from the INVOKES panel under the **Salesforce** category to the plus (+) symbol within this branch. Complete the endpoint configuration using these details:

Tab	Question	Action
Basic Info	**Call your endpoint field?**	Call it `CreateFeedItem`
	What does this end point do?	Add the description: `create a new FeedItem to report arrival update`
	Which Salesforce service you like to design with?	Select option **Standard application delivered by Salesforce.com**
Operations	**Select and Operation Type**	Select **CRUD** in the operations list. Select **create** in the types list.
	Select Business Objects	Select **FeedItem** and tick the single arrow. You case use the filter to quickly find the object.
Header	**Configure the Header properties for selected operation**	This tab gives a lot of possibilities to configure headers that can be used by Salesforc,e for example triggering an e-mail. In this chapter we are not configuring any of them so leave the default settings.
Summary	**Operation Name**	This tab gives a short summary about the chosen operation, object name and configured headers.
	Object(s) Name	

After closing the dialog we need to configure the map activity. To create a `FeedItem` we need a `ParentId`, for example our profile feed from Salesforce. Just like in chapter 4, *Integrations between SaaS Applications*, retrieve it by following these steps:

1. Open a new tab, log in to Salesforce, and visit your profile page.
2. Investigate the URL of the page; it will include the following pattern: `/sObject/00558000001NCwhAAG/view`.

3. Copy the value after `sObject`, for example `00558000001NCwhAAG`.

4. Return to the mapping in ICS.

Complete the map activity `CreateFeedItem` with the following mappings:

Source Element	Target Element

`concat("Flight ",`
`/nsmpr1:ScheduleUpdate/nsmpr1:ident,`
`" from ",`
`/nsmpr1:ScheduleUpdate/nsmpr1:origin,`
`" has arrived at gate A",`
`/nsmpr1:ScheduleUpdate/nsmpr1:faFlightID)`
	`FeedItem /`
	`Body`

Literal string with value `TextPost`	`FeedItem /` `Type`
Your profile id you just collected	`FeedItem /` `ParentId`

Save the mapping and exit the mapper to return to the orchestration canvas. Lastly we need to complete the **Otherwise** branch. If we receive a social preference other than Twitter or Salesforce, we append an update about the arrival in a file that we write to FTP. Drag and drop the `AirportData_Ch9` connection from the **INVOKES** panel under the **FTP** category to the plus (+) symbol within the **Otherwise** branch. Complete the endpoint configuration using these details:

Tab	Question	Action
Basic Info	**What do you want to call your endpoint?**	Call it `WriteUpdateToFTP`
	What does this endpoint do?	Write update to a file at the target location
Configure File Write	**Select Operation**	Select **Write File**
	Select a Transfer Mode	Set this to **ASCII** as we will be writing a XML file.
	Specify an Output Directory	Set the target to `/tmp/output`

	Specify a File Name Pattern	Specify the name: `FlightArrivals_%yyyyMMdd%.csv` The pattern `%yyyyMMDD%` will dynamically add the current date to the file name.
	Append to Existing File	Tick this box to add flight updates produced on the same day to the same file.
Schema	**Define a schema for this endpoint?**	Choose the option **Yes**
	Create a new schema or select an existing one?	Choose the option **Select an existing schema** from the file system
Format Definition	**Select a New File**	Select the file from book resources: `ICSBook_Ch10_FlightArrivalsFTP.xsd`
	Selected File Name	Will show selected file or none.
	Select Schema Element	Select `FlightArrivals`
Summary		This tab gives a short summary about the chosen operation, transfer options and format definition (NXSD) which you can download for reuse.

WriteUpdateToFTP

Description	Write update to a file at the target location
Operation	Write File
Transfer Mode	ASCII
Append to existing file	Yes
Output Directory	/tmp/output
File Name Pattern	FlightArrivals_%yyyyMMdd%.csv
Format Definition	Schema
Element	FlightArrivals

After closing the dialog configure the mapper with the following mappings:

Source Element	Target Element
`*ScheduleUpdate / ident`	`//FlightArrival / flightId`
`*ScheduleUpdate / origin`	`//FlightArrival / origin`
`*ScheduleUpdate / destination`	`//FlightArrival / destination`
`concat("A", /nsmpr1:ScheduleUpdate/nsmpr1:faFlightID)`	`//FlightArrival / gate`
`*ScheduleUpdate / arrivalTime`	`//FlightArrival / arrivalTime`

Save the mapping and exit the mapper to return to the orchestration canvas. All branches should now be completed and all mappings should be configured and valid. We have one last task before our process can be ready for activation: process response mapping. Click on the map activity **ScheduleUpdate** and configure it using the following source to target mappings:

Source Element	Target Element
`*ScheduleUpdate / faFlightID`	`*ScheduleUpdateResult / parentID`
Literal string with value 1	`*ScheduleUpdateResult / processed`
`"Flight at gate is successfully registered"`	`*ScheduleUpdateResult / message`

After completing this last mapping our process is done. The next steps include activating and testing the process, but before we continue let's look at the last part of the process as shown in the following screenshot:

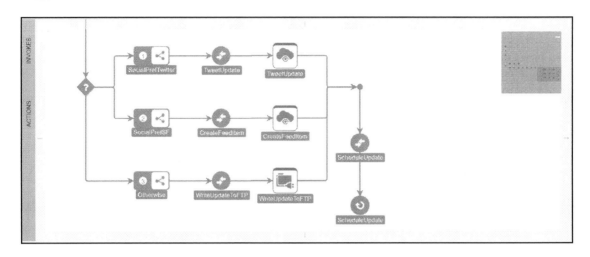

Completing and activating the integration

Now that the logic of our orchestration is finished we only need to add the tracking fields before we can complete and activate the orchestration. At the top right, click **Tracking** to open the **Business Identifiers** dialog. We are going to set two tracking fields: `updateType` and `ident`. Drag and drop both trigger fields to the list and use `updateType` as the primary identifier. Change the tracking name of the `updateType` field to `Flight Update` and change the value of the `ident` field to `Flight Id`. Click **Done** to save the identifiers and, in the orchestration canvas, subsequently click on **Save** and then **Exit Integration** to finish our orchestration. We are returned to the list of all the integrations. Notice that the UI shows most of the connections that we used in the orchestration. To scroll through the connections click on the angle bracket (< or >) as shown in the following screenshot:

Use the **PENDING ACTIVATION** button of the integration we have just created to make it active. To have full insight into the process, you can enable tracing in the **Confirmation** screen, but the process will use more resources. Let's keep it disabled so we can inspect the default features.

Testing the orchestration

Before testing our solution, we need to know the web address for the endpoint our integration is running. Click the information icon on the right side of our entry to view its activation details. Find the **Endpoint URL** within the integration details and copy the address to your clipboard. Notice that the endpoint of an orchestration does not differ from an endpoint that exposes an integration. The URL will look similar to:

`https://xxx-yyy.integration.zzz.oraclecloud.com/integration/flowsvc/soa`
`p/FLIGHTSCHEDULEUP_CH10/v01/?wsdl`.

Invoke a cloud endpoint using SoapUI

To test our cloud endpoint we are going to use SoapUI again to simulate our flight tracking and incident system. Instead of creating a new SOAP project, we have created one for you to use to make these steps easier. Import the SoapUI project from the chapter resources. This can be done through the **File** menu and selecting **Import Project**. Open the project file `FlightScheduleUpdate-Ch10-soapui-project.xml`, which can be found in the book's resources for this chapter. This SoapUI project contains the SOAP binding to send messages to our orchestration and a test suite with two test cases. The first test case includes four calls to the orchestration, each with a different flight identification and a different outcome. Each call takes a different path in the orchestration. The second test case will call the orchestration twice; one call executes the otherwise branch and the other call will result in a fault as shown in the following screenshot:

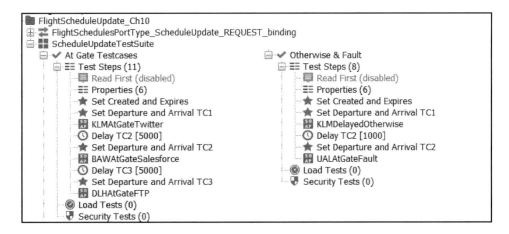

Before we can run the tests we need to set up some project properties. In the preceding project tree, double-click on the project title FlightScheduleUpdate_Ch10. This will show a dialog with a summary overview of project settings. On the bottom find the project properties and edit values for Identity, Domain, and DataCenter to represent your ICS instance, as shown in the following screenshot:

Name	Value
CloudEndpoint	https://${#Project#Identity}-${#Project#Domain}.integration.${#Project#DataCenter}.oraclecloud.co...
Identity	icsinstance
Domain	mydomain
DataCenter	us2

Description **Properties** Load Script Save Script

If you click on `At Gate Testcases` or `Otherwise & Fault` a dialog is shown where we can execute the test steps belonging to this group by clicking on the green play button. Tests can also be run partially by stopping the test run when the delay step is executed. This is how we will run the tests to show the process flow for each individual call to our orchestration. First click on `At Gate Testcases` and subsequently click on the play button to execute the test run. When the test run reaches `Delay TC2` click the stop button. The following result will be executed if the orchestration is built correctly:

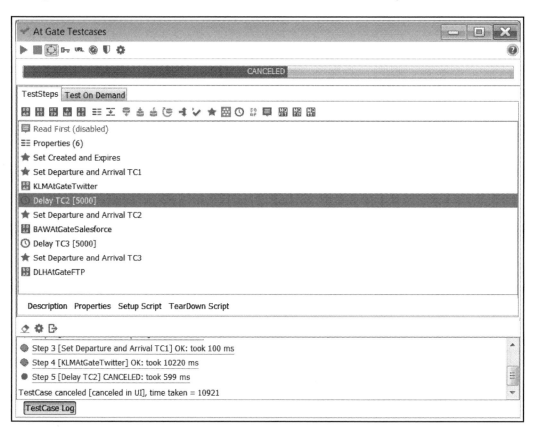

The first four steps should be executed successfully with the expected result. If we inspect the `KLMAtGateTwitter` test step, which can be done by clicking on the name of the test step, we can see that our orchestration responded with a positive result. The message displays the text `Flight at gate is successfully registered` as follows:

```
<ScheduleUpdateResult xmlns:wsdl="http://schemas.xmlsoap.org/wsdl/"
   xmlns:nsmpr0="http://xmlns.oracle.com/cloud/adapter/REST/GetAirlineDetails_REQUEST/types"
   xmlns:nstrgmpr="http://oracle-integration.cloud/soap/IntegratedSourceFlightSchedules/"
   xmlns:soapenc="http://schemas.xmlsoap.org/soap/encoding/" xmlns:http="http://schemas.xmlsoap.org/wsdl/http/"
   xmlns:mime="http://schemas.xmlsoap.org/wsdl/mime/" xmlns:soap="http://schemas.xmlsoap.org/wsdl/soap/"
   xmlns="http://oracle-integration.cloud/soap/IntegratedSourceFlightSchedules/">
   <nstrgmpr:parentID>1</nstrgmpr:parentID>
   <nstrgmpr:processed>1</nstrgmpr:processed>
   <nstrgmpr:message>Flight at gate is successfully registered</nstrgmpr:message>
</ScheduleUpdateResult>
```

Now that we know that the orchestration processed the request successfully we can take a look at the instance flow in ICS. In ICS navigate to the **Monitoring** page and visit the **Tracking** section. Here you will see the completed instance; to see the flow click on the name of the instance `Flight Update: at gate`, as shown in the following screenshot:

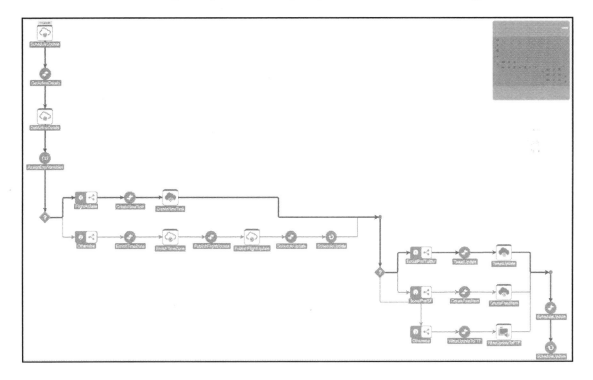

The integration canvas is shown including the path the instance took when executing the orchestration. In this first test we see that the call to apiary to get the `AirlineDetails` returns information about the airline, including the `social` preference, that is, `Twitter`. The response from apiary can be checked in the **Inspector** console when you log in into `Apiary.io` with your account as shown in the following screenshot:

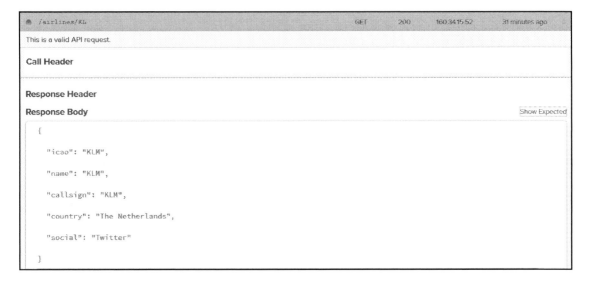

Two values are extracted from the request payload (`updateType`) and from the `GetAirlineDetails` response payload (`social`). Based on the value of `updateType` the `FlightAtGate` branch, of the first switch, is executed and the `CreateNewTask` (that is, Trello API) is invoked. When this call is executed a new task is available for the ground personnel to unload the aircraft. This can be viewed when logged in to Trello as follows:

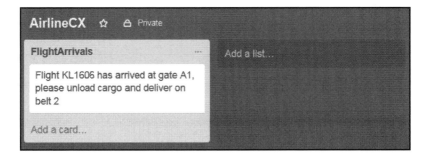

After the `FlightAtGate` branch execution, it follows the route to the second switch. Based on the value of `socialPreference`, the `SocialPrefTwitter` branch is executed and `TweetUpdate` is invoked. When this call is executed a new tweet is posted indicating that the flight has landed and has arrived at its gate, as shown in the following screenshot:

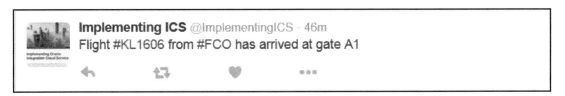

Implementing ICS @ImplementingICS · 46m
Flight #KL1606 from #FCO has arrived at gate A1

The response we get in SoapUI is returned after tweeting the update. Return to SoapUI, go back to the `At Gate Testcases`, and right-click on `Delay TC2`; then click on **Run from here**. When the test run reaches `Delay TC3`, click the stop button. The following result will be executed if the orchestration is built correctly:

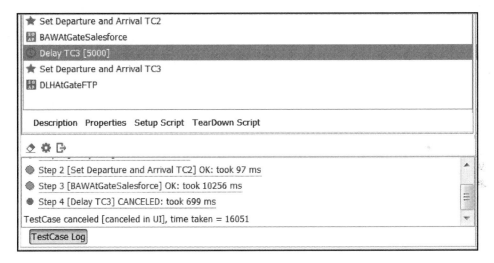

In ICS refresh the Tracking page. The new instance is listed as completed; to see the flow, click on the name of the top instance `Flight Update: at gate` as shown in the following screenshot:

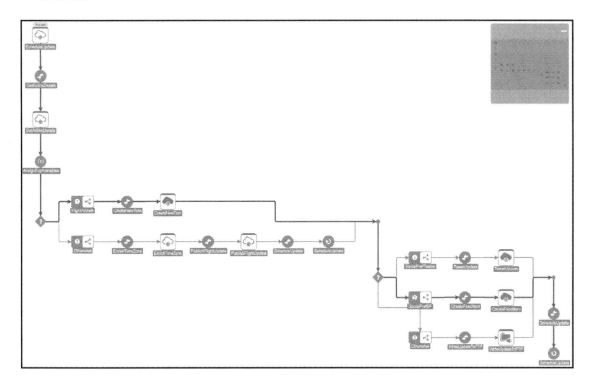

The integration canvas shows the path the instance took when executing the orchestration, which is different this time. The call to `GetAirlineDetails` returns information about the airline, including the `social` preference: `Salesforce`. The two values for `updateType` and `socialPreference` are extracted again and, based on the value of `updateType`, the `FlightAtGate` branch's first switch is executed and the `CreateNewTask` (that is, Trello API) is invoked. When this call is executed a second task is available for the ground personnel to unload another aircraft.

After the `FlightAtGate` branch it follows its route to the second switch. Based on the value of `socialPreference`, the `SocialPrefSF` (Salesforce) branch is executed and `CreateFeedItem` is invoked. When this call is executed a new feed update is posted on your Salesforce user profile to the effect that the flight has landed and has arrived at its gate, as shown as follows:

The response we get in SoapUI is returned after posting the update. Return to SoapUI, go back to the `At Gate Testcases`, right-click on `Delay TC3`, and click on **Run from here**. Let the test finish when it reaches the end of the test run. The following result will be executed if the orchestration is built correctly:

In ICS refresh the **Tracking** page. The new instance is listed as completed; to see the flow, click on the name of the top instance `Flight Update: at gate`, as shown in the following screenshot:

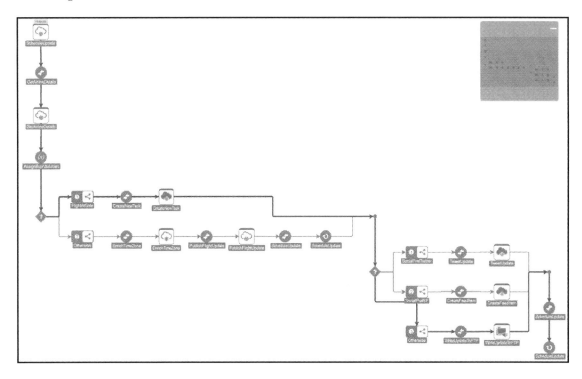

The integration canvas shows the path the instance took when executing the orchestration, which again is different. The call to `GetAirlineDetails` returns information about the airline, including the `social` preference: `LinkedIn`. The two values for `updateType` and `socialPreference` are extracted again and, based on the value of `updateType`, the `FlightAtGate` branch is executed, which creates a third task for the ground personnel to unload another aircraft.

After the `FlightAtGate` branch follows its route to the second switch. Based on the value of `socialPreference` the otherwise branch is executed, because the value does not match any condition, and `WriteUpdateToFTP` is invoked. When this call is executed a new CSV file is created on the assigned FTP server with a record of the flight arrival. When this test is executed multiple times (in one day) the CSV file holds all the records. To check the content of the created record, log in to your FTP server and check the file `/tmp/output/FlightArrivals_%yyyyMMdd%.csv`, as follows:

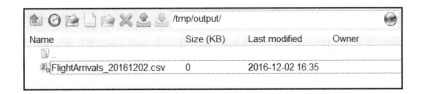

The content of the file should look similar to following screenshot:

	A	B	C	D	E
1	Flight	Origin	Destination	Gate	Arrival Time
2	LH2901	TXL	AMS	A3	2016-12-02T16:54:53Z

The response we get in SoapUI is returned after creating/updating the CSV file. Return to SoapUI and open the `Otherwise & Fault`. Click on the play button to execute a test run. When the test run reaches `Delay TC2` click the stop button. In ICS refresh the **Tracking** page. The new instance is listed as completed; to see the flow, click on the name of the top instance, `Flight Update: delayed`, as shown in the following screenshot:

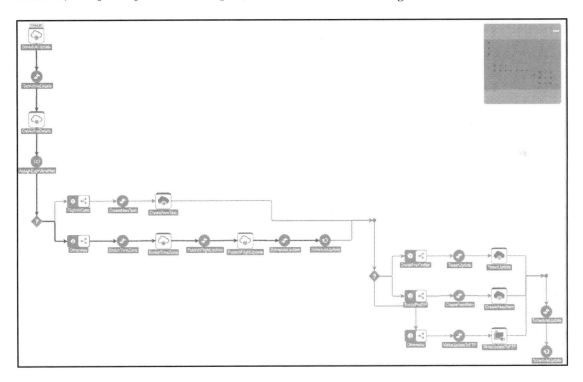

The integration canvas is shown including the path the instance took when executing the orchestration, but this time it takes a different route. The call to `GetAirlineDetails` still returns information about the airline, including the `social` preference, but based on `updateType` the otherwise branch, of the first switch, is executed. This time, no task is created for the ground personnel, but the message is enriched with the correct time zone information by invoking `TimeDB` and it's published to the existing `PublishFlightUpdate` integration we created in `Chapter 3`, *Distribute Messages Using the Pub-Sub Model*. After publishing the message the orchestration returns a response, which afterwards finishes the instances. The second switch is never executed. The response we get in SoapUI is returned after the message is published as follows:

```
<ScheduleUpdateResult
    xmlns:nstrgmpr="http://oracle-integration.cloud/soap/IntegratedSourceFlightSchedules/"
    xmlns="http://oracle-integration.cloud/soap/IntegratedSourceFlightSchedules/">
    <nstrgmpr:parentID>1</nstrgmpr:parentID>
    <nstrgmpr:processed>1</nstrgmpr:processed>
    <nstrgmpr:message>Message published to subscribers</nstrgmpr:message>
</ScheduleUpdateResult>
```

Return to SoapUI, go back to `Otherwise & Fault`, right-click on `Delay TC2`, and click on **Run from here**. Let the test run finish. The call to ICS results in an error called `Internal Server Error: 500`. The orchestration is partially executed, but results in an error because a resource is called on the `FlightAirlines` REST API that does not exist. We can see this error for the first time if we look at the response SoapUI receives from the orchestration.

The following screenshot shows a small part of the fault thrown by apiary responding with a 404 - No Resource Found:

```
   <faultstring>ICS runtime execution error</faultstring>
   <detail>
      <errorCode>OSB-380001</errorCode>
      <reason><![CDATA[Invoke JCA outbound service failed with application error, exception: com.bea.
<html lang="en">
<meta charset="utf-8">
<title>apiary.io—404—No Resource Found!</title>
<body>
<div id="bg"></div>
 <div id="message">
  <h1>The resource you're looking for doesn't exist. <br>Please check the <a href="http://docs.icsfli
  <p></p>
  <ol>
         <section><h2></h2>
                   <li><b>GET</b> /airlines</li>
                   <li><b>GET</b> /airlines/BA</li>
                   <li><b>GET</b> /airlines/KL</li>
                   <li><b>GET</b> /airlines/LH</li>
              </section>
     </ol>
  </div>
</body>
</html>
]]]]>><![CDATA[</instance></genericRestFault>
; nested exception is:
     <genericRestFault><errorCode>404</errorCode><errorPath><![CDATA[G:Application Error]]></reason>
```

In ICS refresh the **Tracking** page. The new instance is listed as `failed`; to see the flow, click on the name of the top instance, `Flight Update: early`, as shown in the following screenshot:

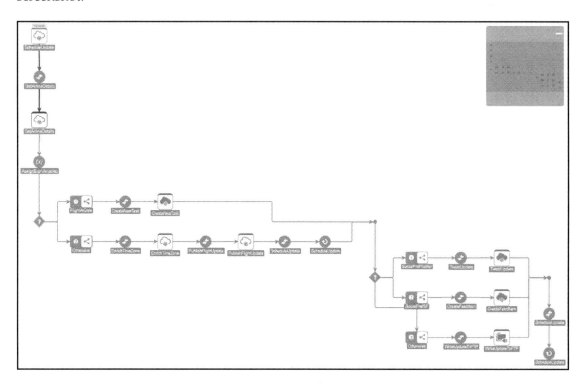

The integration canvas is shown including the path the instance took before failing to execute the orchestration. Because the first invocation failed, no other services are called, but if an invoke within a branch from the second switch fails, the service calls before that will be executed. Adapters do not support rolling back the transaction. If we take a look in the **Inspector** console in apiary, we see an error similar to the one we received back from the integration as follows:

Summary

In this chapter we looked at how ICS provides the means to perform a powerful level of orchestration when creating an integration. We first explained the high-level differences from the integrations we have built up so far. We reused a few connections we built in earlier chapters, but also created a new connection to the SaaS application Trello, which is a Jira-style application. We also updated the existing REST API available at `Apiary.io`. After the initial setup we started building our orchestration and granularly made the process more intelligent. We first looked at the different UI and workflows, compared the basic map data integrations, and explained the available actions, which ranged from simple to more advanced functionality. To give you a basic feel for creating an orchestration, the more common actions were introduced, for example, assign, switch, and branches. Because of the different routes we implemented, we then needed to test the orchestration extensively. Using the given SoapUI project we tested all test cases, each with a different outcome.

In the next chapter, we will look at the underlying factors that can drive the need to connect with on-premise applications and the need to use an agent with ICS to connect to these applications. We will look at the solution ICS provides in the form of an agent and show you how to install and use the agent in combination with an on-premise ERP database.

11
Calling an On-Premises API

In this chapter, we look at what we can do with an on-premises agent, what an agent is capable of doing, and how to deploy an agent. But before we do that, we need to understand the following three topics:

- Why and when an agent can help us
- The different types of agent that ICS offers
- How to get the agent deployed

All our examples so far have illustrated cloud-to-cloud integration or integrations within a single cloud. Whilst this is the likely future of a great deal of IT operations, this is not where things are today when a mix of cloud and on-premises integration exists, and maybe will have to exist this way for a very long time to come; possibly forever. This means that, for ICS to be effective, we need to support accessing on-premises systems and potentially even executing some processing remotely in the on-premises environment.

Once we have understood when an agent is best suited to help us for reasons beyond the simple practicalities, for example, where not all IT systems have been moved into cloud environments, we will work through a scenario. In our scenario, we will have an agent deployed in an on-premises context. This does mean we have some pre-requisites to address. But we will look at those once we understand the agent and deployment options.

With the background completed and having deployed the connection agent, we will create a simple integration taking on-premises data from a database and sending it to **Mockable**, as shown in the following diagram:

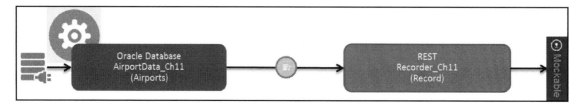

What kinds of agents exist?

ICS offers two types of agents, namely:

- **Connection Agent**: Provides a means to connect to systems and data stores that are on-premises or in networks that need to be treated as if on-premises.
- **Execution Agent**: Sometimes referred to as ICS on-premises or, occasionally, runtime agent. To perform the integration processes in a suitable location other than on the cloud server, for example, when the process starts on-premises and finishes on-premises, do we want to take the data to the cloud?

These agents have different capabilities and environment demands, although there are some basic needs, as you will see as we look through the details.

The essence of the two agents are to provide connectivity to systems running on-premises (or even another cloud) in the case of a connection agent, and to perform the act of executing integration processes on-premises (or someone else's cloud) for the execution agent.

In all of this, there is a downside to the agent model. One of the key benefits of iPaaS and SaaS cloud solutions is that the effort in patching and updating software is in the hands of the service provider. However, the patching and so on of the agents remains in our hands. What is more significant is that the compatibility between server and agent may be a lot more restricted, meaning that we are forced to patch/update agents far more frequently.

Whilst the installation process has some commonality for the two types of agent, including some of the information that needs to be supplied, the actual installation process is different once all the prerequisites are in place. Therefore, the agent installation process will be described for each type of agent when we get to the install stage.

When can an agent help?

There are a few reasons why we may need an agent, covering one or more factors, ranging from technical, security, commercial and legal compliance perspectives, and we will look at these in turn.

From a technical perspective, an agent may be needed to come into play for several reasons. Some connection techniques and technologies are sensitive (relatively speaking) to the time it can take for a call to be made and responded to. This call and response time challenge, or latency, comes from the fact that, regardless of how good the connections are, data takes time to travel, even over fiber optics. For example, for light to travel from London to Sydney takes 5ms. In reality, we do not have fiber from every location directly to every other location by the shortest path. Even the best parts of the Internet backbone are convoluted and involve moving between servers and network infrastructure as the data works its way across the world, and then will need to go through more infrastructure (firewalls and so on) once into your network. You can see this by using a trace command, against a remotely hosted server address (use the `tracert` command followed by an address you know to be physically remote from you). You can see an example in the following screenshot, where we took the web address of the Oxley museum in Wellington, New Zealand (which is unlikely to use Internet acceleration techniques) and traced the steps to contact the website:

```
C:\Users\Phil>tracert www.oxleymuseum.org.au

Tracing route to www.oxleymuseum.org.au [116.0.19.201]
over a maximum of 30 hops:

  1    <1 ms    <1 ms    <1 ms  home [                    ]
  2     *        *        *     Request timed out.
  3     *        *        *     Request timed out.
  4     8 ms     7 ms     8 ms  31.55.
  5     8 ms     7 ms     7 ms  core2-hu0-9-0-0.southbank.ukcore.bt.net [           ]
  6     8 ms     8 ms     7 ms  core4-hu0-2-0-4.faraday.ukcore.bt.net [            ]
  7     7 ms     8 ms     7 ms  213.137.
  8    11 ms     7 ms    13 ms  40ge1-3.core1.lon2.he.net [            ]
  9    75 ms    85 ms    75 ms  100ge1-1.core1.nyc4.he.net [            ]
 10   146 ms   148 ms   149 ms  100ge14-2.core1.sjc2.he.net [            ]
 11   315 ms   314 ms   314 ms  tpg-internet-pty-ltd.10gigabitethernet12-1.core1.sjc2.he.net [            ]
 12   340 ms   342 ms   342 ms  203-219-35-130.static.tpgi.com.au [            ]
 13   317 ms   318 ms   318 ms  203.29.134-132.tpgi.com.au [            ]
 14     *        *        *     Request timed out.
 15   329 ms   329 ms   328 ms  ge-1-0-3-0.bdr2.syd1.bucan.com.au [            ]
 16   330 ms   329 ms   329 ms  ae12.cor1.syd1.bucan.com.au [            ]
 17   329 ms   328 ms   328 ms  odysseus.instanthosting.com.au [            ]
```

As you can see in the `tracert` example, several of the steps had to be attempted several times to perform without the process deciding it was taking too long (steps 2, 3, and 14). As you can see from the output, it took 9 hops before the connection left the UK and reached New York. After one third of a second we have only just made it to Australia (step 12), then we can see the final steps traversing several service providers before reaching the host of the museum's website, which appears to be in Australia rather than New Zealand.

If you look at backbone communications statistics published by the likes of Verizon, dotcom-monitor, and Wondershare, you can see latency times exceeding 500ms and occasionally approaching one second between certain parts of the world.

 For more information about latency measures, you can refer to these sites:
Dotcom-monitor:
`https://www.dotcom-tools.com/internet-backbone-latency.aspx`
Verizon: `http://www.verizonenterprise.com/about/network/latency/`
Wondershare: `https://wondernetwork.com/pings`

Going back to our trusty database, the reason it is sensitive to latency is because the interaction with a database is not a single step, but actually a series of exchanges, a conversation if you like, between the database and the client. Whilst this conversation takes place, resources need to be dedicated to the conversation, as well as potentially blocking or limiting access to the data for other clients. If we have many slow conversations, then a lot of resources get tied up. The solution for this is for the database to limit the time resources held. You could of course extend the amount of time allowed by the database, but you would also soon see all sorts of knock on effects.

By deploying an agent locally, we can have the conversation with the database run very quickly, and then the data flowing to or from the agent can be passed using less time-sensitive mechanisms, using techniques that allow us to share resources between multiple conversations.

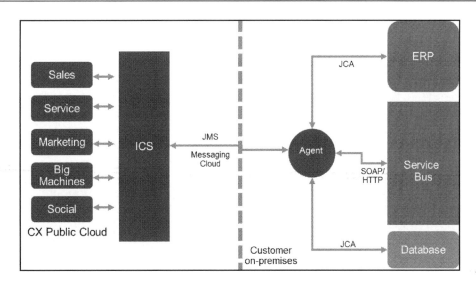

In the previous diagram, we can see a logical presentation showing how the agent fits in. Traditionally, without the agent, the deployment would look more akin to the following diagram:

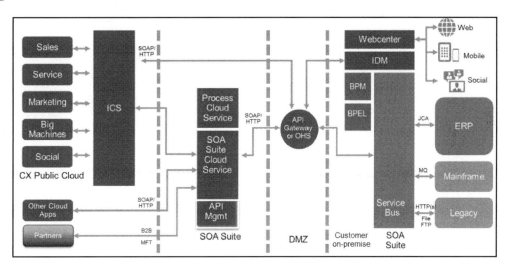

From a security perspective, having systems from outside your network start talking with secure databases is just too dangerous. It would be like allowing anyone to knock at your front door and allow them to go inspect the contents of your safe. Do you trust these visitors? Are they from where they say they are from? Do they have the authority to look that they claim to have? Even if you had an agreement that only visitors who claim to be from the local police station and are wearing a police uniform are allowed, this would be a risk, as you do not know if someone has walked into that police station and borrowed a uniform. It is an IT security person's job to engage and deal with these problems. So, how can we help?

Like using a browser, if we always start the conversation then we can eliminate a range of these concerns as we have chosen when and who we start a conversation with. If we communicate to the outside world through common mechanisms, then the security team do not have to set up any special channels for us. Consider the effort to allow you to use the phone versus establishing a new special courier service. All the security and checks have been done for phones, but not for each special courier. Remember, each time some new mechanism for communicating outside of our environment adds a new risk of error–let's face it, software is complex and written by humans, so it is vulnerable to having bugs that can be exploited; setting up networks is done by people and can be prone to error.

This analogy in IT terms means using web traffic and the security protocols available. Rather than a browser, we use an agent running within our environment.

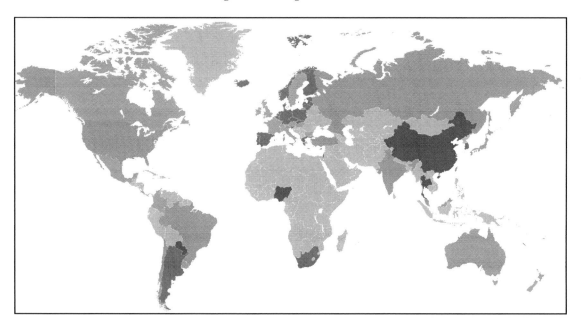

Color Code	Description
	Most restricted
	Restricted
	Some restrictions
	Minimal restrictions
	Effectively no restrictions
	No legislation or no information available

The map source–*US Department of Commerce and country specific legislation ©Forrester Research (All rights reserved).*

The commercial and legal aspects are closely related to the security considerations. In many countries, the location of where information is processed is very simple, to the point that presenting a view of the data using an application or browser means that processing is being performed in the location of where the browser is active. So, as you can imagine, data flowing through a middleware environment, regardless of the quality of hosting and whether it is completely transient, will mean data moving potentially to different countries and agreements and the legality or recognition of agreements is a fairly quickly changing landscape (the previous map helps illustrate the diversity of positions on data security). As a result, particularly in business-to-business and business-to-government arrangements, where data compliance considerations are being cascaded to third or fourth parties, it is often easier commercially to place very simple stipulations on vendors, such as the data can only reside, be processed or be accessed in country *x*. When dealing with very sensitive data, such that clinical information, or that could be considered national security sensitive (and this can often be not the data, but the existence of the data), the drive to restrict data locations is at least desirable, if not necessary.

With such constraints and the cloud meant to remove physical considerations of where and how systems are deployed, there is a clear conflict.

The final driver we need to consider is a blend of commercial and legacy. Whilst we are seeing the adoption of cloud in its many forms, if a company has invested in an on-premises system, the value in moving such a solution to the cloud can be heavily influenced by investment cycles–if a company has acquired infrastructure in the last five years, then there is the commercial benefit in ensuring the investment is capitalized upon, and potentially even having the value of the asset drawn out if possible. This can often lead to the second consideration, which is that the system concerned is too delicate or heavily modified, which means that any combination of cost, effort, or risk (real or perceived), cannot justify doing anything other than leaving it in place.

As you can see from these challenges, there is a need to be able to interact with on-premises solutions in a manner that means communication is driven from somewhere on-premises and potentially have the raw data processed on-premises as well.

Whilst this describes the underlying challenges that the use of an agent is trying to address, we can look at things in a very practical way. The following table provides examples of using the agent and why it is being used (use-case):

Pattern	Use-Case
Synchronous request from cloud to on-premises to retrieve data	Getting the status of an order from **E-Business Suite** (**EBS**) in real time
Cloud events triggers asynchronous message exchange with on-premises events	Creation of an incident in RightNow causes creation of service request in EBS
On-premises events triggers asynchronous message exchange with the cloud	Service request update event results in asynchronous message-based synchronization with RightNow
Synchronize data extracts between on-premises and cloud applications	EBS-based customer data synchronized with **Human Capital Management** (**HCM**)

Prerequisites and deploying an agent

Today, both agents are made available through a bash shell installer (`.bsx`) file. This means you need a bash shell environment that has been certified by Oracle. Presently, this means running a Red Hat or Oracle Linux platform (Microsoft are increasingly incorporating support for Linux within Windows, but it has a way to go before this is production fit and certified by Oracle).

If you are not running one of these environments natively, then the easiest solution is to exploit a virtualization technology. Oracle offers several, in our case **VirtualBox** is the best answer. Oracle even provides a number of prebuilt VirtualBox environments that can be downloaded so we do not have to create a new operating system environment from scratch.

This approach is not the most ideal when it comes to production readiness, where you may wish to consider a Linux instance on native hardware or via a large-scale virtualization platform such as Oracle virtual machine, or Red Hat's equivalent.

 More information about bash shell executables can be obtained at
`http://www.linuxjournal.com/node/1005818`

Those of you who are technically savvy might ask the question: why not use a technology like Docker to create a suitable environment? Whilst Oracle is supporting Docker, presently there is no Docker configuration file for the ICS agent (this may well be offered as an option in the future). The way Docker works on Windows varies today depending upon the version of Windows and whether your CPU is 32-bit (although this is increasingly rare these days) or 64-bit. So, we would end up focusing more on the setup of the basic environment rather than the agent and its use.

The environment pre-requisites differ depending on the agent, as shown in the following table:

Pre-requisite	Connection agent	Execution agent
CPU	Minimum dual core 64-bit CPU.	As per connection agent–however, the potential need for scaling will mean this compute requirement will scale up a lot quicker than a connection agent.
Memory	Minimum of 9GB of RAM–this is made up of 8GB of RAM, which is required for the Agent, plus an additional 1GB to run the VM (this assumes that within the VM we are only running the basic services necessary for this use case).	As per connection agent, but scaling will drive a far quicker growth here.
Network	Visible connectivity to the core server.	Network back to the cloud ICS instance, but also the ability to connect to a web UI on the agent itself.

Storage	3GB.	5GB.
Java Version	Oracle Java 1.7 or later.	Oracle Java 1.7 or later.
Database	None (in fact ensure Derby DB is disabled).	Oracle Database (XE may be sufficient for small scenarios). This is included in the SOA Suite Virtual Box instance (need to ensure Derby DB is disabled).

You will need to download the following:

- VirtualBox–this can be downloaded from `https://www.virtualbox.org/wiki/Downloads`.
- Virtual machine for Virtual Box, a complete list of Oracle provided VMs can be found at `http://www.oracle.com/technetwork/community/developer-vm/index.html`. For our needs the latest SOA Suite VM is recommended as it will have Java.
- The agent will need to be downloaded–we will explain this in more detail shortly.

Setting up and starting the VM

VirtualBox provides a great deal of good documentation, so the following steps here are to provide an overview of what needs to be done. If you have some familiarity with Virtual Box then this will be sufficient. If you need more detailed guidance then we would recommend you review the VirtualBox documentation available at `https://www.virtualbox.org/`.

Before we start the process of getting the VM ready for use, we would recommend you consider copying the downloaded files just in case something gets corrupted during the install process given the size of the downloads.

The downloaded files need to be unpacked from the multipart compression file. Using unzip or 7-Zip, open the first file in the sequence and extract the OVA file. Once successfully extracted, double-click on the .ova file (if you have the file association established) or open VirtualBox and use the **File | Import Appliance** and locate the .ova file to import the file into VirtualBox. As the import starts, you will be asked to agree to the terms of the licensing as there are Oracle products installed onto the VM. With VirtualBox imported, we can start the virtual machine using the **Start** button on the menu bar.

Checking everything is ready

With the VM up and running we would recommend that you double-check that the right version of Java is running and the JAVA_HOME environmental variable is defined and available for you to use. This can be done by using the commands echo $JAVA_HOME and java -version, respectively.

We also need to be able to see the Internet from the virtual machine. The best way to do that is to execute a command such as ping cloud.oracle.com. If the command returns a result, then everything should be fine. If it fails, then we probably have network configuration issues with the virtual machine.

File permissions need to be such that the user you are using has read, write, and execute permissions on the filesystem where the agent will be installed–if in doubt, the easiest step is to sign in with root permissions (sudo root), provide the prompted credentials, then issue the chmod a+rwx * command, as this will grant all the permissions necessary, and then close the root session with the exit command. This is not recommended for a production environment. If you are unfamiliar with establishing roles and permissions in a production environment, I would look to get help from a system administrator.

Agent download

Using the browser within the virtual machine we have got set up, navigate to your instance of ICS, login, and then, within ICS, you need to navigate to the **Agents** part of the **Designer**. At this point, you will see a screen with a header like the following screenshot:

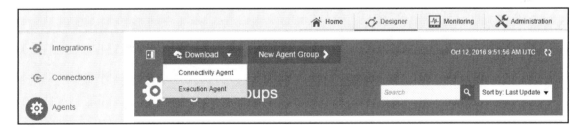

Note in the banner section, the **Download** option, which will offer the download of either the **Connectivity Agent** or **Execution Agent**. For our scenario, we need the **Connectivity Agent**. Clicking on this option will start the download of the installer file.

> Be aware, downloading of either agent involves retrieving a large download and it may take a little time. This is because the download includes a WebLogic container, communications agent, JCA connectors, and the remote agent logic.

Creating the Agent Group

Connection agents need to be associated with an **Agent Group**. As you can see in the previous screenshot, the heading section of the Agents view provides a **New Agent Group** button. By clicking on this, we get a dialog to define the group, as shown in the following screenshot:

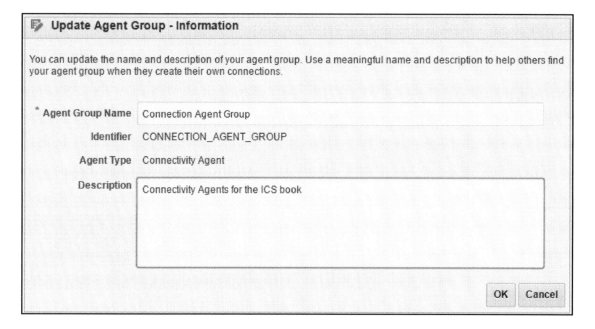

Complete the screen with the details provided in the following table and then click the **OK** button:

Property	Description
Agent Group Name	`Connection Agent Group`
Identifier	This will be determined by ICS for based on the name you provide.
Agent Type	This is defaulted to **Connectivity Agent**.
Description	We would recommend: `Connectivity Agents for the ICS book`

Installing the Connectivity Agent

With everything now ready, we can run the installation process. To do this we need to execute the following command:

```
./cloud-connectivity-agent-installer.bsx -h=https://<ICS Instance
name>.integration.<location e.g. us2>.oraclecloud.com:443 -u=<Oracle cloud
username> -p=<Oracle cloud Password> -ad=<connection group name>
```

Let's break down the command. As you can see, we are asking the `.bsx` file to execute in the local filesystem. We are providing the agent with the address of the server to which the **Connectivity Agent** needs to support, including the port ID for SSL (typically `443`). The port number needs to be explicit as there is a possibility that within the networking environment ports are being redirected (this is sometimes done for security reasons, or to deal with the possibility of multiple servers needing SSL deployed in the same environment). The `-u` and `-p` parameters are the credentials defined to allow the agent to connect with the server–such as your credentials.

We would recommend that, when using connection agents, separate credentials are established within the configuration for Oracle Cloud where you instantiated the ICS instance. (`https://cloud.oracle.com/home`). This means, if you must revoke a user's account, you do not accidentally cut off an agent. It also means that changing security settings will make the impact more easily recognizable in terms of operational processes.

The last parameter shown (-ad) is to link the agent to the **Agent Group** within ICS. This needs to correlate to the identifier of the **Agent Group** (the ICS generated identifier you see when creating the **Agent Group**–which can also be seen by clicking on the group's **name** in the **Agent Group** list view). The following screenshot shows the start of the installation process with the tool verifying the parameters:

```
[oracle@soa-training ICSAgent]$ ./cloud-connectivity-agent-installer.bsx -h=https://
Argument -- -h=https://            .integration.us2.oraclecloud.com:443
Argument -- -u=
Argument -- -p=******
Argument -- -ad=CONNECTION_AGENT_GROUP
minimum free space available requirement is 5 GB
Enough Space Available
Linux Operating System.....Proceeding with installation
Java Home Check Verified OK
Oracle Java is Present,Verified OK
JAVA 64-Bit is Present,Verified OK
Derby Check Verified OK
HOSTURL  = https://            integration.us2.oraclecloud.com:443
USENAME     =
PASSWORD    = ******
PROXYHOST   =
PROXYPORT   =
AGENTDEFINITION = CONNECTION_AGENT_GROUP
DATABASEPASSWORD =
AGENTUSER   =
AGENTPORT   =
AGENTPROFILE =
NOPROXYHOSTS =
https protocol
Valid hostURL provided
            .integration.us2.oraclecloud.com is alive
(Not all processes could be identified, non-owned process info
 will not be shown, you would have to be root to see it all.)
No conflicting Process Running, Verified OK
Checking the installation directory for unwanted files or directories.
Finished checking the installation directory for unwanted files or directories.

Self Extracting Installer

./agentInstaller/
./agentInstaller/wls/
./agentInstaller/wls/wls_jrf_generic.jar
tar: ./agentInstaller/wls/wls_jrf_generic.jar: Wrote only 3584 of 10240 bytes
```

Depending upon the prebuilt VM you start with, `/u01/` may not have sufficient space. This can be addressed either by using VirtualBox to extend the virtual disk or, for the purposes of the demo, utilizing another part of the file system.

If your install does fail because of space issues, then the filesystem being installed to must be cleared out except for the `.bsx` file.

Do not try and install with root permissions, as this will cause the installation to fail.

If the agent is failing to connect to the Internet, it may be that there is a proxy in the way–therefore the agent will need to know about this. You can determine if a proxy is in place if your browser can connect and then examine its Internet connection properties, or visit `http://www.lagado.com/proxy-test`, which uses the HTTP information to determine the existence of a proxy.

Note that the **Connectivity Agent** installer can also utilize additional optional parameters to specify information such as web proxy servers, for example. The complete list of additional attributes is available in the documentation.

The installation process can take a little while, particularly as the agent generates additional meta information about its deployment. You can confirm a successful deployment as the agent will communicate back to the ICS instance and declare its existence, which will increase the agents count, as you can see in the following screenshot:

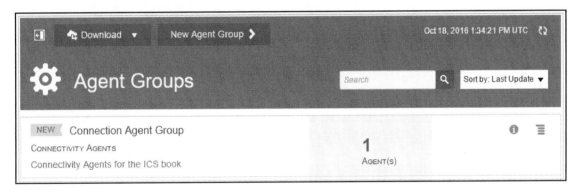

We can see more information about the agents, by clicking on the agent count, which will display the following information:

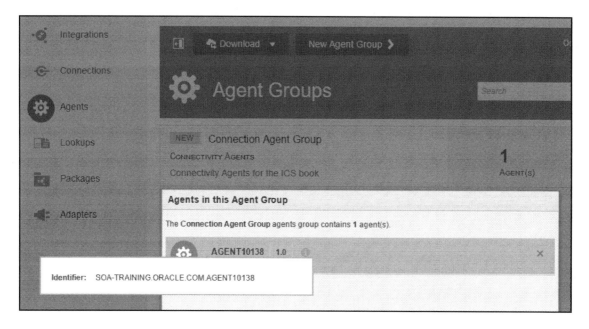

When we click on the information icon for an agent, we can see the agent's unique identifier, which is a composition of the host information and an agent count maintained by the ICS server.

Installing the Execution Agent

Unlike the installation of the Connectivity Agent, the Execution Agent requires no parameters; instead it prompts the user for some of the same information. But it also requires more information. Once unpacked from its zip file in a suitable location, run the following command:

```
./cloud-execution-agent-installer.bsx
```

The following table will explain each of the prompts of the installer and the recommended values to use:

Property	Value
Enter your ICS subscription URL for authentication	This needs to be the web address of your instance of ICS in the Oracle cloud, for example: `https://<ICS Instance name>.integration.<location e.g. us2>.oraclecloud.com`
Enter ICS subscription Username	The installer needs credentials to be able to interact with the server. Ideally separate credentials in `https://cloud.oracle.com/home` will be set up. But in the worst case, provide your username.
Enter ICS subscription password	Provide the matching password to the supplied user name.
Enter HTTPS Proxy Server Host Name	If you have a proxy server between you and the Internet, you need to provide its server name. If there is no proxy, simply press *Enter* and continue.
Enter HTTPS Proxy Server Port Number	As with the proxy hostname–if it does not exist just press *Enter*, otherwise provide it to the port it is using. If your browser is configured to use a proxy, you can extract the information from there.

At this stage, the agent will attempt to contact the server in the Oracle cloud to validate the information provided If successful, then it will start to unpack itself and run the more advanced configuration steps necessary. There are further questions to be addressed to facilitate the installation itself:

Property	Value
Password for <user>	`<user>` will be the name of the user currently being run for the installation, provide the password for this user.
What do you want to call this Execution Agent?	We need to provide a meaningful agent name so we can identify this agent later. We would recommend: `ICSBookExeAgent1`.
Default Install Path for ICS Execution Agent	The installer will display the installation location for the executable agent. You can at this point provide an alternative path. However, we recommend accepting the default by pressing *Enter*.

Default group is	If the installer can determine the correct user group in the OS to use for the installation then it will indicate this in the message, and it can be accepted by hitting *Enter*. It is possible it may not have resolved or you wish to change it. The available groups can be determined by using the command `groups` in a command shell (assuming you are running the command as the installation user). If you need to provide this, the options are going to be very much dependent upon your environment setup–so this will down to good judgment or advice from a system administrator.
Enter Password for the default user WebLogic	As this involves the installation of a WebLogic server, we need to provide the default server user password. For this exercise, we would recommend using `welcome1`.
Enter the Installation Type (compact_domain or expanded_domain?)	This relates to the WebLogic deployment again. For demo and trial purposes a `compact_domain` is sufficient. However, for a production environment we would not recommend this. Answer this prompt by keying `compact_domain`.
Enter Database Type (JavaDB or Oracle DB)?	As with the installation type for a trial or demo we would recommend JavaDB (very much the compact or expanded domain–keep things small, but for production we would recommend connecting to an Oracle Database). Therefore, key in `JavaDB`.

Differences between execution and connection agents

We have identified various aspects of the differences between a connection and execution agent. But let's bring those points together and look at the key differences between the two types of agents, which are summarized in the following table:

Execution Agent	Connection Agent
Contains the core run engine of ICS, but not all the connectors–so it executes logic locally	Connector rich and carries frameworks to deliver and receive data from the core engine
Larger more complex footprint as it needs to persist information	Smaller footprint, persisting only information necessary to deliver the connectivity required
Has the means to define local users	No concept of local users

Upgrading your agent

Whilst we are looking at the installation considerations, we should also look at the maintenance cycle, which will require the agent to be upgraded (or patched depending upon the revision number). This can be done by clicking on the agent in the **Agent** screen as you would when installing the agent.

Once this file is downloaded, we need to unpack the zipped contents, which will contain both the `.bsz` file, but also a `.zip` file for patching called `cloud-connectivity-agent-patcher.zip`. This zip file then needs to be unzipped, which will provide a number of files including a shell script (`.sh`).

You need to then execute the patch script provided with a command as follows:

```
./cloud-connectivity-agent-patcher.sh -
agentInstallDir=AGENT_INSTALL_DIR -icsUn=ICS_username -icsPwd=ICS_password
-icsUrl=https://ICS_host:secure_port -patchZipFile=file_name.zip -
au=agent_username -ap=agent_password -aport=agent_port -pHost=proxy_host -
pPort=proxy_port
```

With the appropriate values substituted in the same way as the original installation.

You can verify that the patching has been completed correctly by examining the agent's folder structure for backup of `soa`, `osb` and `lib` folders, where each backup is post-fixed with `_BAK_PRE_NEW-VERSION`.

Starting and stopping the Agent

We obviously need to know how to start and stop the Agent. This is done by the use of two provided scripts, unsurprisingly called `startAgent.sh` and `stopAgent.sh`, and they can be found in the base folder of the agent installation. The scripts do not fork the process, so if you want to release the command line shell you need to include the `&` in the command.

Troubleshooting

An IT landscape is a complex and many layered thing with opportunities for things to go wrong. ICS will monitor its agents as best it can, but there are scenarios where ICS may experience issues and the ICS core will not be aware of them. Troubleshooting should always start with ICS' **Monitoring** view, but there may be times where this does not give us sufficient insight into what is going on. Let's quickly take a look at some of the possibilities for troubleshooting.

Agent log files

Some problems can be easily spotted by looking at the agent's own log files, which are located a long way into the file structure of the deployment `agenthome/user_projects/domains/agent-domain/servers/AdminServer /logs`. Operationally, it might be worth also trying to monitor this location with a tool.

The agent as a WebLogic container

The agent functionality is delivered through the use of a WebLogic server. As a result we could sign into the WebLogic server console and view what it thinks is going on, for example, is the agent running within the server? This can be determined by navigating the UI through **Deployments** | **agent-webapp** | **Testing** and using the WebLogic tools to examine the agent.

Just start WebLogic

One of the recommended practices when investigating problems is to simplify. As the agent is part of a WebLogic container, we can simply start WebLogic and evaluate whether that works. The scripts for running the deployment as a WebLogic instance can be located within the installation filesystem at `/agenthome/user_projects/domains/agent-domain/bin`.

Sanity check the configuration

It is always possible that something simple has changed within the execution environment. Rather than going through the process of a re-installation, we can apply any corrections to the configuration files directly, which can be the `/agenthome/user_projects/domains/agent-domain/agent/config`. Before making any changes, we would always advocate taking a backup of the current state.

Building the integration

With an agent deployed, having addressed the reasons for having an agent, we can explore our scenario. As mentioned in the introduction in this chapter, we are going to demonstrate the detection of additions or changes to `Airport` data within an on-premises database by a connection agent. The database records that are detected as having been changed by the agent are then sent to the core ICS server running in the Oracle cloud to pass through the integration and be transmitted to the target. This reflects the sort of scenarios you could find when perhaps needing to integrate an on-premises **E-Business Suite** (**EBS**) that uses the idea of open tables as its interface. EBS, like many enterprise solutions, will offer an interface by exposing a view of its data that the outside world can interact with.

When we detect the data change on the on-premises database, the record will be retrieved and concatenated into a string that is sent to a Mockable REST endpoint. This second stage is to help us easily see that we can manipulate the data and see it in Mockable, rather than have a meaningful story. The scenario should look like the following diagram:

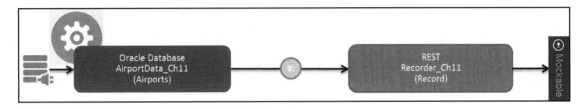

Preparation

This integration does mean that we have some additional setup to do in terms of readying the on-premises database in the same environment (local network, security zone and so on) that we have deployed the agent into. Depending upon the virtual machine that has been used, it is possible that the database has already been deployed. The database can be any of the Oracle DB versions from an XE edition through to an enterprise deployment. As there is plenty of documentation available on setting up an Oracle Database or exploiting an instance on the virtual machine, we are going to skip the step that shows the details of deploying the database. If you deploy the database, make sure you keep a note of the SID or service name. If the database has already been deployed, we need to find these details from the configuration documentation.

With the database ready, the first step is to create a schema with some storage and a user id we shall call `icsbook`. From either SQLNet or from an IDE such as JDeveloper or SQL Developer, for example, we need to run the following command:

```
DROP TABLESPACE icsbookspace INCLUDING CONTENTS AND DATAFILES;
-- DROP USER icsbook ;
CREATE TABLESPACE
   icsbookspace
datafile
   '/u01/app/oracle/oradata/demos/icsbook.dbf'
size   60m autoextend on next 20m maxsize 200m;
CREATE USER icsbook IDENTIFIED BY icsbook
```

```
        DEFAULT TABLESPACE icsbookspace
        TEMPORARY TABLESPACE temp
        QUOTA UNLIMITED ON icsbookspace ;
GRANT CONNECT, DBA to icsbook ;
GRANT create table, create sequence to icsbook ;
GRANT all privileges to icsbook ;
```

This code is provided with the downloads for this chapter, and is called `createUser.sql`. Before running the SQL, make sure the data file path is suitable for your environment.

With the user and the storage established, we can execute the script to create the table that will represent the required data. This is provided within a file called `createTables.sql`, which contains the following code:

```
CREATE TABLE icsbook.Airports
(
airportId int primary key,
ident varchar2 (10),
airportType varchar2 (20),
airportName varchar2 (255),
latitude number (11,5),
longitude number (11,5),
elevation number (6),
continent varchar2(2),
country varchar2(3),
region varchar2(6),
muncipality varchar2(30),
scheduleFlights varchar2(5),
gpsCode varchar2(5),
IATACode varchar2(5) default null,
localcode varchar2(10),
homeLink varchar2(4000) default null,
wikipediaLink varchar2(4000) default null,
keywords varchar2(4000) default null,
icsStatus varchar2(4) default 'new' not null)
TABLESPACE icsbookspace
;
```

Note in the table, in addition to all the columns in the table, matching the data provided for Chapter 9, *Managed File Transfer with Scheduling* is a column called `icsStatus`. This column is important, as you will see.

The final step is to add the first row into the table. This can be done with the following SQL command (which is available in the download set and is called `insertAirportRecord.sql`):

```
INSERT_INTO icsbook.airports
(AirportId, ident, airportType,
 airportName, comm, latitude,
 longitude, elevation, continent,
 country, region, muncipality,
 scheduleFlights, gpsCode, IATACode,
 localcode, homeLink, wikipediaLink,
 keywords ) VALUES
(1, 1, '',
 '', '', 1.1,
 1.1, 0, '',
 '', '', '',
 'no', '', '',
 '',
 null, null, null);
```

With the database populated with a single record, we need to ready things such that we have several records that can be added. This can be achieved by replacing the values in the insert statement with the values from the resources provided in `chapter 9`, *Managed File Transfer with Scheduling*.

The final piece of preparation is to create the Mockable.io stub. Rather than describing each of the steps, as we have done this many times before, the following table should give us all the information necessary to establish a REST configuration:

Property	Description
Path	The path will be prefixed with your Mockable.io domain. Then we want to add `Recorder` as this service is just going to record the calls for us.
Verb	This aligns to the REST convention. So to provide a response we should use `POST`.
Headers	We are not going to handle any headers–so leave this blank.
Response status	We need to provide an HTTP 200 code–so leave this with the default value.
Content-Type	We should supply a JSON structure given that this is a REST service–so select **application/json**.
Content-encoding	We can leave this defaulting to **UTF-8**.

Response Body	Leave the Dynamic Response body setting unset. But we can provide the following JSON sample:
	
	`{`
	`"ResponseStatus": "ok"`
	
	`}`

Display Name	We can leave this blank and allow Mockable to default the value for us.
Enable Request Logger	So, when requests are received, you can control whether the information is logged. For our benefit, we want to see what has been received. So, you want to click on the icon so it shows green.
Set response delay	Leave this as the default.

With the values provided, click on the **Save** and **Stopped** buttons so that the mock is saved and started ready for use. The **Stopped** button should now show **Started**.

With this setup completed, we can now move onto the integration.

Creating the integration

When we create an integration using either execution or connection agent(s), we use the cloud interface to describe the integration and the connections as we would for any integration. Let's start with the database connection first. So, once in the **Connections** list screen, we can create our two connections.

On-premises database connection

As with any new connection, start by clicking on **New Connection** and locate and select the Oracle Database connection within the list of available connections. This will launch the standard dialog to start defining a connection. Use the following table to complete the details:

Property	Description
Connection Name	`AirportData_Ch11`
Identifier	This will be proposed based on the connection name and there is no need to change unless you would like an alternate name.
Connection Role	**Trigger and Invoke**–this will allow us to create the extraction process, but if you choose, also create an insert operation.

Description	Connection via an agent to the airport data within the icsbook database

Completing this screen by clicking on the **Done** button will then display the full connection dialog, as shown in the following screenshot:

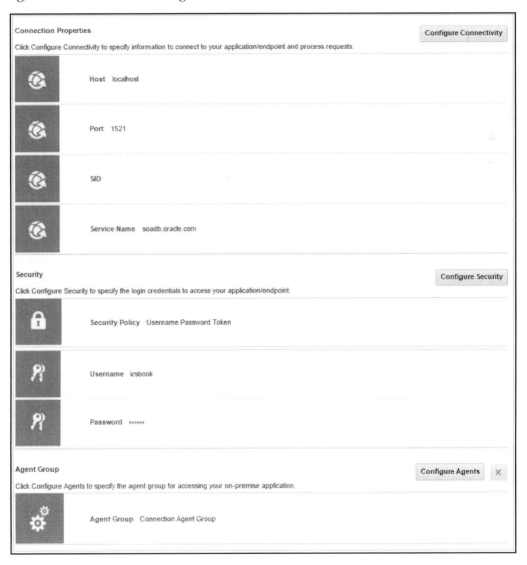

We can use the following table to complete the configuration of the database connection properties:

Property	Description
E-mail Address	Your e-mail address
Connectivity | Host	This is the hostname of the computer that is running the database. Given that the connection is executed by the agent on the same computer and our virtual machine is not too strict with its security, we can use `localhost`. Depending upon how you have set up the database, you may need to use the machine's hostname, its internal IP, or `127.0.0.1`.
Connectivity | Port	We need to identify which port is open for communicating with Oracle; typically this is `1521` for an Oracle Database as is the case in this example. But sometimes this will not be the case, as the ports can be changed for reasons of security.
Connectivity | SID	The final part of the connection is either the SID or service name being offered by the database. SID is commonly used, but the Oracle VM we took also has a service name. In this example, we have left this blank.
Connectivity | Service Name	If a SID is not provided then a service name needs to be. The example database used had the service name documented so we choose to use that.
Security | Security Policy	From options provided we are going to use a username and password, so select **Username Password Token** from the drop-down list.
Security | Username	Having used the create user script provided, we know that the credentials will be `icsbook` as a username.
Security | Password	Having used the create user script provided, we know that the credentials will be `icsbook` as a password.
Configure Agents | Agent Group	This will offer a list of the agent groups setup. Here we need to select the group that was previously set up that is, `Connection Agent Group`, and click on the **Use** button.

If you want to understand more about the differences between Service Name and an **System ID (SID)** then read `https://docs.oracle.com/cd /E11882_01/network.112/e41945/concepts.htm#NETAG177`

With these details provided, it just remains for us to click **Test** to ensure connectivity can be established, click **Save** and **Exit Connection**.

REST connection

Using the details of the previously created Mockable.io endpoint, we can create a REST connection with the following information:

Property	Description
Connection Name	`AirportDataRecorder_Ch11`
Identifier	This will be proposed based on the connection name and there is no need to change unless you would like an alternate name.
Connection Role	**Invoke**–this will allow us to call the REST endpoint with the simplified details of the airport record.
Description	`Connection via an agent to the airport data within the icsbook database`

And the connection details themselves are:

Property	Description
E-mail Address	Your e-mail address
**Connection Properties	Connection Type**	We have defined with Mockable.io a REST API, so you need to select the **REST API Base URL** option from the list.
**Connection Properties	Connection URL**	The connection URL is simply the server address of the Mockable.io account being used. For example, `http://demo1234567.mockable.io/`
**Security	Security Policy**	When the Mockable.io end of the integration was configured, we did not set up any security, so the option of **No Security Policy** can be selected.
Agent Group	As this end of the integration is not running on-premises, we do not need to define an agent group.

With these details provided, it just remains for us to click **Test** to ensure connectivity can be established, click **Save** and **Exit Connection**. We now have the connections for either end of our integration, so now for the last step in the integration itself.

Basic Map Data integration

Having navigated to the integrations list screen, we can start the creation of the integration using the **Create New Integration** button, and then select the **Basic Map Data** pattern. This takes us to the first screen for defining the integration, and the following values can be used to complete this step:

Property	Value
Integration Name	`MoveAirportDataToTheCloud_Ch11`
Identifier	This will be proposed based on the connection name and there is no need to change unless you would like an alternate name.
Version	01.00.0000
Package Name	`ics.book.ch11`
Description	`This integration takes new airport records from an on-premises database when they are first detected or changed and sends them to a REST service that is used for recording such events`

With these details, provided and the **Create** button clicked upon, we can start creating the integration by locating our `AirportData_Ch11` connection and dropping it onto the **Trigger** pad on the canvas. When the wizard is displayed, we can start to configure the endpoint for this integration with the following details:

Tab	Question	Action
Basic Info	**Call your endpoint field?**	To keep it simple, call it `Source`.
	Operation type	This will display a poll for **New** or **Changed** records, as this is the only thing that can be done when a database connection is being used as a source.

With these details the **Next** button can be used to access the next screen. We will then be presented with a screen like the following:

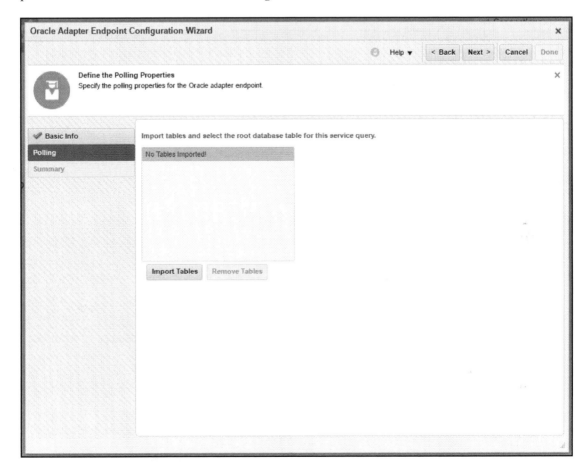

This part of the wizard is a little less conventional than many we have looked at. The objective is to first tell ICS which table we want to track for new records and changes. The wizard can first help us by retrieving some of the database metadata and letting us select the table of interest. The metadata can be retrieved by clicking on the **Import Tables** button.

If the agent is not running, then this process will fail and you will get a pop-up message, but with the agent running the metadata is retrieved, and the screen is updated to offer a drop-down selection of schemas, shown as follows:

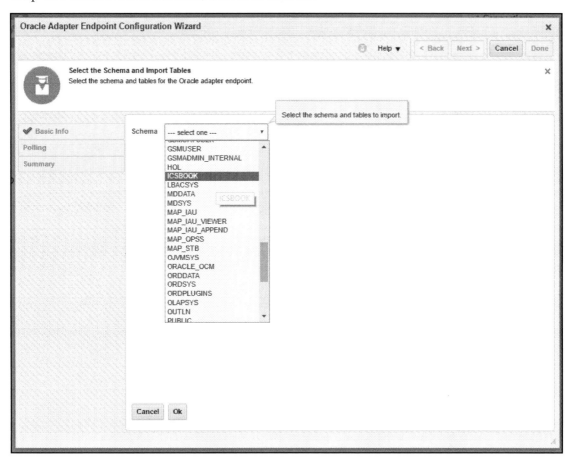

We should select the schema that was created earlier, which was called `icsbook` (but capitalized for the display). Once selected, the screen is again updated to show the available tables in the schema. As we only had one table, the screen will now appear like the following:

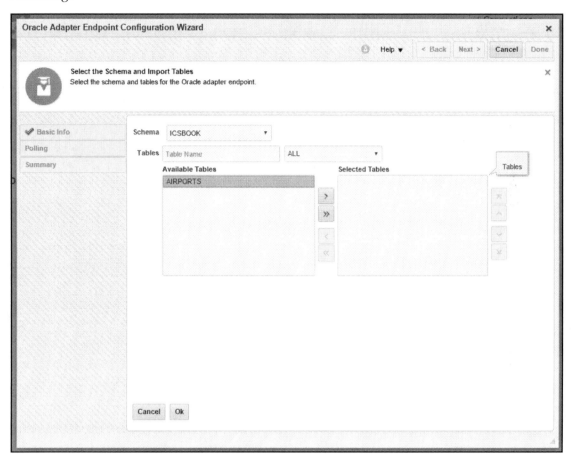

With only one table we should select it and use the **center arrow** to move it to the selected list of tables. Note how there is also a double arrow pointing right–this means multiple tables could also be selected. With tables selected, it is also possible to deselect them as well. At this point, we have now told ICS we want to know about changes to records in the `Airports` table within our `icsbook` schema, and we can progress to the next screen by clicking on **OK**.

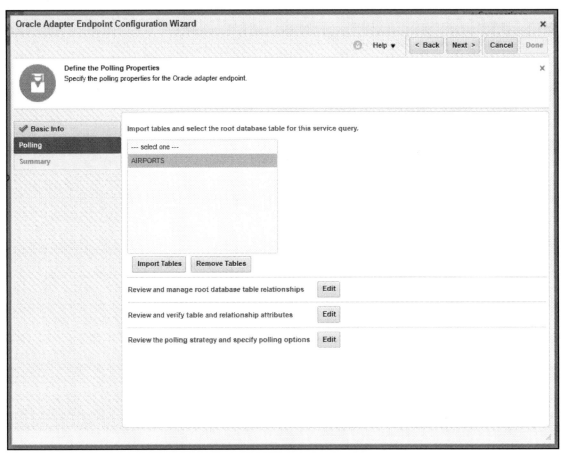

Now ICS knows which table(s) we are interested in monitoring and additional questions are presented, which allows us to describe table relationships, define how the agent knows which records to get, and the speed and frequency by which the data is checked for and sent back. Click on the **Edit** button for the **Review and manage root database table relationships** and we will see the following screen:

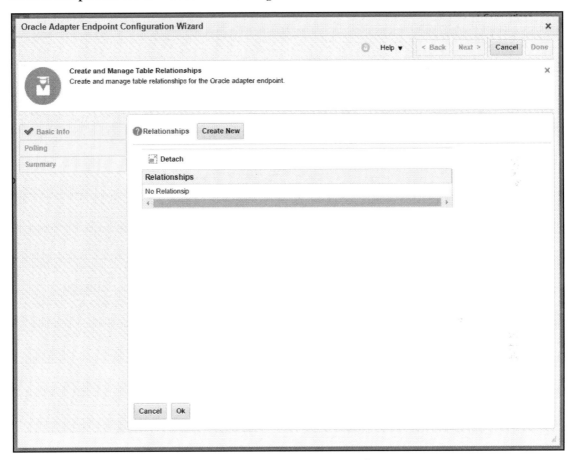

This screen offers us the chance to describe a **Relationship** to another table. This is important as you may wish to have data from related tables (such as when there is one too many relationships being stored within the data through a normalized schema). Another factor here is the possibility that the means by which you determine whether a record needs to be read is managed through a separate table, which matches the table of interest with primary keys and then an attribute field. The two tables are then kept in an aligned state using triggers on the source. The following diagram illustrates this idea:

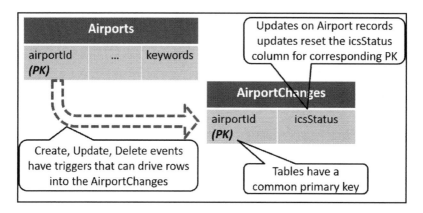

This approach means that the structure of the `Airports` table can remain unmodified. However, for our example, we have kept things nice and simple and incorporated the `icsStatus` field into our `Airports` table. This means we can retreat from this step using the **Cancel** button.

Select the **Edit** button for the **Review and verify table and relationship attributes** option. This will display the following dialog:

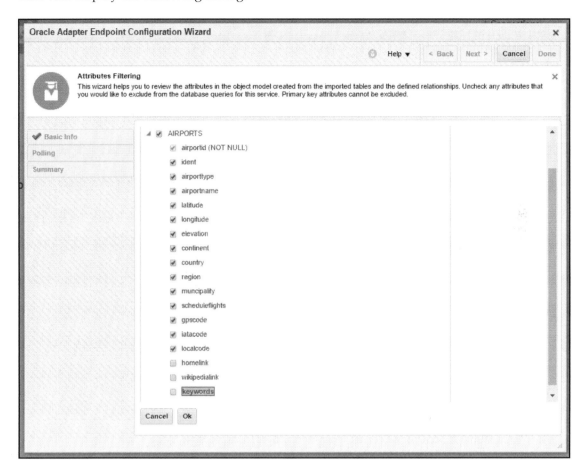

As you can see from the preceding screenshot, the metadata of the database includes each of its columns and we have the option to select which fields will be extracted from the table. To illustrate the point, we should deselect homeLink, wikipediaLink, and keywords. This step can then be completed by clicking on the **OK** button, which will return us to the previous screen.

We can now click the **Edit** button for the last area–**Review the polling strategy and specify polling options**. This will take us to the following screen:

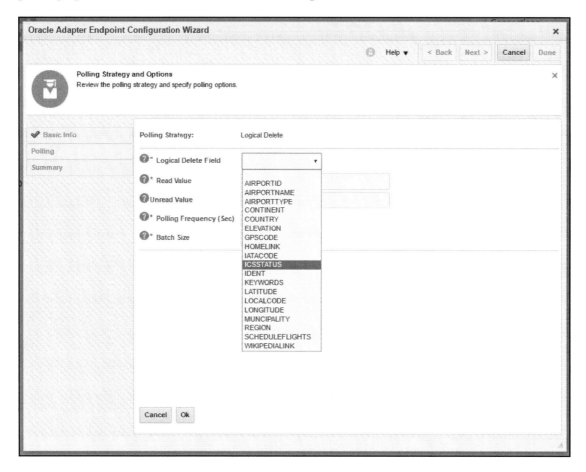

Here we have several values to help ICS determine which records need retrieving. The **Logical Delete Field** (so named as the state of the selected field and its value will mean that the record is no longer relevant–or logically deleted for the detection algorithm) defines the field that is used to track the record status and whether it should be picked up. As previously mentioned, in our example we are using icsStatus for this purpose, so it needs to be selected from the list.

With that column identified, we now need to tell ICS what value indicates that the record has been read already–we can provide the DONE value in this field. Correspondingly, we can also tell ICS what value to expect if it has not yet been read–note that, if the field was to represent multiple states, we can avoid setting this value, but we would suggest that it is set, so use the READY value. If this column has its value changed from DONE to READY, then it would be reread by ICS.

The last two values are about how much data collects in each inspection of the database, and how often to inspect it. We can leave these values with the defaults of 1 (record) and 5 seconds. Note how this is considerably quicker than the file polling we saw in Chapter 9, *Managed File Transfers with Scheduling*. The following screen shows us the completed values:

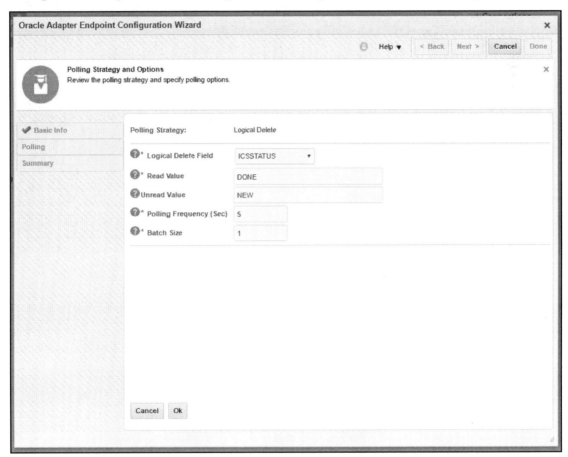

We can complete this screen by clicking on the **OK** button. When we return, we can click the **Next** button to move onto the **Summary** view. The **Summary** view provides information about the table, frequency, and so on. But it also provides a link that can be used to pop up a dialog showing the SQL that will be used by ICS' agent on the database. This is shown as follows:

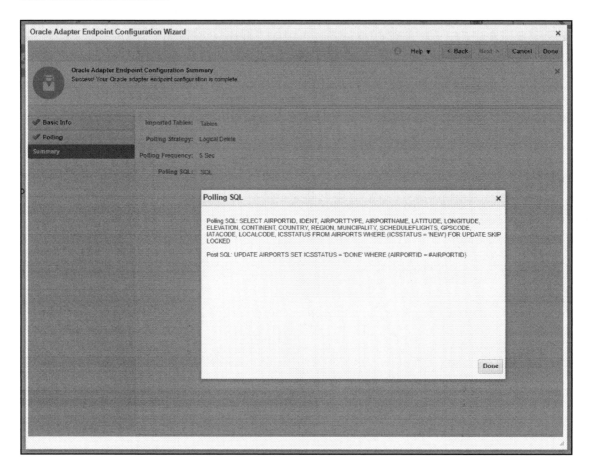

We can close the **Polling SQL** dialog with the **Done** button and then complete the configuration of the database side of our integration with the wizard's **Done** button as well.

Now we are looking at the canvas, we should drop the `AirportDataRecorder_Ch11` connection on to the **Invoke** pad on the canvas. The wizard for this end of the integration can be completed using the following table:

Tab	Question	Action
Basic Info	**Call your endpoint?**	To keep it simple, call it `Target`.
	What does this endpoint do?	Calls a Mockable.io endpoint for recording what was received from the Airports source.
	What is the endpoint's relative resource URI?	`/Recorder`
	What action does the endpoint Perform?	Select the `POST` option.
	Add and review parameters for this endpoint	Leave this checkbox unset.
	Configure a request payload for this endpoint	Set this checkbox here.
	Configure this endpoint to receive the response	Set this checkbox here.
	Configure Request Headers?	Leave these checkboxes unset.
	Configure Response Headers?	Leave these checkboxes unset.
Request	**Send attachments in request**	Leave these checkboxes unset.
	Request is HTML form	Leave these checkboxes unset.
	Select the request payload file	Select **JSON Sample**.
	Schema Location-OR-enter sample JSON	Click on the **Choose file** button. In the file browser navigate to where the downloaded files for this chapter are and select the `RecorderOutput.json` file and **OK** the dialog.
	Element	There is only an open option offered here, so there is no need to change it from request-wrapper.
	Select the type of payload with which you want the endpoint to receive	This should be set to **JSON**.

Response	Select the request payload file	Select **JSON Sample**.
	Schema Location-OR-enter sample JSON	Click on the **Choose file** button. In the file browser navigate to where the downloaded files for this chapter are and select the `RecorderResponse.json` file and **OK** the dialog.
	Element	There is only an open option offered here, so there is no need to change it from request-wrapper.

With this, we should now see the **Summary** view with the REST Service URI matching what was configured earlier. We can complete this wizard with the **Done** button as well.

Connecting endpoints and tracking

The last steps to perform for the integration are to complete the source to target mapping and establish the **Tracking** information.

Select the mapping icon on the canvas; the target only has one attribute called **Recorded**. What we are going to do is use the **concat** function to build a single string to display. Select the **Recorded** field on the right of the mapper and it will launch the **Build Mappings** screen. As we have done before, locate the **concat** function and drop it onto the statement side of the screen. We then drop the first source field we want in the string to be sent to Mockable, such as `airportId`, into the first child. Then, for the second child field, we should add a deliberate separator character to make the output easier. We would suggest adding |. With this done, we need to right-click on the field and select the **Insert Sibling After** option twice. We now repeat this for all the fields we wish to see in the output. Once we are happy that all the fields wanted are mapped, complete the dialog by clicking on **Save** and then the **Close** button.

The mapping screen should now look something like the following:

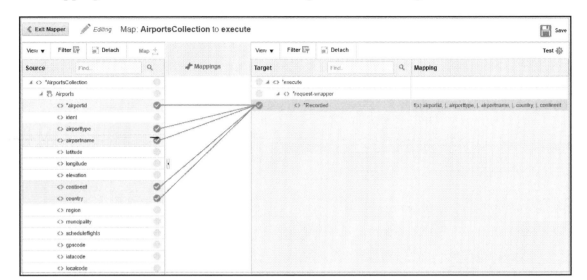

Click on **Save** and then **Exit Integration**. We can activate this integration ready for testing. If we are happy with this, then we can proceed by clicking on the **Save** button, followed by the **Exit Mapper** button. Our integration should now look like this:

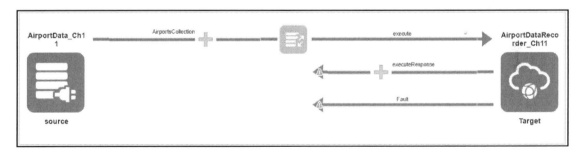

The final step, as you will know, is setting up the tracking. Click on the **Tracking** button, and then we can set the tracking to `airportId` and `airportName`. With that, we can close the tracker settings with the **Done** button. Now we can **Save** the integration and close the editor with **Exit Integration**.

With the integration complete, we can **Activate** the integration on the **Integrations** list.

Testing the integration

With the integration activated, we will see activity quickly, as the database will detect the records we have already added into the database. This can be confirmed by opening up the **Request Inspector** page in Mockable.io (available at the top of the site once we have logged in). We can use the left-hand side of the **Request Inspector** view to select the endpoint we want to see calls for.

The **Request Inspector** will show details along the lines of the following:

We can look more closely at the posted payload in Mockable:

X-Appengine-CityLatLong 51.262991,-1.093609
X-Cloud-Trace-Context 0c052e3a7cdc4b9fae0c34cc82bc81bb/6119334148502156466
X-Appengine-Default-Namespace
Content-Length 71
X-Appengine-Region eng
User-Agent
Host mockable.io
X-Zoo app-id=tomate-premium,domain=gmail.com,host=*.mockable.io
Content_Type application/json
Content_Length 71
X-Appengine-City
X-Appengine-Country
Content-Type application/json

Payload:

```
{
    "Recorded": "7962|small_airport|Cavage Personal Use Airport|NA|US"
}
```

We can trigger the integration by either using the SQL insert script we used earlier on, or by modifying the status value of the records already processed.

Summary

In this chapter, we looked at the underlying factors that can drive the need to use an agent with ICS. Some thought was given to how we can deploy an agent, both for production purposes and to deploy an agent for demo and development purposes. The differences between a connection and execution agent were reviewed. Once the theoretical aspects of agents had been completed, the chapter then quickly walked through the deployment and configuration of a connection agent that ran on-premises (depending on how you deployed the agent in a virtual machine as well). We then created an integration on ICS running in Oracle's cloud that used the agent pushing data from the on-premises database to the Mockable web service. Finally, we initiated the integration to see the agent in action.

In the next chapter, we move away from connecting systems or mocks of systems and concentrate on how we can ensure that our integration platform is running smoothly, along with the integrations it is executing. We will also look at what to do in the event of an error and how to go about identifying and resolving the problem.

12

Are My Integrations Running Fine, and What If They Are Not?

In this chapter, rather than understanding how to build integrations, we are going to examine what information is available that tells us whether or not our integrations, connectors, and agents are working or not; and how to get information that can point to the source of the problem.

Integrations can experience difficulties as a result of many issues, caused by a range of factors such as:

- The systems being integrated are not running or functioning correctly
- Data definitions have changed, resulting that your transformations stop working
- Connections fails as credentials get changed
- Tokens and/or SSL certificates are revoked or expire
- Networks are not performing properly

Trying to provide guidance on how to identify every possible issue or permutation of issues would turn this book into many thousands of pages, and becomes rather unwieldy. So, in the following pages we will look at what the monitoring information ICS offers, and what is available to allow us to understand and diagnose problems that could exist in the design side of ICS (defining integrations, and so on) or the runtime (execution of integrations). In a perfect world everything would work flawlessly forever, but ultimately software, hardware, and data centers are all impacted by humans, and we do occasionally make mistakes. So we do need to know how we can rule out these issues.

In addition to monitoring, ICS offers some administration capabilities such as adding certificates, setting logging information, and emailing reports, all of which directly relate to recognizing errors and resolving them.

Core monitoring information

To help understand what is going on and start any possible problem identification and resolution, it is first best to understand the information that is provided. So we will start by looking at the status indicators and views into what is happening with ICS and the integrations that have been activated.

ICS – all is well

Although problems are more likely to originate within an integration, there is always the possibility that ICS itself has experienced a problem. We can check on the wellbeing of ICS from several places, all of which lead to the **System Health** view shown as follows:

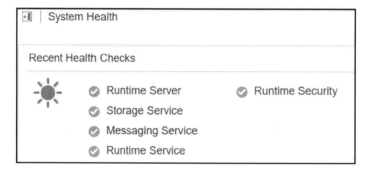

As you can see, the **System Health** is broken down into several different areas. Some of these measures, if indicating a problem, are likely to have a blanket impact, such as the **Storage Service**, others such as the **Messaging Service** will only impact some services.

The quickest route to the information is the summary indicator; we can see it is visible all the time at the top right of the screen, with a color-coded symbol that reflects the total status, so if anything is degraded then this status will degrade.

By clicking on the icon we will see the **System Health** view shown in the preceding screenshot. We can also navigate to the **System Health** from the monitoring dashboard which we will explore in a moment.

Dashboard

The dashboard is the home screen for all monitoring activities for ICS. From the perspective of someone concerned with the health of a production instance of ICS, this is a great tool, but in a development context the dashboard view is going to be of relatively limited value and you will need to drill into the detail to see how the integration(s) you are working on are performing.

It is worth noting that the dashboard and the majority of views that represent aggregated data will have a drop down menu that allows you to view data over several time periods, which are:

- **Last 1 Hour**
- **Last 6 Hours**
- **Last 1 Day**
- **Last 2 Days**
- **Last 3 Days**
- **Since First Activation**

As you can see in the preceding screenshot, the **Integration Dashboard** comprises a menu to access more detailed views on the left and a set of largely graphical status views on the right. The left-hand side can be characterized as three rows of aggregated statistics. The top row describes how well those integrations that have been activated are performing. The second row reflects how much of the resources available are being utilized, and the final row provides some time series insight into how much activity is occurring in the environment.

If you are familiar with Oracle's Alta UI style, then you will quickly recognize that the different graph representations will provide additional information in tool tips if you hover the cursor over something – such as a column in a graph. But also, in most cases, there is the means to drill down into more detail by clicking on the UI component. Most of the dashboard components here have some form of drill down. As with all good user interfaces, we do have within the monitoring views multiple ways to reach the same information. Rather than describe them, we have overlaid the navigation points onto the dashboard graphs in the following diagram:

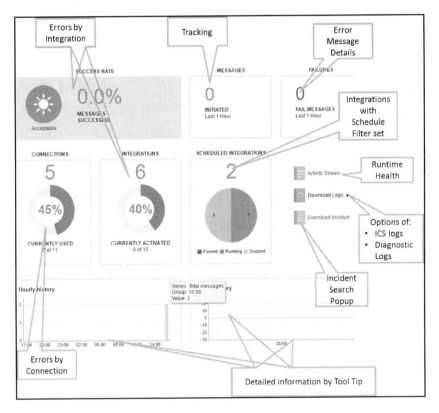

You can get more information about Oracle's Alta UI at
`http://www.oracle.com/webfolder/ux/middleware/alta/index.html`.

The left-hand menu provides one of the alternate routes to more detailed information. Most of the menus expand to a set of sub menus. The following diagram shows how the menus expand:

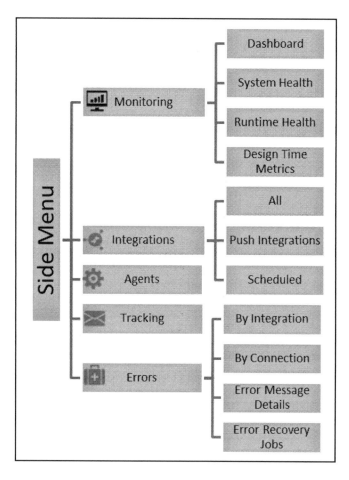

Inducing errors for integrations

Before we can start looking at errors, it helps if we can induce problems to ensure the expected behavior is performed when testing an integration, otherwise proving that our error handling is OK is going to be very much by chance. Some easy scenarios to create are:

- Configuring the endpoint to return an error code (this is generally going to be easier with REST endpoints in Apiary)
- Completely disabling the endpoint (in the case of Mockable, as we have seen in previous chapters, stopping and starting endpoints is a simple action)
- Change the credentials for the endpoint, such as Twitter or Google, so the credentials passed are incorrect

For the purposes of creating the illustrations of errors, we will use Mockable to stop endpoints in order to create errors that demonstrate what ICS does.

Runtime health

If you click on the **Runtime Health** option in the **Monitoring** menu, you will see a view that is a hybrid, based on the Integration views and the dashboard, as shown in the following screenshot. Like the dashboard, the figures reflect all integrations within the environment, but the headline statistics of the number of messages received, processed, and so on, are the same as those provided at the integrations level – where we will explain the meaning of the numbers. Clicking on these statistics will take you to different filtered views of integration instances, which we will describe in more depth shortly. The important point is that we can drill into the meaning of these numbers as necessary.

The following screenshot shows the **Runtime Health** view:

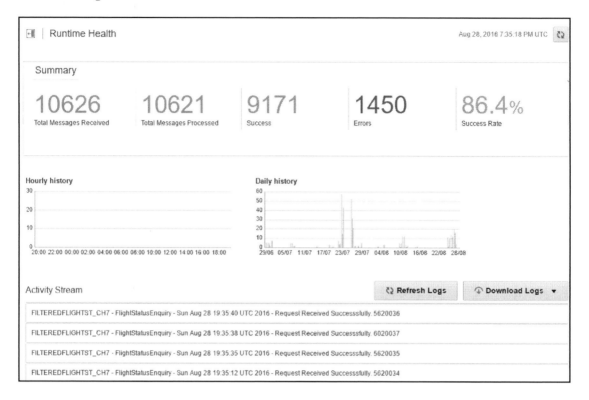

The charts and log links are the same as the dashboard. The distinct part of this view is the **Activity Stream**, which will reflect key events up to the moment within ICS on the screen each time it is refreshed. For example, as you can see in the **Activity Stream**, the `FilteredFlightStatus_Ch7` integration was triggered several times, just prior to the view being refreshed (which must be performed manually).

Design time metrics

The design time metrics provide some insights into the state of the ICS, from the perspective of the design state and design characteristics of the integrations and connections, such as how many integrations are in the different states between draft and active. This is useful, as it will help with housekeeping; in a development environment it is easy for people to create artifacts and then not clear them down once they have determined that they do not do what is required:

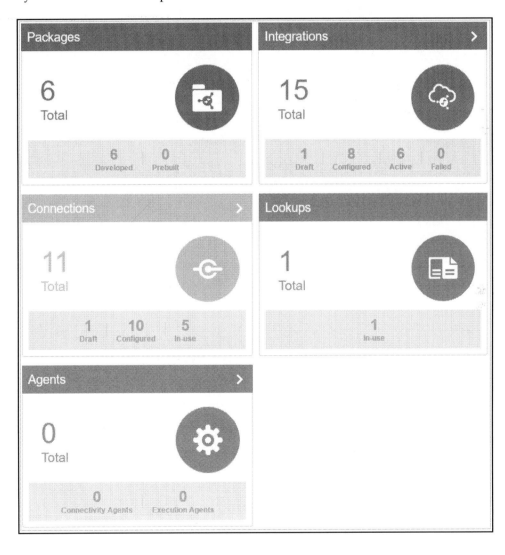

You may note in the preceding screenshot, that the heading has an arrow on the right. By clicking on the arrow, you can click a number of additional statistics. For example, with integrations you can examine how the integrations are split across the different patterns, and by the different adapters being used. As you click through the different views you will see an additional arrow displayed, to scroll back as appropriate as shown in the following screenshot:

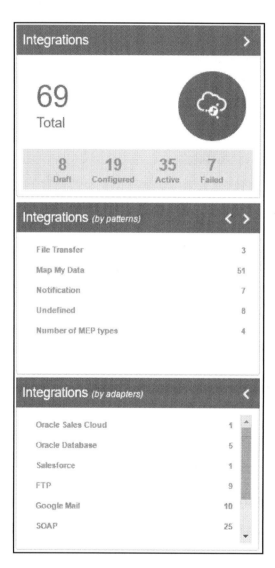

Looking at integrations

Within the integrations menu we can look at all the integrations and use the menus to filter them down, initiated by a scheduler or via push, that is to say, the integrations are triggered by something calling the integration, such as an external application.

All of these views present a list of appropriate integrations showing:

- Received triggers: The number of time the integration has been requested
- Integrations processed: This reflects the possibility that some integrations that are asynchronous in manner may take a time to complete (therefore the received triggers may be greater than those processed)
- Success: That is integrations that completed, not following any error paths
- Integrations that have failed: This is either because of ICS or an external connection not working

You may have also noticed that, like most other views, you can filter down the list of integrations by name in the same way as you can in the designer. In addition to this, the data displayed is filtered by what has occurred in the selected time period as previously mentioned. An example can be seen in the following screenshot:

As you can see in the preceding screenshot, we have filtered the list of **Push Integrations** down to those related to Chapter 7, *Routing and Filtering* (by setting the filter field to `Ch7`) and one of the integration has experienced an error.

To see the views, we will look at the test scenario for the `FilteredFlightStatusEnquiry` service that we produced in Chapter 7, *Routing and Filtering*, which will need to be run a number of times. The service was tracked using the attribute `faFlightID`, and we have added the `ident` and `prefix` to this now (Refer to `Chapter 2`, *Integrating Our First Two Applications*, if you need to see how this is setup). The filter worked on whether the `suffix` element had a value of `BA`. Most of the executions should have that value set to `BA`. Each time you trigger the integration, make sure that at least the `faFlightID` is different. So that errors can be seen, log into Mockable and stop the appropriate mock and then trigger the integration again (with the `suffix` set to `BA`) and we will be able to see an instance of the integration reporting an error. Having run SoapUI several times, you should be able to navigate to the monitoring part of ICS and click on the **Push Integrations** sub menu. We have chosen `FilteredFlightStatusEnquiry_Ch7` so we can illustrate what happens when a filter eliminates an event.

We can focus on the instances of the integration that have run by clicking on the different measures, as it will filter the list of instances displayed accordingly (for example showing everything that was received, succeeded, or caused an error). To best illustrate things, click on **Received**. With this we get a view like as follows:

This list is in time series with the latest instance at the top. In this case, the last instance that was executed had failed as we had disabled the `Mockable.io` on that occasion. Note how the heading for each instance reflects both the `faFlightID` but also a unique **Instance ID**. The **Instance ID** is provided by ICS to each instance of the integration that is run, and is unique across all the integrations on this instance of the ICS service.

We can examine more detail and see visually what has happened with each instance of the service by clicking on the instance name (For example, `faFlightID: 130`). This will present a variation of the editor view, as you can see in the following screenshot:

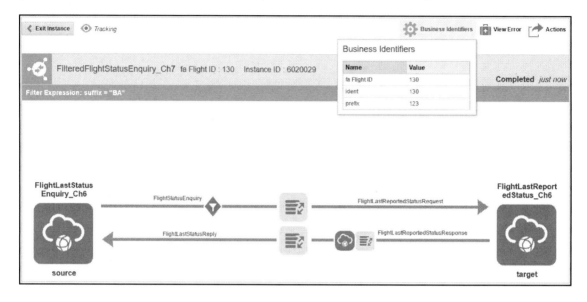

As you can see in the preceding screenshot, the arrows showing the direction of flow are green to show the successful route taken. We can also display all the business identifiers being tracked with each instance, if we click on the **Business Identifiers** button. If we click on **Exit Instance** to return to the instance list and then click on the failed instance name (faFlightID: 150), we would see something like as follows:

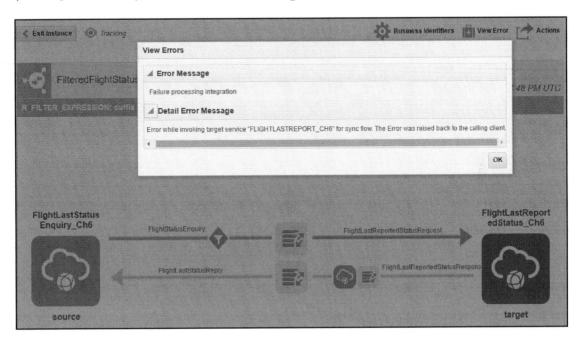

Note that in this screenshot we have clicked on the **View Error** button in this instance to see the error details. In the background integration image, we can see at what stage things failed. In this case, the mapping process completed, but the invocation of our Mockable.io endpoint failed as we had disabled it.

This does leave us with the question of what is the outcome of the situation where the integration can run properly (that is the Mockable endpoint is running and ready), but our filter has prevented the integration from continuing to invoke the endpoint. This situation is shown in the following screenshot:

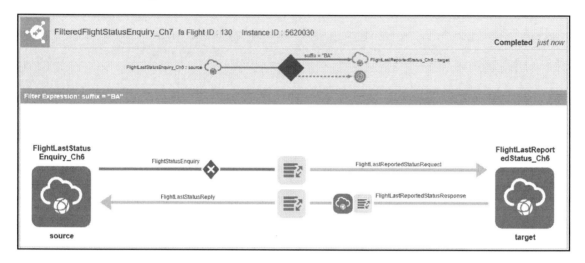

As you can see in the screenshot diagram, the filter in the upper part of the diagram is shown in red, as this is where the integration effectively stopped. As a result, the flow to the transformation did not work, as reflected in the lower part of the diagram. However, as the integration behaved as it should do, the integration counts as a success.

Agents view

If you have agents deployed to connect to on-premises solutions as we illustrated in Chapter 11, *Calling an On-Premises API*, then you need to know that the agent running on the on-premises is operating as expected. This is done by each agent keeping a heartbeat signal going every so often. If data is flowing, the ICS server knows the agent is alive and able to communicate. This does mean that there can be a little bit of latency between the agent failing, and it being reported on the dashboard. The following screenshot shows agents both healthy and unhealthy states (as a result of not receiving any communication):

As you can see from the previous screenshot, where agents are grouped, the group is shown with an aggregated status. Unlike the other views, other than using the agent count in the agent group to expand the view to show the child agents, there is not any further drill downs.

Any further diagnostics to determine the issue with the agent will involve a more detailed investigation, which may include examining the agent's own logs. As the agent is a deployment of a managed WebLogic Server, you examine what is going on through the normal management consoles. Details of the management console can be found at `https://docs.oracle.com/cd/E24329_01/web.1211/e24446/adminconsole.htm#INTRO 151`.

Tracking view

The **Tracking** view, which is accessed from the left-hand menu, is very much like the integration instances view, though all integration instances are shown in time order (based on completion time). The navigation options are also the same in terms of being able to view the integration instances.

Errors view

Like the integrations view, this has several ways to present the errors as shown as follows:

Click on the errors count or integration name (that is `FilteredFlightStatusEnquiry_Ch7`) and you will be given a list view that is the same as the **Error Message Details** menu, except the list is filtered to the relevant integration.

As with the other previous view of integration instances, you can drill into to see what happened in the instance execution. In addition to the filtering of the view, the ability to resubmit the integration or discard the partially executed integration can be achieved by clicking the tick box to the left of the integration icon (or clicking on **Select All** at the top) and clicking on either the **Discard** or **Resubmit** buttons. Using the **Resubmit** button will cause the integration to try to execute again; confirmation of the request will result in a status message acknowledging the request. Resubmitting an integration more than once will result in the subsequent resubmissions being notified as not possible. Only integrations that can operate in an asynchronous manner (such as Orchestrations) can benefit from the **Resubmit** option.

Clicking on **Errors by Connection** will group the integration instances that have had an error related to each specific connection, as shown next. As with the **Errors by Integration**, you can drill down into the specific instances:

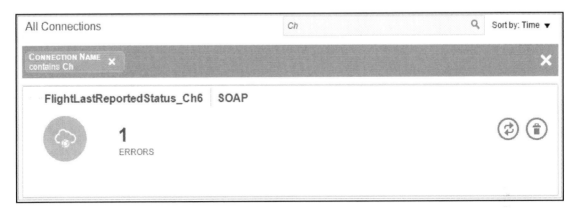

You may have observed that in this connections example, to the right of the connection are two icons. These provide the means to bulk resubmit or discard the execution of integrations that are true to this grouping. This ability is also offered in the integrations view.

The benefit of being able to see **Errors** via integration and by connection, is to help identify where the problem may lie, particularly if it is intermittent (for example, a connection to a service intermittently times out as it is overloaded), as you are able to easily spot a correlation to a connection used by lots of integrations, for example.

The final distinct view for errors is the **By Status Message**, which presents the integrations that have been resubmitted, and their status, which could be in progress, success, or failure.

Advanced resolution

Having explored the monitoring, we can see how error information can be seen, and as a result determine if integrations are failing, or whether there is an issue between ICS and the systems involved in the integration, or something wrong within one or more integrations. Sometimes this alone is sufficient to help identify the problem and its resolution, but not always. This section looks at common causes, and things to check (you may know from the **Monitoring** views a particular connection is the source of problems, but not why). We also explore how to look at the most detailed information available – the log files – and where to get more information on cause and resolution.

Things to check

Before we dig into the logs, the following is a brief list of things you might consider checking if integration(s) stop working:

- ICS system and service health
- Are we in a planned maintenance period?
- Has ICS been updated – if you have deployed any extra logic via the uploading of mappings and so on, is it possible the update may have broken them?
    - Connection errors
    - Third party service status – it might be the service is temporarily not working
    - Certificates (have they expired?)
    - Have service credentials been changed?
    - Service changes (API changes) – have APIs changed?
    - Revoked permissions or check for changing permissions
- Is the schedule for an integration running (deactivating an integration does stop the schedule)?
- Capacity and sizing factors:
    - Are the service calls coming in with payloads that are considered to be too large – the ICS documentation indicates the maximum size of a message is 512 KB
    - Is ICS being challenged in terms of the number of messages being sent within the time period?
    - Is it possible that the throughputs are too much for the target system (you need to understand the performance constraints of those systems)?
- Within an integration:
    - Are your lookups missing values?
    - If you have an enrichment service, is this connecting and producing expected results?
    - Integration (has expected version) has been activated?

Examining logs

As we have seen, it is possible to lock at the error information for a specific integration instance. This information is normally a brief extract from the logging information. The alternative approach to this is to retrieve the log files from the underlying server(s); an approach that requires a great deal more effort.

When errors are not obvious, such as connection losses or subtle errors in your service, it will be necessary to examine the log files. The log files, as you will have seen, can be accessed from several locations. When retrieved, you will have a ZIP file downloaded that contains all of the log files from the servers that are running the ICS service. This will typically be two servers and an admin server. The admin server runs the UI for ICS, so any errors resulting from creating and editing integrations will appear here. Errors that could occur during the running of an integration could show up in any of the server logs. If you connect multiple ICS integrations together, as you do in a publish and subscribe, there is no guarantee that all the related integrations will appear in one log file.

This is presently a challenge, if you want to see what happened in what order when examining complex cases, but there are tools that can merge log files easily, for example LogDistiller (`https://sourceforge.net/projects/logdistiller/`).

Having located the error, the next step is to locate the initial error for our integration. It is a common mistake to look at the last error, as it will be the closest to the end of the log – but often this is a reflection of a subsequent error, rather than the initial problem that will have caused subsequent problems.

Reporting incidents and downloading incidents information

There is always the possibility with any sophisticated software that something will not behave as expected or a problem will occur. While we hope that this will not happen, it is better to be prepared and to make it easier for the Oracle support team to investigate. To this end, ICS has a mechanism to raise an incident within the user's drop down menu, as you can see in the next diagram. This option will create a popup where you can capture information about the incident to advise Oracle what the problem is. When the incident process is started behind the scenes, a range of valuable pieces of information are captured.

When the incident details are completed and you click the **Create** button, the incident is given a number and it is reported to you on the main screen, as you can see in the following diagram:

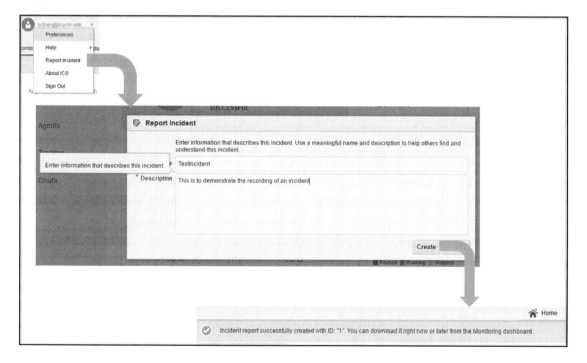

It is then possible to download all the details by clicking on the **Monitoring** dashboard's **Download Incident**, which will present a popup dialog to identify the incident number. Once the number is provided and **Download** button is clicked, then a ZIP file with all the relevant captured information is provided. This information can then be passed back via Oracle's support portal as shown in the following diagram:

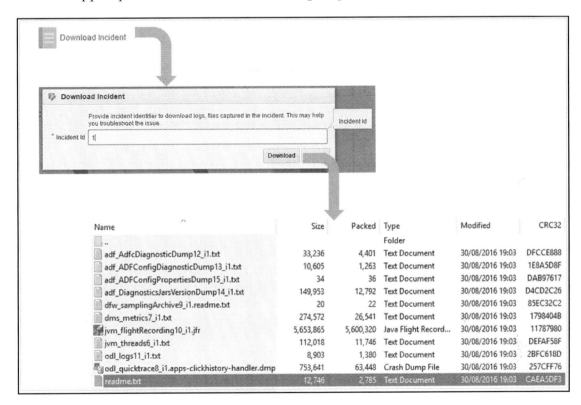

Where to go for information about errors

As with newer products, information on how to troubleshoot errors, and building into the software actions to try prevent users making mistakes, tends to lag a bit behind the features being offered (which is understandable, would you rather have lots of connectors that can cover 90% of use cases or a couple of connectors that help you though those esoteric 10% of situations?).

All of this means we do need to source information to help address those more troublesome cases. The following table describes the different places that can be used to help. It is worth remembering that ICS has been built on top of some core Oracle technologies, so some of the resources will relate back to the underlying areas. As previously mentioned, the most significant contributing technology to ICS is Oracle Service Bus.

Resource name and location	Nature of information
ICS Error Codes	Oracle publishes a document that contains all the ICS error codes. You can look up in this document the details of the different codes. This document only covers the specific ICS codes, not those that can arise from the fact that ICS, as previously mentioned, utilizes other Oracle components. Many of these codes will relate to the UI aspects of ICS, as these are unique to the product, whereas the core engine leverages existing technologies, `https://docs.oracle.com/cloud/latest/intcs_gs/ICSEM/`.
Oracle Cloud Documentation	If you go back to the main Oracle Cloud web pages for ICS (`https://cloud.oracle.com/integration`) you will find access to online documentation, which will allow you to see how certain aspects of the product work – and therefore understand potentially why you have a problem. One of the challenges today in this area is that the documentation is not yet exhaustive in nature. We should also see overtime the documentation being linked and made contextually aware with the different parts of the ICS. This closer linkage between the cloud service and documentation is happening across all the cloud products, `http://docs.oracle.com/cloud/latest/intcs_gs/`.
Oracle Support	Oracle has a very extensive support portal that holds knowledge articles, details of updates. You can examine existing Service Requests (SR) and raise them as well. Most importantly, when dealing with a problem the support portal is best for examining the service requests and Knowledge Base to see if work around or issues have already been posted. Obviously, if an issue has not been raised then it helps everyone to get a problem raised. The portal can be accessed via, `https://support.oracle.com`.

Oracle Community	Oracle actively encourages people to share knowledge and questions through its community site (`https://community.oracle.com`). Once registered, you can interact with the site and the other community members. Most Oracle products or product families have an area within the community site for themselves. In ICS case it is: `https://community.oracle.com/community/cloud_computing/platform-as-a-service-paas/oracle-integration-cloud-service/overview`.
Known Issues log	When issues are identified with releases, Oracle will publish the details online. It is always good to check in here if you think you may have found a problem before trying to raise the issues, `https://docs.oracle.com/cloud/latest/intcs_gs/ICSKI/index.html`. As issues can originate from underlying components, knowing about problems from these areas as well is important – therefore the following is worth checking: `http://www.oracle.com/technetwork/middleware/soasuite/documentation/releasenotes121300-2124738.html#servbus`.
A-Team blog	The A-Team is a specialist team within Oracle that are the leading consulting subject matter experts. This is the team that Oracle will fly in if you have a challenging problem. For us, the A-Team are important as they blog about the more advanced concepts and use cases of the different technologies Oracle offers, including ICS. The A-Team blog is recommended reading regardless of whether you have a problem or not, `http://www.ateam-oracle.com/`.
The site for this book	The authors of this book both actively blog about integration and have a website that contain articles on advanced features, updates, and compile useful resources on ICS, `http://oracle-integration.cloud`.

System maintenance windows

Like all systems, eventually a level of maintenance is necessary – this could be to replace components that are at risk of failing or have failed, deploy new software upgrades that could deliver new features, or to address security issues. While the overall management of Oracle Cloud is not in the scope of this book, it can impact and potentially create the perception of operational issues, so we do need to acknowledge it. Today, Oracle has identified set times each month where it may run routine maintenance. What (if any) maintenance occurs will be notified to the administrator of the service being used by e-mail. The e-mail typically will look something like as follows:

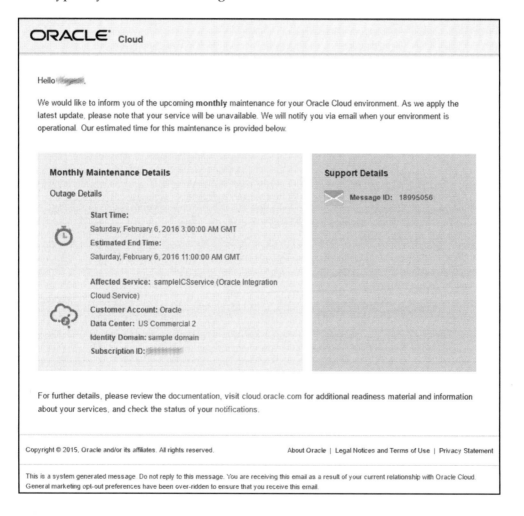

Where possible, Oracle has taken to advising of the consequence of the maintenance activity, which may mean some services stop – such as the Oracle management cloud UI, or the integration designer, for example, this does mean that during a maintenance period potentially activated integrations may continue that is maintenance does not automatically mean the service stopping.

This does mean if you require around-the-clock operations even during a maintenance cycle that will require down time, some extra services within the overall Oracle Cloud portfolio will be needed, in the same way as additional services are needed to mitigate against a data center level outage; but that is a subject beyond this book.

Incorporating ICS monitoring into the enterprise

In some circumstances, it would be desirable to integrate the error reporting and performance information into an enterprise-wide monitoring platform, such as:

- Oracle Enterprise Manager Cloud Control (OEM) (`http://www.oracle.com/technetwork/oem/enterprise-manager/overview/index.html`) or
- Log Analytics (`https://cloud.oracle.com/log-analytics`) Manager

Today, ICS does not provide the means to connect to OEM directly, but the API does provide the means to capture this information and it can be fed into OEM or any other enterprise monitoring product of your choice.

OEM documentation provides guidance on how to implement custom monitors, which can be found at `https://docs.oracle.com/cd/E24628_01/doc.121/e25159/intro.htm#EMPRG107` and `https://docs.oracle.com/cd/E24628_01/doc.121/e25161/plug-inbuilder.htm#EMPRF12911`.

Administration

ICS administration capabilities cover several areas, specifically:

- Managing SSL/TLS certificates

- System logging levels
- E-mail status reporting

These areas are more technical than the rest of ICS and can have implications for the behavior and performance of ICS, for example:

- Removing or changing certificates can result in connectors failing
- Changing the logging can impact ICS performance, but also makes the log files potentially harder to work with

As a result, the actions taken in this area should be done with care, and we would always advocate that before doing anything you understand and have the resources to allow you to revert configurations back to how they were.

Certificate management

The majority of the **Administration** view is given over to the management of SSL/TLS certificates. ICS has a range of preinstalled certificates reflecting the services that the adapters provided require, including the adapters to other Oracle Cloud services as you can see in the following screenshot:

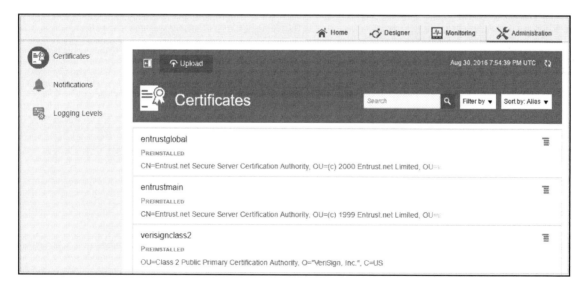

The preinstalled certificates cannot be changed, and Oracle will maintain and update these as necessary. As it maybe necessary to also add our own certificates for when we are using technology adapters with third parties, we need to have the ability to upload and manage them. As you can see in the preceding screenshot, the ability to upload certificates is provided through a menu in the header section of the view. This will provide a dialog to help select the correct file and upload it. As certificates can expire or be revoked, there is a need to therefore upload replacements. This can be done through the use of the menu on the right-hand side of the list view (which in many respects looks a lot like the integrations view). Likewise, if you create your own adapter you may wish to add an additional new certificate, which can be done through the **Upload** button at the top right of the page.

By clicking on the **Certificate** icon or name, you see the details of the certificate as shown in the following screenshot:

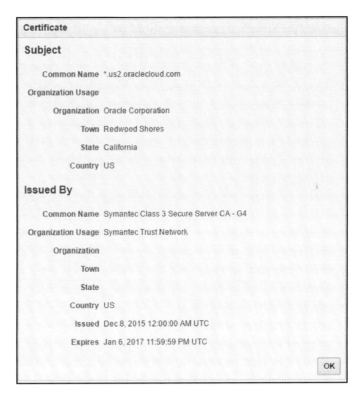

It is important to remember that if you add your own certificates it is necessary to ensure that the certificate has not expired. Ideally, if a service provider (or owner of your own systems) revokes a certificate the provider would inform you, at which point it will be necessary to act by replacing the certificate, otherwise the integration will fail.

If you are wondering why it is necessary to hold SSL certificates within ICS, it is worth remembering that when you visit a website which wants to use SSL, the web server and your browser go through a handshake process to establish the of an SSL certificate. This does not happen within an application, and rather than going through the process of negotiation the certificate can be deployed in advance, which is what is managed here.

Changing log levels

When developing custom adapters or trying to diagnose a particularly challenging issue, sometimes it is desirable to tailor the log information recorded into the system log files. As Oracle (or any other user) does not want people trying to access the underlying technology platforms and manipulating configurations, a dashboard has been provided by which the log levels can be tailored. As the following screenshot shows, the log level can be changed to provide varying levels of information from the most critical incidents to very fine trace information:

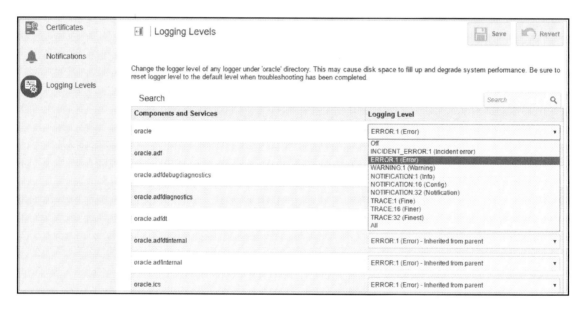

The preceding screenshot does not cover all the classes that can have logging levels configured for. To exploit these controls, it will be necessary to understand the different technologies that Oracle has used to build ICS.

E-mail reporting

ICS provides the means to configure the emailing of activity and service failure notifications, such that in the event of a service failure the administrator(s) or delegated user(s) can be quickly informed of an issue that has been detected and appropriate intervention can be undertaken as shown in the following screenshot:

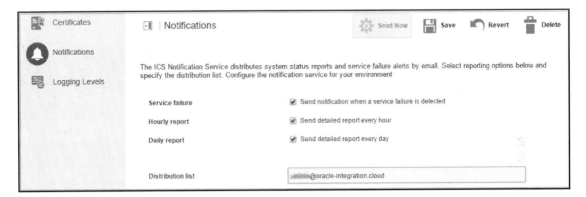

In addition to this, as the preceding screenshot shows, we can also receive daily or hourly activity reports. If you have just resolved an issue or have observed that a backlog of processing is occurring, it may be helpful to have hourly reports, otherwise daily reports should be sufficient. Of course, you can always use the API if you need bespoke reporting regimes (Next chapter covers the APIs). An example of an hourly report is shown in the following screenshot:

Summary

In this chapter, we have looked at the monitoring information available to us in ICS and how to drill into the information to help diagnose problems. We have also looked at how to process the log files to help understand events in a time series manner. Using this knowledge, we have then looked at sources of information to help get an appropriate diagnosis and resolution to the problem.

With the foundations of problem identification and resolution completed, we then explored how ICS could have its monitoring incorporated into the wider enterprise monitoring tools. The last step has been to understand how certificates can be managed within ICS as part of the **Administration** view.

In the next chapter, we complete the book by examining how we can import and export our integrations, and how they can be examined using developer tooling to provide a means to use develop tools to extend details such as lookups and transformations.

13
Where Can I Go from Here?

In the previous chapter, we looked at monitoring and some elements of administration. In this final chapter, we are going to look at core administration capabilities, particularly the use of the importing and exporting of integrations and what this enables you to achieve, including the availability of a marketplace of extensions. We shall discuss the ICS API and the Cloud Adapter Software Development Kit as the foundations to extend the management of ICS, as well as how to build your own adapters.

Finally, the integration space is an ever-evolving part of IT and is becoming the core foundation of nearly all software solutions. Within this, the rapid growth of cloud technology has meant this is perhaps one of the quickest evolving areas of software technology. So, we shall take a look at how we can keep abreast of developments, particularly for ICS, as well as where to get more information that will help with using ICS and understanding the key underpinning technologies.

Import and export

The ability to be able to import and export either individual integrations, connections, lookups, or groups of integrations (known as packages), provides us with the means to achieve a number of different things; the most common of those being the following:

- Keeping integrations and related objects under configuration management
- Separation of the development of integrations from production environments
- Exploiting prebuilt integrations from vendors other than Oracle
- Synchronizing configuration of lookups across many environments
- Distributing integrations into different environments, or making them available for others to use

In addition to importing and exporting whole integrations, you will have noticed through our journey in this book that parts can be discretely imported and exported separately. For the purposes of this chapter, we are only going to concentrate on the larger import and export activities, but the motivations for performing a focused operation are often the same as when you are performing the same process at coarser grained levels.

Import and export scenarios

In the following sections, we can examine these points a bit more closely.

Controlling change in a live environment

Once you have developed your ICS services and they are running as desired, you are going to quickly reach a point where you will want to separate development and testing from your running integrations, so that any additions or changes do not disrupt or create inconsistencies in the target systems you have integrated. The worst thing would be to need to resolve data consistency and integrity issues in your target solutions, as lots of small changes will mean a lot of inconsistency in a live environment. So, separating your test and development from a live setup means no consistency issues, but raises the question of how we move our integrations from development to production? This is where import and export comes into play.

Configuration management

This scenario leads neatly onto the consideration of using a configuration management repository. As you develop the service configuration, you may wish to create milestone copies of the service implementation. So, if as you make further changes and you decide things are not satisfactory, you can always retrieve the milestone from the repository and deploy it back into ICS.

Common service deployment around the world

It is possible that you want to run the same integrations for different instances of the same systems in another part of the world; these instances may then cooperate. This approach of clouds working together can be described as a federated deployment model. Rather than those systems sending data across the world to be manipulated and inserted into a system that may also be in another part of the world, you may choose to deploy the integration logic to the different data centers Oracle offers. As a result, the data does not take so long to reach the integration or destination and reduces the risk of having problems such as data residency (also known as **data sovereignty**).

The additional benefit of duplicating the integrations to different data centers is that, if you have external routing, in the unlikely event of a whole data center failure, it is possible to continue processing. This is not to say that we expect Oracle data centers to fail, but it does happen, and when it does often with dire consequences, Even the most experienced providers, such as Amazon AWS, have been caught out.

Pre-built integrations

Oracle is actively encouraging the user community, as well as third party software vendors, to offer pre-built integrations for ICS through their marketplace (`https://cloud.oracle.com/marketplace/`), where you can buy, and in some cases get for free, additional features that you can run in Oracle's cloud. In this situation, you will be given a package of integrations that you will then want to load into your environment.

Synchronizing lookup data

Within integration flows, it is possible to have lookup values that can be used to swap the presentation of information from one format to another. In an organization with good data governance, it is possible that these lookup values will be mastered somewhere outside ICS. This might be with Oracle SOA Suite and the **Domain Value Mappings** (**DVM**s), or even a completely different third-party tool. In these situations, to keep the mappings up-to-date, or at least synchronized between different tools, you need the ability to export and import these values so different solutions operate with consistent lookup values.

Complex editing and using developer tooling

In some circumstances, it can be more practical to work through a tool that can edit XML directly, particularly when need to edit complex expressions. This kind of scenario was briefly illustrated in Chapter 5, *Going Social with Twitter and Google*. Ultimately, many editors will make life easier for you in most cases, but occasionally it does become quicker, although more error prone, to avoid the helping hand, or to use a more powerful tool such as JDeveloper or XML Spy. Even today, there are times when dropping into raw HTML or XML views to make a minor change can be easier.

Exporting and importing integrations

ICS offers two approaches to this – either the export of a single integration, which will result in an .iar file, or to export a package, which is a means by which you can group related integrations together to export and results in a .par file.

Individual export

Starting from the designer part of ICS, open the **Integrations** page. You can see the list of integrations available. To the right of each integration is the actions menu. Click on this and then click on the **Export** menu option, as shown in the following screenshot:

This will result in the downloading of a file with an .iar extension; the filename reflecting the identifier provided when you created the integration and its version number. This is actually a special type of ZIP file and can be opened accordingly.

If we look into the file, we will find a file structure that contains a collection of XML files and properties files. These files describe the integration, its connections, the state of the different parts and their version numbers, as given in the following screenshot:

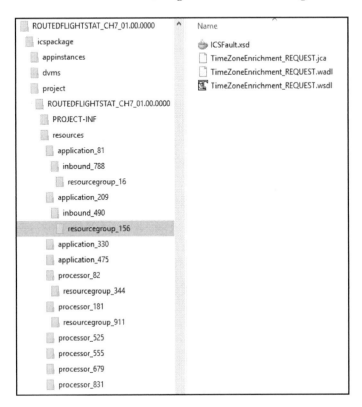

This file can now be imported into another instance of ICS if you want. It is important to remember that there are a couple of constraints:

- Connection definitions are not carried through in their entirety – this is because the connector information includes sensitive credentials
- An imported integration will not be activated, even if the original integration was active

This does raise the question of how the integration gets the connections? If the connection already exists (that is, there is a connection by the same name), then that connection is assumed to be the one to use. If the connection does not exist, then the information within the .par file is used to generate a connection, although the connection will need to be completed.

Illustrating import and export

Rather than importing to another ICS instance, we are going to apply a change that is simple to spot and then import the integration back into the same environment. In the rest of this section, we are going to make the changes to the integration you have already downloaded.

When making changes this way, we should think of it as opening up a black box. Oracle makes no guarantees about the content and structure of the `.iar` files. They do recognize that, at times, a desktop application such as JDeveloper may be better suited to performing the development of very complex mappings and transformations; editing this way can be achieved because ICS has been built making use of industry standards such as XSL. To help in these cases, Oracle have put into the files XML comments such as:

```
< -User Editing allowed BELOW this line - DO NOT DELETE
  THIS LINE-->
```

So, you can see where changes may be applied, but we would advise being careful before making changes (that is, make a backup of our `.iar` file before making any modifications to return to if everything goes wrong). We would suggest when you first open up the `.iar` file that you explore the file contents. Within the resources part of the folder tree, you will find XSL files with the mappings we have previously defined.

Having taken the appropriate precaution of making an unmodified `.iar`, we can edit the `.iar` file. With any form of zip capable tool will be sufficient – WinZip or 7-Zip if you are using a Windows platform and p7zip for Linux and Mac users.

These tools can be found at the following URLs:
WinZip: http://www.winzip.com/
7-Zip: http://www.7-zip.org/
p7zip: http://p7zip.sourceforge.net/

Within the `.iar` file, we want to edit the `project.xml` file; it should be located in `icspackage\project\<integrationname>_<version number>\PROJECT-INF` (where integration name will represent the integration exported and its current version number). The content of this file should look familiar to you, as it relates back to the new integration panel you will have seen before. For example, the **projectDescription** element will match the project description you will have given the integration process. For simplicity, go ahead and change the description (and remember the content has to be valid XML). Once the file has been changed, replace the existing `project.xml` with your new one in the `.iar` file.

Before we progress, it is worth also noting that the `.iar` file also contains the information about the connections needed. These can be found in the `icspackage/appinstances` folder. If you examine any of the XML files describing the connection, you will see that there are no credentials or properties of interface, such as the WSDL directly. But there is sufficient information for ICS to tell you about the connection name and the location of the WSDL (if it is a SOAP based endpoint).

We can now import the modified integration back into ICS, which we will walk through in the next section.

Individual import

To perform an import, unless you have already got several environments, we are going to need to import to our original environment. To import, you need to be on the **Integrations** page, where above the list of integrations and filter options is a menu button showing **Import**. Clicking on this will pop up a file selection dialog – select the modified `.iar` file and click on the **Import** button.

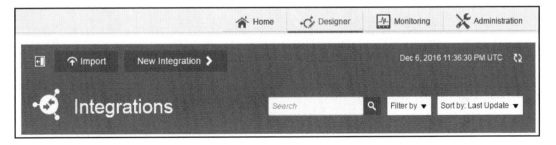

When importing into ICS when it is an existing integration, ICS will challenge you if you import an integration that already exists, as follows:

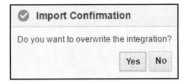

To avoid this, you can of course take the step to delete the existing integration. To perform the delete, you simply need to go the same action menu that we used to perform the export and select **Delete**. You will get a confirmation dialog which you will need to confirm the deletion action. Once confirmed, you will see the integration disappear from the list of integrations available. We can now perform the import process.

Having done this, take a look at the integration description on the page – it should reflect your changes. Further, using the information icon at the top right on the integration information, it should pop up a dialog showing the updated time and who performed the update. With the import process complete, you can verify the changes you made to confirm the integration has been correctly imported.

Regeneration

When performing the import, you might be combining the integration with a different configuration of a connector; for example a connector points to the development instance of an application, but you have exported your integration to run it inside the production environment. In these circumstances, you need to get ICS to refresh the WSDL if a SOAP based connection is involved. This can be done by clicking on the arrow icon at the top right-hand part of the Integration screen. Which will pop up a menu as follows:

Click on the Regenerate artifacts... option. This will provide a pop-up dialog with a warning. Click on the OK button to force the regeneration. With this complete, we can click on Save and Exit Integration, and then the integration will be ready for activation.

Lookup export

The exporting of lookups is very much like the export of an integration. Rather than going into the integrations part of the designer, you need to access the **Lookups** page. On this page, you will see the different lookups that have been created. You can then use the action menu icon to drop down the available options, which includes **Export to CSV**. Selecting this option will trigger the download of a comma-separated value file which will contain a line before the mapping values which match the column headers in the definition provided.

To demonstrate a change for the import process, select a lookup; for example, the one we created in Chapter 6, *Creating Complex Transformations*, and add an additional row of values to the end of the CSV.

Be careful when editing the CSV, particularly when using something like Excel as the editor, as it is possible to damage the file by accident. For example, changing the way the underlying operating system represents line termination. Between Linux and Windows there are subtle differences in how line endings are recognized. It is also possible to accidentally make the document tab-separated.

Note that, presently, you can export from within the **Lookup** editor or from the **Lookups** page, but an import can only be done from the **Lookups** page, rather than the editor today.

Lookup import

With the changes applied, we can import the lookup. Select the **Import Lookup** button on the **Lookups** list page. This will provide you with a popup to select the file to import. The import file needs to follow the pattern of the first two rows containing descriptive information. If you change the first cell in the table which contains the lookup name, then a new lookup will be created regardless of the filename. If the lookup already exists, then ICS will prompt for a confirmation of overwriting the existing lookup. For this exercise, this is what we want to do, so proceed with selecting **Yes**.

You should now see that the number of values being reported will reflect the additional rows provided.

 Lookups today are not versioned within ICS, but changing a lookup may have a material impact on the integrations running. So it is helpful to know when the lookups have changed. Rather than creating new lookups each time there is a change, as this would mean going through all the Integrations and updating the lookup reference, we would suggest you consider recording into the Lookup description when a change is uploaded, or what the change made is.

Packaging

Packaging provides a means to group a number of integrations and connectors together. This may be of our own integrations but, just as easily, it could be for a third-party set of capabilities. Ideally, the grouping will make some sort of logical sense (that is, a collection of related integrations, for example, integrating all the different aspects of Oracle E-Business Suite and Oracle ERP Cloud).

The common use of packages is to facilitate the import and export of multiple elements, but it can be just as easily used to delete groups of items at once (so handle with care). If you have followed the book chapter by chapter then you will have noticed that all the integrations have had their integrations given package names using the pattern of `ics.book.ch<X>`, where `<X>` represents the chapter number.

Package export and import

To see the packages available, in the **Designer** view, click on the **Packages** icon on the left-hand menu. This will display a view very similar to the integrations list. Like the integrations view, it is possible to filter the list of packages using the package name. In the following example, we have used the filter to isolate the `ch2` package (*Chapter 2*, *Integrating Your First Two Applications*). Having located the package you wish to export, you can click on the menu icon on the right to be able to click on the **Export** option, as shown in the following screenshot:

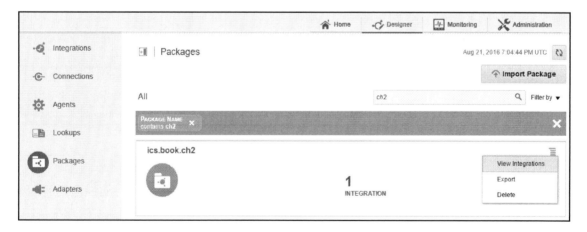

Once you have clicked on the **Export** button, a `.par` file will be downloaded. As previously mentioned the `.par` file is a special form of zip file. If you open the `.par` file up, within it you will find a file called `ics_package_attributes.properties` which provides details of the package, and then a set of `.iar` files representing all the integrations within the package.

You will note that, just as with the integrations page, the top right also provides the means to upload packages (as shown in the preceding screenshot). Clicking on this button will pop up the dialog to select and import the `.par` file.

Alternate tools

As you develop integrations within ICS, you may find that you would prefer an alternate tool for the development of content such as mappings. With the preceding guidance, it is possible to export, modify and reimport mappings and other artifacts now. So, the following are tools that are well established products that could be used to help with this:

Product	Description	URL
JDeveloper	The main developer tool provided by Oracle. This is not a lightweight tool and is focused on meeting the needs of full-time developers.	`http://www.oracle.com/technetwork/developer-tools/jdev/`
Eclipse	Eclipse is one of the leading developer IDE with a large range of extension plugins to enable it to work with a range of different languages, syntax, and software platforms. Like JDeveloper, its focus is on meeting the needs of full-time developers.	`https://eclipse.org/`
NetBeans	NetBeans is another major open source IDE focused towards meeting the needs of developers. It is also sponsored by Oracle.	`https://netbeans.org/`
Altova XML Spy	The Altova family of tools is one of the industry's leading productions when it comes to working with XML-based standards including XSLT. As a tool, it is not purely focused on the core developer community, which makes it attractive for Citizen Integrators.	`http://www.altova.com/xmlspy.html`

ICS API

ICS has its own API that provides a range of REST services focused on the control and monitoring of ICS. The API provides a range of operations, from being able to deploy connections and integrations, to activating and deleting them, through to getting details of any errors: the monitoring metrics we saw in the previous chapter.

The details of the APIs can be obtained from the Oracle documentation online (`https://docs.oracle.com/cloud/latest/intcs_gs/ICSRA/`), which is also linked to the ICS tool itself. While the APIs lend themselves to extending your preferred enterprise monitoring tool, it is also very easy to build some basic management scripts through the use of tools such as cURL.

To illustrate this point, we are going to use the API to retrieve some information about an instance of ICS:

- Retrieve the monitoring metrics so you can see the high-level stats regarding your environment. This is the sort of thing that could be your first step to incorporating ICS into the enterprise monitoring capabilities the IT are likely to be operating.
- Retrieve the monitoring log files – having a little script handy to pull these logs down when you need them to help debug integration development saves on having to navigate between the **Designer** and the **Monitoring** views. Note, these logs are slightly different to the system level logs.
- Issue a command to deactivate a specific integration.

Before we illustrate these cases, let's first talk a bit about cURL and get it into place, and the general principles that have been applied to the ICS APIs.

Getting and using cURL

cURL is an open source tool that is mostly associated with Linux platforms but, over time, has been adapted and implemented for just about every operating system you can think of. cURL serves as a tool with which you can communicate with web servers using the HTTP/HTTPS syntax. This makes it ideal for formulating REST-based calls from a command line. cURL can go a long way beyond this, but for our purposes, HTTP is sufficient.

You can download the right platform implementation for cURL from the cURL website – ht tps://curl.haxx.se/. You can retrieve the binaries, source files, or installer packs such as MSI or DEB files. Given the variety here, we are not going to describe the installation process; there is plenty of documentation on how to achieve this on the net. Ultimately, you need to invoke the cURL command from a shell (DOS/PowerShell/Bash, and so on). For the purposes of this book, we have downloaded a binary and ensured that it is the system path.

You can confirm that cURL is running fine by issuing the curl -help command, which should result in the help information being displayed, as you can see in the following screenshot:

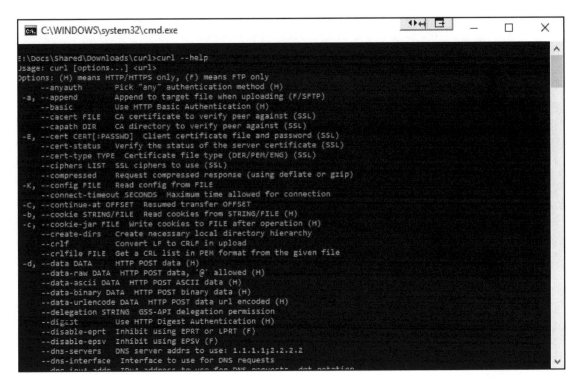

With this, we know cURL is available and will run. Let's talk a bit about the cURL command structure. The command is defined as a series of parameters that will define the following details:

- User credentials – these are the same credentials that you will use when signing into the web interface
- The HTTP header attributes such as the nature of the payload being sent or wanted back
- A reference to a file as the contents for the body – although we do not need this except when uploading integrations and so on
- The HTTP operation to perform such as GET, POST, and so on, as we explained in Chapter 1, *Introducing the Concepts and Terminology*
- The complete target URL that will execute the call

ICS is happy with being sent and being asked for, in most cases, with both XML and JSON formatted payloads. The documentation for each service will confirm whether both formats are supported. With that, we can start to look at the construction of the cURL commands, which in most cases will be as follows:

```
curl -u username:password -H "HTTP header attribute settings in  quotes" -
X HTTP operation e.g. GET target URL
```

To bring this to life, our first example would look like this:

```
curl -u myusername:mypassword -H "Accept:application/XML" - X GET
https://integrationtrial12345-
deoracleem12345.integration.us2.oraclecloud.com/icsapis/v1/monitoring/integ
rations
```

As you can see, we express whether XML or JSON is wanted through the use of -H "Accept:application/XML" (that is, we will accept XML), and what we are providing is formatted as by -H "Content-Type:application/json". For most requests, there is no provided body content, so we can disregard the **Content-Type** header information, hence it is not in the example.

Let's execute this cURL command. The following screenshot shows the outcome:

As you can see from the screenshot, we do get a stream of XML back, which is not practical from a readability view. So we would recommend that you direct the output to a file and then use a pretty printer app. The output can be done either by piping the log content or using an -o option for example -o integrations.txt. Note that the moment a file is involved, the display showing the execution changes, with stats regarding the download presented instead as follows:

Applying this means we get a result that can contain information like:

```
<flowId>8d1261af-7c24-4d19-8c24-41532621d9d4</flowId>
<flowName>TweetFlightScheduleChanges_Ch5</flowName>
<flowCode>TWEETFLIGHTSCHED_CH5</flowCode>
<flowVersion>01.00.0000</flowVersion>
<description>This integration will take the ScheduleUpdate request and send
out a tweet returning a result or fault as response.</description>
<noOfMsgsReceived>54</noOfMsgsReceived>
<noOfMsgsProcessed>54</noOfMsgsProcessed>
<noOfErrors>21</noOfErrors>
<noOfSuccess>33</noOfSuccess>
<errorsInQueues    xmlns:xsd="http://www.w3.org/2001/XMLSchema"
xmlns:xsi="http://www.w3.org/2001/XMLSchema-instance">
```

```
  <errorObjects xsi:type="xsd:string">
    Unable to reach target.
  </errorObjects>
  <errorObjects xsi:type="xsd:string">
    Unable to reply back.
  </errorObjects>
  <errorObjects xsi:type="xsd:string">
    Unable to send error back.
  </errorObjects>
</errorsInQueues>
<successRate>61</successRate>
<avgRespTime>0</avgRespTime>
```

Taking our second scenario of using the API to retrieve the logs, we need to observe that the output is documented as an octet-stream not XML or JSON. So, if we invoke the service with:

```
curl -u myusername:mypassword -H "Accept:application/XML" -o log.txt -X GET
https://integrationtrial12345-deoracleem12345.integration.us2.oraclecloud.c
om/icsapis/v1/monitoring/logs/export
```

then we will see any empty file, as the header (-H) parameter says we want XML, but the service can only supply an octet-stream. So, correcting this to be:

```
curl -u myusername:mypassword -H "Accept:application/octet-stream" -o
log.txt -X GET
https://integrationtrial12345-deoracleem12345.integration.us2.oraclecloud.c
om/icsapis/v1/monitoring/logs/export
```

will result in a file called `log.txt` being populated.

Neither of these examples target specific instances of things in the environment such as an integration or a connection, and are also requests rather than commands. The API adopts the proper REST strategy by incorporating the identifiers within the URL. So, let's look at a command, for example, the activation or deactivation of an integration.

The first step is to choose an integration to activate or deactivate (the only difference being the last part of the URL is activate or deactivate). We will need the integration identifier and the version number, so if you navigate into the integration and pop up the details, you will see something like:

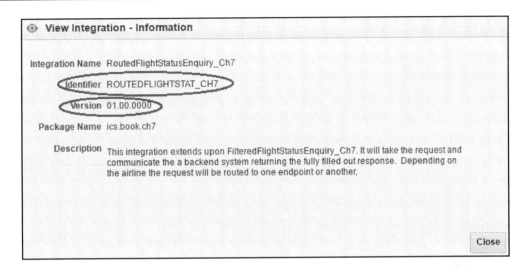

We will need the ICS generated identifier and the full version number of the selected integration, as highlighted in the preceding screenshot. Note that in the API documentation, the identifier is often referred to as the code. We need to incorporate these values into the URL, as the following code illustrates:

```
curl -u myusername:mypassword -H "Content-Type:application/XML" -H
"Accept:application/XML" --write-out %{http_code} -X POST
https://integrationtrial12345-deoracleem12345.integration.us2.oraclecloud.c
om/icsapis/v1/integrations/ROUTEDFLIG_CH7/01.00.0000/deactivate
```

Within the code, you may also observe several differences; the HTTP operation is now a POST rather than GET as we are issuing a command rather than asking for information. We have also added `--write-out %{http_code}`. This cURL parameter means that we can see the HTTP response code and response message. Without the additional write parameter, we would not get any indication of the command having been successful, or having failed. For example, as a result of using an incorrect integration, we can see the wellknown 404 error as follows:

```
E:\Docs\Shared\Downloads\curl>curl -u                              -H "Content-Type:application/XML" -H "Accept:appl
ication/XML" --write-out %{http_code} -X POST https://icssandbox-a167512.integration.us2.oraclecloud.com/icsapis/v1/integrat
ions/ROUTEDFLIGHTSTA_CH7/01.00.0000/deactivate
Integration not found.404
E:\Docs\Shared\Downloads\curl>
```

Or, in the case of deactivating the same service twice, the service deactivates correctly (resulting in a `200` code) and then the second time generates an error as the service is now no longer active, as shown in the following screenshot:

```
E:\Docs\Shared\Downloads\curl>curl -u ███████████████ :████████ -H "Content-Type:application/XML" -H "Accept:appl
ication/XML" --write-out %{http_code} -X POST https://icssandbox-a167512.integration.us2.oraclecloud.com/icsapis/v1/integrat
ions/ROUTEDFLIGHTSTAT_CH7/01.00.0000/deactivate
200
E:\Docs\Shared\Downloads\curl>curl -u ███████████████ :████████ -H "Content-Type:application/XML" -H "Accept:appl
ication/XML" --write-out %{http_code} -X POST https://icssandbox-a167512.integration.us2.oraclecloud.com/icsapis/v1/integrat
ions/ROUTEDFLIGHTSTAT_CH7/01.00.0000/deactivate
Integration "{0}" is not active so it cannot be deactivated.412
E:\Docs\Shared\Downloads\curl>_
```

Cloud adapters software development kit

The connectors used by ICS are actually built using a framework known as **Cloud Adapters Software Development Kit** (sometimes shortened to **Adapter SDK**). The SDK is freely available as a download so that anyone can use it to build their own adapters. This means it is very much possible to have customer adapters created for your own applications to simplify connectivity – as Oracle has done with Salesforce, for example (hiding the handshake process when connecting to Salesforce). It can be used to overcome integrations that have interfaces that are not realized through standards such as web services; for example, when integration is only offered through the use of a set of libraries.

As using the SDK is very much a Java development activity, we are only going to look at what is involved, rather than going through the process in detail, as it would warrant several chapters in its own right. We will walk through what is involved and how the different elements relate so that it is possible to understand what is involved.

Before we can understand the specific parts of an adapter and the tools needed, let's first look at ICS from the perspective of how it works. As you have seen in `Chapter 12`, *Are My Integrations Running Fine, and What If They Are Not?*, ICS has a design time side of things, which is the user interface that allows you to create the integrations, define the configuration for the connections, and so on. Then there is the runtime side, which actually takes the integration definitions and executes them. ICS's design time elements have a lot of building blocks that allow you to create a lot of the adapter's design time elements through configuration. You can see the two aspects in the following diagram, where the upper half reflects design time, and the lower half represents runtime. When both parts are brought together, it represents the complete adapter:

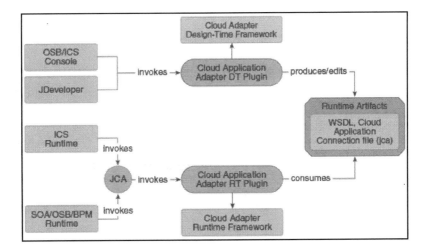

Starting with **JDeveloper** on the design time side, it is used to build upon the design time framework, which provides the means to create the building blocks for your user interface to capture the necessary information for connectors, applying the connections to integrations and so on. Within this framework are standardized interfaces that are then invoked by ICS to present the UI. The metadata created by the user is then used by the **Runtime Artifacts**. JDeveloper has a set of extensions as part of the SDK to help build the relevant artifacts.

For the adapter to then perform the runtime operations, you obviously need to have libraries that can be invoked that can interact with your application. The means to do this is incorporated into the functional runtime part of the adapter and is achieved by implementing a collection of classes based on standard interfaces. With this, the ICS engine then only needs to pass the execution payload from runtime component to the next for execution.

With all the relevant pieces built, they then need to be packaged into JAR files and be deployed and registered with the server – all of which can be done with JDeveloper and its SDK extensions.

As you can see, the process of building adapters is very code-centric. Oracle provides a simple worked example as part of its SDK documentation, which can be found at `https ://docs.oracle.com/cloud/latest/intcs_gs/CCCDG/toc.htm`.

Keeping up to date

When it comes to IT, things develop and change at a tremendous rate and cloud services are likely to increase this tempo. The thing that impacted the rate of change was the speed by which customers could apply updates. Vendors do not want to upset customers by changing so quickly that, as soon as they have deployed the latest edition, there is already another version released. Not only do you want to avoid frustrating users with the tempo of deploying updates, but also, as a software vendor, you do not want to be trying to support too many versions of a product. All of this disappears when offered as a cloud service, as the vendor will be conducting the updates for you. As the vendor has control of the deployment of updates, they can keep everyone up-to date, simplifying things for them. This means that we will see a heightened arms race by cloud providers. This is great for us as customers, as we will see more and more capability in the short term; but for us as authors, and Packt as our publisher, it risks this book appearing to date quickly.

To help with this, the book has dealt with stuff that is unlikely to change much, so you may find that elements of capability appear to be missing. So how do you find out about how to get the most of these newer features? Well, the authors have committed to having their own site to support this book, which can be found at `http://oracle-integration.cloud`. As things evolve, the authors will endeavor to write articles about the new capabilities added, plus reference known resources that we are aware of.

This does not mean that the only point of information is the book's website. Oracle provides a raft of channels for information. Not only that, Oracle support a number of community channels where you can go find information and ask questions. This is all in addition to the more formal channels that Oracle offers, such as the formal support (`http://support.orac le.com`), account management team, and so on. You might consider also exploiting the information at:

- Author's blogs: both authors have their own blogs (`https://blog.mp3monster.o rg`, `http://soa-iot-and-beyond.blogspot.co.uk/`) and write about related subjects such as integration strategies and related cloud products that you might want to use alongside ICS.
- Oracle has an extensive catalog of YouTube videos known as **Oracle Learning Library (OLL)** – `https://www.youtube.com/user/OracleLearning`, this includes a channel for Oracle Cloud – `https://www.youtube.com/user/OracleCloudVid eos`.
- Oracle training solutions – `https://apexapps.oracle.com`.

- The `https://community.oracle.com`– this is a community site provided and maintained by Oracle with both Oracle staff and community members such as the authors of this book (and a number of others by Packt) who will share advice and answer questions. This a section dedicated to PaaS at, `https://community.oracle.com/community/cloud_computing/platform-as-a-service-paas`.

- The Oracle A-Team is a group of subject matter experts that Oracle will use to help its customers on challenging situations. This team also have their own blog at `http://www.ateam-oracle.com/` and write about Oracle Cloud including ICS.

- Oracle Integration blog which covers a wide range of integration areas including ICS can be found at, `https://blogs.oracle.com/integration/`.

- **Virtual Technology Summits** (**VTS**) a cross between a webinar and a one day conference are run regularly and the webinars are kept so that you can browse them and replay the sessions as desired. To keep up with VTS start at, `http://www.oracle.com/technetwork/community/developer-day/index.html`.

- A number of Oracle partners such as AMIS and Capgemini have their own active blogs and will publish articles on the technologies that they typically work with – such as `https://technology.amis.nl/`.

- User groups such as IOUG (`http://www.ioug.org/`), UKOUG (`https://www.ukoug.org`) and others keep presentation material available on their sites – although typically you do need to be a member of the user group to have access to these resources.

In addition to ICS related resources, you may be interested in knowing about, the following resources look at broader integration concepts and techniques that can be used with ICS or any other integration capability, for example SOA CS:

- Within IT the idea of patterns has been around for a while and the various areas of IT have developed their own catalogs of patterns. In the integration space the definitive source is the *Enterprise Integration Patterns* book by *Gregor Hohpe* and *Bobby Woolfe*. The book has a website (`http://www.enterpriseintegrationpatterns.com`) to go with it, that contains the essential pattern information, but if you want more explanation and detail then you will need the book. If you are going to be creating a lot of integrations then having the book maybe worthwhile. But, a word of warning, it is not a book for reading from cover to cover.

- Going beyond the *Hohpe* and *Woolfe* material into broader design considerations that impact integration are the books by *Thomas Erl* published/associated with Arcitura which is Erl's training company. These books have been published through *Addison Wesley*. The books from *Erl* cover a wide range of related technologies from web services to cloud and typically each aspect has a concepts/principles and a patterns book, with supporting website. The most directly relevant of these is SOA Patterns (`http://SOAPatterns.org`). These texts are a lot more abstract and architectural in view point, so do not expect them to provide detailed implementation guidance. But they are leading texts in these subject areas.

In addition to providing information about developments on ICS and its capabilities, the authors will seek to also provide a catalog of potentially helpful sites to help with a deeper understanding of the standards ICS supports such as SOAP and WSDL, but also web-based tools that will also help with development activities. There is no doubt that purely cloud-based tooling is still developing, so we shall seek to keep a list of sites and tools that may help you going forwards updated.

In terms of broader technical resources that may help you in the future:

- World Wide Web Consortium (best known as W3C) is the standards body that has driven the development of many of the central web standards we use today covering things like SOAP, WSDL among many. All the information can be seen at `https://www.w3.org/`.
- **Internet Engineering Task Force (IETF)** is another key standards organization. Some of the web standards have been developed in conjunction with other organizations such as the W3C for example HTTP. It should be noted, that the IETF documentation does tend to be very textual and specification driven with limited elaboration. In addition to HTTP, the IETF also have the SMTP (standard underpinning e-mail). The IETF site is at `https://www.ietf.org/`.
- Whilst REST is not a standard, there are a number of standards as you will have seen in the book covering the description of APIs that utilize REST including:
  - API Blueprint – `https://apiblueprint.org/`
  - Swagger – `http://swagger.io/`
  - RAML – `http://raml.org/`
  - WADL (although now rarely used) – `https://www.w3.org/Submission/wadl/`

- W3Schools is a good reference site for many of the web and XML standards, providing quick reference and illustrations of simple, common applications of the standards such as XSLT, HTML, XSD, and so on, `http://www.w3schools.com/`.
- When it comes to the APIs to other applications, whilst the ICS adapter will simplify much of the work, it is worth being able to refer to the originating provider and their API definitions, as this will provide access to rich additional information on what the data represents, and can go as far as providing test tools to help establish the expected behavior as you will have seen mentioned in the book.

In addition to this of course, there a broad range of Packt books and online educational material available at `https://www.packtpub.com`.

Summary

In this chapter, we have taken a look at the processes involved in importing and exporting integrations and packages and the reasons how you might want to perform such activities. With this, we have looked at the makeup of an `.iar` (integration archive) and `.par` (package archive). So, from here, you can see how to make local modifications and redeploy the changes. We moved onto the ICS API to understand how we can script or code, the means to control and manage our ICS instance. This led us onto the SDK and how to add custom adapters that can be used by ICS or even SOA CS. Finally, a number of potentially helpful resources have been identified that can help with thinking about how integrations may be implemented (for example, patterns), where you can go to look for more information on ICS and, if needed, the possibilities for reaching out for help (although we hope that this book will mean that is a great deal less necessary). Then, finally, we referenced documentation for industry standards, so that you can appreciate the art of the possible.

As a result of reading this book, we hope that you have got a grasp of the foundations of ICS, but more importantly, been given the means by which you can explore and learn more about ICS alone, or as part of a wider community.

Index

X

Made in the USA
Lexington, KY
14 August 2019